The International Relations of the Contemporary Middle East

D0224285

The Middle East, a few decades ago, was seen to be an autonomous subsystem of the global international political system. More recently, the region has been subordinated to the hegemony of a singular superpower, the US, bolstered by an alliance with Israel and a network of Arab client states.

The subordination of the contemporary Middle East has resulted in large part from the disappearance of countervailing forces, for example, global bipolarity, that for a while allowed the Arab world in particular to exercise a modicum of flexibility in shaping its international relations.

The aspirations of the indigenous population of the Middle East have been stifled by the dynamics of the unequal global power relationships, and domestic politics of the countries of the region are regularly subordinated to the prerogatives of international markets and the strategic competition of the great powers.

Employing the concept of imperialism – defined as a pattern of alliances between a center (rulers) in the Center (developed) country and a center (client regime) in the Periphery (underdeveloped country) – as an overall framework to analyse the subordination of the region, this book is essential reading for students and scholars of the Middle East, International Relations, and Politics in general.

Tareq Y. Ismael is Professor of Political Science at the University of Calgary, Canada and is the Secretary General of the International Association of Middle Eastern Studies. He has published extensively on the Middle East, Iraq and international studies. His most recent works include *Government and Politics in the Contemporary Middle East: Continuity and Change,* with Jacqueline S. Ismael (Routledge, 2011), and *The Sudanese Communist Party: Ideology and Party Politics* (Routledge, 2012).

Glenn E. Perry is Professor Emeritus of Political Science at Indiana State University. Reflecting interdisciplinary interests that often extend beyond political science to history and religion, his books include *The Middle East: Fourteen Islamic Centuries* (Prentice Hall, 1997), and *The History of Egypt* (Greenwood Press, 2004).

The International Relations of the Contemporary Middle East

Subordination and beyond

Edited by
Tareq Y. Ismael and Glenn E. Perry

LONDON AND NEW YORK

First published 2014
by Routledge
2 Park Square, Milton Park, Abingdon, Oxon OX14 4RN

Simultaneously published in the USA and Canada
by Routledge
711 Third Avenue, New York, NY 10017

Routledge is an imprint of the Taylor & Francis Group, an informa business

British Library Cataloguing in Publication Data
A catalogue record for this book is available from the British Library

Library of Congress Cataloging in Publication Data
A catalog record for this book has been requested

ISBN: 978-0-415-66134-8 (hbk)
ISBN: 978-0-415-66135-5 (pbk)
ISBN: 978-0-203-73023-2 (ebk)

Typeset in Times New Roman
by Taylor & Francis Books

To the memory of **FRIEDEMANN BÜTTNER**
(*18.5.1938; †4.9.2012),
Scholar, gentleman and friend.
He will be missed.

Contents

Contributors

Karen Aboul Kheir studied political science at the American University in Cairo, where she obtained her BA and MA degrees. As managing editor of *Al Siyassa Al Dawliya* (*International Politics*) from 2005 to 2012, she closely followed regional and international relations. She is currently an editorial consultant to several scholarly publications in Arabic on regional and international relations. She is Executive Manager and Academic Adviser on International Relations at the Regional Center for Strategic Studies, an independent think tank based in Cairo.

Tozun Bahcheli is Professor of Political Science at King's University College at Western University, London, Canada. He has written widely on ethnic conflict in Cyprus, secessionist conflicts in divided societies, and Turkish foreign policy. During 1995–96 he was a senior fellow at the United States Institute of Peace in Washington, DC. He is the author of *Greek–Turkish Relations Since 1955* (Westview Press, 1990) and co-editor (with Henry Srebrnik and Barry Bartmann) of *De Facto States: The Quest for Sovereignty* (Routledge, 2004).

Fran Cetti is researching securitization of asylum in the European Union. Her PhD, from the University of East London, UK focused upon forced migrants, discourses of threats and European identity. Recent publications include: "Asylum and the Discourse of Terror: the European 'Security State'," in B. Brescher, M. Devenney, and A. Winter (eds), *Discourses and Practices of Terrorism* (Routledge, 2010), and "Asylum and the European 'Security State': the Construction of the Global Outsider," in L. L. S. Talani (ed.), *Globalisation, Migration and the Future of Europe: Insiders and Outsiders* (Routledge, 2012).

Richard Falk is Albert G. Milbank Professor Emeritus of International Law and Practice at Princeton University and a research professor at the University of California, Santa Barbara. His many important roles in global affairs include his current position as Special Rapporteur on human rights in Occupied Palestine for the UN Human Rights Council. His recent books include *The Declining World Order: America's Neo-imperial Foreign*

Policy, with Howard Friel (Routledge, 2004); *International Law and the Third World: Reshaping Justice*, with Jacqueline Stevens and Balakrishnan Rajagopa (Routledge, 2008); *The Record of the Paper: How the* New York Times *Misrepresents American Foreign Policy*, with Howard Friel (Verso, 2007); *Israel–Palestine on Record: How the* New York Times *Misreports Conflict in the Middle East*, with Howard Friel (Verso, 2007); *Achieving Human Rights* (Routledge, 2009); *At the Nuclear Precipice*, with David Krieger (Oxford University Press, 2008); *The Path to Zero: Dialogues on Nuclear Dangers*, ed. with David Krieger (Paradigm, 2012); and *Legality and Legitimacy in Global Affairs*, ed. with Mark Juergensmeyer and Vesselin Popouski (Oxford University Press, 2012), as well as the fourth edition of his *International Law and World Order: A Problem-oriented Coursebook*, with Burns Weston *et al.* (West Group, 2006).

William W. Haddad is a Humanities Distinguished Professor, Department of History, California State University, Fullerton. He is also co-editor of the *International Journal of Contemporary Iraqi Studies*. His books are *Nationalism in a Non-national State: The Dissolution of the Ottoman Empire*, ed. with William Ochsenwald (Ohio State University Press, 1977); *The June 1967 War after Three Decades*, ed. with Ghada H. Talhami and Janice J. Terry; *Iraq: The Human Cost of History*, ed. with Tareq Y. Ismael; and *Barriers to Reconciliation: Essays on Iraq and the Palestine/Israel Conflict*, ed. with Jacqueline Ismael (UPA, 2006).

Tareq Y. Ismael is Professor of Political Science at the University of Calgary, Canada and is the Secretary General of the International Association of Middle Eastern Studies. He has published extensively on the Middle East, Iraq and international studies. His most recent works include *Iraq: The Human Cost of History*, ed. with William H. Haddad (Pluto Press, 2003); *The Iraqi Predicament: People in the Quagmire of Power Politics*, with Jacqueline S. Ismael (Pluto Press, 2004); *The Communist Movement in the Arab World* (Routledge, 2005); *The Rise and Fall of the Communist Party of Iraq* (Cambridge University Press, 2008); *Cultural Cleansing: Why Museums were Looted, Libraries Burned and Academics Murdered*, ed. with Raymond Baker and Shereen T. Ismael (Pluto Press, 2010), *Islam in the Eyes of the West: Images and Realities in an Age of Terror*, ed. with Andrew Rippin (Routledge, 2010), *Government and Politics in the Contemporary Middle East: Continuity and Change,* with Jacqueline S. Ismael (Routledge, 2011), and *The Sudanese Communist Party: Ideology and Party Politics* (Routledge, 2012).

Philip Marfleet is Professor of Migration and Refugee Studies at the University of East London, UK. He has published widely on migration issues and on social and political change in the contemporary Middle East. His latest book, ed. with Rabab El Mahdi, is *Egypt – the Moment of Change* (Zed, 2009).

Glenn E. Perry is Professor Emeritus of Political Science at Indiana State University. Reflecting interdisciplinary interests that often extend beyond political science to history and religion, his books include *The Middle East: Fourteen Islamic Centuries* (3rd ed., Prentice Hall, 1997), *Palestine: Continuing Dispossession,* ed. (AAUG, 1986), *The Palestine Problem: An Annotated Bibliography* (AAUG, 1990), and *The History of Egypt* (Greenwood Press, 2004). He has also contributed dozens of articles and chapters – all on Middle Eastern affairs, involving such topics as international law, the one-state solution to the Palestine question, historical memory, cultural cleansing, Islamic political concepts and movements, the paucity of democracy and the Western promotion of authoritarianism in the region, and misconceptions about Huntington's "clash of civilizations" idea – to academic journals and multi-authored volumes.

Jasamin Rostam-Kolayi received her PhD at the University of California, Los Angeles and is an Assistant Professor in the Department of History at California State University, Fullerton. Her research interests focus on themes in modern Iranian history, including women's education, religious minorities, and US–Iran relations.

Ghada Hashem Talhami is D.K. Pearsons Professor Emerita of Politics at Lake Forest College. Her works include *Palestine in the Egyptian Press: From al-Ahram to al-Ahali* (Lexington Books, 2007); *Palestinian Refugees: Pawns to Political Actors* (Nova Science Publishers, 2003); and *Syria and the Palestinians: The Clash of Nationalisms* (University Press of Florida, 2001).

Stephen Zunes is a Professor of Politics at the University of San Francisco. He serves as an advisory committee member and Middle East editor for the Foreign Policy in Focus Project and as an associate editor of *Peace Review.* He is the author of scores of articles for scholarly and general readership on Middle Eastern politics, US foreign policy, international terrorism, social movements, and human rights. He is the principal editor of *Nonviolent Social Movements* (Blackwell Publishers, 1999) and the author of the highly acclaimed *Tinderbox: US Middle East Policy and the Roots of Terrorism* (Common Courage Press, 2003) and *Western Sahara: War, Nationalism and Conflict Irresolution in Northwest Africa,* with Jacob Mundy (Syracuse University Press, 2010).

Preface

Although *The International Relations of the Middle East: Subordination and Beyond* is the fourth general work in the field published by one of the authors (Ismael), this volume is an entirely original enterprise and in no sense represents a mere revision of earlier efforts. Likewise, we believe that our analysis of the region's international politics departs significantly from any previous texts, offering a novel approach to the subject matter.

Intended for use by policy makers, journalists with a serious interest in Middle East politics, and graduate or upper-level undergraduate students, the chapters focus on important aspects of the international relations of the Middle East. Space limitations and the thematic focus prevent uniform coverage of all states active in the region, but countries and organizations central to the Middle East's international relations – including Syria, Iraq, Hamas, and Hezbollah – receive considerable coverage both in our extensive introductory chapter, "Toward a Framework for Analysis," and in various other chapters throughout the volume.

The renewed subordination that the Middle East has experienced in the global arena during the past quarter century, though in the broader context of signs that the "West's" quarter millennium of dominating the "rest" may finally be waning, has resulted in large part from the disappearance of countervailing forces – that is, global bipolarity – that for a while allowed the Arab world in particular to exercise a modicum of flexibility in shaping its international relations. The current subordination of the region is characterized by the hegemony of a singular superpower, the US, bolstered by an alliance with Israel and a network of Arab client states. In keeping with the framework suggested by Johan Galtung in his classic article on the subject, we make use of the concept of imperialism – defined as involving a pattern of alliances between a center (rulers) in the Center (developed) country and a center (client regime) in the Periphery (underdeveloped country) – as an overall framework for our analysis. We believe this framework continues to be useful for conceptualizing the relationship of most Middle Eastern states with major powers long after the former gained recognition as sovereign states. Indeed, Western imperialism in the Middle East mostly took the form of de facto domination of "independent" Middle Eastern states even during the nineteenth and early twentieth centuries. The contributors follow this framework flexibly and with much eclecticism in using complementary theoretical prisms, including realism.

The terms "Center" and "Periphery" are borrowed from dependency theory, which emphasizes the exploitative economic relationship between the Center and Periphery as the cause of development and underdevelopment. But our emphasis is on political ties, and only sporadically do some of the contributors apply the fundamentals of *dependencia*. Any potential objection by those who dislike the term "imperialism" – and prefer to speak in terms of "dominant world orders" or whatever – may in some respects be making little more than a semantic argument.

Following an extensive introductory chapter that develops the theme and ties the other chapters together and an historical overview of imperialism in the region, Part II of the volume focuses on the existing imperial order. This includes chapters on the roles of the US and Israel. Although space prohibits inclusion of separate chapters on all the regimes aligned with the existing order (e.g., Saudi Arabia, Jordan, the UAE), the dynamics of these individual countries appear in the general discussion of the Middle East's subordination.

The last part of the book focuses on some possible countervailing forces within the region This includes chapters on three key Middle Eastern states: the Islamic Republic of Iran, which vies with the US and its allies – Israel and client Arab regimes – for hegemony in the region; Turkey, whose challenge is more subtle under AKP leadership; and Egypt, whose alliance with the Center has been shaken since 2011 and whose future position is now up in the air. Also, we have included chapters on the EU, which has some future potential for not playing second fiddle to the present hegemon, and on the UN, an arena in which the legitimacy (in Gramscian terms, hegemony) of otherwise-prevailing double standards bolstering the imperial order sometimes gets challenged.

We wish to thank all the contributors for the enormous amount of work they put into the project. They showed amazing patience with our critiques of their chapter drafts and responded with alacrity to our many requests for revision. The value of the volume largely results from their research and expertise.

Last but not least, we want to thank Aisha I. Biberdorf for her creativity and skill in designing a cover that so well captures the spirit of the book.

Tareq Y. Ismael
Calgary, Alberta, Canada
Glenn E. Perry
Terre Haute, Indiana, USA

Part I
Broad patterns

1 Toward a framework for analysis

Tareq Y. Ismael and Glenn E. Perry

Owing to the Middle East's immense resources and critical geostrategic position, it continues to play a crucial role in international affairs. This, however, occurs within the context of subordination – and sometimes resistance – to Western powers. The aspirations of the indigenous population of the region long have been stifled by the dynamics of unequal global power relationships, with the domestic politics of the countries of the Middle East regularly subordinated to the prerogatives of international markets and the strategic competition of the great powers. The wave of protests that developed from 2010 onward should be interpreted, at least in large part, as a rejection of elite complicity in perpetuating this subordination and as an attempt by the masses to seize control over the political and socioeconomic direction of their countries.

Identifying the "Middle East"

The "Middle East" is not a geographical or cultural category created by its own people. Some writers famously deny its existence, but if we did not have such a term we undoubtedly would have to invent another one for the region overlapping the African and Eurasian continents. It is a term coined by American naval theorist Alfred Thayer Mahan at the dawn of the twentieth century, initially with reference to the area between the Near East and the Far East, but it subsequently – in large part resulting from the whims of British strategists at the outset of World War II who set up a "Middle East Command" in Cairo – acquired a meaning that is now familiar.

Although the geographical extent of the Middle East is ambiguous, our definition includes at least the predominantly Arab (that is, Arabic-speaking) countries of Southwest Asia and Egypt. The other Arabic-speaking countries of the African continent – the Sudan, Libya, Tunisia, Algeria, Morocco, and Mauritania – constitute integral parts of the Arab world too but lie outside the area of our main focus. The term "Middle East" also extends to two major non-Arab Muslim countries that lie north and east of the Arab world, namely Turkey and Iran. We propose to call them the Outer Circle, although they more often have been labeled "the Northern Tier" or "non-Arab periphery."

The region also includes the state of Israel, whose identity is defined in terms of Jewishness ("the state of the Jewish people," potentially involving all of those still living abroad). Unless we treat the territories it has occupied – and established settlements in – but not formally annexed since 1967 as parts of it, Israel is indeed primarily Jewish, with a 20 per cent Arab Palestinian minority. The clash between this state (and the broader Zionist movement that brought it into existence) and the Arab world, particularly the Arab masses, has provided a special coloring to the region's politics.

In the modern era, the Arab and Islamic world has conceived itself in different ways. First of all, the ascendant type of identity in the Arab world during much of the twentieth century – in contrast to the division into religious communities that historically prevailed – was pan-Arabism, the idea that the whole region, "from the Ocean to the Gulf," regardless of state boundaries or religion (not including ethnic non-Arab minorities, of course, largely the Berbers, southern Sudanese, and Kurds) was one nation. This conception always competed with state, religious, and other identities but was particularly powerful in some areas, notably in the Fertile Crescent. As a result, political movements were able to cut across state boundaries. During the mid 1950s, President Gamal Abdul Nasser of Egypt emerged as a charismatic figure throughout the Arab world, with millions seeing him as a deliverer from the balkanization imposed by colonial powers and from corrupt, servile, and exploitative regimes. Nasser, in turn, was able to stir up the masses when their rulers were accused of disloyalty to the idea of Arab unity and to the Palestinian cause.

During this period, as Michael Barnett shows, Arab leaders threatened one another with ideas rather than military force, that is, accusations of disloyalty to these all-Arab concerns – "the norms of Arabism and not the balance of power"[1] – while presenting themselves as the true champions of these principles. Barnett maintains that while they did not really expect to give up sovereignty to a pan-Arab entity or to challenge Israel militarily, they repeatedly got entrapped by their rhetoric. For example, Syrian leaders put Nasser to a test in 1958 with a risky offer for unification he could not refuse without undermining his aura of pan-Arab leadership. In 1967 when Egypt's leader took the necessary actions to restore his position as champion of the Arab cause in Palestine, he accomplished little more than precipitating an Israeli attack.

Another feature of the classic Arab system was the way non-Arab states were relatively insulated from participating in it. There was a strong Arab taboo on joining with non-Arabs against another Arab state. As a case in point, fear of the consequences of violating this principle forced Saudi Arabia and other Western client regimes to give up on a scheme to cooperate with Turkey in a US-backed invasion of Syria in 1957.[2] Similarly, while Arabian Peninsula monarchs were glad to have the shah of Iran acting against revolutionaries in the Dhofar Province of Oman in the early 1970s, the norms of Arabism prevented them from openly endorsing this; their concerns are said to have got in the way of an Iranian intention to attack Southern Yemen in 1976.

The taboo against breaking ranks with other Arabs in relation to Israel was even stronger than in the case of the Outer Circle. The Arab regimes, notably the Hashemite rulers of Transjordan/Jordan, who collaborated with the Zionist movement before 1948 and thereafter with Israel, tried to keep this secret,[3] as did those non-state groups, notably some Maronites in Lebanon, who had ties with the Israelis and saw them as potential allies against an Arab world with which many of them did not identify.[4]

Increasingly from the 1960s the fundamentals of the Arab system eroded. After Nasser, there was no new charismatic figure in the Arab world that could play the same role. Already during his last years – starting with the breakup of the United Arab Republic (UAR) in 1961 and continuing with the failure of Iraq to merge with the new pan-Arab entity following its revolution in 1958 and then with the defeat by Israel in 1967 – Nasser's ability to lead a cohesive Arab world had weakened.[5] Moreover, the non-Arab Muslim countries of the region – Iran and Turkey – became increasingly integrated into the region's politics. Even the taboo against cooperation/peace with Israel broke down, at the level of the Arab regimes if not amongst the Arab public.

The region's subordination intensified with the fading of Nasserism and pan-Arabism. Increasingly, Nasser's successors aligned themselves with Washington and, in the case of Egypt and Jordan, openly broke the taboo on Arab cooperation with Israel. The parallel – if somewhat weaker – taboos on Arab alliances with non-Arabs in general against other Arab states and on military action against other Arab states likewise collapsed. For instance, the US attacks on Iraq – in 1991 and 2003 – brought in various levels of Arab cooperation, both overt and covert. More recently, joint military intervention by Europeans and Americans, along with Arab client regimes, enabled rebels to overthrow the Libyan regime of Muammar al-Qaddafi. In the case of the 2012 civil war in Syria, American clients in the Arab world (notably the rulers of Saudi Arabia and Qatar) have cooperated with Turkey to overthrow the Assad regime, alongside various kinds of "non-lethal" aid by the US for the rebels,[6] amid increasing calls for further military intervention. Fearing that otherwise it will not have "influence" amongst post-Ba'athist rulers,[7] the US also has striven to organize the rebels into a more cohesive force dominated – in line with our definition of imperialism – by pro-US elements.

Patterns of continuing imperialism

As noted in William Haddad and Jasamin Rostam-Kolayi's chapter, "the Imperial State still exists." The notion of a Middle East still subjected to imperialist rule may seem odd to someone whose image of imperialism is that of formal colonial status of territories, once often clearly indicated by their colors on world maps, as when countries such as India were officially parts of the British Empire. But, again in Haddad and Rostam-Kolayi's words, Western imperialism in the Middle East often involved "semi-independent regimes dependent on the Center [Britain, France] for protection." While there is room for such complex concepts as "imperialism" to be used in different ways, this generally corresponds to the definition used in this volume and is drawn from Johan Galtung's classic theory (or model) of imperialism.[8] The kind of indirect domination through backing a dependent local oligarchy that we refer to represents an age-old practice that Machiavelli, in Chapter V of *The Prince*, recommended as one important technique for maintaining empires. A scholarly study of how the US – contrary to its rhetoric – engaged in systematic "democracy prevention" in Egypt during the Mubarak era concludes that the elites of the two countries "promoted shared elite interests over popular opposition with an effectiveness that rivaled the British protectorate" (of 1914–22).[9]

Galtung also portrays imperialism as collaboration between the centers (elites/ruling classes/dominant groups) in the Center – that is, developed countries – and those in the Periphery, i.e., underdeveloped countries. (Note that upper case indicates countries, while lower case signifies parts of countries.) Thus Saudi Arabia exemplifies a Periphery country, while the Saudi regime is the center in the Periphery or cP. The masses in Saudi Arabia form the periphery in the Periphery or pP. Galtung stresses that there is greater disharmony of interest between center and periphery in Periphery nations than in Center nations. But situations exist in which the center of a Periphery country has the backing – notably when sectarian or ethnic divisions enter the picture – of parts of its periphery in particular situations, as in Saudi Arabia in its conflict with Iran, and in which an anti-imperialist center, as in Syria in 2012, faces rebellion from elements of its periphery that seek imperial intervention. The center in the Periphery does not always – or even usually – act as a mere puppet of its ally in the Center nation, which it sometimes manipulates for its own purposes and vis-à-vis which it often demonstrates a considerable amount of bargaining power. The center of the Periphery sometimes defies its patron in symbolic ways, as in the case of United Nations votes, often in ways that serve the interests of the Center by bolstering the legitimacy of the client regime at home and in the broader Arab world.

The term "imperialism," as Galtung uses it, would seem to exclude – arbitrarily, one might argue – expansion by a Periphery nation to control another Periphery nation (or, if such is imaginable, a Center nation) and domination of one Center nation by another Center nation seems not to fit his definition either. In our view, Galtung's analysis is not beyond criticism, and the realities of Middle Eastern politics are at odds with one part of his model, that is, the absence of interaction among centers in the Periphery. But he does provide a useful framework for analyzing the modern relationship between Western countries and those in the Middle East.

Galtung classifies imperialism as only one type of domination, the kind that "cuts across nations," with the center in the Periphery constituting a bridgehead for the Center nation and serving their common interest. His writings clearly fall into the category of dependency theory, which emphasizes the way economic ties between Center and Periphery countries created and perpetuate global inequality. However, he also identifies five types of imperialism (economic, political, military, communication, and cultural) and, in contrast to the Marxist idea of the preponderance of economic determinants common amongst dependency theorists, Galtung insists that imperialism can start with any of these types and then proceed to one or more of the others. As this is a work in international politics, we focus on the political type of imperialism rather than on dependency theory as such while recognizing that the other types of relationships are always interwoven with politics.

One dramatic marker of the subservient status of Middle East countries is the relationship of their domestic politics to international relations and foreign policy. In the case of independent Center countries, foreign policy derives from internal factors: a country's assessment of its power within the international system and attendant threats; its ideological/intellectual conception of its role within the international system; and the nature of historic ties with other countries. In the case of subservient Middle East regimes – excluding revisionist powers like revolutionary Iran – the relationship is nearly inverted, with these countries' foreign policies often bound to that of their American patron and with their domestic politics representing a struggle to defend these policies against popular opposition. Hence the domestic politics of the Middle East tends in many cases to be colored by popular opposition to a regime's foreign policy and by the regime's attempt to suppress this opposition (and hence, continued foreign patronage).

The Middle East in a world of unbalanced power

Interpreting the international relations of the Middle East and the geostrategy of the singular great power, the US, is impossible without a treatment of the centrality of Israel in the region's politics. Israel's role as a bridgehead of the Center is unique in several respects. In the first place, the level of Washington's commitment would be hard to overstate. US aid, now almost entirely military, long has exceeded $3 billion per year and, according to a report to Congress, had cumulatively added up to $115 billion by 2012.[10] In terms of current US dollars, the US Agency for International Development calculated a figure just under $186 billion in 2010.[11] Considering the various ways in which much aid is disguised, the total amount, according to some estimates, has exceeded even that. In addition to its own arms industry (which enabled it to rank fifth in arms deliveries to less developed countries in 2011),[12] Israel is provided the most advanced, sophisticated weapons that are available. Add to this that Israel is a highly developed – i.e., rich – Center country (not including the territories it has incorporated de facto into the state since 1967). Unlike in 1957, when the Eisenhower administration demanded unconditional withdrawal from newly occupied territories, the US has allowed the occupation to continue since 1967, ostensibly until peace agreements are concluded.

Beginning with the Johnson administration, the US has totally excluded Israel from its commitment to stopping nuclear proliferation. With a double standard applied to other Middle Eastern states, this has allowed Israel to create a nuclear "iron wall" (a term the revisionist Zionist, Ze'ev Jabotinsky, coined to describe his concept of Zionist strategy long before the nuclear age), making it a veritable regional superpower. In the face of Israeli and American pressure, the International Atomic Energy Association (IAEA) repeatedly has succeeded in getting Arab states to withdraw proposals for that organization to put Israel's nuclear weapons on the agenda.[13]

One cannot meaningfully portray Israel as just another small state in the region that is connected to the superpower in the same way as Saudi Arabia or Jordan. In the first place, Israel is more than a Middle Eastern state. It is the manifestation of a global political movement, Zionism, the name given to Jewish nationalism, which emerged in the context of other European nationalisms in the nineteenth century and flowered in reaction to historic anti-Semitism, culminating with the horrors of the Nazi Holocaust.

In the early twentieth century, the Jewish population in historic Palestine was small (one twelfth of the total as late as 1917), although millions eventually were recruited as settlers, mainly after the Zionist movement succeeded in establishing the Jewish state in 1948. The Israeli novelist, A. B. Yehoshua[14] concluded that this created "a conflict unprecedented in human history," as no other people ever tried "to return to its ancient homeland and re-establish sovereignty there." Yehoshua goes on to note that the people already inhabiting the country, the Palestinians, "also have been forced to face a unique phenomenon that no other nation has confronted."

The Jewish population of the US is roughly the same as Israel's – not far from six million each, depending in part on how Jewishness is defined – with the total of Jews in the world barely exceeding 13 million. Polls show that Jewish Americans tend to be relatively dovish with regard to the Arab–Israeli conflict, and some are anti-Zionist. Still, the concentration of the Jewish diaspora in the US has made it the center of the contemporary Zionist movement, which is closely tied to the state of Israel through such organizations as the Jewish Agency and Jewish National Fund. Politically, the American Israel Public Action Committee (AIPAC) has long been the primary pro-Israel lobby in the US, although this provides just one example of a vast network of pro-Israel activism. AIPAC is rightfully regarded as one of the most powerful political organizations in the US. Members of Congress who criticized Israeli policies in the past were "targeted" for defeat. While this type of behavior is not unusual for political lobbies, as with domestic lobbies like the National Rifle Association (NRA) and its targeting of gun-control advocates, it is highly unusual for an advocate of a foreign government to carry such power within the US. And while the agenda of such a group as the NRA regularly faces denunciation by many political leaders and in the mainstream press, the essentials of the pro-Israel narrative generally go unchallenged in such circles in the US. Also, AIPAC has considerable powers of socialization; American politicians, who typically have little previous understanding of or interest in the Middle East conflict, are generously courted by AIPAC, with no comparable counterbalance by an Arab/Palestinian "lobby."

The influence of the Israel lobby in the US is attributable, in large part, to the general public's low level of understanding of events in the Middle East. Many Christian Americans have been led to put the Arab–Israeli conflict in the context of past Western mistreatment of Jews rather than of Western colonialism. Others view today's Israel as a fulfillment of Biblical prophecy. Some influential preachers have further developed the political force of this narrative with the demonization of Muslims within an "end-time" narrative that sees the necessity of the Israeli state as a prelude to the return of Christ. This "Christian Zionist" narrative has been ably exploited by pro-Israeli forces in the US.

While proponents – and some critics – of the American–Israeli relationship point to certain ways Israel is used to enhance American power, notably by providing intelligence, others see the relationship as having great cost, namely in inspiring popular backlash against the US throughout the region. Aside from its support for Israel itself, it is its backing of authoritarian clients – in large part because of a realization that democratically elected leaders would be more responsive to popular anti-Israeli sentiment – more than anything else that has created resentment and thus endangered the American position in the region. During the Gulf War of 1991 it is notable that Baghdad sought to undermine the coalition supporting the US by provoking Israeli military involvement, while Washington desperately pressured the Israelis not to retaliate against missile attacks. The Iraqi leader hoped[15] – and others apparently feared – that Arab regimes finding themselves fighting on Israel's side against an Arab state would be overthrown, and while King Hussein secretly assured the director of Israel's intelligence agency, Mossad, that he would not give Iraqi aircraft permission to cross his territory to attack Israel, his fear of being perceived as being in collusion with it would prevent him from opening his skies for an Israeli attack on his Arab neighbor.

More than two decades later, an Israeli proponent of an American attack on Iran – to destroy its alleged nuclear weapons program – inadvertently pointed to the same phenomenon. He argued that an Israeli attack would "inflame animosity" and "would rally the Arab and Muslim world behind Iran, strengthen radical Islamists, neutralize potentially sympathetic regimes, and further distance Turkey from Israel and the West."[16] But he failed to note that the cost to the US of attacking Iran in order to preserve the Israeli nuclear monopoly in the region, if such occurs, would likely also be profound. The occupation of Iraq in 2003, propelled in large part by many of the same policy makers and pressure groups now advocating an attack on Iran, already has proved highly expensive, economically – and ultimately costing more than $3 trillion, according to some estimates – and otherwise, for the imperial enterprise.

Client regimes in the Arab world

The American–Israeli relationship results in anomalous political dynamics for the Arab states in the region. The subordinate Arab regimes have superficially proclaimed their loyalty to the "Arab cause" while typically more or less allying themselves in a de facto way with their purported enemy. The "Wiki-Leaks" documents released in 2010 confirmed what astute observers already understood, that is, that most Arab leaders cared little for the Palestine issue as such, regarding it as just an "annoying nuisance" and that they "publicly attack Israel while warning against Iran in closed forums." Some Israelis, notably Prime Minister Benjamin Netanyahu, confused these American client dictators with the Arab public and picked up on this "doublespeak" of Arab rulers in an attempt to belie the claim that Palestine has broad regional significance.[17]

A case in point of the way the centers in the Periphery states betray their own peripheries relates to nuclear proliferation. An observer of Iran's nuclear program points out that with regard to Israel's well known large nuclear arsenal:

> ... any call for [an] international probe ... should primarily come from Israel's neighboring countries as, more than any other country in the world they are endangered by [it]. However, autocratic Arab rulers have historically placed the survival of their regimes above their national interests and popular preferences. Given the lack of democratic account-ability in the Arab world, conservative authoritarian Arab regimes [centers in the Periphery] have refrained from seriously pushing for international scrutiny into Israel's nuclear weapons program and calling for nuclear disarmament in the Middle East region, as demanded by their publics. These regimes have instead defined their interests in close har-mony with Israeli and U.S. interests in the region by calling [instead] for international pressure on Iran's IAEA-monitored nuclear program [rather than on Israel].[18]

Secret cooperation between Israel and some Arab regimes has long existed. WikiLeaks documents revealed that the king of Bahrain talked to the American ambassador in 2005 about his contacts with Mossad and about his willingness to "move forward in other areas."[19] While the Saudis publicly opposed Washington's plans for invading Iraq in 2003 and avoided publicizing any help to their patron, they (along with the Mubarak regime) earned inclusion in the Pentagon's later category of "silent partners" who allowed attacks to take place from a secret base on their territory.[20]

The WikiLeaks revelation that the Saudi ambassador in Washington told his counterparts that his king was calling for beheading "this snake" – not Israel, but rather a rising Iran – came as no surprise to those who understand the position of such peripheries in the Periphery. The Arab client monarchies generally, as well as Mubarak, took similar positions.[21] And in response to "a symbolic moment" when Sheikh Muhammad bin Zayed al-Nahyan of Abu Dhabi expressed his worries about Iran, the American ambassador commented that this "strategic view of the region ... is curiously close to the Israeli one."[22]

Overall, this typifies the Saudi position within the region. While Riyadh consciously presents itself as the "custodian of the Two Holy Mosques" – i.e., a leader of the Islamic world – its position is ultimately one of subordination to the American regional strategy. The nature of the American–Saudi relationship was made explicit in 1981 in the "Reagan corollary to the Carter Doctrine," which stated that America would intervene to protect Saudi Arabia (and implicitly other Persian Gulf allies) from internal threats to their security. This was an extension to the Carter Doctrine, which promised protection of the region from external threats. Thus America explicitly committed itself to the stability of such autocratic regimes from popular challenges.[23] Consequently, while the Saudi regime attempts to placate and co-opt internal and regional opposition through distribution of oil money, it follows a regional policy at odds with both Arab nationalism and Islamism.

Indeed, on the central question of Arab politics – Israel – Saudi Arabia and other US client monarchies are hardly less effectively allied with their purported enemy than would be the case if they had open diplomatic ties and a formal treaty with the Jewish state.[24] Admittedly, public support for modest Palestinian aspirations – a state limited to territories occupied since 1967 – provides a legitimizing tool for these Arab regimes, and the continuing occupation of Palestinian territories threatens to stir up popular dissatisfaction. Although denied by the Saudis, there are reports of an agreement between Tel Aviv and Riyadh allowing Israel to access Saudi airspace – without interference – in the event of an Israeli attack on Iran.[25] In any case, Saudi regional policy is explicitly tied to American – and by extension Israeli – designs, with Saudi Arabia playing the role of a chief regional antagonist to Iranian influence, as is the proxy struggle in the Syrian civil war.

The Saudi dynasty – closely tied to the militant puritanical *Wahhabi* religious movement since the 1700s – has deep roots in the central Arabian region of Najd. But the early twentieth century saw it attached to the British and later to the Americans, making it a crucial and long-lasting example of a center in the Periphery tied in an imperialist fashion to a center in the Center. The Najdi emir, Abdul Aziz – oddly called "Ibn Saud" in the West– lost power to a rival dynasty, the Rashidis of northern Arabia, in the late nineteenth century, and his return from exile in Kuwait in 1902 seems largely to have been a function of British policy, as was his expansion into the Persian Gulf region of al-Hasa in 1913. He was one of the Peninsula rulers who collaborated with the British during World War I, fighting against the Rashidis, who were loyal to Istanbul. The other main ally of the British in the Peninsula during the early 1920s, King Hussein of the Hijaz, who – as Sharif of Mecca – had joined with them against his Ottoman overlords in World War I, displeased them so much in the mid 1920s that they allowed the Saudis to invade and annex his kingdom as well as other territories that came to constitute Saudi Arabia, although they continued to maintain client monarchies ruled by Hussein's sons in Transjordan and Iraq, both of which remained fierce rivals of the Saudis until the late 1950s.

One can trace the beginnings of US interests in Saudi Arabia to the 1930s, when American oil companies (later known as Aramco) obtained a concession there. Military and economic ties developed further during World War II, and the US obtained an air base at Dhahran. A meeting of US President Franklin D. Roosevelt and King Abdul Aziz in February 1945 symbolized and marked the acceleration of such cooperation. In effect, the Saudi–American relationship came to constitute an oil-for-protection pact, that is, access to Saudi oil resources in exchange for US political and military support. The Saudis ended their long-time alliance with Egypt against the Hashemite kingdoms in 1957, as Nasser's popularity as a pan-Arab leader came to be seen as the overriding threat to Western-backed monarchies and as the diplomatic blow the British and French took following their invasion of the Suez Canal the previous year allowed the US increasingly to take over the imperial role in the region.

A shared fear of Arab nationalism[26] fuelled cooperation between the US and Saudi Arabia during subsequent years, although this often was put in terms of resisting "communism." They joined in opposing Soviet influence, as in supporting the Mujahidin in Afghanistan in the 1980s – and also the Contras in Nicaragua and anti-Marxist UNITA forces in Angola. By that time, the Iranian Revolution had created a new ideological threat to the region's regimes, and Saudi resources became a key factor in its containment. Saudi efforts currently focus on preserving the status quo forces in the region in the face of the Arab Spring. By Autumn 2012, they pledged nearly $18 billion – and had already disbursed $3.4 billion – to regional governments: $4 billion to Egypt, $5 billion to Bahrain and Oman, $3.6 billion to Yemen, $2.65 billion to Jordan, $750 million to Tunisia, $1.25 billion to Morocco, and $340 million to the occupied Palestinian territories.[27] In the case of Bahrain – where the "Arab Spring" manifested itself as a revolt of the largely Shi'ite population against Sunni rulers closely aligned with the Saudis and the US, as demonstrated by the location of the US Fifth Fleet there – Saudi Arabia and other Arab client regimes in the Gulf Consultative Council sent armed forces to crush the opposition movement.

US and Saudi foreign policies for the region share a vision of "stability." This includes a perpetuation of the implicit – and sometimes explicit – accommodation between Israel and Arab regimes, staving off Iranian regional influence and nuclear ambitions, and protection of the monarchical regimes in Saudi Arabia and the other Gulf Cooperation Council (GCC) countries. Ideologically, this requires the neutralization of democratic forces in the region whose demands for reform could eventually increasingly threaten them. The US and Saudi Arabia deploy diplomacy, financial aid, and ultimately, military intervention to arrest any such developments. Saudi and GCC regional policy in large measure represents an extension of US regional preferences. Arguably one of the real world's nearest approximation to Galtung's model of imperialism, the alliance between the centers of the US and Saudi Arabia has grown into the most important pillar of American hegemony in the region.

The Palestinian Authority (PA) established following the Oslo Accord provides an example of a national movement that was co-opted by those against whom resistance was once directed. Papers revealed by WikiLeaks in January 2011 provided damning evidence of PA–Israeli collaboration.[28] As a case in point, Israelis apparently consulted with PA President Mahmoud Abbas, and also with Egyptian officials, before the attack on Gaza in December 2008. PA leaders later cooperated with the US in an attempt to postpone referral of the Goldstone Report, with its conclusion that Israel had committed war crimes, to the Security Council. The PA negotiator, Saeb Erekat, spoke of the PA's having to kill its "own people" to demonstrate its commitment to order. The documents revealed details of Israeli–PA coordination in security matters, jointly planning such actions as the assassination of an al-Aqsa Martyr's Brigade commander. PA officials opposed opening border crossings to Gaza. So keen was Abbas – as Erekat boasted to American officials – to demonstrate the PA leadership's usefulness to the dominant order that he asked a businessman to donate $50 million to establish a radio station for the opponents of Iranian President Ahmadinejad in 2009.[29]

Relationships between Center nations and regimes in the Periphery vary from case to case, with not all of the latter consistently characterized by either zealous pursuit of independence or full collaboration. Libya under the regime of Muammar al-Qaddafi provides a case in point. Leading a coup in 1969 against one of Washington's most important client monarchies, who hosted the Wheeler Air Force Base, Qaddafi appeared to represent an idealistic commitment to the rights of the Arab/Islamic world (and the broader Third World). His first years in power were characterized by the obsessive pursuit of a unified Arab nation that would have meant sacrificing Libyan independence and presumably his own power, although he may have fancied himself as ultimately taking the reins in such a union.

Cornered by their own rhetoric about unity, some more cynical Arab leaders entered into unity agreements with Qaddafi that soon turned out to be meaningless – just as was his later pretense of having set up the world's only real democracy – and eventually forgotten. He emerged as an enemy of the US during the 1980s because of his regime's support of armed movements, as well as his weapons programs and purported backing of terrorist attacks. He proclaimed such disgust with the other Arab regimes that eventually he gave up on the Arab world and aspired to lead the African continent instead. But the struggle to stay in power – and the temptations of power – resulted in resort to the same sort of cronyism, favoritism, and despotism that were found in other dictatorships, if not likely worse. However, following the invasion in Iraq in 2003, Qaddafi dramatically changed course in his foreign policy, establishing a client relationship with Washington. He agreed to dismantle his chemical and biological weapons and his nuclear weapons program and proceeded to cooperate with Washington's "war on terrorism."

Qaddafi continued of course to denounce and ridicule the treason of other Arab rulers and to engage in other extravagant attacks on imperialism. But he was frightened when he saw revolutionary movements coming to the surface in 2011, even coming out in support of Tunisia's suddenly beleaguered President Zine al-Abidine Ben Ali. Qaddafi's newfound Western patrons and de facto allies among the centers of Arab countries were, in fact, never as dependable as he might have hoped. And so Arab absolute monarchs – "the primary enthusiasts" – and Western "democratizers" quickly joined in massively with his local opponents when revolt broke out in 2011. Elsewhere in the non-Western world the "reaction ... ranged from quiet disgust – India and Brazil – to vocal opposition from China, Russia, South Africa and the African Union."[30] Unlike the threatening cases of Tunisia, Egypt, and Bahrain during the uprisings of 2011, Libya's proved "a 'convenient' revolution" for the West.[31] While the ultimate results of the fall of the Qaddafi regime remain uncertain, Western countries may be looking for new military bases, and American and European companies immediately were engaged in a virtual "gold rush."[32] Assurances passed on by rebel leaders to the Israelis during the uprising that their future regime would "not be hostile toward them" were quickly disavowed when made public.[33]

Client Arab regimes provide services to their patrons in ways that Israel could not. According to William Norton-Taylor, a key factor in the overthrow of the Qaddafi regime – in this case, a formerly rebellious leader who had come to terms with the Center in the expectation that this would guarantee his survival – was secret services provided by the absolute monarchies of the Persian Gulf. In Norton-Taylor's words, this

> ... gave birth to a new kind of covert intervention involving military advisers and special forces, not from the US – not only from European countries, notably Britain's SAS [Special Air Service] but those of Arab countries, notably Qatar and the United Arab Emirates ..., supported ... by Gulf money and weapons.[34]

The military intervention in 2011 to protect their fellow autocrat in Bahrain from popular demands for democracy provides a better known example of the way such centers in Periphery nations in the Arab world collaborate for mutual preservation and to protect the imperial interests of the center in their patron Center nation. During the 1980s, Washington and Riyadh joined together in large-scale financial support for anti-communist movements such as the UNITA in Angola, and – demonstrating how alliances with such authoritarian centers in the Periphery can be used to evade constitutions in the Center nation – the Reagan administration was able to circumvent a Congressional cut-off of funds for the Nicaraguan Contras by replenishing its treasury with Saudi contributions. In 1981, Reagan declared that the US would never allow the Saudi regime to be overthrown. With American troops located in the client monarchy a decade later, it thus appeared to those who subsequently joined al-Qaida that – as Vali Nasr put the matter – "the United States is part of Saudi's [sic] domestic politics," with the American forces now becoming "the 'Republican Guards' of Saudi Arabia. ... to protect the Saud family from its population."[35]

Hossein Askari argues that a key factor in autocrats' survival has been the extent to which they can buy the support of influential Westerners through personal consulting contracts, gifts to their favorite universities or foundations, and lucrative contracts for influential oil, defense industry, engineering and financial corporations, who then lobby for them, with "the 'watchdog' media reveal[ing] little." All the while, Western support for Arab autocracies is "justified on the basis of empty phrases such as 'national interest' and 'access to oil.'"[36] Askari believes that the way such corrupt rulers have inhibited the sort of economic progress required for survival following the eventual drying up of oil revenues through sharing their wealth with Western elites represents the equivalent of the blatant robbery that occurred during classic colonialism.

Countervailing forces: the emerging Periphery and a multipolar world

In Shelley's celebrated portrayal of Ozymandias's broken statue, the pedestal proclaimed "Look on my works, ye Mighty, and despair." The message reminded the rulers of the British Empire at one of its high points two centuries ago that imperial orders are transient. While we cannot know in what direction the world will change during subsequent decades, prognosticators of various stripes recently sense that a move toward a multipolar global system is on its way. The Center is weakening as a result of recent expensive, ill-considered, counterproductive imperial undertakings that have bled its economy and thus its power. As Karen Aboul Kheir's essay persuasively argues, the uncontrollable popular revolt in the Arab world against authoritarian rule in 2011 reflected the weakening of American hegemony but also further contributed to the process. According to one report,[37] Israeli military intelligence views the "Arab Spring" as representing both the rise of Islamism and the decline of American influence, with other powers "now meddling in the Middle East." At the same time, some nations and civilizations that were in decline in recent centuries seem to be on their way back.

Europe, the location of the original "Center" of the modern world system, has undergone economic and political integration in the form of the European Union. Will this create a countervailing power for a multipolar world or, in light of economic setbacks, is this a non-starter? Short of the emergence of a united Europe as a military power, the same European countries that for centuries constituted the great powers – notably Britain, France, and Germany – are likely to play an important role alongside several other emerging powerful states during the rest of this century. As the power of the US slowly recedes, European countries can be expected to act more independently.

Refusal to follow Washington's lead on Middle Eastern issues, though, has so far proved the exception, not the rule. We saw this when France and Germany declined to participate in the American-led war against Iraq in 2003, although it is now known that Berlin eventually cooperated in important ways, e.g., by obtaining and passing on Iraq's defense plans to Washington.[38] For that matter, the British government's participation in the American war was essentially the result of one man, Prime Minister Tony Blair, who supported Bush's policies against the instincts of his own party and those of the public at large. But the subsequent Conservative government of David Cameron eagerly pushed ahead of Washington in the Libyan intervention of 2011.[39] By this time, France had an equally interventionist President, Nicolas Sarkozy, who also joined in the push to overthrow the Libyan regime – but whose brash style in such matters may have contributed to his failing to win reelection the next year. Germany had a more interventionist chancellor Angela Merkel, who nevertheless refrained from participating in this action.

In addition to the growing European role, there is much reason to believe that a more balanced world order is now beginning to emerge for the first time in roughly three centuries, in which power will be more evenly distributed across different regions and cultures. The center of world wealth and power – i.e., the Center – increasingly was Europe and recently European-settled lands, notably the US, during this era, and by the late nineteenth century the rest of the world – now reduced to Periphery status – appeared permanently subdued. Aside from Japan's rise as another great power about a century ago, the world has been dominated by what historically was known as Western – or, in the case of Russia, Orthodox – Christendom.

In the words of Samuel P. Huntington,[40] the recent period of Western domination represents no more than a "'blip' on the world economy" that likely "will be over" by *c.* 2050. As for the US, many writers, both in the popular press and in scholarly circles have argued that its power already is ebbing. Political scientist Chalmers Johnson, for instance, in his tetralogy of books on the subject,[41] provides notable evidence of this process of decline. He focused his attention on overlooked structural factors, namely military Keynesianism and the growth of unchecked executive power. Military Keynesianism is identified as the economically stimulative effects of foreign militarism on the American domestic economy. Referring to Germany, the Polish economist Michal Kalecki defined this phenomenon as "[g]overnment spending on arms [that has] a multiplier effect on general consumer spending"[42] while absorbing low-skilled individuals into work that is more remunerative and socially-prestigious than would otherwise be available. In the case of the American economy, this gave rise to the huge "military-industrial complex" of President Eisenhower's dire warning.

Vast spending on military hardware and technology arguably creates a demand for its deployment. In the absence of war, such weaponry serves as a monument to one's power. And indeed, in the post-Cold War era, a renewed messianism in American foreign policy arose that was packaged ideologically as "neo-conservatism." Foreign-policy neo-conservatism, which came to theoretical maturity in the 1990s, gained ascendency following the terrorist attacks of 9/11. Thus the US set out on a global "war on terror" whose financial costs would rise into the trillions, all the while leaving inadequate resources to confront a global economic meltdown in 2008 that threatened to paralyze the financial system. The decade of the "oughts"/ "noughts" for the US represents the point at which the economic logic of military Keynesianism and global dominance began to unravel in the face of fruitless adventures abroad and of economic turmoil.

Multiple writers have elaborated on the emergence of a multipolar world. In Johnson's telling, the concomitant decline of the US and the rise of new global powers can be exemplified in the accumulation of credit owed to other nations. Notably, by the end of the first decade of the current millennium, China held $854 billion of US dollar reserves and Japan $850 billion. Other writers, including Fareed Zakaria and David Mason,[43] have elaborated on the coming of a world in which America is in relative decline as great powers emerge again in the non-Western world, while a joint report of US intelligence agencies issued in December 2012 predicted that – while the US would probably "remain 'first among equals'" – by 2030 there will no longer be "a hegemonic power" and that the "historic rise of the West since 1750" would be essentially reversed, "restoring Asia's weight in the global economy."[44] There has even been talk – perhaps exaggerated – of the "American century" now making way for the "Chinese century"[45] or possibly the "Indian century."[46]

The global environment of the Middle East is likely to include several other important powers, although economic and political problems[47] could prevent this. Russia has retained its nuclear superpower status and may play a more important role again, although demographic decline threatens to hinder it. Japan suffers the same weakness but has already become a military power and may join the nuclear club in a future world in which it cannot look to others to provide its security. Brazil and South Africa show some potential of becoming major world powers, as does at least one predominantly Muslim country far from the Middle East, namely Indonesia.

The rise of China and India portends a fundamental change in the world's power structure. The former lays claim to having occupied the central role in the world for much longer than any of the other great powers. Its remarkable recent record of economic development – dropping somewhat in 2012 – and its high rate of savings already have made China a major player. One student of world history[48] has noted that even the second millennium CE was one of Chinese leadership, with only the final centuries providing an exception. At one extreme is the prediction that China not only will reach parity of power with the US but that it will attain the status of "nearly sole superpower" by 2030,[49] while others foresee a much slower process that will leave the US still the preeminent pole in a truly multipolar system, perhaps into the next century.

The Resistance Bloc

Western domination has of course always evoked resistance among Middle Eastern peoples. A confluence of factors, including costly American misadventures in Afghanistan and Iraq, the relative decline of American power globally, and the destabilization of the Middle East in light of the "Arab Spring" increased the leverage – at least initially – of the "Resistance Bloc" within the region. This force has often been simplistically characterized by invoking a "specter" of "the Shi'ite Crescent." The "specter" was presaged, of course, by the Iranian Revolution of 1979. This momentous event provided a rare instance – at least until the "Arab Spring" of 2011 – of a successful popular uprising of the periphery in a Middle Eastern Periphery nation against a crucial client (the shah) of the center in the Center. The theocratic nature of the new regime provided a special coloring to it, but the essence of the revolution was the overthrow of a dictator seen as a collaborator with the Center. It seems likely that even if secular groups among the revolutionaries had prevailed, the results in many ways would have been the same, although their lists of assets and liabilities as they set out to inspire other revolutions against centers in the Periphery allied with the main Center nation would have been different.

Revolutionary Iran has provided the most significant challenge to the status quo in the region. With its combination of massive oil and gas reserves and a population similar in size to those of Turkey and Egypt – roughly 80 million in each case – Iran possesses some important components of a medium-sized power. In the words of two commentators writing after the emergence of the Arab Spring, revolutionary Iran's specter is most feared where there is "entrenched authoritarianism, where it has exploited the illegitimacy of Arab rulers by highlighting their dependence on the US and their impotence (or ambivalence) on pan-Arab issues, such as the conflicts in Iraq, Lebanon, and the Palestinian territories,"[50] Iran's emergence as a major Middle East force opposed to the Center and the centers in the Periphery echoes that of Nasser a generation or so earlier, though invoking religious (i.e., Islamic) identity as opposed to ethnic (Arab) nationalism.

While the term, as elucidated by political scientist Joel Migdal, applies first of all to its effectiveness in governing at home,[51] a country mobilized by a "strong state" – rare in the Third World but which revolutionary Iran shows signs of having created – also possesses an enormous advantage internationally. This strength was seen not only in the incredible fierceness of Iran's fight in its war with Iraq during the 1980s but also in the case of the strong de facto state ruled by Hezbollah that the Iranian Revolution inspired and Iranian Revolutionary Guards helped to create in the predominantly Shi'ite parts of Lebanon following the Israeli occupation in 1982. Hezbollah guerrillas arguably provided the first defeat that Israel has ever experienced, forcing it to withdraw from Lebanon in 2000. Six years later Hezbollah mobilized the population as no other Arab entity had ever done, giving a severe blow to Israel's reputation as an invincible regional superpower.

Iran's Islamic regime was notably fortuitous in the gifts it received from three outsiders, namely Saddam Hussein, George H. W. Bush, and George W. Bush. The Iraqi leader faced a threat to his regime in the form of an Islamic Revolution in Iran in 1979 that claimed to represent the beginning of a movement that would spread beyond its borders to the whole Islamic world. Some of his majority Shi'ite population saw revolutionary Iran as a beacon. His response was to invade Iran in order to nip this threat in the bud. Saddam calculated that a weakened Iranian military and Western hostility toward the Islamic Revolution provided a golden opportunity to make Iraq the dominant power in the Gulf region and the Arab world. He apparently also hoped the removal of the danger on his eastern flank would allow him ultimately to defeat Israel, whose use of nuclear weapons he could deter by developing his own.[52] He mainly succeeded in rallying Iranian support for the new regime, exemplifying Huntington's generalization[53] first articulated in 1967, that an essential asset of revolutions in general is foreign intervention, which creates nationalistic support and radicalization.

A decade after the beginning of the war with Iran, Iraqi forces occupied Kuwait. This temporary elimination of an important center in a Periphery country frightened the other centers in the Periphery and in the Center itself. But a renewed alliance led by Bush Sr brought other Center countries and centers in the Periphery together to launch a military blow that left Iraq drastically weakened. However, it was kept intact, except for the now-de facto independence of the Kurdish north, as a dyke to stem the flow of the Iranian tide that continued to endanger the hegemony of the Center and its allied centers in the Periphery. Barely more than a decade later, however, Bush Jr, influenced by ideologically rigid neo-conservatives, proved himself an inept player in the game of *realpolitik,* overthrowing the Iraqi state and unwittingly destroying a major constraint on Iranian power.

The struggle for hegemony in the region grew increasingly vicious by the second decade of the twenty-first century. With the issue of nuclear proliferation occupying center stage, hawks in Israel and the US identified Iran as the primary threat to their strategic domination of the region. Iran was therefore subjected to various kinds of economic warfare by Western countries, including sanctions adopted by the Security Council, and by the Arab League, which remained dominated by centers in the Periphery aligned with the center in the Center. Washington announced stringent sanctions in 2012, and the EU committed itself to boycott Iranian oil, while Iran spoke of retaliating by closing the Strait of Hormuz and thus of disrupting shipments of oil from other countries in the Persian Gulf region.

The threat of an armed attack on Iran either by the US or by Israel hovered in the air. It was widely recognized that a land invasion likely would meet ferocious resistance from both supporters and critics of the regime. Although the Netanyahu government, some of the client Arab autocracies, and right-wing elements in the US were pushing at least for a massive air attack on Iranian nuclear facilities, the possibility that Iran would react by disrupting oil shipments provided a powerful deterrent. Even Meir Dagan, the former head of Mossad, warned that such an attack would be "the most stupid idea." There was widespread calculation that an attack would set back any nuclear weapons capability for only a few years and guarantee that Iran would develop the "bomb" if it had not done so already.

A Pew poll of global Muslim opinion in 2012 provides insight into the obstacle that sectarianism poses to Iranian leadership of the Islamic world. Asked the question "Shias [sic] are Muslim/not Muslim," 53 per cent of Egyptians answered "not Muslim," as did 40 per cent of Palestinians and 43 per cent of Jordanians. In part, this likely reflected both a lack of familiarity with different sects among some less educated people in certain areas and the impact of headlines about sectarian conflicts in, say, Iraq or Syria. Interestingly, Sunnis in countries with significant histories of sectarian violence showed high levels of support for Shi'ites as authentic Muslims – 82 per cent in Iraq and 77 per cent in Lebanon – likely owing to long histories of coexistence, including intermarriages. Considering that these countries have experienced sectarian tension and violence, this has primarily been a political construction – i.e., a battle for political control between sectarian parties affiliated with, and backed in many cases by, external states – rather than deep-seated prejudice.

Public opinion polls have demonstrated the ability, however limited, of Shi'ite leaders to find admirers in Sunni countries. For a while, Hasan Nasrallah of Hezbollah was found to be the most admired leader in the Arab world, notably following his organization's ferocious resistance to Israel in 2006. But a poll, conducted in 2010, revealed that Turkish Prime Minister Recep Tayyip Erdoğan had overtaken him, possibly representing temporary euphoria following reports of Ankara's anger over Israeli policies (and not necessarily based entirely on sectarian considerations per se).

At the same time, a considerable minority, 18 per cent, saw Iran as a threat, although President Mahmoud Ahmadinejad continued to get favorable ratings from nearly two-thirds of those who were interviewed.[54] A Pew poll in 2012 demonstrated continuing pro-Iranian sentiment in heavily Sunni countries, although less than before.[55] The Iranian revolutionary regime's clerical leadership has accentuated its image in much of the Sunni world as a specifically Shi'ite movement despite attempts to present itself as broadly Islamic and to play down sectarian differences. Aside from sectarianism, Arabs – including some Shi'ites – often see the Islamic Republic of Iran as representing Persian/Iranian particularism despite its lip service to Islamic universalism.

The extreme movement in Sunnism, whose devotees call themselves Unitarians but are known by others as Wahhabis, constitutes a special case. The movement – which rose in the 1700s and was embraced by the Sa'udi family, leading to the establishment of the Kingdom of Saudi Arabia in the twentieth century – has always seen Shi'ites, as well as Sufis (Muslim mystics), as heretics. They attacked the Shi'ite shrines in Iraq when they went on the offensive in the early 1800s. The "Wahhabis" have influenced a broader constituency of anti-Shi'ite Salafis (relating to predecessors/ancestors), especially in the Gulf region, but further afield too, as demonstrated by their considerable success in the Egyptian parliamentary elections of 2011–12.

The extent to which post-1979 Tehran attracted support among Arab Shi'ites, who almost invariably had reasons to see themselves as victims of discrimination, raised barriers to its potential appeal to broader constituencies. The Iraq–Iran War of the 1980s can be understood in large part as the effort of President Saddam Hussein to defend Iraq's Sunni-dominated center from its Shi'ite periphery, within which the appeal of Ayatollah Khomeini found considerable receptivity. But this specific attraction of the Islamic Revolution in Iran to Shi'ites dictated that it would find no support among Iraqi Sunni Arabs – nor among the Sunni Kurdish rebels in northern Iraq, who however entered into an alliance of convenience with Tehran. The post-2003 follow-up saw the bitter resistance of Sunni Arab groups to a new order dominated by Shi'ite parties with close ties to Tehran. The removal of Saddam Hussein and his regime eliminated an important counterweight to the Iranian-led "Resistance Bloc" and allowed pro-Iranian parties to control the government – and gave pro-Iranian militias much more real power. There were also new economic ties between the two countries. However, some observers report a widespread backlash against Iranians that is allowing such countries as Turkey, Kuwait, Lebanon, and China – though not the US – an advantage in the competition for trade and investment.[56]

During the "Arab Spring" of 2011 protests in the American client states in the Persian Gulf largely were confined to Shi'ite minorities. These disturbances, while threatening to the regimes, could be downplayed in regime propaganda by emphasizing Shi'ite "otherness" and implied disloyalty. The Saudi regime was able to contain the protests at least in large part because they erupted among the Shi'ites of the Eastern Province, making it less likely that the majority Sunnis would join in. Massive increases in spending also helped to distract potential critics of the regime. In the case of Bahrain, the Sunni monarchy was able to hold back protests from the state's large Shi'ite majority at least in part by virtue of the dominant Sunnis' view of the opposition as a threat to their own primacy but also by the military intervention mainly of Saudi Arabia – and other client regimes forming the Gulf Consultative Council – in support of their fellow monarchy. Such joint action by centers in the Periphery with at least the tacit approval of the center in the Center nation helped to preserve the existing structure of imperialism.[57] Washington expressed its usual concern over repression carried out by its client in Manama but soon resumed arms sales after announcing a halt. But such blatant hypocrisy exhibited by a self-proclaimed supporter of democracy also threatened to undermine its hegemony in the long run, for as a victim of the repression told an American journalist: "When Obama sells arms to dictators repressing people seeking democracy, he ruins the reputation of America. It's never in America's interest to turn a whole people against it."[58]

Its geographic location has made Syria a key link in the Resistance Bloc. As in the case of Iraq until 2003, Syria has been under the control of the Ba'ath Party since the 1960s, but the Syrian leadership in fact is made up of a clique – centered on the Assad family – belonging to the historically marginalized Alawi sect, an offshoot of Twelver Shi'ism, causing some observers to see its alliance with revolutionary Iran as representing sectarianism. But the highly unorthodox – some would say "heretical" or even completely beyond the pale of Islam – doctrines and practices of the Alawites, as well as the regime's secularism, make that interpretation problematic. In reality, the alliance is based on pragmatism. The enmity between the Assad regime and that of Saddam Hussein dictated an alliance with Iraq's eastern neighbor and provides a modern manifestation of the ancient Indian "realist" statesman Kautilya's *mandala* (wheel) theory of international politics, in which each prince fears his immediate neighbor and forms an alliance with the latter's neighbor.

There are limits to this sort of geographic determinism. The failure of Iraq to ally with Israel – some reports of an attempt to do this during the 1980s notwithstanding – points to the powerful countervailing effect of the onus Arabism and Islamism put on such a relationship. The close ties between the Assad regime and a post-Saddam Iraqi government led by pro-Iranian Shi'ite parties also demonstrate that Kautilya's theory cannot always accurately predict alignments, but this is partly explained in "realist" geopolitical terms by the present military weakness of Iraq that has deprived it of effective statehood. Whether explained by its own Shi'ite particularism, the need to keep on good terms with Tehran, or the important economic ties it had developed with its western neighbor, the regime in Baghdad provided the most important example of official Arab backing for the Damascus regime during the latter's increasing travails in 2011–12. Criticism by the Arab Sunni member of the three-member Iraqi presidential council, Vice President Tariq al-Hashimi – he soon afterward took refuge in the de facto separate Kurdish region following accusations of organizing a terror plot – of Baghdad's backing for Assad further pointed to the sectarian aspect of the situation.[59]

A foremost objective of Syria – making continuing adherence to the Resistance Front a no-brainer – is recovery of its southwestern territory, the Golan Heights, which Israel occupied in 1967. Since its failed attempt to retake most of this area in 1973, the Syrian–Israeli frontier has been quiet – and it intervened, as part of an Arab League force, in Lebanon in 1976 in what looked like an indirect tacit alliance with Israel by saving the latter's Phalangist allies from defeat – and there is reason to think that Syria would be ready to make a separate peace with Israel and break its alliance with Iran in return for full withdrawal from Golan. Negotiations in 2000 came close to achieving this.

The Israeli invasion of Lebanon in 1982, as Damascus was supporting Iran in the war that was beginning to turn against Iraq, led to air battles between Israeli and Syrian forces. Aside from historic ties between the two countries – many, particularly Lebanese Sunnis, did not think of them as two countries – Syria sees any hostile pro-Israeli control of Lebanon – as seemed to be emerging in the immediate aftermath of the 1982 War – as a dire threat. All of this meshed with the role of the Shi'ites in Lebanon, concentrated in the south and east as well as in parts of Beirut – the bottom of the sectarian heap but now the country's largest religious community.

The civil war that had begun in 1975 pitted a "leftist" alliance mainly of Palestinian refugees and Sunni Lebanese against a "rightist" coalition made up primarily of Maronite Christians, itself split into mutually feuding factions. The position of most Shi'ites was unclear at first, and indeed by 1982 those in the south resented the Palestinians, whom they blamed for Israeli retaliation. Their hostility to Palestinians reached such a point that many Lebanese Shi'ites welcomed the Israelis. But they soon turned against the invaders and became their most feared enemies. The Syrian imperative of keeping the Israelis out of Lebanon meshed with the dream of the Islamic revolutionaries in Tehran of taking the lead in a pan-Islamic struggle against Israel. Iranian Revolutionary Guards created an elite al-Quds (Jerusalem) Force, and some appeared in Lebanon in 1983 to organize the resistance to the Israeli occupation. Out of this initiative emerged the Party of God (Hezbollah) that eclipsed the older Shi'ite party, Amal. Hezbollah has since grown into the most powerful force in the country, and although it forms essentially its own de facto state in parts of the country, it has become an important force in the anemic *de jure* Lebanese government as well.

The popular revolt against the Assad regime in Syria beginning in 2011 created a quandary for other members of the Resistance Bloc, demonstrating the way such actors are subject to the same hypocrisy as is the imperial order. While Iran and its allies rejoiced over the fall of American client regimes in Cairo and Tunis, as well as in Tripoli – and proclaimed the "Islamic Spring" of 2011 a too-much-delayed sequel to the Iranian Spring of 1979 – they could ill afford to lose their key ally in Damascus and indeed saw the Syrian rebellion as being instigated to destroy the Resistance Bloc. There were accusations, denied by Tehran, that Revolutionary Guards were helping repress protesters and even establishing bases in Syria, and weapons for use by Assad's forces found their way from Iran through Iraqi airspace despite Baghdad's sporadic attempts to placate Washington by agreeing to stop this.[60] Hezbollah backed the Assad regime against demonstrators, and its leader, Hasan Nasrallah, declared his support, blaming its troubles on an Israeli and American plot. This development caused many of Assad's opponents, particularly in the majority Sunni community, to turn against it.

Hamas (the Palestinian Islamic Resistance Movement), the most important Sunni organization in the Resistance Bloc, reacted differently. It had won the Palestinian legislative elections in 2006 and gained control of the Gaza Strip the following year. With civil war breaking out in Syria, it broke with the regime in Damascus, where its Political Bureau had previously been located, but it continued to receive aid – apparently somewhat reduced – from Iran as well as to maintain amicable ties with Arab regimes in conflict with Tehran.

As the Syrian protests turned into armed conflict, and then into full-scale civil war, sectarian dimensions of the conflict intensified[61] and showed signs of spreading to adjacent countries. Demographically, Syria is divided, with Sunnis forming a large majority (perhaps 74 per cent), while the Alawites, who predominate in the regime, constitute roughly 12 per cent while various other Shi'ite and Christian groups make up the rest of the population. While most of the members of these sects are Arabs, Syria also has one large ethnic minority (about 10 per cent), the Kurds – generally Sunnis – notably in the areas adjacent to Kurdish areas of Turkey and Iraq as well as in urban areas.

Sunni militants – Salafis, both Syrian and others from the larger Arab world – gained prominence within the Free Syrian Army, the main rebel umbrella group, making it difficult for Western powers to intervene on its side until they can isolate such elements. Domestically, significant Sunni Islamist factions participating in the opposition – and sometimes launching suicide bombings – include *Ahrar al-Arour* and *Sukur al-Sham* – who have issued anti-Alawi religious proclamations and are accused of kidnapping Shi'ites – as well as *Jabhat al-Nusra*, "a direct offshoot of Al Qaeda in Iraq" that surpasses all other rebel groups in in its "boldness and skill" in battle.[62] The overt and covert intervention of regional players has intensified these sectarian tensions (both in Syria and in the larger region). Aside from the above-mentioned expected Iranian support for the Syrian regime, the Western client monarchies, notably the Saudis, have provided massive support for the opposition, much of which is said to have fallen into the hands of the most militant groups. Under such increasingly sectarian circumstances, the Alawi/Shi'ite and Christian minorities have mostly found themselves bound to the regime in order to survive and sometimes have come under attack from rebel extremists. These circumstances bode poorly for any post-Assad political arrangement, and fear abounded that the country would split into a patchwork of sectarian and ethnic entities. By the end of 2012, the number of deaths resulting from the conflict was estimated at more than 60,000, and more than half a million Syrians had fled, mainly to Lebanon, Turkey, Jordan, and Iraq[63] – including Iraqis who had taken refuge in Syria following the invasion of 2003.

Facing a setback to its appeal in the Arab world and the prospect that the Assad regime would not survive unless it reformed itself, Iranian leaders began to hedge their bets. President Ahmadinejad called on the Syrian government to respect its people's "legitimate demands" and hold free elections. Tehran reacted favorably to Egyptian President Muhammad Morsi's proposal in August 2012 for its participation, along with Cairo, Ankara and Riyadh, in a "committee of four" to mediate the conflict.[64] Iranian leaders also took into account the possibility that – if he could – Assad would pull the rug out from under them in return for regaining the occupied Golan Heights.[65] In any case, the prospect of the Assad regime's downfall made the future of the Resistance Bloc problematic, and both Hebzollah and the Iranian government remained committed to preventing a rebel victory.

Several factors have converged that increasingly seem to be transforming Turkey's role in the Middle East. It was the heart of the last great Islamic state, whose Padishahs/Sultans indeed by the nineteenth century came to be widely recognized by Sunni Muslims as the latest successors – i.e., caliphs – to the Prophet Muhammad as head of the Islamic world. But the newly established Republic of Turkey – ironically, under a leader, Mustafa Kemal (alias, Atatürk) who initially fought fiercely in the name of Islam to resist Greek and Western encroachment in Anatolia – adopted a concept of "modernization" that implied aping Western civilization and turned away from the rest of the world's Muslims. Such a move could be made only by a Kemalist political elite centered in the bureaucracy and, especially, the military, which set limits and sporadically intervened directly after the transition to a multiparty "democracy." Even during an era when purely secular nationalism was believed to be gradually gaining ascendency in the Arab world, the recalcitrant acquiescence of the periphery in Turkey to Kemalism recurrently showed its head, but the center kept putting a lid on it by banning Islamist parties, which were deemed to threaten the secular system. In addition, the Cold War provided a distraction that diverted Ankara's attention from the Middle Eastern stage, aside from efforts closely tied to the "containment" of Soviet influence such as membership in the Baghdad Pact (later called CENTO, "Central Treaty Organization") and threats to invade Syria in 1957. Turkey became a member of NATO in 1952 and – indicative of a strong aspiration shared by its government and public to anchor itself with the West – has participated in various European institutions. It seemed at least for a while to have had reason to believe that it was going to gain admission to the European Union – which, however, recurrently rationalized its exclusion of this Muslim country in various unconvincing ways.

Persisting Islamic influence provided an important factor in making ordinary Turks generally anti-Israeli from the beginning. However, the political elite eagerly established diplomatic relations with the Jewish state, partly as a way of asserting their difference from the Arabs and other "backward" peoples. This inclination fit into the Israeli "periphery" strategy of countering Arab opposition by establishing close ties with the Outer Circle of Middle Eastern countries, which tended to have conflicts with Arab states, as in the case of Syrian support for militant Kurdish rebels in Turkey. Close relations between Turkey and Israel developed into a strategic alliance in 1996, as proponents of Kautilya's *mandala* theory might have predicted. The opening years of the twenty-first century ushered in a new situation. With the largest economy in the region, Turkey became an economic powerhouse. During the first half of 2011 it surpassed China as the country with the highest rate of growth, exceeding 10 per cent.[66] The growth of the Turkish economy has been matched by increasing ties with the region. Trade with Egypt in particular reached $US3.7 billion a year by 2011.[67] By 2011, trade with the Arab world had been multiplied six times over during the Erdoğan government's watch,[68] and plans called for major increases in both trade and investment.

As Tozun Bahcheli shows in his essay in this volume, Turkey during recent years has undergone tremendous change in its outlook, which now calls for a more active policy in the Middle East. It has not renounced Kemalism, but the rise to power of a moderate Islamist party, the Justice and Development Party or AKP, led by Prime Minister Erdoğan, since 2002, has changed the country's politics. His critics point to his authoritarian tendencies and have accused him of abusing Turkey's legal system to silence critics of his government. In any case, he has broken the power of the military in domestic politics and has improved democratic standards in the country. More to the point, he has given it a new face in the Middle East. With the parliament casting a vote on the matter, Ankara enraged its long-time American ally in 2003 by refusing to allow the invasion of Iraq to be launched from its territory and again in 2010 by voting against the US-led call for a Security Council resolution to mandate new economic sanctions against Iran. A series of actions by the Likud-led government of Israel in 2010 – notably the killing of eight Turkish citizens and a Turkish-American by Israeli troops forcibly boarding a vessel carrying relief supplies to Gaza and the Israeli government's refusal to apologize – seriously damaged Turkish–Israeli relations. Erdoğan's increasing championship of the Palestinian cause and his strident anti-Israel rhetoric has put him ahead of Hezbollah's Hasan Nasrallah and Iran's President Ahmadinejad as the Arab public's most admired leader. A public opinion poll conducted in five Arab countries in October 2011 revealed that approximately 50 per cent of the people considered Turkey the country that recently had played "the 'most constructive' role," putting it far ahead of any rival for this honor, and that Erdoğan was "the most admired among world leaders."[69] A Turkish academic, Aysan Dey, summed up the changes by advising Tel Aviv to learn about the "new Turkey" in which the Turkish military and the state no longer "showed disdain for what the public really wanted."[70] Reminiscent of Huntington's suggestion[71] 15 years earlier that Turkey might "reject Ataturk's legacy" of begging to join the West and instead provide the "core state" that Islamic civilization has recently lacked, Israeli historian Benny Morris in 2011 bemoaned Turkey's "gradual divorce from the West and its steady realignment with the world's other Islamists." Referring to the recent revolt against the Israel-aligned Mubarak regime in Cairo, he concluded that "The Turks may soon find an emulator in Egypt."[72] Erdoğan's visit to Cairo received a broadly positive response from Egyptians, although some Muslim Brotherhood leaders criticized him for his comments on the balance of religious tradition and the secular state and expressed wariness about any Turkish attempt to teach them how to establish a democracy.

So far, there are limits to the transformation. Turkey remains a member of NATO and hosts American bases, including the important Incirlik Airbase. Despite its growing ties with Iran, it agreed to allow US radar stations – over the protests of Iran, against which they were fully understood to be designed in the event of a future military clash – to be located in eastern Anatolia. And following several years of growing friendship between Ankara and Damascus (and important economic ties), the Assad regime's repression of demonstrators in 2011–12 brought condemnation from Erdoğan and his government. He announced a cut-off of military sales to Damascus and then imposed more serious economic sanctions. In addition, Turkey provided sanctuary for refugees and rebels on its side of the border. There was some talk of the possibility of military intervention to set up "safe areas" within Syria. Iranian resentment over Turkish aid to Assad's enemies threatened to undermine Tehran's previously amicable relationship with Ankara. Allusions by Iranian officials to the possibility of retaliating against radar bases and other sites in Turkey – and to the drastic impact a disruption in trade would have on the latter – in the event of a military assault demonstrated some of the cards that still might be played.[73] The Syrian crisis threatened to overflow into Turkey too, as Assad was losing control over the Kurdish region of his country and possibly considering the use of his Kurdish card by restoring his former alliance with Kurdish guerrillas in Turkey. Also, the Alavi minority in Turkey showed signs of siding with Assad, creating the danger of inflaming sectarianism there.

Revolt of the masses: less complicit elites?

The vulnerability of authoritarian Arab rulers may provide a new threat to American hegemony within the region. Immediately after the overthrow of Mubarak in February 2011, Netanyahu is said to have spoken fearfully to the Knesset.[74] Bernard-Henri Lévy, the philosopher who takes credit for convincing the French government to overthrow Qaddafi, has told of how obviously "scared" and pessimistic Israeli Foreign Minister Avigdor Lieberman was about the situation and how his face and body movements expressed "a cry for help."[75] At a meeting of supporters of Israel in 2011, during the early days of the "Arab Spring," Martin Kramer, a hawkish Israeli specialist on the Islamic world, proclaimed that "we believe the status quo is sustainable" and – nicely illustrating the usual kind of alliance between the centers in Center and Periphery Nations that was threatening to fall apart – that "it's the job of the US to sustain it."[76] Noting that the "rejuvenated embrace of the Palestinian cause" that "confirm[s] its status as a barometer of social justice and freedom" in the Arab world during the recent uprisings, a report on the new mood concluded that "the demands of an empowered public" point to an end to "policies which, at least tacitly, capitulated to the dictates of the US and Israel."[77] In connection with renewed Israeli air attacks in Sinai in retaliation against rocket attacks by militant Palestinian groups in August 2011, Akiva Eldar warned that

... the encounter between Israeli arrogance (and its sister, euphoria) and ousted Egyptian President Hosni Mubarak's duplicitous policy regarding the Israeli–Palestinian conflict facilitated maintaining relations with Egypt, as though there were no occupation in the territories, and maintaining the occupation as though there were no Camp David agreement.[78]

Eldar went on to indicate that "this time, the Israeli arrogance is encountering the honor of an Arab street that is undermining the old order." Pointing to the new phenomenon of democratic elections in Egypt, Gideon Levy warned that the "new Egypt ... would not stand by in the face of another brutal [Israeli] assault on Gaza."[79] Patrick Seale concluded in September 2011 of the continuing "Arab Spring" against dictators that a revolution of "equal significance" was "proceeding against American and Israeli hegemony."[80] Seeing the new threat from ordinary Arabs, even a key member of the Saudi royal family[81] warned that his kingdom's close relationship with its long-time patron would take on a "toxic" character and – expressing a fear that still had not been realized a year later – might not survive an American veto of Palestine's membership in the United Nations.

Admittedly, some observers began to reassure themselves and others that Arab democracy would be tolerable. And some moderate Israelis argued that by not being so collaborative a democratized Arab world would make Israel see the need for settling the Palestine question, which would be to its own benefit. Even when popular revolt spread to Syria, whose alliance with Iran, Hezbollah, and Hamas evoked suspicions that this represented a counter-offensive by the hegemonic powers, both Israel and Washington began to demonstrate fear that the outcome could work against them. They were mindful of how the Assad regime had so long quietly kept the peace on the Golan front and feared that the likely alternative would be more hostile, whether led by Islamists or by secular nationalists. In fact, WikiLeaks cables, not surprisingly, reveal that Washington had already been financing Syrian opposition groups and a satellite television station that broadcast anti-regime propaganda during the George W. Bush and Obama administrations.[82] With violence in Syria intensifying to the point of civil war, American President Barack Obama authorized the CIA to provide support to Syrian rebels, the extent of which is not entirely clear.[83] The ongoing threat to the Assad regime may exemplify what to Washington is "a 'convenient' revolution" like Libya's, as opposed to "'dangerous' ones"[84] against client regimes. But the reality of radical Salafi involvement in the Syrian revolt, as well as the prospect that direct military intervention would prove extremely dangerous, seemed to temper the enthusiasm of some policymakers in Washington.

The "democracy" established in Iraq after the 2003 invasion – if only because Ayatollah Sistani stood up against plans for a "caucus" chosen by occupying military forces – demonstrated how relatively free elections undermine American hegemony.[85] In 2011, while the struggle to maintain US influence had not ended, the elected parliament refused to accept a new Status of Forces Agreement giving American soldiers immunity from Iraqi law beyond the end of the year. With a contingent of guards – for the largest

US embassy in the world, planned at a time of grandiose expectations for Iraq as a center of American hegemony in the region – as one exception, the American military presence would soon be over. In the words of one commentator:

> And so that is the way the war ends. ... The US will receive no benefit from its illegal war of aggression, no permanent bases, no bulwark against Iran, no new Arab friend to Israel, no $14 a barrel petroleum – all things Washington had dreamed of. Dreams that turned out to be flimsy and unsubstantial and tragic.[86]

But withdrawal from Iraq was making way for plans to strengthen military ties with the Gulf monarchies. Washington is said to be planning not just for continuing bilateral ties – it already had 40,000 troops in these states, including 23,000 in Kuwait – but also a more integrated "security architecture," involving coordinated training exercises.[87]

Mubarak's fall from power put a key part of the dominant arrangement in question. Even with free elections, there was reason to wonder about the extent to which the military would give up power. Much of the old repressiveness remained in place, but continuing pressure from below could not easily be ignored. Following the first round of parliamentary elections in December 2011, a member of the "transitional" junta headed by Field Marshal Muhammad Tantawi declared that they were not truly representative of the popular will, that the elected body would not be allowed to write the new constitution, and that public scrutiny of the military budget would be unthinkable.[88] With the Muslim Brothers' newly established Freedom and Justice Party (FJP) and other Islamists winning the lion's share of the seats, the military, backed by a judiciary made up of holdovers from the *ancien régime*, dissolved the newly elected parliament, and when the FJP candidate, Muhammad Morsi, was elected president, the military revoked the powers of his office. He calmly and adroitly struck back – apparently playing off the resentment of junior officers against the military leadership – in August 2012 by retiring Tantawi and other top generals, but the struggle between the elected leaders and the "remnants" of the Mubarak era did not seem to end.

So far, there was no revolution in foreign policy. It seemed that Turkey's Erdoğan in some ways had gone further in breaking with Israel than had the new Egyptian leaders, who found themselves between the Scylla of renewed conflict and losing Washington's – and the Persian Gulf monarchies' – vital assistance and the Charybdis of public demands for ending Mubarak's coziness with Israel. The transitional military regime and then the newly elected president not surprisingly reaffirmed Cairo's commitment to the peace treaty with Israel, but that could gradually erode if democratization proceeds, particularly if Palestinian expectations are not met.

There is room for an Egyptian center whose distance from the country's periphery is narrower than before to challenge Israel more strongly – with regard, say, to the issue of nuclear weapons[89] and the interminable "peace process" – in ways that come within both the letter and the spirit of the peace. Already, some changes have occurred – allowing Iranian warships to use the Suez Canal for the first time since 1979, some moves toward restoring diplomatic relations with Tehran, and mediating differences between Hamas and the Fatah-controlled PA. Allegedly reflecting the extent to which channels of communication between Egypt and Israel have been reduced, Israel had to send messages via Washington when elements of the Egyptian public, following the deaths of six Egyptian soldiers in an incident on the Israeli border, attacked the Israeli embassy in Cairo in September 2011.[90] With Mubarak and others in his regime accused of having agreed to sell oil to Israel at lower-than-market prices in return for kickbacks, Egypt demanded a renegotiation of the deal amid repeated sabotage of the pipeline by unknown persons.

Renewed attacks by Israel on the Hamas-ruled Gaza Strip in November 2012 pointed to the changed circumstances created by the overthrow of the Mubarak regime. The Israelis no longer had a center of the Periphery in Cairo to wish them well and to hope Hamas would be crushed. Egypt's newly elected Islamist leaders were not in a position to support the Gazans to the extent that some might have hoped or feared. From their beginnings in the 1920s, the Muslim Brothers had fervently opposed Zionism and Israel, and President Morsi now faced the danger of losing to more militant Islamist groups if he moderated his principles too much now that he held office. But he was severely constrained by his country's desperate need for financial assistance from the US, the International Monetary Fund (IMF), and the oil-rich Arab monarchies, as well as by a continuing fear of intervention by the Egyptian military. And there was no appetite for suddenly ending the peace with Israel. But without a Mubarak in Israel's pocket, Washington was frightened and, together with Cairo, succeeded in working out a cease-fire but left underlying issues, notably the blockade of the Hamas-dominated territory, for further negotiations.

The crisis coincided with stunning new developments within Egypt. The prestige of both Hamas (notably in relation to the Fatah-dominated PA that had looked on as the Palestinians in Gaza stood so firm) soared, as did that of the new Islamist leader in Cairo, who seized the moment by decreeing the termination of the authority of the judiciary – holdovers from the Mubarak dictatorship who previously had deprived the country of its popularly elected parliament – to challenge presidential actions until the new constitution drawn up by a constitutional assembly – whose large Islamist majority reflected the result of the parliamentary elections but faced dissolution by the holdover judges – was in place. It was not clear in the immediate aftermath of this daring step whether his removal of checks on presidential power constituted either a timely strike against those who were determined to thwart the new Islamist-led democracy or a long-term return to authoritarianism under his leadership. Nor could one tell whether this would make way for a radical turn away from Mubarak's foreign policy or – alternately – as reflecting

Morsi's assessment that Washington was so pleased with his role in the Gaza crisis and his general alignment with the Persian Gulf monarchies against the Resistance Bloc that he saw it as willing to co-opt him as its new client to replace Mubarak. There was suspicion that Washington had provided a "green light" for the emergence of a "new pharaoh"[91] – that is, a restoration of the imperial pattern with a mere change of leadership in the center of the Periphery. And one could only wait to see whether Morsi's enraged opponents – both the remnants of the old regime and those who thought the leadership of the revolution had been stolen from them and took to the streets anew – could win the day. In any case, a new constitution – quickly adopted by the assembly and violently opposed by secularists and *ancient régime* remnants – won a large majority in the popular vote that followed in December 2012.

The outcome of the "Arab Spring" remains in doubt. Whatever the revolutionaries at the center of the protests may have intended early in 2011, subsequent free elections – with Libya a possible exception – demonstrated a continuing popular Islamist tide. Whether this would undermine domination by the Center remained unclear. Would Islamist forces work together, or would internecine divisions between moderate and extreme Islamists and between Shi'ites and Sunnis – and Arabs and Iranians – provide new opportunities for the classic *divide et impera* strategy? To the annoyance of Washington and Tel Aviv, Morsi flew to Tehran to participate in the Non-Aligned Movement summit meeting of August 2012, but – apparently more tellingly – he also condemned the repression being carried out – with Iranian support – in Syria. Would the continuing influence of a military – notably in Egypt – aligned with the Center guarantee the perpetuation of the imperial order? Would selective intervention by the Center and some of its client monarchies – whose support for "the goal of democracy" one scholar[92] called "completely laughable" – rid them of such irritants as Assad and Qaddafi while keeping or restoring the client autocracies in places like Riyadh, Abu Dhabi, and Cairo? There was a beginning of suspicion that Ankara's spats with the Israelis, however authentic, were enabling it to act as a Trojan Horse in support of the now-threatened Israeli–American hegemony. Reminding us of "an Arabic phrase [portraying] a drowning man hang[ing] by ropes made of air," one suspicious commentator[93] believed that in 2011 these were

> ... being held out to the Arab world by the modern-day successors of Kitchener and McMahon ... through assistance to Sunni Arab Islam and with prominent Turkish-Ottoman support, in the hope that the new regimes will counter the increasingly strong Shi'ite Islam at Iran's helm.

Evoking what might represent the most ancient version of the "blowback" concept, the author concluded, however, that "this is just another *golem* [an artificial creature in Jewish folklore] that is liable to turn on its maker."

Conclusion

The political disposition of the Middle East is at its most unstable state in the post-World War II era. The strategic prerogatives of the American–Israeli regional project find themselves in simultaneous conflict with revisionist powers in the region – chiefly Iran and perhaps Turkey and an emerging new Egypt – and the masses in revolt, who have succeeded in overthrowing some American clients and have attempted to launch a new order within the region, one less favorable to American interests. This volume examines these fluid and dramatic developments through a series of case studies.

Focusing on broad patterns, Part I begins with our broad analysis of the Middle East's international politics in this chapter. Chapter 2, by William Haddad and Jasamin Rostam-Kolayi, provides a historical and theoretical overview of imperialism in the Middle East, emphasizing its European origins as background to the subsequent American and Israeli regional projects.

Part II deals with today's global and regional hegemons in the Middle East. In Chapter 3, Stephen Zunes examines the post-1945 power of the US in the Middle East, highlighting its role in militarizing the region and preventing democratic outcomes. Special attention is given to the American response to the challenge of radical Islamist movements and the recent popular insurrections, as well as to US relations with Israel, Iraq, and Iran. In Chapter 4, Ghada Talhami examines Israel's evolution from a vulnerable siege-state in 1948 to a regional superpower within the theoretical construct of its being a bridgehead of the American Center.

Focusing on selected actors that offer some possibility for providing the region respite from hegemony, Part III begins with Chapter 5, in which Mojtaba Mahdavi charts and critically examines the growth of Iranian power from the 1979 revolution onward, identifying the major political and theological fault lines Iran's expansion has revealed. In Chapter 6, Karen Aboul Kheir considers the Egyptian case, particularly its decline from regional leadership, and interprets the causes of the political protests from 2010 onward. In Chapter 7, Tozun Bahcheli discusses Turkey's search for a new political identity in the past decade, which has seen it chart an increasingly independent path and has made it an important player in the politics of the Middle East. Turning to an important neighboring region in Chapter 8, Philip Marfleet and Fran Cetti analyze European relations with the Middle East, particularly the efforts of the European Union to develop a "neighborhood policy" based on close relations with governments across the region – including those removed by revolutions in Egypt and Tunisia – and by the conflict in Libya. In Chapter 9, drawing on such case studies as Iraq and Libya, Richard Falk demonstrates the failures of the United Nations in its role as an authoritative international venue for the negotiation of collective problems facing the Middle East as a result of the global organization's domination by the permanent members of the Security Council.

Notes

1 M. Barnett, *Dialogues in Arab Politics: Negotiations in Regional Order*, New York: Columbia University Press, 1998, p. ix.

2 See D. Eisenhower, *The White House Years: Waging Peace, 1956–1961*, New York: Doubleday, 1965, pp. 197–203; P. Seale, *The Struggle for Syria: A Study of Post-War Arab Politics*, London: Oxford University Press, 1965, pp. 296–306; and G. Perry, "The Arab System and Its Erosion," *Asian Profile*, 1984, vol. 12, 271–99.

3 See G. Perry, "Israeli Involvement in Inter-Arab Politics," *International Journal of Islamic and Arabic Studies*, 1984, vol. 1, 11–31 and Perry, "The Arab System and Its Erosion."

4 L. Eisenberg, *My Enemy's Enemy: Lebanon in the Early Zionist Imagination, 1900–1948*, Detroit: Wayne State University Press, 1994.

5 M. Doran, "The Heirs of Nasser: Who Will Benefit from the Second Arab Revolution?" *Foreign Affairs*, 2011, vol. 90, 17–25.

6 M. Hosenball, "Obama authorizes secret CIA support for Syrian rebels," *The Globe and Mail*, August 2, 2012. URL: <http://www.theglobeandmail.com/news/world/obama-authorizes-secret-cia-support-for-syrian-rebels/article4457317/> (accessed August 24, 2012).

7 D. Sanger and E. Schmitt, "U.S. is Weighing Stronger Action in Syria Conflict," *New York Times*, November 29, 2012, pp. A1, A12.

8 J. Galtung, "A Structural Theory of Imperialism," *Journal of Peace Research*, 1971, vol. 8, 81–117.

9 J. Brownlee, *Democracy Prevention: The Politics of the U.S.–Egyptian Alliance*, Cambridge and New York: Cambridge University Press, 2012, p. 176.

10 J. Sharp, "U.S. Foreign Aid to Israel," Washington, DC: Congressional Research Service, September 16, 2010. URL: <http://www.fas.org/sgp/crs/mideast/RL33222.pdf> (accessed August 26, 2012).

11 U.S. Overseas Loans and Grants (Greenbook). U.S. Agency for International Development. URL: <http://gbk.eads.usaidallnet.gov/index.html> (accessed September 6, 2012). Also see J. Mearsheimer and S. Walt, *The Israel Lobby and U.S. Foreign Policy*, New York: Farrar, Straus and Giraux, 2007, pp. 24–40.

12 R. Grimmot and P. Kerr, "Arms Transfers to Developing Nations, 2004–11," Congressional Research Service, August 24, 2012. URL: <http://www.fas.org/sgp/crs/weapons/R42678.pdf> (accessed September 1, 2012).

13 Y. Melman, "IAEA won't discuss Israel's 'nuclear capabilities' after Arab proposal dropped," *Haaretz*, September 23, 2011. URL: <http://www.haaretz.com/news/diplomacy-defense/iaea-won-t-discuss-israel-s-nuclear-capabilities-after-arab-proposal-dropped-1.386334> (accessed August 26, 2012).

14 A. Yehoshua, "Why the Israeli–Palestinian conflict refuses to be resolved," *Haaretz*, April 26, 2011. URL: <http://www.haaretz.com/print-edition/features/why-the-israeli-palestinian-conflict-refuses-to-be-resolved-1.358095> (accessed September 1, 2012).

15 E. Helevy, *Man in the Shadows: Inside the Middle East Crisis with a Man Who Led the Mossad*, New York: Saint Martin's Press, 2006, pp. 31–32.

16 C. Shalev, "Will a U.S. attack on Iran become Obama's 'October Surprise'?" *Haaretz*, December 27, 2011. URL: <http://www.haaretz.com/blogs/west-of-eden/will-a-u-s-attack-on-iran-become-obama-s-october-surprise-1.403898> (accessed August 26, 2012).

17 A. Benn, "WikiLeaks cables tell the story of an empire in decline," *Haaretz*, December 1, 2010. URL: <http://www.haaretz.com/print-edition/opinion/wiki-leaks-cables-tell-the-story-of-an-empire-in-decline-1.328145> (accessed September 1, 2012).

18 K. Ziabari, "Israel and the Futility of Attacking Iran: Interview with Abolghasem Bayyenat," *Foreign Policy in Focus*, July 18, 2011. URL: http://www.fpif.org/articles/israel_and_the_futility_of_attacking_iran_interview_with_abolghasem_bayyenat> (accessed August 26, 2012).

19 Y. Melman, "According to latest trove of documents revealed by WikiLeaks, the Bahraini King instructed that official statements stop referring to Israel as the 'Zionist entity' or 'enemy'," *Haaretz*, April 8, 2011. URL: <http://www.haaretz.com/print-edition/news/haaretz-wikileaks-exclusive-bahrain-king-boasted-of-intelligence-ties-with-israel-1.354728> (accessed August 26, 2012).

20 M. Gordon, "German Intelligence Gave U.S. Iraqi Defense Plan, Report Says," *New York Times*, February 27, 2006. URL: <http://www.nytimes.com/2006/02/27/politics/27germans.html?pagewanted=all> (accessed August 26, 2012).

21 I. Black and S. Tisdall, "Saudi Arabia urges US attack on Iran to stop nuclear programme," *The Guardian*, November 28, 2011. URL: <http://www.guardian.co.uk/world/2010/nov/28/us-embassy-cables-saudis-iran?INTCMP=ILC-NETTXT3487> (accessed August 26, 2012).

22 R. Fisk, "Now we know. America really doesn't care about injustice in the Middle East," *The Independent*, November 30, 2010. URL: <http://www.independent.co.uk/opinion/commentators/fisk/robert-fisk-now-we-know-america-really-doesnt-care-about-injustice-in-the-middle-east-2146971.html> (accessed August 26, 2012).

23 N. Gvosdev and R. Takeyh, "Triumph of the New Wilsonism," *The National Interest*, January 4, 2012. URL: <http://nationalinterest.org/article/decline-western-realism-6274?page=show> (accessed September 5, 2012).

24 A. Oren, "For Saudi Arabia, Israel is turning from foe to friend," *Haaretz*, April 15, 2012. URL: <http://www.haaretz.com/opinion/for-saudi-arabia-israel-is-turning-from-foe-to-friend-1.424278> (accessed September 5, 2012). For a particularly blunt articulation of this reality, see C. Zambelis, "Unspoken Israeli-Saudi alliance targets Iran," *Asia Times Online*, September 8, 2012. URL: <http://atimes.com/atimes/Middle_East/NI08Ak01.html> (accessed September 8, 2012).

25 Haaretz Service, "Israel denies Saudis gave IDF airspace clearance for Iran Strike," *Haaretz*, January 1, 2009. URL: <http://www.haaretz.com/news/israel-denies-saudis-gave-idf-airspace-clearance-for-iran-strike-1.267118> (accessed September 5, 2012).

26 See M. Kerr, *The Arab Cold War: Gamal 'Abd al-Nasir and His Rivals, 1958–1970*, 3rd ed., London: Oxford University Press, 1971.

27 AFP, "Saudi aid to Arab Spring countries $3.7 bn: IMF," *AFP*, September 19, 2012. URL: <http://www.google.com/hostednews/afp/article/ALeqM5h5N0F1HOpCQBGctZM4qb4el5xpSg?docId=CNG.da4e80c9d12ac6c38b0b2b0c3ce9687c.301> (accessed November 11, 2012).

28 J. Khoury, A. Issacharoff, and A. Pfeffer, "'Palestinian Authority closely coordinating security operations with Israel'," *Haaretz*, January 26, 2011. URL: <http://www.haaretz.com/news/diplomacy-defense/palestinian-authority-closely-coordinating-security-operations-with-israel-1.339205> (accessed August 27, 2012). Also see B. Ravid, "WikiLeaks exposé: Israel tried to coordinate Gaza war with Abbas," *Haaretz*, November 28, 2010. URL: <http://www.haaretz.com/news/diplomacy-defense/wikileaks-expose-israel-tried-to-coordinate-gaza-war-with-abbas-1.327487> (accessed August 27, 2012).

29 I. Black and S. Milne, "Palestinian distrust of Iran revealed in leaked papers," *The Guardian*, January 26, 2011. URL: <http://www.guardian.co.uk/world/2011/jan/26/palestinian-distrust-iran-leaked-papers> (accessed August 26, 2012).

30 P. Lee, "China: the West's bogeyman in Libya," *Asia Times Online*, September 17, 2011. URL: <http://www.atimes.com/atimes/Middle_East/MI17Ak03.html> (accessed August 26, 2012).

31 Z. Bar'el, "The next stop on the Arab freedom train is Damascus," *Haaretz*, August 22, 2011. URL: <http://www.haaretz.com/news/middle-east/the-next-stop-on-the-arab-freedom-train-is-damascus-1.380068> (accessed August 27, 2012).

32 S. Shane, "West Sees Libya as Opportunity for Businesses," *New York Times*, October 28, 2011. URL: <http://www.nytimes.com/2011/10/29/world/africa/western-companies-see-libya-as-ripe-at-last-for-business.html?pagewanted=all> (accessed August 30, 2012).

33 S. Hendler, "Libya War Logs" (review of "*La guerre sans l'aimer*," by Bernard-Henri Lévy), *Haaretz*, December 16, 2011. URL: <ttp://www.haaretz.com/weekend/week-s-end/libya-war-logs-1.401754> (accessed August 27, 2012).

34 R. Norton-Taylor, "Libya: a new breed of military intervention," *The Guardian*, August 25, 2011. URL: <http://www.guardian.co.uk/commentisfree/2011/aug/25/libya-military-intervention> (accessed August 27, 2012).

35 V. Nasr, "Interview with Vali Nasr," *Frontline*, October 25, 2001. URL: <http://www.pbs.org/wgbh/pages/frontline/shows/saudi/interviews/nasr.html> (accessed August 27, 2012).

36 H. Askari, "Arab Spring's cruel truth," *Asia Times Online*, August 27, 2011. URL: <http://www.atimes.com/atimes/Middle_East/MH27Ak02.html> (accessed August 27, 2012).

37 A. Harel and A. Issacharoff, "Warning: More shake-ups ahead," *Haaretz*, December 16, 2011. URL: <http://www.haaretz.com/weekend/week-s-end/harel-and-issacharoff-warning-more-shake-ups-ahead-1.401763> (accessed August 27, 2012).

38 M. Gordon, "German Intelligence Gave U.S. Iraqi Defense Plan, Report Says," *New York Times*, February 27, 2006. URL: <http://www.nytimes.com/2006/02/27/politics/27germans.html?pagewanted=all> (accessed August 27, 2012).

39 A. Oren, "Defeat into victory," *Haaretz*, August 26, 2011. URL: <http://www.haaretz.com/weekend/week-s-end/defeat-into-victory-1.380813> (accessed August 27, 2012).

40 S. Huntington, *The Clash of Civilizations and the Remaking of World Order*, New York: Simon & Schuster, 1996, p. 88.

41 C. Johnson, *Blowback: The Costs and Consequences of American Empire*, New York: Metropolitan Books, 2000; *The Sorrows of Empire: Militarism, Secrecy, and the End of the Republic*, New York: Metropolitan Books, 2004; *Nemesis: The Last Days of the American Republic*, New York: Metropolitan Books, 2007; and *Dismantling the Empire: America's Last Best Hope*, New York: Macmillan Books, 2010.

42 C. Johnson, "Republic or empire: A National Intelligence Estimate on the United States," *Harper's Magazine*, January 2007. URL: <http://www.harpers.org/archive/2007/01/0081346> (accessed August 27, 2012).

43 F. Zakaria, *The Post-American World*, New York: W.W. Norton, 2008; D. Mason, *The End of the American Century*, Lanham, MD: Rowman & Littlefield, 2009.

44 National Intelligence Council (US), "Global Trends 2030: Alternative Worlds." URL: <http://www.dni.gov/files/documents/GlobalTrends_2030.pdf> (accessed December 11, 2012).

45 R. Cornwell *et al.*, "The Year of the Tiger: The Chinese century," *The Independent*, February 14, 2010. URL <http://www.independent.co.uk/news/world/asia/the-year-of-the-tiger-the-chinese-century-1899131.html> (accessed August 27, 2012).

46 Z. Abdoolcarim, "The ChIndian Century," *Time*, November 10, 2011. URL: <http://www.time.com/time/specials/packages/article/0,28804,2099180_2099179_2099178,00.html> (accessed August 28, 2012).

47 N. Sheva, "Cracks in the BRIC wall," *Haaretz*, December 29, 2011. URL: <http://english.themarker.com/forecasts-for-2012/cracks-in-the-bric-wall-1.404261> (accessed August 28, 2012).

48 F. Fernandez-Armesto, *Millennium: A History of the Last Thousand Years*, New York: Touchstone, 1995, p. 735.

49 A. Subramanian, "The inevitable superpower," *Foreign Affairs*, 2011, vol. 90, 66–78.
50 D. Kaye and F. Wehrey, "Response: Arab Spring, Persian Winter: Will Iran Emerge the Winner from the Arab Revolt?" *Foreign Affairs*, 2011, vol. 90, 183–86.
51 J. Migdal, *Strong Societies and Weak States*, Princeton, NJ: Princeton University Press, 1988.
52 A. Baram, "Saddam Hussein's dreams of an end to the Zionist nightmare," *Haaretz*, January 12, 2011. URL: <http://www.haaretz.com/weekend/week-s-end/saddam-hussein-s-dreams-of-an-end-to-the-zionist-nightmare-1.405806> (accessed August 29, 2012).
53 S. Huntington, *Political Order in Changing Societies*, 2nd ed., New Haven and London: Yale University Press, 2006, pp. 300ff.
54 S. Telhami, "The 2011 Arab Public Opinion Poll," Brookings website, November 26, 2011. URL: <http://www.brookings.edu/reports/2011/1121_arab_public_opinion_telhami> (accessed August 29, 2012).
55 Pew Global Attitudes Project, 2012 Spring Survey Topline Results, July 10, 2012 Release, *Pew Research Center* website. URL: <http://www.pewglobal.org/files/2012/07/Pew-Global-Attitudes-Project-Arab-Spring-TOPLINE-Tuesday-July-10-2012.pdf> (accessed September 2, 2012).
56 T. Arango, "Vacuum Is Feared as U.S. Quits Iraq, but Iran's Deep Influence May Not Fill It," *New York Times*, October 9, 2011. URL: <http://www.nytimes.com/2011/10/09/world/middleeast/if-united-states-leaves-vacuum-in-iraq-disliked-iran-may-not-fill-it.html> (accessed August 29, 2012).
57 H. Amirahmadi and K. Afrasiabi, "The west's silence over Bahrain smacks of double standards," *The Guardian*, April 29, 2011. URL: <http://www.guardian.co.uk/commentisfree/2011/apr/29/bahrain-saudi-arabia-iran-west?INTCMP=ILCNETTXT3487> (accessed August 29, 2012).
58 N. Kristof, "Repressing Democracy with American Arms," *New York Times*, December 18, 2011. URL: <http://www.nytimes.com/2011/12/18/opinion/sunday/kristof-repressing-democracy-with-american-arms.html> (accessed August 29, 2012).
59 J. Cole, "Iraq's al-Maliki Seeks Arrest of Sunni VP as Terrorist, Parliament in Uproar," *Informed Comment*, December 18, 2011. URL: <http://www.juancole.com/2011/12/iraqs-al-maliki-seeks-arrest-of-sunni-vp-as-terrorist-parliament-in-uproar.html> (accessed August 29, 2012).
60 M. Gordon, E. Schmitt, and T. Arrango, "Iraq Hampering Effort to Slow Arms for Syria," *New York Times*, December 2, 2012, pp. A1, A11.
61 See P. Seale, "The Destruction of Syria," *Agency Global*, July 24, 2012. URL: <http://www.agenceglobal.com/index.php?show=article&Tid=2840> (accessed September 2, 2012).
62 T. Arango, A. Barnard, and H. Saad, "Syria Rebels Tied to Al Qaeda Play Key Role in War," *New York Times*, December 9, 2012, p. 1.
63 "Number of Syrian refugees registered in region tops 500,000 mark," UNHCR: The UN Refugee Agency website, December 11, 2012. URL: <http://www.unhcr.org/50c70ca36.html> (accessed January 1, 2013). Also see Los Angeles Times Staff, "Syrian refugees raise tensions in Lebanon," Los Angeles Times, August 17, 2012. URL: <http://www.latimes.com/news/nationworld/iraq/complete/la-fg-syria-violence-20120818,0,2636410.story> (accessed August 30, 2012). On loss of life, see: "Data suggests Syria death toll could be more than 60,000, says UN human rights office," UN News Centre, January 2, 2013. URL: <http://www.un.org/apps/news/story.asp?NewsID=43866#.UOeZ1W9QXzQ> (accessed January 4, 2013).
64 D. Kirkpatrick, "Egyptian Asks Rivals of West to Peace Plan," *New York Times*, September 27, 2012, pp. A1, A6.
65 K. Afrasiabi, "Iran makes a u-turn on Syria," *Asia Times Online*, September 1, 2011. URL: <http://atimes.com/atimes/Middle_East/MI01Ak01.html> (accessed August 28, 2012).

66 E. Hava, "Robust private sector gives Turkey fastest H1 growth worldwide," *Today's Zaman*, September 12, 2011. URL: <http://www.todayszaman.com/news-256556-robust-private-sector-gives-turkey-fastest-h1-growth-worldwide.html> (accessed August 30, 2012).

67 "Turkish–Egyptian Business Council requests earlier trade liberalization," *World Bulletin*, September 12, 2011. URL: <http://www.worldbulletin.net/?aType=haber&ArticleID=78767> (accessed August 30, 2012).

68 J. Shenker, "Egypt threatens to use live rounds in security crackdown," *The Guardian*, September 12, 2011. URL: <http://www.guardian.co.uk/world/2011/sep/12/egypt-live-rounds-protest-crackdown> (accessed August 30, 2012).

69 Telhami, "The 2011 Arab Public Opinion Poll."

70 Z. Bar'el, "Turkey set to sign military pact with Egypt, after cutting trade ties with Israel," *Haaretz*, September 7, 2011. URL: <http://www.haaretz.com/print-edition/news/turkey-set-to-sign-military-pact-with-egypt-after-cutting-trade-ties-with-israel-1.382955> (accessed August 30, 2012).

71 Huntington, *The Clash of Civilizations,* pp. 178–79. Also see G. Perry, "Huntington's 'clash of civilizations': rumours and clarification," in T. Ismael and A. Rippin (eds), *Islam in the Eyes of the West: Images and realities in an age of terror,* London: Routledge, 2010, pp. 226–50.

72 B. Morris, "Turkey's Islamic Revolution," *The National Interest*, August 1, 2011. URL: <http://nationalinterest.org/commentary/turkeys-islamic-revolution-5685> (accessed August 30, 2012).

73 See Z. Bar'el, "In Syria crisis, Turkey is caught between Iran and a hard place," *Haaretz*, December 7, 2011. URL: <http://www.haaretz.com/print-edition/features/in-syria-crisis-turkey-is-caught-between-iran-and-a-hard-place-1.400036> (accessed August 30, 2012).

74 Y. Verter, "The Arab Spring turned Netanyahu into the national fearmonger," *Haaretz*, December 16, 2011. URL: <http://www.haaretz.com/weekend/week-s-end/the-arab-spring-turned-netanyahu-into-the-national-fearmonger-1.401760> (accessed August 29, 2012).

75 Hendler, "Libya War Logs."

76 M. Duss, "Letter from Herziya, Neocon Woodstock," *The Nation*, February 14, 2011. URL: <http://www.thenation.com/article/158547/letter-herzliya-neocon-woodstock> (accessed August 30, 2012).

77 A. Eldar, "When Israeli arrogance meets Arab honor," *Haaretz*, August 22, 2011. URL: <http://www.haaretz.com/print-edition/opinion/when-israeli-arrogance-meets-arab-honor-1.379926> (accessed August 30, 2012); A. Shadid and D. Kirkpatrick, "In Tumult, New Hope for Palestinian Cause," *New York Times*, August 9, 2011. URL: <http://www.nytimes.com/2011/08/10/world/middleeast/10palestinians.html?_r=1> (accessed August 30, 2012).

78 Eldar, "When Israeli arrogance meets Arab honor."

79 G. Levy, "Israeli war drums ignore Hamas move for change," *Haaretz*, January 1, 2012. URL: <http://www.haaretz.com/print-edition/opinion/israeli-war-drums-ignore-hamas-move-for-change-1.404822> (accessed September 1, 2012).

80 P. Seale, "The Middle East's New Geopolitical Map," *Middle East Online,* September 21, 2011. URL: <http://www.middle-east-online.com/english/?id=48148> (accessed August 30, 2012).

81 Turki al-Faisal, "Veto a State, Lose an Ally," *New York Times*, September 11, 2012. URL: <http://www.nytimes.com/2011/09/12/opinion/veto-a-state-lose-an-ally.html> (accessed August 30, 2012).

82 C. Whitlock, "U.S. secretly backed Syrian opposition groups, cables released by WikiLeaks show," *Washington Post*, April 17, 2011. URL: <http://www.washingtonpost.com/world/us-secretly-backed-syrian-opposition-groups-cables-released-by-wikileaks-show/2011/04/14/AF1p9hwD_print.html> (accessed August 30, 2012).

83 Hosenball, "Obama authorizes secret CIA support."

84 Bar'el, "The next stop on the Arab freedom train is Damascus."

85 G. Perry, "Imperial Democratization: Rhetoric and Reality," *Arab Studies Quarterly*, 2006, vol. 28, 55–87.

86 J. Cole, "This is the Way the Iraq War Ends, with Bangs and Whimpers," *Informed Comment*, October 16, 2011. URL: <http://www.juancole.com/2011/10/this-is-the-way-the-iraq-war-ends-with-bangs-and-wimpers.html> (accessed August 30, 2012).

87 T. Shanker and S. Myers, "U.S. Is Planning Buildup in Gulf After Iraq Exit," *New York Times*, October 29, 2011. URL: <http://www.nytimes.com/2011/10/30/world/middleeast/united-states-plans-post-iraq-troop-increase-in-persian-gulf.html?pagewanted=all> (accessed October 31, 2012).

88 D. Kirkpatrick, "Military Flexes Its Muscles as Islamists Gain in Egypt," *New York Times*, December 7, 2011. URL: <http://www.nytimes.com/2011/12/08/world/middleeast/egyptian-general-mukhtar-al-mulla-asserts-continuing-control-despite-elections.html?pagewanted=all> (accessed August 30, 2012).

89 R. Pedatzur, "Israel must change its nuclear policy," *Haaretz*, October 10, 2011. URL: <http://www.haaretz.com/print-edition/opinion/israel-must-change-its-nuclear-policy-1.389074> (accessed August 30, 2012).

90 B. Ravid, "Diplomatic ties with Egypt down to bare minimum," *Haaretz*, September 11, 2011. URL: <http://www.haaretz.com/print-edition/news/diplomatic-ties-with-egypt-down> (accessed August 30, 2012).

91 See O. Basharat, "Egypt's American-controlled pharaoh," *Haaretz*, November 27, 2012. URL: <http://www.haaretz.com/opinion/egypt-s-american-controlled-pharaoh.premium-1.480768> (accessed November 27, 2012).

92 H. Cobban, "Further thoughts on Syria, Turkey, and democracy," *Just World News*, November 25, 2011. URL: <http://justworldnews.org/archives/004237.html> (accessed August 30, 2012).

93 S. Masalha, "Recent revolutions are neither Arab nor Spring," *Haaretz*, December 5, 2011. URL: <http://www.haaretz.com/print-edition/opinion/recent-revolutions-are-neither-arab-nor-spring-1.399552> (accessed August 30, 2012).

2 Imperialism and its manifestations in the Middle East

William W. Haddad and Jasamin Rostam-Kolayi

Our purpose is to provide a historical backdrop to the continuing subordination of the Middle East by providing a sketch of the emergence of Western imperialism in the region. We will briefly focus on two important theories of imperialism and then examine the past two centuries of that phenomenon through these lenses, with major emphasis on the earlier periods, when it took on a more blatant form than today. Finally, we show what occurred rather than trying to prove the veracity of one theory or another. This should set the stage for the micro chapters that follow.

Historians, economists, political scientists and others have been interested in the origins, reasons, and permutations of "imperialism" – implying, from an ethnocentric point of view, the expansion of the "civilized" polity to barriers beyond its ethnic homeland. Throughout history we identify empires and their imperial past. However, early in the twentieth century President Woodrow Wilson seemed to sound the death knell for this phenomenon when he proclaimed that the Age of Empires was over and that the world was entering the Age of Nations. Imperialism was to be studied, not lived. According to one of his Fourteen Points, the self-determination of peoples in their respective nation-states was to replace multi-national states. This same Wilsonian principle of self-determination was invoked after World War II, this time to end colonialism. Though this was a hopeful assumption, and though many multi-ethnic empires – such as in the Austro-Hungarian, Russian, and Ottoman cases – have made way in both Europe and the Middle East for more-or-less ethnically based nation-states, the imperial state still exists – particularly the informal variety in which subordinate entities are legally sovereign – much to the pleasure of some and the sorrow of others.

Wilson later admitted that he had not intended for self-determination to be applied everywhere, since many areas of the world, in his estimation, were not ready for self-rule. Since the Peace of Westphalia of 1648 which legitimized the sovereign state in Western Christendom, it was to be limited to the "more advanced" Europe and did not include the Middle East. It was this mindset that guided the European powers to colonize the Middle East after World War I.

Some theories of imperialism

In order to understand the roots of imperialism, scholars have suggested that early civilizations, in order to protect themselves from the warlike nomads beyond their frontiers, were forced to expand to defensible positions. This view is flawed. For example, the Greek empire was not established because of a need to defend against "barbarians." The Ottoman Empire did not come into being because of threats from the outside but was impelled by Islam to expand. It needed to control the three holy cities of Mecca, Medina and Jerusalem in order to be recognized as the leader of the Muslim world. And this certainly was not a concern of the Mongols when they conquered most of the Eurasian continent in the fourteenth century. One does not hear the fear of outsiders in Genghis Khan's famous declaration that Man's greatest joy is to kill his enemy, mount his horse and embrace his woman. Notwithstanding the flaws of interpretations of imperialism and our inability to completely understand their origin, they continue to exist into the twenty-first century. Recent explanations, which are more sophisticated and that help us understand the reasons for them, have been dominated by two opposing interpretations: Marxian and Neo-Conservative.

Marx and Lenin offered an economic theory of the origins of imperialism. One of Marx's fundamental ideas is that economics is the foundation of everything in history, but he did not develop a theory of imperialism as such. Lenin argued specifically that imperialism was the last, monopolistic stage of capitalism as it searched for overseas investment of surplus capital backed by the military power of the state. For the Marxist, the connection between imperialism and capitalism is clear.

Since Marxism argues that imperialism is an economic necessity, it is therefore inevitable in societies with advanced capitalism. Put in more stark terms, in order to understand imperialism, one follows the money. Students do not need to study Shakespeare for his Great Man theory, nor does one read Tolstoy, who argued that a force necessary to move one million people required one million people, for economic forces constitute the foundation of everything.

Another writer, J. H. Hobson, preceded Lenin in providing an important analysis of the importance of economics to imperialism. Though Hobson was not a Marxist, his *Imperialism: A Study,* which appeared in 1902, influenced Marxists, including Lenin.[1] Hobson argued that as capitalistic societies advance there is a tendency toward monopoly. The result is that more and more money is concentrated in fewer and fewer hands and that the opportunity to invest declines. As more money accumulates because of a lack of investment opportunities, the capitalistic society begins to look abroad for markets and places to invest. Once capital is invested in a foreign country there is pressure to occupy it or make it a colony or protectorate in order to safeguard the investment and to limit competition from other industrial countries.

Lenin, under the influence of Hobson, published his monograph, *Imperialism*, in 1916. Lenin wrote that Hobson gave "a very good and accurate description of the fundamental economic and political traits of imperialism." Lenin continued that capitalism is

> ... that stage of development in which the dominance of monopolies and finance capital has established itself; in which the export of capital has acquired pronounced importance; in which the division of the world among the international trusts has begun; in which the division of all territories of the globe among the great capitalist powers has been completed.[2]

Thus for Lenin and other Marxists, World War I was not a surprise. As the developed capitalistic countries required colonies they inevitably came into conflict as they sought to divide up a finite world. Hobson had anticipated this result and suggested that these kinds of conflicts could be avoided by redistributing wealth at home to make everyone more productive and have more purchasing power. Lenin rejected this possibility, saying that a capitalistic country would never agree to a more equal distribution of wealth amongst its people. Put in other terms, Lenin argued that moderate economic reform was a non-capitalistic idea and therefore could not be implemented in a capitalistic country. Thus, in the Marxist view, imperialism seeks to provide an answer to declining profits, social unrest caused by unemployment, and the need for more markets and raw materials.

At the time of its propagation, there was a reaction to the Marxist focus on economic determinism; for example in the writings of Joseph B. Schumpeter. In his famous article titled "Imperialism has a social basis," the Harvard economist argued that a capitalistic society offers no fertile soil for imperialist impulses.[3] His disciples further argued that if one examines the movement of capital, one will be surprised to learn that it did not flow to the colonies. Nor were the colonies a source of raw materials, thus refuting Hobson and Lenin. Rather, imperialism is an atavistic throwback to pre-capitalist eras – something that cannot be explained by what exists today. It predates capitalism. Imperial conquests happen for the sake of conquest, for victory, for glory. But while the Marxist interpretation of imperialism has serious flaws, its emphasis on economics as an imperial catalyst makes it a useful analytical tool.

At the other end of the political spectrum are those who say that it is the duty of advanced peoples to help to bring progress and well-being – from "the true faith" to democracy – to others, a rationalization that assures themselves and others at home and abroad that their motives are "pure." A prime example of this is the current Neo-Conservativism. This view evolved as the imperial imperative changed over time, becoming less concerned with defense of the Center. Thus Neo-Conservatives perforce adopted another, older justification to validate their cause: altruism. This altruism had echoes in previous ideas which justified imperialism as a way to combat the slave

racism

trade in Africa or to spread Christianity – and, more generally, what was termed "the White Man's Burden." Thus the Neo-Cons and others who echo some of their views, argue that a benevolent global hegemon – and this requires an "exceptional nation," of which there is only one – is required to protect "public goods" such as freedom of the seas and indeed world peace and even justifies violations of the UN Charter and other rules of international law that are binding on others.

The American Neo-Conservatives – and, not always easily distinguishable from them, the "liberal interventionists" – who favor imperialism are fond of recalling that though America has preached self-determination for a century, on the one occasion when it was invoked in the US, called at that time Secession, it was put down with great loss of life. As a corollary to their support of imperialism, contemporary Neo-Conservatives argue that no matter the violence associated with the subjugation of a population, the imperial venture has brought subsequent generations of the colonized the benefits of the *imperium* – order, safety, modernization, Christianity, private property, and the rule of law. The Neo-Conservative imperialists – whose version of altruism emphasizes the need to "promote democracy" and to protect human rights – further argue that since they are motivated by the best of intentions, if the results – for example, in Iraq in 2003 and after – are not what they hoped for, the outcome can be dismissed. In this way, Dick Cheney, Condoleezza Rice, Paul Wolfowitz, Richard Perle, and Donald Rumsfeld never have to say they are sorry.

There are many other theories of imperialism. What they all hold in common is that they were invented in the Center, were Eurocentric, and though their spokespeople believed they were helping the world, took little heed of the impact on the colonized. This includes the impact of subservience, the failure to encourage education, the denial of basic human rights, and the exclusion from the "universal" concept of equality. Compounding the negative results for the Periphery, the Western intellectual defense or explanation of the imperial process has been suffused with the racist pseudo-science of social Darwinism ("the White Man's Burden") and Messianic determinism (*dieu veut*) which permit no agency for "The Other."

In large part, Western imperialism in the Middle East has been motivated by the region's strategic location, although this does not necessarily belie the economic interpretation. The "crown jewel" of British imperialism in particular, long was India and thus, London was intensely concerned with protecting its "road to India." When General Bonaparte carried out his reckless invasion of Egypt in 1798, he saw this as a step toward conquering India, which the French had lost to the British a few decades earlier. And the imperative was of preventing czarist Russia from gaining access to the "warm-water" ports in the Eastern Mediterranean and the Persian Gulf and the essence of the so-called "Eastern Question" throughout the nineteenth century. The British recurrently acted to limit czarist imperialism through friendly backing of the Ottomans and Qajars but could not avoid the temptation of

British Empire was strategic ~ui South Africa

engaging in economic penetration, perpetuating the Capitulations, and occupying territories like Egypt and Cyprus that helped to push Ottomans and Iranians into backing Germany during World War I. That in part explains the tendency to rely on local collaborators and avoid direct rule whenever possible. Only in the period immediately before World War I did the additional factor of access to oil and to profitable oil concessions gradually come to compete with the "road to India" motive.

Types of imperialism

Until the late fifteenth century, Islamic states were the dominant force in Europe, and the future seemed to belong to them. As late as 1683, Ottoman forces besieged Vienna and came close to conquering it. The Mediterranean Sea long was an Ottoman lake on which, as one British diplomat put it, no European could float a plank without asking Istanbul. Christian Europe dreaded this Muslim empire and feared that its children would soon be the reading the Quran, not the Bible. Further aggravating relations was Muslim control of the water and land trading routes to East Asia. Western Europe was acquainted with the luxuries of the East, such as tea, silk and porcelains and wanted access to them without having to deal with Muslim inter-mediaries. It was a desire to bypass the Muslim monopoly on the trade routes that motivated the Spanish to sail west to reach the East and the Portuguese effort to circumnavigate Africa to reach China.

A setback to the Muslim monopoly on trade occurred when Vasco da Gama circumnavigated Africa in 1498 and landed at the Arab merchant city of Calicut in India. This set the stage for the subsequent Portuguese blockade of the Red Sea and the Persian Gulf, thus impeding Muslim maritime commerce between Europe and East Asia. Realizing the importance of their discovery of a new route to East Asia, in 1507, the Portuguese took control of the entrance to the Red Sea and followed this up in 1515 with a blockade of the Straits of Hormuz. The victories in the Indian Ocean were followed by the naval victory of an alliance of European Catholic maritime states at the battle of Lepanto, west of Greece, in 1571. Though the Ottomans recovered from the loss at Lepanto, which one Istanbul official described as no more than a shave, after which the hair would grow back, the Muslim Empire never again engaged in a major naval battle with a Western European state. And it emboldened the West to think that the Ottomans were not invincible. Western Christendom's domination of the seas – at a time when Muslim empires continued to expand on land, where they remained superior – would make way within about two centuries for the decline of Islamic power in general in the face of a Western world that had enriched itself through control of the seas and the Americas, and massive enslavement of Africans.

The imperial adventure of which the "Age of Discovery" was the opening salvo had as its goal economic domination. This was exemplified by Western Europe's attempt to weaken the Islamic world and was part of a phenomenon now conventionally known as the old imperialism. Under the old imperialism, Western European Center Nations created wealth as they moved from mercantilism to capitalism, sought markets in and raw materials from the Periphery, and fought amongst themselves and others to prevent competition. This resulted in an immeasurable transfer of wealth, whether gold, silver, or human beings, to the Center. Put in its most stark terms, during the period of the old imperialism, the Center developed by underdeveloping the Periphery.

The term "new imperialism" is used to describe the renewed colonial expansion that began in the late nineteenth century. It continued the policy of economic domination but added to it the political control of the Periphery in Africa, Asia, and the Middle East. European countries – but also the US, Japan, and Australia – began to control wide swaths of territory.

Hobson dated the new phase back to 1871, when Europe's first significant physical appropriation of African territory occurred. Lenin put the beginning in 1876, when capitalism in Europe entered a new phase and, as a result, Belgian King Leopold II called together a group of geographers and explorers to determine the best way to conquer Africa. Others argue that the new imperialism can be dated to 1884–85, when the Congress of Berlin on Africa met and agreed to a set of regulations for exploring that continent. Among other items, the conference established rules for the recognition of European colonial claims, one case in point being that it was no longer enough to plant a flag and proclaim that all of the territory around it belonged to such-and-such country. Rather a European country that signed on to the Act that came out of the Congress had to physically occupy and develop resources in the country that it claimed. With this new system, the scramble for African territory was energized. By the post-World War I era, only Liberia and Ethiopia were not incorporated officially as parts of European empires.

The causes of this accelerated overseas expansion are generally accepted. The second industrial revolution, characterized by the use of fossil fuels rather than steam to produce energy, transformed Western Europe and to a lesser extent the US and Japan, making them more powerful economically and militarily. Further, the growth of industrialized cities put new pressures on countries to look abroad.

Defenders of colonialism often voiced their support in altruistic terms. John Stuart Mill was perhaps the most famous of them, arguing that many peoples were not ready for self-government and therefore that England, for example, should support white settler colonies. These colonies could serve to alleviate the problem in the Center of limited land for agriculture and population pressure.

Cecil Rhodes, an avid nineteenth-century imperialist, dreamed of building a railroad from Cape Town to Cairo that would never leave British territory. He was said to espouse expansion after attending an English village meeting in which everybody cried for "bread, bread, and bread"[4] He concluded that Empire was necessary to avoid a class-based civil war in England. This economic interpretation closely resembled those later enunciated by Hobson and Lenin.

Evelyn Baring – later known as Lord Cromer – the longtime British Consul General – and effective proconsul – in Egypt, opined that "The special aptitude shown by Englishmen in the government of Oriental races pointed to England as the most effective and beneficent instrument for the gradual introduction of European civilization into Egypt." He believed that the Western model, with its emphasis on empiricism and rationalism, was needed to improve what he called "the Oriental mind."[5]

The new imperialism was reinforced by Charles Darwin's theory of evolution. Elucidated in his *On the Origin of Species* (1859), it explained that over time, and largely by sexual selection, living things evolved from simple forms to more complex ones. This idea, under the rubric of social Darwinism, was then appropriated by racists and imperialists, with its adherents arguing that the principles of evolution could be applied to whole groups of peoples and nations. Some, it was argued, were more advanced than others, and those less evolved needed tutelage in order to move up the evolutionary scale. A determining factor was skin color – with the lighter races more advanced. Though originally a neutral idea positing that living things evolved from simple structures to more complex ones, Darwin's theory was seized by racists. The morphing of a scientific theory to one that rationalized discrimination based on skin color assuaged the Western Europeans and permitted without remorse the conquest of those who were less technologically advanced. Charlatans and even men of science toured cities and showed, ostensibly by the size or weight of craniums, that darker races were less evolved, thus excusing domination under the disguise of civilizing the Other. Proselytizing Christianity too was an integral part of the imperial process, what the French called "*notre mission civilicatrice.*" In the special case of Palestine, strategic concerns were reinforced by a sentimental association of the modern Zionists as the successors to popular heroes from the Old Testament and disregard for the indigenous population as "mere natives" who did not really matter or as the successors to Canaanites whose extermination was said to be divinely approved.

Of course, supporters of the new imperialism attempted to soften the impact of the colonial project by couching it in terms like "The White Man's Burden," immortalized in a poem by Rudyard Kipling. Subtitled, "The United States and the Philippine Islands," an allusion to the territory recently won in the Spanish-American war, the poem exhorted Americans to empire and purported to justify for them the imperial enterprise. Kipling's poem reflected a commonly held opinion of the late nineteenth century that it was the obligation of the rich and more advanced Center to help the poor and underdeveloped Periphery.

Citizens in the industrialized states supported the imperial imperative. Incited by the appearance of yellow journalism and convinced that the application of social Darwinism would prove their nation superior, the public was the greatest supporter of imperialism. They believed rivalry would inevitably mean a reduction in the number of imperial powers until only the fittest one survived. The rise of nationalism added a new and dangerous element to the mix.

The new imperialism also saw the establishment of colonial settlements – the attempt to change the demographics of the conquered state by encouraging settlers from the Center to take up new lives in the Periphery. The period between the mid nineteenth century till World War I is considered the golden age of the New Imperialism. During that time perhaps a quarter of the globe came under colonial rule, mainly that of Britain, France, Germany, and Belgium.

World War I, the Ottoman Empire and its dissolution

Ruling the Ottoman Empire at the beginning of the twentieth century was Sultan Abdul Hamid II. He has been variously described as an intelligent, able politician, a modernizer, an early Stalin and mad. He was famous for his desire to build railroads, most notably dreaming of one that would connect the Turkish Straits and the Persian Gulf. Leland Stanford was approached to take the lead, but engrossed in similar efforts in the US, he declined. Realizing that the results of building such a railroad would lead to prosperity in Greater Syria, Iraq, and the Empire generally, the Sultan turned to a syndicate led by the Germans. In April 1909, he was deposed in the Young Turk Revolution dominated by the triumvirate of Jemal, Enver and Talat Pashas. The alliance Abdul Hamid had formed with the Germans would influence the decision to enter World War I on their side.

Early in the fighting, the British attempted to seize the Turkish Straits in what was dubbed the Dardanelles Campaign. It was a colossal failure, one that set back the political career of Winston Churchill, First Lord of the Admiralty. As a result, the British began to fear a German-Turkish attack on Suez. No longer fearful of losing the Straits, the Ottomans went on the offensive against British invaders of southern Iraq and imposed horrible casualties on them but a new British offensive succeeded a year later.

However, when the armistice was signed in 1918 the Ottomans still held the northeastern area of what we now call Iraq, essentially the province of Mosul. According to the terms of surrender, Turkish forces were to lay down their weapons, but the British violated the terms of the armistice by marching north to complete their physical control of what eventually would form the new country of Iraq.

The destruction of the Ottoman Empire completely changed the makeup of the Middle East, resulting in the loss of the Arab provinces and eventual emergence of new states there.

The victorious Allied Powers initially supported a Greek attempt to occupy Asia Minor. The Turks, however, rallied around General Mustafa Kemal – later known as Kemal Atatürk – an Ottoman military commander and the hero of the Dardanelles Campaign, and organized military resistance. This meant defeating Armenian, Italian, and French attempts, and most importantly driving out the Greeks and overseeing the removal of the British from Istanbul in 1923.

Thus were established the borders of today's Republic of Turkey in the predominantly Turkish areas of the former Empire.

The Arabs of geographic Syria, through their participation in the Ottoman Parliament in Istanbul and their long association with the caliphs in Istanbul, were largely loyal to the Ottoman Empire throughout the war. Though the elites argued tepidly for the use of Arabic in the Arab provinces, there was no large Arab nationalist movement prior to World War I. To the sophisticated Muslim Syrian urbanite living in Damascus, an Arab then was thought of as a desert dweller who lived in a tent.

The Christian Arab minority also remained loyal, at least until after the war began. An agreement with Istanbul in 1861 guaranteed the Maronites in Lebanon the right to local economic autonomy as well as religious and social self-rule as part of the *millet* system, which arranged citizens by religion. The Maronites benefited from these special considerations not only because of Ottoman benevolence but also from the centuries of Western European concessions wrested from Istanbul. Known collectively as the Capitulations, these were laws, regulations and procedures granted to foreigners living in or trading with the Ottoman Empire. The Capitulations essentially gave foreigners a trade advantage, since they were exempted from local taxes, had beneficial tariff structures for their exports and imports, and enjoyed extraterritoriality when they disregarded Ottoman law. Negotiated when Istanbul was strong, the Capitulations were exploited as the Empire weakened. Many Christians and Jews, as well as some Sunni Muslims in Damascus and the port cities of geographic Syria, obtained citizenship in Western European nations that they had never even traveled to. In this way – illustrating another form of Western imperialism – the Center cultivated and even created small bridgeheads in the Periphery for mutual financial benefit and ultimately used these ties to control the Middle East.

In conjunction with the Capitulations was the penetration of western missionaries. For example, the American Board of Commissioners for Foreign Missions, a Protestant agency founded in 1810, first arrived in Anatolia in 1839. Their representatives established scores of schools there, as they did in Lebanon. The French actively, though on a smaller scale, imitated this process of winning supporters through education. Thus there developed in the Ottoman Empire a dual system of education: Ottoman state schools were used by Muslims and successfully increased their literacy rate in the nineteenth century but Christians – for example, the Armenians in Asia Minor and the Maronites in Lebanon – tended to gravitate to the missionary schools. When American missionaries established the Syrian Protestant College (later to become the American University) in Beirut, the formula changed. Maronites went to French schools and ultimately the University of St. Joseph, while Protestant and Muslim students attended the American University of Beirut.

Since the mission schools originally served Christians rather than Muslims, a question arises concerning what role minorities had in the rise of Arab nationalism and the Arab Revolt. The defining work on this subject was George Antonius's *The Arab Awakening*.[6] He argued that it was largely Christian secret societies, educated in mission schools about the blessings of Western civilization that gave rise to an Arabic literary revival and the growth of Arab nationalism. The leaders of the secret societies, as this narrative goes, organized opposition to the Ottomans, and this in turn gave rise to the Arab Revolt, which was largely responsible for the failure of the Ottoman effort in the Arab provinces. Antonius has been proven wrong in asserting that the Arabic literary revival and the growth of Arab nationalism was the result of the mission schools, as were his claims about the success of the Arab Revolt.

To find an answer to the question of why nationalism began to emerge in the Middle East it is probably better to look elsewhere, especially the emergence of newspapers and printing presses in Cairo and Beirut. The most famous was the Egyptian Bulaq Press, established early in the nineteenth century, which published on average 100 books per year. The publisher and the daily press certainly accelerated the rise and spread of Arab nationalism. Nevertheless, Arab separatism was at a nascent stage in World War I and had a minimum impact on the outcome of the war. In fact, the Ottomans were able to defend Syria until December 1917, when the British and their Arab collaborators took Jerusalem, followed in September 1918 by the capture of Damascus and Aleppo.

Syria was quiescent also because of the harshness of Jemal Pasha, named by the ruling triumvirate to govern the Syrian provinces. If the few calls for autonomy before 1914 were viewed by Istanbul as harmless dissent, after World War I began Jemal saw pleas for regional autonomy as rebellion. Though considered the weakest of the triumvirate that included Enver and Talat, he was given the task of keeping the Empire in line by being its policeman. To emphasize his position in 1915, 11 Arab nationalists were executed in what came to be called Beirut's Martyrs Square. A year later some 200 Syrians were arrested and convicted of treason, and 22 were put to death in Damascus and Beirut. Shocked by the deaths of moderate leaders, who were generally loyal to the Empire, Syria did not rise in a rebellion fueled by Arab nationalism. It was the Ottoman decision to enter the war on the side of Germany, the impressment of Arab males into the Ottoman military, Jemal's heavy-handedness in dealing with Istanbul's Arab subjects, and – most importantly – the defeat of the Turks and the imperial ambitions of Britain and France that led to the territorial division after the war.

The wartime agreements

The Hussein-McMahon correspondence, 1915

The apprehension that followed the Dardanelles disaster induced the British to look for an Arab ally that would prevent an attack on Suez. Perhaps the Arabs could even aid in the capture of geographic Syria by opening a southern front against the Ottomans and thus help the United Kingdom after its initial attempt to capture Baghdad ended in failure. British imperial interest in attacking Ottoman Syria should be seen through the lens of India. Egypt, including the Suez Canal, had come under British control in 1882 and constituted a vital point on the "road to India." It was a cornerstone of British policy to let no European power near the Canal or even into the southern portions of geographic Syria. Britain also had a secondary interest in the Middle East, as its navy was changing from coal to oil.

In the Arabian peninsula, the Arab Hashemite family, descendants of the Prophet Muhammad, as the title "sharif" indicates, were Ottoman governors of the Hijaz, including Mecca, Islam's holiest city. The Hashemite holder of the office since 1908, Sharif Hussein, was restive and ambitious. Thus there was a congruence of interests: the Hashemites wanted to establish an Arab caliphate under Hussein, and the British were eager to gain Arab allies to prevent the Ottomans from threatening geographic Syria, Egypt and the Canal. In October 1915, Sir Henry McMahon, the British High Commissioner in Egypt, began negotiations with Sharif Hussein's son, Abdullah. Representing the center of the most powerful Center nation, McMahon's negotiations should be seen as an alliance-forming opportunity that helped to create a new bridgehead in the Periphery.

The French, as a British ally, had to be consulted since they had long-standing interests in Syria, especially with the Maronites in Mount Lebanon. As a result, McMahon insisted in his letter of October 24, 1915 that the area "lying to the west of the districts of Damascus, Homs, Hama, and Aleppo" were to be excluded from the promised area of Arab independence.[7] This exclusion was necessary to satisfy the French desire to create a Christian Lebanon. While Sharif Hussein refused to accept this, he would not allow it to stand in the way of a deal. Also apparently excluded were the provinces of Basra and Baghdad, where British "special measures of administrative control" were necessary. There was a third caveat, that the areas around Mersin and Adana – subsequently called Hatay and annexed to Turkey in 1924 – were not "purely Arab" and therefore were excluded. Otherwise, the British would "recognize and support the independence of the Arabs." And they would welcome "the resumption of the Caliphate [headed] by an Arab of true blood."

Those who later argued that Palestine was excluded from the promise made to Sharif Hussein pointed out that there was no district of Damascus and so it must have meant the province of al-Sham, a name that can be applied either to Syria or Damascus. The problem with this is that Homs and Hama also were listed, and they were not provinces. And the province of Aleppo had as its western border the Mediterranean – it had no land to its west. The logical conclusion is that "districts" meant the enumerated cities and perhaps their environs, not whole provinces.

On October 24, 1915, the Hussein-McMahon correspondence was completed, tying the Hashemites to the idea of Arab nationalism for the first time and creating a center of the Periphery tied to an imperial British Center. The Arab Revolt began in June 1916 with attacks against the Hijaz railroad, which it was able to sever. This was a blow to the Ottoman war effort, since the railroad supplied men and materials between Damascus and Medina. Other attacks did not go so well; for example, the Arab forces were never able to take Medina. Still, they succeeded in tying down tens of thousands of Ottoman troops and forcing them to be almost constantly on the defensive. Otherwise, the Arab Revolt was largely a guerilla effort, although Britain's Arab allies did participate in the capture of Aqaba. They also were able to take advantage of the British defeat of Ottoman naval forces in the Red Sea and convinced some 700 Ottoman Arab officers and men, including the future pro-British leader of Iraq, Nuri al-Said, to join the revolt rather than languish in prison. Faisal, Hussein's third son, led the Arabs out of the peninsula, where they joined in Sinai with the more professional British forces from Egypt. Together they advanced steadily through Greater Syria. Often resistance was minimal, due to Enver Pasha's decision to withdraw Ottoman troops from the Arab provinces to invade the Caucasus. Syrian popular support for the Ottoman cause waned as well because of Jemal Pasha's ruthlessness in putting to death even moderate Arab nationalists.

Though the British had initially overestimated their ally's military ability, the Arab forces improved over time and often distinguished themselves in battle. They believed that they were fighting for a future independent from the Turks.

In December 1917, General Edmund Allenby's forces captured Jerusalem, and he established a British military administration in Palestine. On the first day of October 1918, although small contingents of Arab camel cavalry and Australian soldiers had entered unauthorized, Faisal and his army symbolically entered Damascus, which was festooned with flags of the Arab Revolt. He became the military governor of Syria.

The Sykes-Picot Agreement, 1916

Britain and France traditionally had pursued a policy of propping up the Ottoman Empire as a foil against Russian ambitions. However, as early as 1904, when they signed the *Entente Cordiale*, the discussion turned to the partition of the Ottoman Empire. Already, there were overlapping desires that may be summarized as follows: Germany wanted Asia Minor, France wanted Greater Syria, and Britain wanted Egypt, the Suez, the Red Sea, the Persian Gulf and the Basra area. Russia wanted the Turkish Straits, Istanbul and eastern Asia Minor, with its largely Orthodox, mostly Armenian population. Italy wanted southwestern Anatolia as a sphere of influence, and the Greeks dreamed of restoring the Byzantine Empire in all of Asia Minor. Almost as soon as war broke out in 1914, the *Entente* began more serious negotiating over potential spoils. Early negotiations resulted in an understanding that Russia would get Istanbul, the Straits, and their hinterland on both sides of the water route. The Pact of London, concluded in 1915, promised concessions to Italy in Asia Minor and Libya – with recompense in other, unnamed territories in case the Ottoman Empire avoided dismemberment – in order to bring it into the war.

Of these conflicting claims, those of France and Britain were the most important because of their joint war effort and longstanding aspirations in the Arab world. The French were interested in the western portion of the Middle East, specifically the provinces of Beirut – including Mount Lebanon, Aleppo, Syria – which encompassed Damascus, and the Sanjak (subprovince) of Jerusalem which included most of Palestine. French interest in these areas reflected their desire to protect the Maronites and the Catholic institutions in the Holy Land, an assertion dating to the Crusades. Apart from missionary activity, they also could claim a sort of imperial primacy in the need to protect their "citizens" under the Capitulations and because of their ownership of a small number of railroads in Palestine as well as part of the silk production in Lebanon. The French imperial mind envisioned a sphere of influence along the Mediterranean from the Taurus Mountains in the north to the borders with Egypt and the Arabian peninsula. The French realized that their claims would be much stronger if they had a military presence, but they were able to introduce only a token number of soldiers into the area because of their preoccupation with fighting the Germans over Alsace-Lorraine. The Middle East was secondary, and as a result they were no match for the British in backing up their claims after the war.

The British, of course, had different ideas. They were adamant in their rejection of having any foreign power close to Egypt and the Suez Canal. Also, they had signed agreements with petty states in the Arabian peninsula and were fighting during World War I to control the Persian Gulf, the refinery at Abadan, and the province of Basra, with its vital seaport.

In order to solidify the Allies' understanding of what each was to receive, the British and French began secret negotiations in 1915–16. Representing the British was Sir Mark Sykes, a member of parliament and an advisor on Middle Eastern affairs in the Foreign Office. On the French side was the diplomat Francois Georges-Picot. The talks lasted more than a year and were approved, with the adherence of czarist Russia, in mid May 1916. Under the terms of the Agreement, the Arab provinces of Greater Syria and Mesopotamia were divided by France and Britain into what became known later as mandates. The basic parts of the Agreement and other related secret agreements can be described as follows:

1. The province of Lebanon and the coastal area of Syria to its north, along with a small part of south East Asia Minor, was to be detached from Greater Syria and come under direct French control.
2. A large portion of inland Syria and northern Iraq/Mesopotamia in a diagonal line extending from the southeast to the northwest, including

the former province of Mosul, was to be a French sphere of influence. The British agreed to this because they wanted to have the French as a buffer between themselves and the Russians.

3. The British were to control Syria and Mesopotamia to the south and west of the diagonal line that was French territory.
4. Palestine was to be an international zone.
5. Italy, which joined the Allied Powers in 1915, was given Antalya and the Mediterranean region adjoining it.
6. Even though Greece did not join the Allies until 1917, its share of the pie was Smyrna and a small portion of territory to its north.
7. In order to come into force, Britain and France agreed that Russia must also accept the Agreement. This was accomplished when Sykes and Picot traveled to Petrograd and, with minor border changes in the Mosul region and concessions in the Armenian areas of Asia Minor to satisfy Russian desires, the Agreement was signed in mid May 1916.

As we have noted, the wording of some provisions of the Hussein-McMahon letters are ambiguous, and, as if they were a holy text, remain a source of contention into the twenty-first century. We have mentioned the confusion associated with the "districts" of Damascus, Homs, Hama, and Aleppo. The Sykes-Picot Agreement added further complications. As an example of the contradictions contained in the two separate agreements, consider Palestine. If in the Hussein-McMahon correspondence it was promised as part of an Arab state, the Russians, the Greeks, Armenians, and especially the French as protectors of religious shrines in the Holy Land could be expected to object. If, on the other hand, Palestine was excluded from being part of the area of Arab independence then the Arabs had a legitimate interpretive complaint. As a result of this tension, and particularly to please the Russian claims, it was decided that the Holy Land would be administered by an international body. The British were also acting out of imperial interest in keeping Palestine, so close to the Suez Canal, from any one ally or the Arabs.

For obvious reasons, the Sykes-Picot Agreement was secret. When the Bolsheviks published a copy in 1917 in order to discredit the former czarist regime and the Entente, Sharif Hussein demanded an explanation from David Hogarth, who headed the Arab Bureau in Cairo. Hogarth responded by literally denying the existence of the Agreement, adding duplicitously that the population of Syria would have to consent in any case. Hussein's options were few, and so the Arab Revolt continued. The Greeks and the Italians were not happy either to learn of the Agreement and were able to negotiate a new set of promises. Pledges and counterpledges multiplied in such a contradictory fashion that each adherent could claim whatever it wished. Arab sympathizers and most scholars agree that the Sykes-Picot Agreement contradicted promises made to the Arabs in the earlier Hussein-McMahon correspondences.

The Balfour Declaration, 1917

The growth of political Zionism, that is the movement to form a Jewish state, can be attributed to such late nineteenth-century manifestations of anti-Semitism as the Dreyfus affair in France and pogroms carried out by Russian and Polish peasants against Jews living in their midst. In the latter case, poor Slavs were incited to attack the Jewish population centers in difficult economic times or amid rampant disease – much as Jews were falsely blamed during the Black Death during the late Middle Ages. In the case of the Dreyfus affair, the trial of a Jewish French officer falsely accused of being a spy showed that secular nationalism was not going to end the European, Christian hatred of Jews.

Theodore Herzl, a reporter who covered the Dreyfus trial, is generally regarded as the father of political Zionism, which he promoted in a pamphlet titled *Der Judenstaat* (1896). Soon afterward, in August 1897 he convened the first Zionist Congress in Basle, Switzerland and formed the World Zionist Organization. A scheme of settlement eventually emerged that focused on Palestine as the location of the future Jewish state. Though there had been similar Zionist ideas earlier, Herzl's lasting legacy was that he formed an organization that united Jews of different nationalities throughout the world into an enterprise with the clear objective of forming a Jewish state.

The focus of Zionist activities after Basle was to get somebody to provide a territory for a Jewish state. The Pope and the Ottoman Caliph were solicited but demurred. The British were also approached and offered Uganda or part of Argentina. These offers were an embarrassment to the organization, and it was with some relief that leadership of the Zionist movement passed to others following Herzl's death in 1904. In the early twentieth century, the center of Zionist activity was Berlin, but with the outbreak of war London emerged as another locus under the leadership of Chaim Weizmann. With the support of the *Manchester Guardian* and the British Rothschilds, the idea slowly gained favor in the United Kingdom. In December 1916 in the midst of the war, Lloyd George became Prime Minister. He was a Christian Zionist who believed that the Jewish people must be gathered in the Holy Land before there could be a second coming of the Messiah. He was also opposed to a French presence in Syria, especially areas close to the Suez Canal. Taking advantage of George's fear, the Zionists pledged that if they were to receive Palestine it would be in the British sphere of influence, a new outpost to control the Periphery as it were. As support mounted for the enterprise, Lord Balfour, the British Foreign Secretary, wrote a letter to Lord Lionel Roths-child in November 1917. The letter, now known as the Balfour Declaration, began, "His Majesty's Government view with favour the establishment in Palestine of a national home for the Jewish people."[8] Though both the Palestinians and the Israelis continue to debate the meaning of the Balfour Declaration, especially the definition of the term "national home," it is considered by Zionists to be the movement's birth certificate. When it was written, this was the intent of its authors. The British did not ask the Arabs their opinion, just as no Arabs were solicited about the Sykes-Picot Agreement. In this sense Palestine was similar to other imperial enterprises – the colonizer could do as it wished and could dispose of territory whimsically.

The Arabs of geographic Syria were aware of the Zionist project long before Balfour as a result of the influx of Jewish settlers and the purchase of Arab land, largely from absentee landlords. Newspapers in Beirut, Jaffa, Haifa and Damascus were strongly anti-Zionist even prior to 1917. In the late nineteenth and early twentieth centuries, Arab members of the Ottoman Parliament pressured Istanbul to outlaw Jewish land purchases.

The Balfour Declaration is unique in that it was a governmental document directed to a private person. The question is, why was it written? There are several interpretations:

1. This was just the latest manifestation of the imperial mindset in which powerful men make decisions based on personal prejudices and not necessarily based on national interests.
2. It was part of the British plan to scuttle the international zone that had been agreed to in the Sykes-Picot Agreement. In this scenario, the French and Russians would be kept at a distance from Egypt (and notably the Suez Canal).
3. It was a Machiavellian attempt – based on the idea that Jews had great influence – to rally Jewish support to keep Russia in the war and to get the US to increase its war effort in support of the Allied Powers.

Of the three interpretations, perhaps it is the first two that have the greatest legitimacy. According to this explanation, the British had long planned to keep Palestine without consideration of their promise to Hussein. The Arabs could not be allowed to rule themselves, and France and Russia had to be kept away from the Suez Canal. In this scenario, the first step was to make Palestine an international condominium as provided for in the Sykes-Picot Agreement. The next step was to remove Russia and France from Palestine, using Zionism as an excuse. This nicely meshed with Prime Minister Lloyd George's religious beliefs about the need to gather the Jews in the Holy Land.

As the war came to a halt, Palestine was the Thrice Promised Land; once to the Arabs in the Hussein-McMahon correspondences, a second time to the Allies in the Sykes-Picot Agreement, and finally to the Zionists in the Balfour Declaration.

The situation in the Middle East at the end of the war may be summarized as follows:

1. The Ottoman Empire was defeated and its forces ordered to disarm. Turkish military remnants were preparing to defend Asia Minor against an anticipated partition amongst the victors.

2. Though Faisal was the governor of Greater Syria, Britain had complete military control of the Middle East except for Asia Minor. Lloyd George, a Zionist, was the Prime Minister.

3. The French had no significant military force in Greater Syria, an area that they hoped to control. They had strained to station troops there but were so tied down in Europe that they could not do so. This allowed the British to achieve their aims through the weight of arms.

4. With the czarist regime overthrown, Russia had withdrawn from the war. This meant that from the British point of view, the need for the French to serve as a buffer in Mesopotamia between Britain and Russia, as promised in the Sykes-Picot Agreement, had vanished.

5. Using the Balfour Declaration as an imperial instrument, British Zionists committed themselves to putting inordinate pressure on Britain to maximize its presence in Greater Syria, especially Palestine, which was to be excluded from any future Arab state.

6. Georges Clemenceau had become the Prime Minister of France in November 1917. He was only marginally interested in the Middle East. During the war and after he focused on regaining Alsace-Lorraine.

The post-war settlement

Geographic Syria and the establishment of the mandate in a truncated Syria

In 1919, the victors met at the Paris Peace Conference to divide the spoils of war and to determine the resulting national borders. Tensions rose when Faisal pushed for the complete independence of the Arab Kingdom in Syria. As a compromise, the Americans proposed a commission of inquiry to go to the Middle East to determine the wishes of those who would be most affected. Though only slightly warm to the idea at the beginning, the British and the French ultimately saw a fact-finding commission as a threat to their imperial designs and so declined to participate. George Clemenceau was irritated by the upstart American attempt to have some say in the final disposition of the Middle East. Only the Americans appointed representatives, who thus formed what came to be called the King-Crane Commission and proceeded to interview Arab notables.

In May 1919, the two remaining partners of the old Triple Entente agreed that they alone would decide the future of Syria, no matter what the King-Crane report might say – or the Syrians or the Hashemites. Under prodding from Britain, which argued it had done all the fighting, France gave up any claim to Mosul and Palestine in return for unfettered control of northern geographic Syria from a line roughly north of Palestine east to Iraq. The British agreed to withdraw their military from the portion of geographic Syria that had been allocated to the French.

Thus, without including Faisal or the Hashemites, the fate of the Arab Kingdom was doomed. The British had decided that they had a greater need of French support, as iterated in the Sykes-Picot Agreement, than of the Arabs, as elucidated in the Hussein-McMahon letters.

The agreement between the British and the French to divide geographic Syria violated the Anglo-French declaration of 1918 that promised the Arabs their independence and the right to choose their own leaders. This hastened the response of the Arabs, who attempted to foil the division. In June 1919 a call for a Syrian Congress to convene in Damascus went out. A few weeks later, the members of the King-Crane Commission arrived. In testimony before it, members of the Congress objected to a mandate, as did Arab notables who appeared before the commission. The King-Crane findings were that the Arabs preferred no tutelage, but that if there had to be some form of mandate it should involve assistance only and be assigned to the US, which at that time Arabs tended to see as devoid of imperial aspirations in their region. When the fact-finding commission submitted its report, its conclusions and recommendations were suppressed.

The British and the French, pre-empting King-Crane, issued their joint declaration. Faisal was forced to negotiate with Clemenceau and from a position of weakness accepted French tutelage in return for recognition of the Syrian state. The news of this compromise led to anti-French demonstrations in Damascus, and Faisal was forced to renounce the agreement. The nationalists went further and, meeting in March 1920, declared the formation of the "United Syrian Kingdom," with Faisal as its monarch.

This unilateral action was immediately condemned by France and England. The two allies pressured the League of Nations to call a conference at San Remo, Italy, where it was resolved to immediately give the mandate for Syria to the French. In its Covenant adopted the previous year, the League had defined the category of Class A mandates as applying to former Ottoman and German territories:

> To those colonies and territories which as a consequence of the late war have ceased to be under the sovereignty of the States which formerly governed them and which are *inhabited by peoples not yet able to stand by themselves* under the strenuous conditions of the modern world, there should be applied the principle that the well-being and development of such peoples form a sacred trust of civilization. ...
>
> ... [T]he *tutelage of such peoples* should be entrusted to advanced nations who by reason of their resources, their experience or their geographical position can best undertake this responsibility, and who are willing to accept it, and that this tutelage should be exercised by them as Mandatories on behalf of the League [Emphasis added].[9]

Fearing a protracted and bloody confrontation with the French, Faisal capitulated and fled through Palestine to England. His defense minister,

Yusuf al-Azma, refused to do the same and led a small contingent of Arabs to face the French forces at Khan Maysalun. Al-Azma was killed in the battle, and the French, under General Henri Gouraud, captured Damascus in July 1920, thus destroying the Arab Kingdom, beginning the period of the French mandate in Syria and Lebanon and becoming their High Commissioner. Compounding the Syrian hatred of Gouraud for the force he used in conquering Syria was the allegation that he had stood on Saladin's grave in a moment of extreme colonial hubris and announced that the Crusades were finally over, with the victory of the Cross over the Crescent.

The Syrian resistance at Khan Maysalun soon took on epic proportions. It was viewed as an Arab attempt to stop the imperial avalanche. Al-Azma became a hero with statues of him throughout the Middle East. More importantly, the defeat of his forces had a psychological impact on the Arab world. It led to a general feeling in the Middle East that continues till today that the West is not honorable in its commitments, speaks with a forked tongue about issues of democracy that are perhaps only suitable for light-skinned people, and will oppress anyone who stands in the way of its imperial designs.

Mandatory Lebanon

Unlike the rest of geographic Syria, France had a long relationship with the Maronites of Mount Lebanon that dated to the Crusades. The Ottomans had ceded protection of the Maronites – who united with the Roman Catholic Church while keeping their own Syriac-language liturgy during the previous decade – to the French in 1649. Thus almost immediately after taking Damascus, General Gouraud issued a decree splitting Mount Lebanon, the former Ottoman subprovince which had been granted semi-autonomy in 1861, from the Syrian mandate. To it he added the largely Muslim coast which contained the urban areas of Tripoli, Beirut, Sidon and Tyre. Further, the decree added the fertile Biqa' Valley, thus creating what was termed *"Le Grand Liban."* Gouraud assumed the title of High Commissioner, and a Frenchman was named governor of Lebanon under Gouraud.

The reasons for the additional territory were based on the realization that Lebanon was not viable as a landlocked mountain fortress. Nor could it thrive without the agricultural production from the Litani River-fed Biqa' Valley. The addition of the Muslim coastal areas and the religiously mixed valley diluted the power of the Maronites and provided the Christians only a slight majority in the new country. The French viewed this development positively, thinking that the Christians would become more dependent on them and not want to see an end to the mandate.

Mandatory Palestine

British forces defeated the Ottomans in Palestine, taking Jerusalem in December 1917. The British army ruled Palestine till July 1920, when it passed to a civilian administration, and in 1922 it became a British Mandate.

With the end of the war, the population consisted of approximately 600,000 Arabs (Muslims and Christians) and perhaps 50,000 Jews, most of whom belonged to *Haluka* communities, that is, Jews who had come to die in the Holy Land and who lived on charity. The three-year period of military occupation saw maneuvering by the Arabs on the ground and by the Zionists in London to get a headstart in the coming struggle. The British had their own agenda.

The Palestinians viewed themselves as part of Greater Syria. Thus they depended on the implementation of the Hussein-McMahon correspondence. Their view was reinforced by the King-Crane report. They also called for the implementation of Wilson's Fourteen Points (notably self-determination) since they were over 90 per cent of the population and Jews owned only one per cent of the land. They also fell back on the belief that the Anglo-French declaration of 1918, which promised independence and self-government for the Arabs, would not be abandoned.

The Zionists after the war, especially Weizmann, acted as if Palestine were already a Jewish state. There was a triumphal march in Jerusalem in 1918 to celebrate the one-year anniversary of the Balfour Declaration. In London, the Zionists and their supporters in the government spoke derisively of the Palestinians as non-Arabs – Levantines who needed the benefit of Western civilization and instruction in the value of hard work. And once again the British view that France and Russia needed to be kept from Suez dominated the narrative. The Zionist plan served as a cover for the British to occupy Palestine as part of their imperial adventure.

With the agreement of the French to give up their claim to Palestine, and with other minor players like the Papacy and the Greek Orthodox pushed aside, the mandate for Palestine was established. The Preamble of the mandate for Palestine included the Balfour Declaration, which called for "the establishment in Palestine of a national home for the Jewish people, it being clearly understood that nothing should be done which might prejudice the civil and religious rights of existing non-Jewish communities in Palestine," a curious way to refer to the population that was 13 times as large as the Jewish one.

With the mandate established and Sir Herbert Samuel, a Zionist, named High Commissioner, the plan to make Palestine a Jewish state gained new impetus. Weizmann proclaimed that he hoped the British would stay in Palestine and encourage Jewish immigration until such time as it was as Jewish as England was English. When that time arrived, the English would leave and a Jewish state would be proclaimed.

Mandatory Transjordan

The mandate for Transjordan was entirely unplanned. An untamed, sparsely-populated area, half of whose inhabitants were Bedouin, it had no tradition of being a separate entity. However, once the borders of Syria, Lebanon, Palestine and Iraq had been defined, what was left was Transjordan. It was technically part of the League of Nations mandate for Palestine, but the area to the east of the Jordan River was removed since it had clearly been promised to the Arabs in the Hussein-McMahon correspondence. It could have been added to Iraq or to the Hijaz. The only imperative for London was that it remain in the British sphere of influence.

That Prince Abdullah would become the ruler of Transjordan was even less clear. It seemed in 1920 that the second son of Hussein had no future. His reputation had suffered during the Arab Revolt, when in 1917 he was put in charge of the unsuccessful siege of Medina, essentially doing nothing except collecting British subsidies. In 1919, he and his Hashemite forces were defeated by the Saudi kingdom in Najd (central Arabia) in a confrontation over taxation rights over a particular tribe. The ultimate humiliation occurred when Iraqi notables were polled over the prospect of having him as their king, and they rejected him. Undaunted, he set off in July 1920 in a quixotic attempt to become king of Syria after the deposal of his younger brother by the French. Abdullah arrived in Ma'an in November with several hundred armed supporters. When Sir Herbert Samuel, the British High Commissioner for Palestine and Transjordan, heard the prince would soon be there, he was asked what he was going to do. Samuel responded that he was going to go out onto the front steps of his residence with his hat in hand to say, "Welcome to Amman, Your Highness."

Abdullah's arrival in Amman solved the problem of what to do with Transjordan. He met several times with Winston Churchill, now the Colonial Secretary, and Churchill offered him the country for a six-month probationary period. Abdullah worked well with the British and collaborated with the French in Damascus and so, in 1923, was recognized as the Amir of Transjordan. Providing a classic example of the relationship between the center in the Center and the center in the Periphery that this volume has stressed as central to imperialism, the British gained a competent collaborator who helped them rule the country during the period of the mandate and afterward.

Mandatory Iraq

Defining Iraq is more difficult than "Greater Syria." There was no Ottoman designation for such an administrative entity – but rather separate provinces of Basra, Baghdad, and Mosul. The term Iraq in the nineteenth century did not quite coincide with the entity emerging after World War I – in what was the only large area of the former Empire with a Shi'ite majority.

Calls for autonomy were rare before 1914, and the population generally remained loyal to Istanbul. Compared with their counterparts in Greater Syria, Christians in Iraq made up a smaller percentage of the population and were not in close contact with Europe. It is fair to say that, via Basra, there was more contact with India than with Europe. Further, the most prominent minority in Iraq were the Jews, who were generally supportive of the Ottoman Empire but not politically active. Sunni tribal leaders did not participate in the government of the Ottoman Empire, nor did the Shi'ite socioeconomic elite. Opposition to British rule did not generally represent Iraqi nationalism as such. Many Iraqis fought with the Hashemites in the Arab Revolt, participated in the Congress in Damascus, and thought of themselves as Syrians.

The ethnic and religious composition of the new Iraq did not bode well for its future. Basra was largely Shi'ite and close to its Persian co-religionists. The former province of Baghdad was Sunni, with large Jewish and Christian populations in the urban area. Mosul was a largely Sunni Kurdish area with small numbers of Christians and other minorities. Oil had been discovered there earlier in the century but remained untouched, although this increased British interest.

The British took Basra and the Abadan refinery early in the war. In 1915, they moved toward Baghdad but were defeated in April of the following year. They pushed north again in order to take pressure off the Russians and in March 1917 succeeded in capturing Baghdad. Mosul fell in November 1918 in violation of the Armistice of Mudros – thus completing the composition of what would constitute Iraq.

The war had devastated Iraq. The British found few to welcome them and were viewed as invaders who were hostile to the indigenous culture. Even after the war the majority of Sunnis remained loyal to the Ottoman Empire. The Shi'ites also viewed the British as *kuffār*, non-believers. Thus a major problem for the British was to find a conspirator – a collaborative center – to help them rule.

The mandate in Iraq was given to Britain at San Remo in 1920 in violation of the Anglo-French declaration of November 1918 that promised "national governments" established by "free choice" of their citizens. The mandate lasted until 1932. Iraq now constituted part of an imperial system, with bases allowing the British to control the Persian Gulf and safeguard the Iranian oil that their navy had come to depend on.

The Great Iraqi Revolt broke out in July 1920 in the lower Euphrates. It united Shi'ites and Sunnis, tribes and urban dwellers, and had spread north by October of the same year. It was suppressed by British and Indian troops only at a high cost to both sides. It was at this point and in light of the Hussein-McMahon and Sykes-Picot agreements that the British decided that Iraq should have an Arab face. With Sharif Hussein's son Faisal having lost Syria to the French, the British arranged for him to take the throne of Iraq instead. He understood of course that he owed his kingdom to the British, and he and his family – together with a larger oligarchy made up of landlords and veterans of the Arab Revolt – constituted a loyal center allied with the British both under the mandate, which ended in 1932, and during the subsequent era of "independence" under a treaty relationship that allowed the British to maintain troops and airbases there and generally perpetuated their sway over the country. As a case in point, each Iraqi minister had a British advisor who actually ran the department.

Domestic politics between the great wars became increasingly dysfunctional. Political parties had begun to form around charismatic elites who typically put forward their views in a new newspaper they owned. Alliances shifted with opportunities. The most prominent among the political leaders was Nuri al-Said, an Ottoman officer who later served in the Arab Revolt and remained one of the most conspicuous symbols of the British-allied oligarchy, serving as Prime Minister four times until the outbreak of World War II. His opponents formed an opposition party, the National Brotherhood, which ran on a platform stressing opposition to British influence and to corruption. Quite popular, it was able to hold power from 1932 to 1936.

A third group, the Reform Party, also emerged. Its adherents were younger and largely Western educated and wanted to emulate Western democracy. They formed an alliance with the army and in 1936 overthrew the National Brotherhood and dissolved the parliament – the first instance in the post-World War I Arab world of a military coup.

Thus began a series of coups that continued through World War II. Nationalists who temporarily took power in Baghdad during this period flirted with Germany as a counterweight against continuing British domination but were ultimately put down by another British invasion in 1942, in which the "Arab Legion" from Transjordan participated. In this manner the Center controlled the Periphery by force when necessary. For the next 15 years Baghdad was firmly in the Western sphere of influence. Its public face was Nuri al-Said, who sided with the British and the new superpower, the US, purportedly out of a fear of an expanding Soviet Union, while in reality this center of the Periphery understood that the real threat to it emanated from the nationalistic periphery in its own country and throughout the Arab world. Symbolic of this period was the Baghdad Pact, an alliance of pro-Western Middle Eastern regimes with Great Britain that confronted Arab nationalism, of which by the mid 1950s Gamal Abdul Nasser of Egypt was becoming the main symbol.

Despite periodic domestic distractions, the Center preferred economic control through oil, increasingly focusing more attention on the Mosul district and less attention on the Basra-Persian Gulf-India nexus. The first oil concession had been granted to the Turkish Petroleum Company (TPC) in 1925, and oil was discovered in 1927. The TPC was owned by British, Dutch, French and US oil companies. In 1929 the TPC was renamed the Iraqi Petroleum Company, and its concession covered most of Iraq. Exports went from under one million barrels annually in 1932 to over 40 million a decade later. But with all of Iraq's oil production in the hands of the IPC, Iraq's ability to tap this resource for national development was limited. Still, one may say that relations between the oil conglomerate, representing the Center, and the Hashemite center of the Periphery were cordial. The monarchy was dependent on the British military for protection, an arrangement that had been solidified with the adoption of the Baghdad Pact.

The untenable position of the regime's alignment with the West was high-lighted in the defeat of the Arabs in 1948 and the formation of Israel. Also anti-Western, and by extension anti-Hashemite, strains reached their apogee when France, Britain and Israel invaded Egypt in 1956. The resulting political tension reached a climax when Egypt and Syria joined to form the United Arab Republic in 1958. In response, Jordan and Iraq federated in an attempt to stem the tide of Abdul Nasser's leadership. But it could not be stopped, and in July 1958 the military struck. King Faisal II and Nuri al-Said were drawn and quartered by delirious revolutionary crowds, and a Republic of Iraq – nationalist and presumed to be pro-Nasser – was proclaimed. But while the Center's devoted local ally now made way for a nationalist regime, the face of imperialism would continue to show itself in various forms during succeeding decades.

The British in Egypt

More than other parts of the Middle East, Egypt had a territorial national identity that went back thousands of years. It also had a past that included many different faces. For example, when it was necessary or convenient it could claim to be Arab, Muslim, African, or Pharaonic.

It was also unique, starting with Muhammad Ali at the beginning of the nineteenth century, in having a central government in Cairo and a national bureaucracy that organized the state. Muhammad Ali was a junior officer, probably Albanian, in an army organized by the Ottoman Empire in 1798 to remove General Napoleon Bonaparte from Egypt. As the French evacuated Egypt, he was able to drive out the Ottoman governor, defeat the Mamluks – the military class composed of manumitted slaves – and end their 600 year control that had reasserted itself even after the Ottoman conquest, and be proclaimed by the Cairenes as their Governor. When he pledged fealty to Istanbul, the Porte named him Governor of Egypt in 1806.

As Governor, Muhammad Ali created an Egyptian army, established a bureaucracy and generally improved living standards. An ambitious ruler, he conquered the Hijaz and the Sudan, and ultimately sent an expedition under his son Ibrahim to invade geographic Syria which went on in 1831 to cross the Taurus Mountains into Anatolia. Threatened with European intervention, Muhammad Ali agreed to retreat in return for allowing Ibrahim to rule Syria in his father's name. Things did not go well in Syria, however, since Ibrahim and his father were viewed as carpetbaggers by the local population. Their control of Syria also frightened Western European powers, which feared the emergence of a threat to their primacy in the Mediterranean. British naval forces bombarded the Syrian coast and Alexandria, forcing Muhammad Ali in 1840 to withdraw from Greater Syria in return for European recognition of him and his descendants as hereditary viceroys of Egypt and the Sudan.

Muhammad Ali's progeny dreamed of building a canal to connect the Mediterranean with the Red Sea and the Indian Ocean, thus cutting by two-thirds the sailing time from England to India. Not only would time be saved, but also money. The Suez Canal was completed in 1869, during the reign of the Khedive Ismail who was known for his extravagance. He had several solid gold dinner services, commissioned operas, built an opulent opera house, and made repeated expensive trips to Europe that strained the Egyptian treasury. As a result, Egypt went bankrupt and stopped paying its debts. European banks demanded their money, and Ismail was deposed in 1879. In the guise of bringing solvency back to Egypt, Dual Controllers from France and Britain moved to Cairo and were given the responsibility of fixing Egypt's finances. The Dual Controllers could attend Egyptian cabinet meetings, collect data, and report to their respective governments. As they reduced the debt, they cut spending for the military, pensioned bureaucrats, and generally reduced the budget. Acting as representatives of the Center, they essentially ruled Egypt and controlled the Suez Canal.

When in 1882 the Egyptian army took control of the cabinet and threatened the ruler, Britain and France saw this as a threat to their primacy and decided to use force. However, a change in the French government meant that Britain alone intervened. Alexandria was bombarded, the British Navy occupied both ends of the Suez Canal, and the British army took Cairo. Thus began the occupation of Egypt that lasted over 90 years. Shortly after the conquest of Egypt, Evelyn Baring – later Lord Cromer – returned to Egypt as the British Consul General and ruled the country until he retired in 1907. When the Ottoman Empire, of which Egypt still was nominally a part, declared war on the United Kingdom in 1914, the British responded by formalizing their role there, declaring Egypt a protectorate. The descendants of Muhammad Ali remained as puppet rulers, and the civilian prime ministers bowed to the demands of the British.

Still, Egyptian nationalism grew apace, and a delegation (*wafd*) of leading figures asked for permission to travel to London to ask for independence. This led to a general rebellion against British rule, known by Egyptians as the 1919 Revolution. Finding some malleable politicians to collaborate with them, Britain unilaterally declared Egypt "independent" in 1922 on their own terms – but reserving defense, the Sudan, protection of minorities and foreigners, and communications for their own exclusive control.

With the declaration of "independence," Sultan Fuad I took title of "King." Power in Egypt became tri-polar – involving the British, the King, and the Wafd Party, which dominated parliamentary elections whenever they were free but which the British and the King never allowed to govern long, was anti-British and castigated the monarchy as a willing tool of London. A fourth contender, the Muslim Brotherhood, calling for an Islamic state, would enter the fray within a few years.

When Fuad died in 1936, his son Farouk ascended the throne. Although named King with great hope, he was corrupt, grew increasingly corpulent, and became closely identified as a British puppet. The ultimate blow to the monarchy occurred during the 1948 Arab-Israeli war, in which the Egyptian army performed miserably and profiteering was rampant. In one infamous case, it was discovered that members of the royal family were involved in selling sand as gunpowder that was loaded into artillery shells. The end of the war saw Egypt in occupation of Gaza but humiliated as leader of the newly formed Arab League. The military blamed the politicians and the monarchy for the defeat and plotted to regain its honor.

The military struck in 1952, sending Farouk into European exile. The monarchy was abolished the following year, and Egypt was declared a republic. The Egyptian determination after World War II to end domination by the Center was successful in 1956, when the last British military forces reluctantly withdrew from the Suez Canal on terms agreed on two years earlier and then, along with their French and Israeli allies, had to succumb to international pressures to withdraw following their attack on the Suez Canal and Sinai in the autumn of that year. Thus ended more than 90 years of British imperial control of Egypt.

But the Center eventually was able to reassert itself again following Egypt's defeat by Israel in 1967 and Nasser's death three years later. His successors, Anwar Sadat and Husni Mubarak, chose to align their regimes with Washington, which bolstered their dictatorial rule and, after reluctantly giving in to popular demands for free elections during the Arab Spring of 2011, attempted to maintain the power of their allies in the military.[10] The US had already gradually replaced the British as the main imperial power in the region, particularly after the Suez fiasco of 1956. As we will see below, the gradual transition from British to US imperialism had begun in the 1930s with the Saudis granting an oil concession to an American company.

The Arabian peninsula

In the nineteenth-century Arabian peninsula, there were dual outside contenders for power: the Ottomans and the British. And there were various local tribal chieftains and princes who sought alliances with one or the other of these contenders. In the western Arabian peninsula, the Ottoman Empire with its religious prestige focused on controlling Mecca and Medina, and symbolized by the Hijaz railroad, supported the Hashemites with men, material, and money.

In the eastern portions of the peninsula, British agents associated with the colonial government of India – known as the Raj – controlled the foreign affairs of petty local chieftains and princes along the Persian Gulf. Oman (then called Muscat and Oman) retained formal independence in a legal sense but entered into a treaty relationship with London that left it a de facto protectorate. Other chieftains – in Kuwait, Bahrain, Qatar, and the so-called Trucial States (today's United Arab Emirates) – became formal British protectorates that allowed the rulers to maintain control of domestic affairs insofar as the British did not wish to intervene.

The same kind of relationship with the British emerged in southern Arabia in the case of local rulers in what made up the Aden Protectorate. Together with the port city of Aden – a rare case of formal colonialism in this region – these entities, later known as Southern Yemen, gained independence under a revolutionary Marxist regime in 1967, following a long struggle against British attempts to create a federation of client rulers.

The US increasingly replaced the British as the dominant Center power and protector of the rulers in all of these states after the British withdrew during the 1960s and 1970s. Southern Yemen's close ties with Moscow provided an exception until the end of the Cold War and the breakup of the USSR, at which time it united with North Yemen to form one state. While asserting its independence in such actions as opposing the authorization of force against Iraq in 1990, when it was a member of the Security Council, the Yemeni regime – now increasingly beleaguered in the face of various rebel movements, including al-Qaeda in the Arabian peninsula – lined up in support of the US "War on Terrorism" in 2001.

A similar treaty relationship emerged in the early twentieth century between the British and the Saudi dynasty in Najd. The Saudis' rivals, the Rashidi family of Shammar, remained loyal to the Ottomans and thus lost out when Britain won the war and emerged as the hegemon of the entire peninsula. Two local allies of the British – the Hashemites of the Hijaz, led by Hussein, the sharif of Mecca (who had joined the British to lead the "Arab Revolt" during the war) and the Saudis of the Najd – were left to fight with each other, but British backing – or the lack thereof – provided the key to this contest between rival centers in the Periphery.

The issue came to a head in 1924 when Hussein proclaimed himself caliph. This smacked of arrogance to many in the Islamic world and evoked jealousy among other petty princes. The British did not like this assertion of independence in a client ruler and failed to defend him when their other client dynasty, the Saudis, attacked the Hijaz and soon occupied it. Hussein fled, and Saudi Sultan of the Najd, Abdul Aziz, added "King of the Hejaz" to his former title. He cemented his ties with the United Kingdom in two treaties, the second of which recognized him as an "independent" ruler. In 1932, he assumed the title "King of Saudi Arabia."

A new actor, the US, was appearing on the Saudi stage. The entry of this new Center was facilitated by oil. In 1931 Abdul Aziz granted an oil concession for exploration to the Standard Oil Company of California. It soon joined with other US companies to form the Arabian-American Oil Company (Aramco). Oil in large quantities was discovered in 1938 and the first tanker of Saudi oil set sail a year later.

Demand for oil increased dramatically during World War II, and the US recognized that Saudi Arabian petroleum would be crucial in the future. The US relationship, as Saudi Arabia's new patron, was formalized when President Franklin Roosevelt met with Abdul Aziz aboard the USS *Quincy* on February 14, 1945. The two leaders concluded a still-secret agreement. It has been in force for almost 70 years, but its broad outline – at least as it later emerged – can be discerned with near certainty: the US would be responsible for Saudi Arabia's military security and maintaining the royal family in power in return for protecting American interests in its oil. The center of the Center and the center of the Periphery in this case have hardly ever waivered in their support for each other.

Iran between Russia and Britain

Even though Iran – as was typical for this region – was not formally colonized, it did not escape Russian and British interference and incursions in the nineteenth and early twentieth centuries, coinciding with the rise and fall of the Qajar dynasty (1795–1925). Both Russia and Britain considered Iran of strategic importance as a buffer state and an arena of economic and political influence through diplomacy, trade, and concessions. Both agreed on the need to preserve the Qajar state in order to maintain a balance of power in the region, an arrangement similar to the one made in the Ottoman Empire. However, this did not preclude either from undermining Qajar sovereignty in domestic policymaking and violating its territorial integrity. This state of affairs produced a complicated history of foreign relations and economic and political interactions between the Qajar state and British and Russian officials. Scholars have often portrayed the Qajars as hapless victims in the Great Game. However, Qajar rulers, such as Nasser al-Din Shah (on the throne from 1848 to 1896), exercised leverage from the Periphery and sought to play the two Center powers against each other through granting economic capitulations and concessions in order to acquire much needed state resources. In this way, collaboration between local Iranian elites and imperial Russia and Britain more aptly represents the usual Periphery–Center dynamics.

Notable Russian–Iranian encounters began in the 1600s when the Safavid rulers of Iran sponsored 15 diplomatic and trade missions to Russia and received ten Russian missions. In the early nineteenth century, Iran began to feel the weight of Russian military superiority in humiliating defeats – 1813 and 1827 – and the subsequent loss of territory in the Caucasus, Azerbaijan, and Central Asia. In the face of victory, the Russians imposed the Treaty of Turkomanchai (1828) on Iran, which included clauses granting capitulations, such as extraterritorial rights and favorable tariffs, to Russian merchants. While imperial Russia was the predominant foreign presence in the Qajar court and throughout the country, Iran's most famous nineteenth-century protest movement against economic concessions was driven in part by anti-British sentiment.

Although Iran and Britain had enjoyed infrequent diplomatic contact before the nineteenth century, the Qajar period witnessed more sustained ties. British imperial interests in Iran were concerned primarily with the security of colonial India and the acquisition of trade, communications, financial, and other concessions. By the early twentieth century, oil exploration in southern Iran became a decisive factor as well, leading to the creation of the Anglo-Persian Oil Company in 1908. As early as the nineteenth century, British policymakers regarded Russian advances in Iran as a threat to its Indian colony and to their commercial interests. In 1841, the British secured a treaty in which the Qajar government promised to give their merchants the same capitulatory privileges as their Russian counterparts. This treaty opened the way for the export of British manufactured goods to Iranian markets, initiating a shift in Iran's foreign trade to exportable cash crops.

The reign of Nasser al-Din Shah witnessed a series of struggles over concessions that introduced a new stage of British financial and economic activity. British policymakers viewed the strengthening of commercial and economic ties with Iran as a bulwark against Russian expansionism and the creation of new markets for British goods. In 1872, the Shah and his reform-minded premier, Mirza Hussein Khan, granted Baron Julius de Reuter, a German-born naturalized British citizen, an all-embracing concession, which included a monopoly over the construction of railroads, mining and exploitation of natural resources, finance, and banking.

The Shah and his premier considered the British investment in Iranian infrastructure as a protection against Russian influence and a source of personal wealth. Due to opposition within the Qajar court, the Shah cancelled the Reuter Concession, which however did not deter the British from future economic penetration. The establishment of the Imperial Bank of Persia in 1889 served the British well in terms of controlling Iranian public and private finances.

Despite the success of the Imperial Bank, granting the 1890 Tobacco Concession to a British company led to widespread anti-British sentiment and Iranian opposition against Nasir al-Din Shah, even from within his harem – i.e., the quarters of the palace reserved for wives, mothers, and children. Under the terms of the agreement, the British company would retain the exclusive right to produce, sell, and export Iran's entire tobacco crop. Protests and a lack of support from British policymakers, now wary of destabilizing Qajar rule and their longstanding strategic objectives in Iran, led the Shah to revoke the concession in 1892. Nasir al-Din Shah never recovered from this political defeat, raising concerns that Qajar Iran was no longer a dependable buffer state.

This episode marked a shift in British-Russian relations concerning Iran, encouraging a rapprochement leading to the 1907 secret agreement partitioning Iran into two zones of influence, with the Russian sphere in the north and the British in the south. The Qajar government viewed the partitioning as a violation of Iranian sovereignty and as indicating the failure of its longtime policy of balancing the two imperial powers and keeping them apart to prevent the annexation of its territory. The new British and Russian alliance was also prompted by the rise of an imperial Germany in the Middle East at the turn of the twentieth century, just as the Qajar state's maneuvering was proving less effective. Thus, Iranian relations with imperial Russia and Britain during the nineteenth and early twentieth centuries were characterized by a Peripheral state's commercial, financial, and diplomatic cooperation with two

Center imperial powers, which vied for increasing influence and authority in this buffer state perceived as strategically significant.

The new Center in the old Periphery: the US and Iran

While Russia and Britain competed for economic leverage and influence in Iran and were thus perceived by Iranians as untrustworthy, the US was viewed as a benevolent country from the nineteenth century until the end of World War II. Iran-US relations began in the early nineteenth century with the dispatch of American Protestant missionaries, sponsored by the American Board of Commissioners of Foreign Missions, who focused medical and educational activities in northwestern Iran. Diplomatic contacts between Iran and the US came later in the nineteenth century with the exchange of envoys. During the Iranian Constitutional Revolution of 1905–11, which established a constitutional monarchy and a series of elected parliaments, Iranian nationalists who had assumed British support against Russian opposition to constitutionalism saw their hopes dashed with the 1907 partition. Iranian officials then looked to the US as an ally in their cause, appointing two Americans – Morgan Shuster in 1911 and Arthur Millspaugh during 1922–27 and 1942–45 – as financial advisors. During World War II, Britain and the Soviet Union, whose armies had invaded Iran, forced Iranian monarch Reza Shah Pahlavi – who ruled during 1925–41 – to abdicate power due to his German sympathies. Even though the US was allied with Britain and the Soviet Union, Iran-US relations remained cordial. Because the US did not interfere in Iranian policymaking, Iranians continued to view it positively. The US military sent 30,000 soldiers to Iran by 1944 to protect supply routes, construct infrastructure, and train the local army and police. Thus, it was not until the 1950s, when Cold War imperatives reshaped the global balance of power to produce a new center – the United States – did Iran's relationship to the US change.

World War II ended the long reign of British and Russian dominance in Iranian economic and political affairs and witnessed the emergence of the US as a global superpower. When Prime Minister Muhammad Mossadeq nationalized the British-controlled Iranian oil industry in 1951, the Truman administration offered its support and tried to broker an agreement between the Iranians and British. However, a shift in US Cold War policymaking prioritizing the security of the Middle East as a bulwark against Soviet expansionism drove the Eisenhower administration to sponsor a coup overthrowing Mossadeq in 1953 and reinstating the son of ousted Reza Shah, Muhammad Reza Shah Pahlavi (1953–79). Thus, in the 1960s and 1970s, US economic, military, and security aid to Iran supported the Shah's autocratic and repressive regime. US support for the Shah generated a deep well of Iranian resentment towards the US government, expressed most dramatically in the anti-Shah and anti-American demonstrations – the revolt against the center of their Periphery nation and against the center of the Center nation that had put it in power in this case being inseparably intertwined – that led to the Iranian Revolution of 1979 and the subsequent hostage crisis.[11] Hostility and animosity between the US and the revolutionary government of Iran have continued to characterize relations between the two countries.

Conclusion

We have examined the way the contemporary countries of the Middle East came into being, usually as a result of efforts of the Center to control the Periphery. Even when Center countries have succumbed to popular demands for "independence," this in most cases has been within the framework of a political map resulting from imperial domination. Often portrayed in altruistic terms of advancing those less civilized, the Center's motivation was usually more covert and sinister: to assert the superiority of one culture over another and to ultimately control its resources.

Several aspects of Western imperialism in the region differentiate it in large part from patterns found in many other parts of the world's Periphery. Aside from the Maghrib, where the French – and, in the case of Libya, Italy – engaged in formal colonialism – sometimes even there, as in Tunisia and Morocco, leaving "protected" titular rulers in place – imperialism in the Middle East mostly was informal even at the height of the Western imperial age in its classic form. Arguably, this was the worst of both worlds, demonstrating the benefits neither of true independence nor of the kind of positive influences that, say, India experienced under outright British rule. One particularly malign feature of Western imperialism – both in the past and in the present – has been its reliance on authoritarian centers. Center countries penetrated states – the Ottoman Empire and Iran – that remained formally "independent." Aside from the city of Aden, there were no British "crown colonies" in the Middle East. Instead, there were "spheres of influence" – as in Iran during the early part of the twentieth century and as planned by the Allied Powers for Anatolia after World War I. Egypt was formally a part of the British Empire only during 1914–22 (with a "protected" sultan on the throne), while in other periods the fiction was maintained that it still was under Ottoman sovereignty or – after 1922 – that it had its own sovereignty. There were League of Nations mandates in the Fertile Crescent, but these gave way to formal independence fairly soon. Except for Palestine, in which case the West has facilitated the displacement and subordination of the indigenous population, settler colonialism of the kind found in southern Africa and in Algeria has been absent from the area this volume focuses on.

But when imperial powers agreed to "independence," much of the essence of imperialism continued. The US emerged in the post-World War II period as the new Center dominating the Periphery through alliances with local elites, including some – as in the case of Persian Gulf monarchies – that remained British protectorates until the 1960s. Those leaders who rose to power and tried to break the pattern of subservience to the Center were denounced as new "Hitlers" or as "rogues" – starting with a liberal democrat, Muhammad Mossadeq in Iran and continuing with authoritarian secular nationalists such as Gamal Abdul Nasser and Saddam Hussein as well as those of the current Islamist variety. Challenges to the "stability" of Western client regimes continue to rise, though. One of the most important American clients – who had been entrusted to police the Persian Gulf region – fell in 1979 to be replaced by a radical regime fiercely devoted to anti-imperialism. The "Arab Spring" now has overthrown others – as in Tunisia and Egypt – while Western powers actually intervened to overthrow an untrusted and disliked rebel-turned-client regime in Libya, and the rest – including such classic cases as the Saudi royal family, the Hashemites in Jordan, and all the dynasties in the Persian Gulf – remain in peril. But the Center possesses numerous ways – ranging from replacement to co-option – of attempting to preserve or to reassert its domination.

Notes

1 J. Hobson, *Imperialism: A Study*, London: James Nisbet & Co., 1902.
2 V. Lenin, "Imperialism, the Highest Stage of Capitalism," in *The Essentials of Lenin*, Vol. 1, Westport, CT: Hyperion Press, 1973, p. 709. URL: <http://www.marxists.org/archive/lenin/works/1916/imp-hsc/> (accessed March 14, 2013).
3 J. Schumeter, "The Sociology of Imperialisms," *Imperialism and Social Class: Two Essays by Joseph Schumeter*, Cleveland and New York: World Publishing Co., 1955, pp. 2–98. URL: <http://mises.org/books/imperialism.pdf> (accessed March 13, 2013).
4 Quoted in V. Lenin, *Imperialism, the Highest Stage of Capitalism*, London: Lawrence and Wishart, 1948, p. 304.
5 E. Baring, *Modern Egypt*, New York: Macmillan Company, 1908, p. 328.
6 G. Antonius, *The Arab Awakening*, Philadelphia: J. P. Lippincott, 1939.
7 See "The McMahon–Hussein Correspondence 14 July 1915–10 March 1916." URL: <www.mideastweb.org/mcmahon.htm> (accessed March 14, 2013). All quotations in this article are taken from that same letter.
8 "Balfour Declaration-Text/Non-UN Document," United Nations Question of Palestine website. URL: <http://unispal.un.org/UNISPAL.NSF/0/E210CA73E38-D9E1D052565FA00705C61> (accessed March 14, 2013).
9 "The Covenant of the League of Nations," The Avalon Project: Documents in Law, History and Diplomacy, Lillian Goldman Library, Yale Law School. URL: <http://avalon.law.yale.edu/20th_century/leagcov.asp> (accessed March 14, 2013).
10 For a remarkably frank scholarly analysis of this reality, see J. Brownlee, *Democracy Prevention: The Politics of the U.S.-Egyptian Alliance*, Cambridge and New York: Cambridge University Press, 2012.
11 See M. Gasiorowski, "US Foreign Policy Toward Iran During the Mussadiq Era," in D. Lesch and M. Haas (eds), *The Middle East and the United States: History, Politics, and Ideologies*, 5th ed., Boulder, CO: Westview Press, 2012.

Part II

The Center in an age of inequality

3 The United States

A hegemon challenged

Stephen Zunes

Aligning themselves with local elites, foreign empires have sought to dominate the Middle East during the past two centuries but always have found themselves at the receiving end of a popular and oftentimes violent backlash. The US increasingly replaced Great Britain as the dominant imperial power in the region after World War II but was challenged by another superpower, the Soviet Union, during the following half century. Then it was widely assumed following the collapse of the Soviet Union and the American triumph in the 1991 Gulf War that, for good or for ill, the US had emerged as the unchallenged outside power.

Proponents of US policy argued that the same kind of backlash that had undermined earlier ventures would not occur this time. Americans, they maintained, had entered the region eschewing colonial ambitions, championing the rule of law and the authority of the United Nations, and seeking economic growth and political stability. America stood out as a singular and responsible overseer, so went this argument, in using its military and economic power to insure stability and security in the face of despots, terrorists, and religious extremists. Critics of the US role, on the other hand, point out that America's overbearing power has created widespread resentment in the Middle East and the Islamic world generally. The chief complaints revolve around US support for repressive and corrupt regimes, the exploitative practices of American oil companies and other corporations, the prejudicial use of the United Nations, the arming and bankrolling of the Israeli occupation and support for attacks against its neighbors, and destabilization efforts against internationally recognized governments, as well as direct military intervention.

Whatever the nature of the US role, there is little question regarding the region's strategic and economic importance. Lying at the intersection of Africa, Asia, and Europe, it also is the source of most of the world's petroleum reserves. The State Department has described the Middle East as "a stupendous source of strategic power, and one of the greatest material prizes in world history, probably the richest economic prize in the world in the field of foreign investment."[1] As far back as the 1950s, President Dwight Eisenhower described the Middle East as the most "strategically important area in the world."[2] Furthermore, it is the destination of the lion's share of American arms exports and is therefore considered extremely important for politically influential arms manufacturers.

No longer concerned that the region might fall under Soviet influence, the US nevertheless has a continuing longstanding concern about the influence of indigenous movements that potentially challenge American interests. There is a perception of an ongoing threat from radical forces – both Islamic and secular – as well as concern over the instability that could result from any major challenges to the rule of pro-Western regimes, even – perhaps especially – from democratic movements.[3] This has resulted in support for the status quo regardless of a given regime's level of commitment to democracy or human rights as long as it is aligned with Washington. Notwithstanding the George W. Bush administration's rhetoric about championing democracy, US support for autocratic regimes in the region – including security assistance for internal repression – actually increased during that period and has remained high, even as such governments have found themselves challenged by popular pro-democracy movements.

Some analysts have attempted to explain US Middle East policy on factors unique to the region, especially the influential "Israel Lobby," an argument most notably advanced by prominent American political scientists John Mearsheimer and Stephen Walt.[4] Their assertions have been challenged by other political scientists, including those who share their opposition to the strident US support for Israeli policies, who argue that it unfairly exonerates the US government and non-Jewish elites from their role in often misguided and disastrous policies.

Indeed, US policy toward the greater Middle East fits the broader pattern of its policies toward other parts of the Global South, such as Latin America, Africa, and Southeast Asia. The primary criticisms of US policy in the Middle East have focused on support for dictatorships, imposition of blatant double standards regarding human rights and international law, undermining the authority of the United Nations, pushing for military solutions to political problems, transfers of massive quantities of armaments, imposing draconian austerity programs on debt-ridden countries through international financial institutions, and periodically imposing sanctions, bombing, staging coups, and invading countries that challenge US hegemonic goals. However, the history of US foreign relations indicates that such policies hardly are unique in the case of the Middle East. Indeed, US support for Indonesia's former occupation of East Timor and Morocco's ongoing occupation of Western Sahara demonstrates that US support for the Israeli occupation is not unique either.

In short, like any great power historically, the primary goal of the US is to maintain and advance its strategic and economic hegemony. The following analysis illustrates this through examining the American response to two region-wide phenomena – the challenge of radical Islamist movements and the recent pro-democracy insurrections (the "Arab Spring") – and to three key Middle Eastern countries: Israel, Iraq and Iran.

The challenge of radical Islamists

Supporters of American hegemony took advantage of real security concerns following the attacks by Al-Qaeda in 2001. This resulted in a series of policy initiatives – initially with the support of a broad cross-section of US political and intellectual opinion – directly challenging the international legal order. The doctrine of preventive war, the use of extraordinary rendition and torture, the invasion of Iraq, threats against Iran, the war in Afghanistan, backing for militaristic and expansionist elements in Israel, and related policies intensified the US's alienation from Middle Eastern opinion and even from traditional European and Asian allies whose cooperation is needed in the anti-terrorist struggle. The opposition to such policies is both principled – in the sense that there are serious moral and legal implications – and practical, particularly because of the serious ramifications of the overemphasis on military means to address complex problems. Indeed, such policies have emboldened extremists, weakened moderates, and have resulted in a more anarchic international order which makes legitimate counter-terrorism efforts all the more difficult.

Radical Islamist movements have risen to the forefront primarily in countries where there has been a dramatic dislocation of the population as a result of war or uneven economic development. US support for decades of Israeli attacks and occupation not only have torn Palestinian and Lebanese society apart but in turn have provoked extremist movements that were unheard of just a few decades ago. The US-led overthrow of the constitutional government in Iran in 1953 and subsequent support for the Shah's brutal dictatorship succeeded in crushing that country's democratic opposition, resulting in a 1979 revolution led by hardline Islamic clerics. The US directly aided extremist Islamists in Afghanistan when they were challenging the Soviet Union in the 1980s, many of whom have gone on to serve as the core of the Taliban and international terror cells today. To this day, the US maintains close ties with Saudi Arabia, which adheres to an extremely rigid and repressive interpretation of Islam and spreads such intolerance through the establishment of schools preaching its extremist theology, and for many years actively supported governments in Pakistan which tolerated radical Islamist groups while suppressing democratic movements.

US military aid to the Middle East exceeds its economic aid by a ratio of six to one. Arms sales are America's primary commercial export to the region, strengthening militarization and weakening financial support for human needs. Furthermore, while threatening war at the mere possibility of Iran's developing nuclear weapons, the US maintains close strategic ties to states with existing nuclear arsenals, notably Israel, Pakistan, and India. It has failed to support calls by Iran and virtually every Arab state for establishing a nuclear weapon-free zone in the region and its navy has brought its own tactical nuclear weapons into Middle Eastern waters starting in the late 1950s. In a part of the world which has been repeatedly invaded by outside powers in recent centuries, the growing US military presence has created increasing resentment that is manifested in militant religious movements.

While leading efforts in recent years to impose debilitating sanctions against the people of Iraq, Libya, Sudan, and Iran for their governments' violations of UN Security Council resolutions, the US has used its ability to veto otherwise unanimous resolutions to block Security Council enforcement of its resolutions applying to such allies as Turkey, Israel, and Morocco for their occupation of neighboring countries. Such double standards make it hard for the Islamic world to rely on the international community's willingness to apply existing legal norms.

The US has also been at the forefront of pushing neo-liberal economic models of development. These policies have resulted in cutbacks in social services, privatization of public resources, foreign takeovers of domestic enterprises, reduction of taxes for the wealthy, the elimination of subsidies for farmers and for basic foodstuffs, and ending protection for domestic industry. While this has spurred some economic growth in some cases, it has also led to a dramatic increase in social and economic inequality. This growing disparity between the rich and the poor has been particularly offensive to Muslims, whose exposure to Western economic influence has been primarily through witnessing some of the crassest materialism and consumerism from foreign imports enjoyed by local elites while the majority suffers in poverty. The failure of state-centric socialist experiments in the Arab world left an ideological vacuum among those who value economic justice, and this has been filled by certain radical Islamic movements. US-backed neo-liberal economic policies have destroyed traditional economies and turned millions of rural peasants into a new urban underclass populating the teeming slums, who become susceptible to the appeals of radical clerics.

The US has also encouraged Islamic radicalism through large-scale military, diplomatic, economic and financial support of Israel's continuing occupation, repression, and colonization of additional Palestinian territories since 1967. America's failure to be an honest broker in the Israeli–Palestinian dispute has facilitated the dramatic expansion of illegal Israeli settlements which stand in the way of creating a viable Palestinian state. Despite the Palestinian Authority's willingness to accept just 22 per cent of historic Palestine and to live in peace with the Jewish state, US policy has continued to support Israeli expansionism, giving radical Islamists an opportunity to claim that such moderation will never be rewarded.

Despite rhetoric about supporting democracy, the US remains the primary outside supporter of autocratic regimes throughout the Islamic world from Brunei to Morocco. Extremist movements tend to arise in countries where oppressed populations believe there are few legal or nonviolent means of addressing grievances. And it is not surprising that those who suffer under such repressive and irresponsible governments will at least in part blame the West for their suffering.

The standard reason given by US officials and many pundits in the American media for what motivated the attacks of 9/11 is the terrorists' hatred of liberty and of democracy. According to President George W. Bush, "They hate ... democratically elected government. They hate our freedoms – our freedom of religion, our freedom of speech, our freedom to vote and assemble and disagree with each other."[5] In reality, US policy in the Middle East has generally tended not to promote freedom, but to support authoritarian client regimes and occupation armies. The contradiction between the democratic ideals with which most Americans identify and the perceived exigencies of superpower status is not unique to current US policy in the Middle East, and yet its significance is rarely appreciated.

Attention to human rights by successive American administrations has always been relative to the perceived strategic importance of the country in question: the more important an allied regime is strategically, the less attention is given to human rights. Unfortunately for people living under the rule of Middle Eastern governments allied to the US, their location makes their countries of great strategic value in the view of American policy makers. However, there is a price to pay for such priorities.

Terrorism rarely rises out of democratic societies. When it does, terrorist groups are usually suppressed fairly easily, since few people agree with the terrorists' assertion that armed resistance, especially against non-combatants, is the best way to effect political change. It is no coincidence that violent political movements tend to arise within countries where governments rely on violence. The US plays a major role in propping up repressive governments which, in turn, has led to a terrorist backlash.

Indeed, the more the US has militarized the Middle East, the greater the reaction from Islamist extremists using asymmetrical warfare in the form of terrorism has become. Even though only a small percentage of the population supports Al-Qaeda's methods, terrorist networks can expect to grow as long as the grievances espoused by such movements resonate with large numbers.

As most Muslims recognize, Osama bin Laden was not an authority on Islam. He was a businessman who – like any good businessman – knew how to take a popular sentiment and use it to sell a product: in this case, anti-American terrorism. The grievances expressed in his manifestoes – the military presence of the US in the Gulf, the inhumane consequences of US policy towards Iraq (even prior to 2003), U.S. support for the Israeli dispossession and occupation of Palestine, and US backing for autocratic Arab regimes – had widespread appeal. A survey by the *Wall Street Journal* found that even among wealthy elites in Islamic countries – many of whom had business or other ties with the US – there was an enormous amount of anger over and dismay about these policies.[6] As British novelist John LeCarre observed in the aftermath of the 9/11 terrorist attacks, "What America longs for at this moment, even more than retribution, is more friends and fewer enemies."[7]

Some policies pursued by Western governments – such as improved intelligence and interdiction, disrupting financial networks, and the killing and imprisonment of bin Laden and other top Al-Qaeda leaders – have weakened the movement. But far more significant in lessening the threat from such radical groups has been the popular disgust over the methods and extreme ideology of the movement and the realization that such tactics could never succeed. Neither Al-Qaeda nor any like-minded group has come close to overthrowing Arab regimes. Indeed, the most significant decline in active participants, recruits, and financial support for Al-Qaeda may have resulted from the recent resort to the largely nonviolent methods employed by popular movements which have succeeded in bringing down American client dictatorships in Tunisia and Egypt.

The "Arab Spring"

US diplomatic history is replete with examples of strategic analysts, State Department officers, and other Washington officials engaging in detailed policy planning relating to almost any conceivable contingency – except for ordinary people mobilizing to create change. This certainly appears to have been the case regarding the pro-democracy insurrections which began in December 2010 and caught Washington completely off-guard. Furthermore, the US response has not generally endeared many in these largely youthful movements – who may eventually find themselves in positions of power – to the US. During the first weeks of the Tunisian protests, for example, rather than praise the largely nonviolent pro-democracy movement and con-demn the country's repressive regime, US Secretary of State Hillary Clinton expressed her concern over the impact of the "unrest and instability" on the "very positive aspects of our relationship with Tunisia," insisting that the US was "not taking sides" and that she would "wait and see" before even communicating directly with Tunisian dictator Zine al-Abidine Ben Ali or his ministers.[8]

Similarly, during the first week of the Egyptian revolution, Clinton insisted that the country was stable and that Mubarak was "looking for ways to respond to the legitimate needs and interests of the Egyptian people,"[9] despite the miserable failure of the regime in its nearly 30 years in power to do so. Asked whether the US still supported Mubarak in the face of severe repres-sion against pro-democracy activists, White House spokesman Robert Gibbs responded that Egypt remained a "close and important ally."[10] As during the Tunisian protests, the Obama administration equated the scattered violence of some pro-democracy protesters with the far greater violence of the security forces. In Gibbs's words, "We continue to believe first and foremost that all of the parties should refrain from violence."[11] Even when Clinton finally urged "Egyptian authorities not to prevent peaceful protests or block communica-tions including on social media sites,"[12] the administration emphasized reform from within rather than supporting demands that the dictator step down. By the fifth day, however, the Obama administration, apparently not wanting to be on the wrong side of history, started speaking of an eventual transition to democratic rule, telling the regime that large-scale repression of nonviolent protesters – which would presumably be implemented with US-supplied weaponry – would be unacceptable. By the second week, Washington began speaking about a speedy transition to democracy and began quietly pressuring Mubarak to resign. President Obama finally offered eloquent praise for the pro-democracy demonstrators, but only after Washington's allied dictators in Tunisia and Egypt were forced to resign.

As the most militarized region and with the most military-backed dictatorships in the world, the Middle East and North Africa has long exemplified the realist paradigm that power rests with whoever has the guns. These dramatic civil insurrections, however, have permanently challenged that assumption. These largely nonviolent revolutions remind us that even a monopoly of military force and the support of the one remaining superpower may not suffice to retain power in the face of massive popular nonviolent resistance. Indeed, foreign governments now may be less capable of imposing their will than was the case during the past century or more. Even in Libya, the final collapse of the Qaddafi regime came not as a result of NATO air power, but rather from the civil insurrections in working class districts which made Tripoli ungovernable. Instead of a bloody and protracted battle by advancing rebels to conquer the city from loyalist troops, as many predicted, the armored columns of the rebel forces entered the capital essentially unchallenged, limiting the fighting to mop-up operations at Qaddafi's compound and a few other small installations. Indeed, the initial phase of the uprising was overwhelmingly nonviolent and liberated much of the country before the launching of the armed struggle, the subsequent setbacks, and the NATO-backed military campaign that slowly regained lost territory.

These successful and largely nonviolent pro-democracy struggles have challenged not just the narratives of Al-Qaeda and other Salafi extremists but those on the other extreme as well. The neo-conservatives and other supporters of the Iraq War insisted that only through invasion and occupation could democracy take hold. Even putting aside the repressiveness and corruption of the US-backed regime in Baghdad today, it is now clear that there are more effective and far less destructive means of bringing down autocratic regimes.

Defenders of US policy toward Egypt during Mubarak's autocratic rule note that there had been some quiet US government support for dissident groups. Some US Embassy staffers had sporadic contacts with pro-democracy activists and, through such congressionally-funded foundations as the National Endowment for Democracy (NED), there was limited financial assistance to some civil society organizations. But this small amount of US "democracy assistance" did not include support for training in strategic nonviolent action or the other kinds of grassroots mobilization that proved decisive, and the key groups that organized the protests refused US funding on principle. In any case, the amount of US funding for NED and related programs in Egypt paled in comparison with the billions of dollars in military and economic assistance to the Mubarak regime and the close and regular interaction among US officials and leading Egyptian political and military leaders. And most of this limited "pro-democracy" funding was eliminated altogether in early 2009 following Obama's inauguration.

The lack of enthusiasm by the US towards popular indigenous pro-democracy struggles could not be better illustrated than in the case of Bahrain, where the autocratic monarchy brutally suppressed the overwhelmingly nonviolent pro-democracy movement on that island nation in early 2012. In the aftermath of the nonviolent overthrow of Mubarak, President Obama warned other Middle Eastern leaders that they should "get out ahead of change" by quickly moving toward democracy. Even though the February 15 press conference in which he made this statement took place during some of the worst repression in Bahrain, he chose not to mention the country by name. In the face of Bahraini security forces unleashing violence on peaceful protesters, Obama insisted that "each country is different, each country has its own traditions; America can't dictate how they run their societies."[13] He later publicly criticized the regime's mass imprisonment of opposition leaders and refusal to enter into meaningful negotiations with them, but refused to use Washington's considerable leverage to press the regime to compromise. At the height of the protests in Bahrain, US Admiral Mike Mullen, chairman of the Joint Chiefs of Staff, flew to Bahrain to assure King Hamad and Crown Prince Salman of "our strong commitment to our military relationship with the Bahraini defense forces." And, despite the massacres of the previous week, he thanked his hosts "for the very measured way they have been handling the popular crisis here."[14] Indeed, the February 25 *New York Times* reported how the Obama administration had "sent out senior diplomats in recent days to offer the monarchs reassurance and advice – even those who lead the most stifling governments."[15] Also telling was a speech given in April at the annual meeting of the Center for the Study of Islam and Democracy in Washington, DC in which Obama's special Middle East advisor Dennis Ross condemned alleged Iranian support for Bahrain's pro-democracy movement while saying nothing about the military intervention by US-backed Saudi and Emirati forces in Bahrain to help crush the pro-democracy struggle there.

Rather than advocating sanctions, as the President had done with Syria, the US Defense Department announced just a week before Obama's September UN speech a proposed sale of $53 million of weapons and related equipment to Bahrain's military. In defending the arms transfer, the Pentagon praised Bahrain's autocracy as "an important force for political stability and economic progress in the Middle East."[16] Though pressure from human rights groups initially forced the administration to postpone the sale, the administration announced the resumption of arms sales the following May.

The US has been only slightly more open to the pro-democracy forces in Yemen. Between Obama's inauguration in January 2009 and the suspension of aid in response to savage repression of largely nonviolent pro-democracy activists, US security assistance to the Yemeni regime went up five-fold. Despite diplomatic cables going back as far as 2005[17] indicating that Yemen's autocratic President Ali Abdullah Salih could potentially face a popular pro-democracy uprising, Secretary of Defense Robert Gates acknowledged that Washington had not planned for an era without him. As one former ambassador to Yemen put it in March 2011, "For right now, he's our guy."[18]

Eventually, the Obama administration joined its European allies in pushing Salih to step aside. But the US has not been strongly supportive of the pro-democracy protests either. For example, following government attacks in April 2011, which killed a dozen protesters and injured hundreds of others, the US Embassy called on the Yemenis to cooperate with the Saudi-led initiatives for a transition of power – which Salih initially rejected – by "avoiding all provocative demonstrations, marches and speeches."[19]

The emphasis in the West on cultural or religious explanations for the paucity of democracy and liberty in the region tends to minimize other factors that are arguably more important. These include the legacy of colonialism, high levels of militarization, and uneven economic development, much of which can be linked in no small part to the policies of Western governments, including the US. A considerable degree of effrontery is required for American help in strengthening the repressive capability of regimes in the face of human rights movements to be followed by the claim that the lack of freedom in these countries is evidence that their people do not want it. These arms transfers and the diplomatic and economic support play an important role in keeping these regimes in power and thus provide clearcut examples of Johan Galtung's penetrating portrayal of imperialism in terms of collaboration between a Center country and the center or ruling elite of a Periphery country.

Israel: ally and surrogate

The close relationship between the US and Israel has been one of the most salient features in US foreign policy for more than four decades. The well over $3 billion in military and economic aid sent annually to Israel by Washington is rarely questioned in Congress, even by liberals who normally challenge US aid to governments that engage in widespread violations of human rights – or by conservatives who usually oppose foreign aid in general. Virtually all Western countries share the US's strong support for Israel's peace and security, and yet only the US provides such massive arms and other aid, while the occupation of lands seized in the 1967 war continues. No other government comes close to offering the level of diplomatic support provided by Washington. The US often stands alone with Israel at the United Nations and other international forums when objections are raised over ongoing Israeli violations of international law. In sheer volume, American aid to Israel – now passing the $123 million mark – is in a league of its own. No country has ever received as much congressionally-mandated aid as has Israel, not even South Vietnam and Iraq. Indeed, Israel receives more US aid per capita annually than the total annual GNP per capita of several Arab states. What is perhaps even more unusual is that Israel, like its benefactor, is an advanced, industrialized, technologically-sophisticated country, as well as a major arms exporter.

The US was the first country to recognize modern Israel as an independent state, within minutes of its declaration of independence in 1948. During most of its first two decades, however, Great Britain and France were Israel's primary international supporters, with the US attempting to take a more balanced approach vis-à-vis its hostile Arab neighbors. In 1956, for example, the US pressured Israel, Great Britain and France to withdraw their forces from Egypt following the tripartite invasion of that country. Since the late 1960s, however, the US has tried to play the contradictory roles of being the principal military, economic and diplomatic supporter of Israel while at the same time serving as the chief mediator of the conflict.

US aid to Israel began in the early 1950s but accelerated dramatically after the 1967 war, when the US greatly expanded military loans and grants. Economic aid increased greatly in subsequent years, with grants replacing loans for economic assistance in 1981 and with military aid turning exclusively into grants in 1985. During the 1990s, the annual US subsidy for Israel stood at approximately $3 billion in military and economic grants, in addition to assistance from other parts of the budget (or off-budget), which have totaled up to an additional $500 million in recent years.[20] Most US recipients of economic aid are required to use the bulk of the money for specific projects, such as buying certain US agricultural surpluses or finished goods. Normally, among countries receiving US foreign aid, officials of the US Agency for International Development (AID) oversee the actual programs, administered directly either through non-governmental organizations or under co-sponsorship with a government agency. The exception is Israel, where most US aid goes directly into the government's treasury to use at its discretion. The US government sets the funding level, and these become simply cash transfers.

In addition, congressional researchers have disclosed that between 1974 and 1989, $16.4 billion in US military loans were converted to grants and that this was the understanding from the beginning. Indeed, Congress eventually has forgiven all past American loans to Israel. As a result, while other countries struggle under onerous debt loads and repayment programs, Israel can tout the claim that it has never defaulted on a US government loan, as it has never been required to repay them. For decades, US policy proclaimed that economic assistance to Israel had to equal or exceed Israel's annual debt repayment. In addition to the more than $3 billion in annual grants, between 1992 and 1996, the US also provided loan guarantees that originally totaled an additional $10 billion and with an additional $11 billion added to that in 2004.

Furthermore, unlike other countries, which receive aid in quarterly installments, aid to Israel since 1982 has been given in a lump sum at the beginning of the fiscal year, leaving the US government to borrow from future revenues.

Israel even lends some of the money back through US treasury bills and collects additional interest. This special arrangement costs the US government approximately $50–60 million each year.[21] In addition, more than $1.5 billion in private US funds go to Israel annually – $1 billion in private tax-deductible donations and $500 million in Israeli bonds.[22] This ability of Americans to make what amounts to tax-deductible contributions to a foreign government through private charities is not extended to any other country.

For a country that makes up just one-tenth of one per cent of the world's population, US aid to Israel as a proportion of the foreign aid budget is enormous. Approximately one out of every four dollars for foreign aid goes to it, several times all US aid to sub-Saharan Africa. That is not because it is poor – its GNP is higher than the *combined* GNP of its immediate neighbors Egypt, Lebanon, Syria, Jordan, the West Bank, and the Gaza Strip. With a per capita income about $32,000, Israel ranks among the 30 wealthiest countries in the world, higher than oil-rich Saudi Arabia and trailing only slightly behind most Western European countries.

Aid to Israel has often been rationalized as a means to support the peace process. However, it has increased as the peace process stagnated and then collapsed. With repeated US public pronouncements that the aid is unconditional, the recipient state has no incentive to make concessions necessary for peace or to end its human rights abuses and other violations of international law. Henry Kissinger once wryly got to the heart of the matter in relating that when he called for Israeli concessions, the Israeli Prime Minister "says he can't because Israel is weak. So I give him more arms, and he says he doesn't need to make concessions because Israel is strong."[23]

The diplomatic support for Israel is unprecedented as well. In the Security Council, the US has vetoed 42 resolutions critical of Israel, primarily regarding the government's ongoing violations of international humanitarian law. This constitutes nearly a third of all vetoes by permanent members of the Security Council since 1970. Scores of other resolutions never made it to a vote because of a threatened US veto and scores of others were weakened considerably due to US pressure.

For over 30 years, there has been an international consensus on the resolution of the Arab–Israeli conflict. This calls for withdrawal of Israeli forces to within Israel's internationally-recognized (pre-June 1967) boundaries in return for strict security guarantees, establishment of a Palestinian state in the West Bank and Gaza Strip, making a shared Jerusalem the capital of both states, and a just resolution for the Palestinian refugees. During the same period, the Palestine Liberation Organization (PLO), which served for many years as the Palestinians' *de facto* government-in-exile under the leadership of Yasir Arafat, has evolved from openly calling for Israel's destruction to supporting this international consensus. Having hinted at a willingness to accept the emerging international consensus as far back as the mid 1970s, Arafat made this official in 1988 in his unilateral recognition of Israel and renunciation of violence and was followed by PLO signing the Oslo Accords with Israel in

1993. In 1996, the Palestine National Council formally repealed sections in its charter calling for Israel's dissolution.[24]

But the US, along with Israel, long rejected the international consensus. A UN Security Council resolution reflecting this international consensus had the support of virtually the entire international community, including most Arab states and the Palestinians, was put to a vote as far back as 1976 but was opposed by Israel and was vetoed by the US. This strident opposition to compromise was modified when President Bill Clinton, toward the end of his presidency, and President George W. Bush, in a more explicit way in the fall of 2002, declared US support for a Palestinian state in parts of the West Bank and Gaza Strip. However, both administrations made clear that the US was talking about severely circumscribed boundaries along lines that the Israelis were willing to offer, together with restrictions on certain aspects of its sovereignty that would make the prospective Palestinian state independent only in name. Both administrations supported a Jerusalem primarily under Israeli sovereignty, only partial Israeli withdrawal from occupied Palestinian territories, and no right for Palestinian refugees to return. Nor were these administrations willing to demand an end to Israel's illegal confiscation of Palestinian land and construction of Jewish-only settlements and roads within the occupied territories that would otherwise become part of an already circumscribed Palestinian state.

The position taken by President Obama has been somewhat more moderate, calling for acceptance of the pre-June 1967 borders as the starting point for a negotiated settlement. But he has never called for a complete withdrawal of Israeli troops and settlers. He specified that Palestinian borders must be with "Israel, Jordan and Egypt," thereby challenging Israeli plans to retain control of the Jordan Valley (and thus completely surround any future Palestinian mini-state, which would thus lack access to its eastern neighbor) and – since the West Bank does not border Egypt – to prevent the exclusion of the Gaza Strip in the Palestinian state. The unspecified variations from the pre-1967 borders, Obama insisted, should be made through "mutually agreed-upon" land swaps. Unfortunately, despite Palestinian President Mahmoud Abbas's agreement to such reciprocal territorial swaps, Israeli Prime Minister Benyamin Netanyahu has refused to consider trading any land within Israel while simultaneously insisting on annexing large swathes of occupied Palestinian territory. How such "mutually agreed-upon" swaps will take place without the US exerting enormous leverage – such as threatening to withhold some of the annual $3 billion in unconditional aid provided annually, which Obama has ruled out – is hard to imagine. Obama has also insisted that the borders of the new Palestinian state be agreed on prior to negotiations over the status of East Jerusalem, the nominal Palestinian capital and base of leading Palestinian universities, businesses, and cultural and religious landmarks. In addition, Obama has steadfastly opposed any recognition of a Palestinian state by the United Nations or any UN body outside of the parameters agreed to by the Israeli government. A large bipartisan majority of Congress, meanwhile, in an apparent rebuke to Obama's calls for even limited Israeli compromises, has passed a series of non-binding resolutions largely supporting Netanyahu's position on the outstanding issues of the peace talks.

The US also opposes any negotiations with a potential national unity government between the ruling Fatah, long the dominant party of the PLO, and the Islamist Hamas, on the grounds that Hamas refuses to recognize Israel's right to exist or formally endorse previous agreements. The US, however, demonstrates a blatant double standard by not insisting on the same prerequisites for Israel, whose government includes parties that – representing a mirror image of Hamas – both refuse to recognize Palestine's right to exist and reject previous agreements.

A review of the history of the US role in the peace process is revealing, indicating a desire for more of a Pax Americana than a real peace. Despite the widespread portrayal of the US as an honest broker in the Middle East, American opposition to a comprehensive peace settlement between Israel and its Arab neighbors goes back to the late 1960s. Officially, the US has backed UN Security Council resolutions 242 and 338 – that call for Israel's withdrawal from the territories seized in the 1967 war in return for mutual security guarantees – as the basis for peace. However, as far back as 1969, US National Security Advisor Henry Kissinger passed on to the Israelis the advice that they ignore the Rogers Plan – crafted by US Secretary of State William Rogers – that would have required Israel to return, with some minor alterations, to its 1967 borders in return for peace. The Nixon administration did not even encourage the far more modest Allon Plan, proposed by Israel's foreign minister soon after the war, which would have led to an Israeli withdrawal from most of the occupied territories outside of the Jordan Valley. Instead, Kissinger encouraged the Israeli government to hold on to its captured Arab lands. When Egyptian President Anwar Sadat made peace overtures in 1971, Kissinger successfully advised the Israelis to ignore it. As a result, Egypt – along with Syria – attacked Israeli occupation forces in October 1973, advancing into the occupied Sinai Peninsula and Golan Heights before a massive US re-supply operation enabled Israel to mount a successful counter-attack. Only after the war did the US support disengagement talks, and then only under American auspices. It has never pursued peace plans proposed by the Europeans, the United Nations or the Arab states, including such Saudi initiatives as the 1981 Fahd Plan and the very similar 2002 Abdullah Plan that essentially reiterated the principle of land for peace. In the common lexicon in the US, the "peace process" refers only to efforts initiated by the US government.

The US has consistently rejected an international peace conference that would lead to a comprehensive all-parties peace settlement. Instead it has pushed for a succession of bilateral arrangements that could maximize American influence in the region, such as the 1978 Camp David agreement between Israel and Egypt and the 1994 peace treaty between Israel and Jordan. Neither of these effectively addressed the underlying source of the

Arab–Israeli conflict: the fate of the Palestinians. Furthermore, by neutralizing Egypt – by far Israel's biggest military rival – with the Camp David agreement, Israel was emboldened to invade Lebanon in 1982 and redouble its colonization and repression in the occupied Palestinian territories.

Like most Arab governments, the PLO initially ruled out formal negotiations directly with Israel. By the mid 1970s, however, the Palestinians began expressing their desire to be included in the peace process. Both Israel and the US refused to include them. The US insisted that Jordan – a US client state that occupied the West Bank between 1948 and 1967 (although its annexation of the territory failed to get widespread international recognition) and was host to a sizable population of Palestinian refugees – would serve as the Palestinians' representative. Given the traditional hostility between Jordan and the PLO, however, which led to a civil war in Jordan during the early 1970s in which thousands of Palestinian civilians were killed, few Palestinians felt the Hashemite monarchy could fairly represent their interests. The US position was that the PLO could participate in the peace process only if it (1) recognized Israel's right to exist; (2) accepted UN Security Council resolutions 242 and 338 as the basis for peace talks; and, (3) renounced terrorism. While most observers considered these conditions reasonable in themselves, they noted an unfair double standard in Washington's failure to call for Israel – which adamantly continued to reject the Palestinians' right to a state and also rejected the usual interpretation of the relevant resolutions – to reciprocate. Furthermore, only the PLO was asked to renounce "terrorism," even though Israeli forces killed far more civilians than did the various Palestinian militias under the umbrella of the PLO.

For more than a decade, the PLO unsuccessfully tried to convince the US to call for reciprocal declarations in support of the UN resolutions and against violence against civilians. And it called for a simultaneous mutual recognition of Palestine and Israel. However, both the Carter and Reagan administrations refused, and, in 1988, the PLO finally relented and agreed to Washington's three demands without any reciprocity by Israel.

And still the US refused to allow the PLO a role in the peace process. It limited official contact with the PLO to conversations conducted by the US ambassador to Tunisia, where the PLO relocated its offices following its ouster from Lebanon by invading Israeli forces in 1982. These talks were broken off within two years when the US determined that the PLO had not sufficiently criticized an attempted terrorist attack against Israel by a small Palestinian splinter group.

Continuing to reject calls for an international conference under UN auspices, the US set up a major peace conference in Madrid in 1991. While some meetings were to take place on a multilateral basis, Washington determined that the real negotiations would take place bilaterally, with a strong American presence. While most Arab nations were invited to participate, the US explicitly excluded the PLO. It allowed for Palestinian participation only as part of the Jordanian delegation and excluded delegates from the Palestinian diaspora or Israeli-occupied East Jerusalem as well as anyone affiliated with the PLO. This may have been the first time that the convener of a peace conference granted itself the right to choose the delegation from one of the participants.[25] Real progress was made on the Israeli–Palestinian track only when the Israelis did an end-run around the restrictive US formula and met in direct talks with the PLO secretly in Norway in 1993. These were the talks that resulted in the Declaration of Principles, also known as the Oslo Accords, which – while failing to recognize the Palestinians' right to statehood and imposing other limitations, – did provide a framework for substantive progress towards Israeli–Palestinian peace.

Unaware of the secret Israeli–PLO talks in Norway, the US had already put forward what it called a "compromise" proposal for Palestinian autonomy. However, the Israeli negotiating proposal being put forth at the same time and largely incorporated into the Declaration of Principles was actually more favorable to the Palestinians than was the US proposal, which Palestinian officials described as "closer to the Israeli Likud position," referring to the Rabin government's right-wing predecessors. This was only one of more than a half dozen occasions during the 1990s in which the US actually took a harder line towards Israel's Arab adversaries than did the ruling Israeli Labor Party and/or Israeli public opinion. Indeed, while Israel was secretly meeting with the PLO in the summer of 1993, the Clinton administration, Congress, and both major American political parties were on record as opposing the inclusion of the PLO in the peace process.

Peace talks resumed in Washington in the fall of 1993 within the Oslo framework. Under the relatively moderate Labor Party, elected to office in 1992, Israeli negotiators recognized that – in terms of domestic Israeli politics – the peace movement did not have as much political clout as the right wing. As a result, it was difficult politically for them to take the necessary steps for achieving peace, such as bringing Israel into compliance with UN Security Council resolutions and agreeing to Palestinian independence within viable borders. As a result, members of the Israeli negotiating team in Washington privately asked US officials to openly push the Israeli government to compromise further so as to give the prime minister sufficient political cover to proceed with concessions.[26] Demonstrating again that it was more anti-Palestinian than the Israeli government, the Clinton administration refused to do so.

Over the next seven years, the US brokered a series of Israeli–Palestinian agreements that led to the withdrawal of Israeli forces from most of the Gaza Strip and parts of the West Bank. Some of the areas came under control of the PLO-led Palestinian Authority, giving the Palestinians a degree of self-governance in a small area of their own country for the first time. The majority of the West Bank and about 20 per cent of the Gaza Strip remained under Israeli military occupation or some kind of joint administration. During this period, Israel severely limited the mobility of Palestinians within and between the West Bank and Gaza Strip and dramatically expanded its expropriation of land in the occupied territories for colonization by Jewish settlers. In addition, the Israelis refused to withdraw from as much territory as promised in the US-brokered disengagement agreements. Meanwhile, the increasingly corrupt, inept, and autocratic Palestinian Authority – under the leadership of PLO Chairman Yasir Arafat – had alienated much of the Palestinian population and proved itself unable to suppress the growth of radical Islamic groups, which saw the Palestinian Authority as an entity designed to suppress resistance against the ongoing Israeli occupation. On more than two dozen occasions between 1994 and 2000, Islamic extremists engaged in terrorist bombings against civilian targets inside Israel. The US and Israel then used this as an excuse to delay further Israeli withdrawals, a freeze on settlements, or other issues related to a final status agreement.

From the beginning of the talks following the Principles of Understanding negotiated in Norway, it became apparent that the two sides saw the process very differently. The Palestinians saw the Oslo process as a means to end the occupation and establish a Palestinian state in the West Bank – including Arab East Jerusalem – and the Gaza Strip. By contrast, the US and Israel apparently saw it more as a way of perpetuating the occupation of major parts of these territories, with Israel's former enemies now co-opted as collaborators and "enforcers." In this role, the Palestinian Authority would be in charge of administering most major Palestinian population centers and cooperating with Israel in protecting Israel and its settlements in the occupied territories.

In signing the Declaration of Principles, the Palestinians worked on the assumption that this would result in concrete improvements in the lives of those in the occupied territories, that the interim period would be no more than five years, and that the permanent settlement would be based on UN Security Council resolutions 242 and 338. They trusted that the US, as guarantor of the agreement – signed on the White House lawn on September 13, 1993 – would be able to pressure Israel and insure cooperation. However, none of these assumptions were fulfilled.

Indeed, the Clinton administration and Congress faulted the Palestinians for refusing to accept a series of proposals put forward in 2000 and subsequently which would have allowed Israel to hold on to large swaths of Palestinian territory in the West Bank, essentially dividing the Palestinian "state" into a series of non-contiguous cantons with Israel controlling movement between the segments of Palestinian territory, as well as water resources, air space, and international travel. When frustration spilled over into a series of violent confrontations in 2000–2, resulting in large numbers of military and civilian casualties on both sides, the US blamed the Palestinians exclusively for the violence, despite reports from reputable human rights groups that both sides shared responsibility. Even when the US was forced to bring in international partners – Russia, the European Union and the United Nations – to work out a staged plan for peace, the US insisted on taking the dominant role and put the impetus on the Palestinian side, rather than the mutual reciprocal steps as required by the Quartet. The US backed a unilateral initiative by the Sharon government which led to the withdrawal from illegal settlements in the Gaza Strip but increased Israeli colonization and control of large segments of the occupied West Bank, including occupied East Jerusalem.

An attempt by the Bush administration to press Fatah into staging a coup against its Hamas partners in a coalition government in 2005 resulted in a counter-coup which led the Gaza Strip to fall under the control of Hamas, while the non-occupied portions of the West Bank remained under the control of the Fatah-dominated Palestinian Authority. The US then backed a draconian siege on the Gaza Strip, as well as a devastating Israeli military offensive on the Gaza Strip in 2008–9 in response to Hamas rocket attacks. Reports by Amnesty International, the UN Human Rights Council, Human Rights Watch and other groups which documented likely war crimes by both sides were summarily dismissed by the Bush administration and Congress. Despite the deaths of over 800 Palestinian civilians at the hands of Israeli forces – compared with three Israelis killed by Hamas forces – the Bush administration and Congress rejected the reports, defended Israel's actions, and put the blame exclusively on Hamas. Congress also went on record defending an Israeli attack on an unarmed humanitarian aid flotilla bound for Gaza in 2010 in international waters, killing nine crewmen.

This raises questions as to what actually motivates US policy in support of the more hard line and rejectionist elements in Israeli politics. Although US backing of successive Israeli governments, like most foreign policy decisions, typically is rationalized on moral grounds, there is little evidence that moral imperatives play a determining role in US policy in the Middle East or in any other part of the world. Most Americans do share a moral commitment to Israel's survival as a Jewish state, but this would not account for the level of financial, military, and diplomatic support provided. American aid to Israel goes well beyond protecting its security needs within its internationally-recognized borders. US assistance includes support for policies in militarily occupied territories that often violate well-established legal and ethical standards of international behavior.

Were Israel's security interests paramount in the eyes of American policy-makers, US aid to Israel would have been highest in the early years of its existence. That was when its democratic institutions were strongest and its strategic situation most vulnerable. And support would have declined as its military power grew dramatically and its repression against Palestinians in the occupied territories increased. Instead, the trend has been in just the opposite direction, as massive US military and economic aid began only after the 1967 war. Indeed, 99 per cent of US military assistance to Israel since its establishment has come only after Israel proved itself to be far stronger than any combination of Arab armies and after Israeli occupation forces became the rulers of a large Palestinian population.

Similarly, US aid to Israel is higher now than 40 years ago, when Egypt's massive and well-equipped armed forces threatened war. Today, by contrast,

Israel has a longstanding peace treaty with Egypt and a large demilitarized and internationally monitored buffer zone keeping its army at a distance. And while Syria's military formerly was expanding rapidly with advanced Soviet weaponry, Syria now has made clear its willingness to live in peace with Israel in return for ending the occupation of the Golan Heights, and its military capabilities have been declining since the collapse of its Soviet patron.

Also in the mid 1970s, Jordan still claimed the West Bank and stationed large numbers of troops along its lengthy Israeli frontier. But now, it has signed a peace treaty with Israel, renounced its claims to the West Bank, and has established fully normalized relations. And while Iraq once was embarking upon a vast program of militarization, its armed forces have long since been devastated. This raises serious questions as to why US aid has either remained steady or actually increased each year since military threats withered.

Following a hypothetical cut-off of all US aid to Israel, it still would take many years for Israel to come under significantly greater military threat than it is today. It has both a major domestic arms industry and an existing military force far more capable and powerful than any conceivable combination of opposing forces. There would be no question of its survival being at risk militarily in the foreseeable future. What is remarkable is that only after Israel gained an increasingly dominant military position has such consensus for increasingly massive US backing emerged. In short, the growing US support for the Israeli government, like US support for allies elsewhere in the world, is not motivated primarily by what are perceived as the country's objective security needs or a strong moral commitment to the country. Rather, as elsewhere, US foreign policy is concerned primarily with advancing its own perceived strategic interests. And there is a broad bipartisan consensus among policymakers that Israel has advanced US interest in the Middle East and beyond.

- Israel has successfully prevented victories by radical nationalist movements in Lebanon and Jordan, as well as in Palestine, and has subsequently battled Islamist forces.
- Israel has kept Syria, for many years an ally of the Soviet Union and subsequently an ally of Iran, in check.
- Israel's air force is predominant throughout the region.
- Israel's frequent wars have provided battlefield testing for American arms, initially against Soviet weapons.
- Israel has served as a conduit for US arms to regimes and movements too unpopular in the US for it to openly do so itself. Examples include apartheid South Africa, the Islamic Republic in Iran, the military junta in Guatemala, the Nicaraguan Contras, and Colombian paramilitaries.
- Israeli military advisors have assisted allied regimes and movements such as the Contras, the Salvadoran junta, and foreign occupation forces in Namibia and Western Sahara.
- Israel's intelligence services have assisted the US in intelligence gathering and covert operations.

- Israel has cooperated with the US military-industrial complex with research and development for new jet fighters, anti-missile defense systems, and other weapons programs.

The pattern of US aid to Israel is revealing. Immediately following Israel's spectacular victory in the 1967 war, when it demonstrated its military superiority in the region, US aid shot up by 450 per cent. Part of this increase, according to the *New York Times*, was apparently related to Israel's willingness to provide the US with examples of new Soviet weapons captured during the war. Following the 1970–71 civil war in Jordan, when Israel's potential to curb revolutionary movements outside its borders became apparent, US aid increased another sevenfold. After attacking Arab armies in the 1973 war were successfully countered by the largest US airlift in history, with Israel demonstrating its power to defeat surprisingly strong Soviet-supplied forces, military aid increased by another 800 per cent. These increases paralleled the British decision to withdraw its forces from "east of the Suez," which also led to massive arms sales and logistical cooperation with the Shah's Iran, a key component of the Nixon Doctrine.

The same pattern continued in subsequent years. Aid quadrupled again in 1979 soon after the fall of the Shah, the election of the right-wing Likud government, and the ratification of the Egyptian–Israeli Peace Treaty. The latter included provisions for increased military assistance that made as much a tripartite military pact as a traditional peace agreement. (It is noteworthy that the additional aid provided to Israel in the treaty continued despite the Begin government's refusal to abide by any reasonable interpretation of provisions relating to Palestinian autonomy.) Aid increased yet again soon after the 1982 Israeli invasion of Lebanon. In 1983 and 1984, when the US and Israel signed memoranda of understanding on strategic cooperation and military planning and conducted their first joint naval and air military exercises, Israel was rewarded by an additional $1.5 billion in economic aid and another half billion dollars for the development of a new jet fighter.

During and immediately after the Gulf War, US aid increased by an additional $650 million. When Israel dramatically increased its repression in the occupied territories – including incursions into Palestinian territories whose autonomy was provided for in treaties guaranteed by the US government – US aid increased still further and shot up again following the September 11 terrorist attacks against the US, yet again after the US invasion of Iraq, and have continued to increase as tensions have increased between the US and Iran.

The correlation is clear: the stronger and more willing to cooperate with US interests that Israel becomes, the stronger the support. The continued high levels of US aid to Israel come not out of concern for Israel's survival, but as a result of the US desire for Israel to continue its political and strategic dominance. Indeed, leaders of both American political parties long have called not for the US to help maintain a military balance between Israel and its neighbors, but for insuring Israeli military superiority.

A strong case can be made that whatever short-term strategic advantages the US may gain from this kind of relationship are more than offset by the damage the relationship has caused. It is a major source of anti-American sentiment in the Middle East, including terrorists and other extremists who have targeted Americans and US interests. It has made it far more difficult for the US to press such issues as human rights, arms control, nuclear non-proliferation, enforcement of UN Security Council resolutions, and other concerns due to perceived double standards regarding Israel. It has given license for Israel to engage in policies in contravention of widely-accepted international legal norms with which the US is held responsible due to its unconditional military, economic and diplomatic support for the government. However, as is often the case in foreign policy formulation, the longer-term consequences are often ignored by perceived shorter-term exigencies, ideological pre-conceptions, political pressure, bureaucratic inertia, and other factors.

Historically, some of the worst cases of US support for allies engaged in violations of international legal norms have not remained unchallenged, leading to reversals in US policy on Vietnam, Central America, South Africa, and East Timor. In these cases, grass roots movements supportive of peace and justice grew to a point where liberal members of Congress, in the media and elsewhere, joined in the call to stop US complicity. In other cases, such as US support for Morocco's invasion and occupation of Western Sahara, too few Americans are even aware of the situation to mount a serious challenge, leaving it off the radar screen of lawmakers and pundits.

However, the case of Israel and Palestine is different. There are significant sectors of the population that question US policy, and yet there is a widespread consensus among elite sectors of government and the media in support of US backing for the Israeli occupation. Therefore, while the perceived strategic imperative is at the root of US support for Israel, there are additional factors that have made this issue particularly difficult for peace and human rights activists. These include the following:

- Many liberals – particularly among the post-World War II generation in leadership positions in government and the media – have a strong sentimental attachment for Israel. Many Americans identify with Israel's internal democracy, its progressive social institutions – such as the kibbutzim – in its earlier years, its previous reputation for a relatively high level of social equality for its Jewish citizens, and its important role as a sanctuary for an oppressed minority group that spent centuries in diaspora. Through a mixture of guilt regarding Western anti-Semitism, personal friendships with Jewish Americans who identify strongly with Israel, and fear of inadvertently encouraging anti-Semitism by criticizing Israel, there is enormous reluctance to acknowledge the seriousness of Israeli violations of human rights and international law.
- The Christian Right, with tens of millions of followers and a major base of support for the Republican Party, has thrown its immense media and

political clout in support for Benyamin Netanyahu and other right-wing Israeli leaders. Based in part on a messianic theology that sees the ingathering of Jews in the Holy Land as a precursor to the second coming of Christ, the battle between Israelis and Palestinians is, in their eyes, simply a continuation of the battle between the Israelites and the Philistines, with God in the role of a cosmic real estate agent who has deemed that the land belongs to Israel alone, secular notions of international law and the right of self-determination notwithstanding.

- Mainstream and conservative Jewish organizations have mobilized considerable lobbying resources, financial contributions, and pressure on the news media and other forums of public discourse. Although the power of the pro-Israel lobby is often greatly exaggerated, its role has been important in certain tight congressional races and in helping to create a climate of intimidation among those who seek to moderate US policy, including growing numbers of progressive Jews.
- The arms industry, which contributes five times more money to congressional campaigns and lobbying efforts than AIPAC and other pro-Israel groups, has a considerable stake in supporting massive arms shipments to Israel and other Middle Eastern allies of the US. It is far easier for a member of Congress to challenge a $60 million arms deal to, say, Indonesia than the more than $3 billion in military aid granted annually to Israel, particularly when so many congressional districts include factories that produce this military hardware.
- Widespread racism toward Arabs and Muslims has been prevalent in American society and often is perpetuated in the media. This is compounded by the identification many Americans have with Zionism in the Middle East as a reflection of historic experience as pioneers in North America, building a nation based upon noble, idealistic values while simultaneously suppressing and expelling the indigenous population.
- Progressive movements in the US generally have failed to challenge US policy toward Israel and Palestine in an effective manner. For many years, most mainstream peace and human rights groups avoided the issue, not wanting to alienate many of their Jewish and other liberal constituents supportive of the Israeli government. Without countervailing pressure from progressives, liberal members of Congress thus had little incentive not to cave in to pressure from supporters of Israeli policies. Meanwhile, many groups on the far left and others took a stridently anti-Israel position that did not just challenge Israeli policies but were seen as being more based upon a rigid ideological agenda than out of universal concern for human rights, and thereby damaging their credibility. In some cases, particularly among the more conservative individuals and groups critical of Israel, a latent anti-Semitism would come to the fore in wildly exaggerated claims of Jewish economic and political power and other statements that further alienated potential critics of US policy.

As a result, the US government has had little incentive to change its policies towards Israel and its neighbors.

Iraq: the destruction of an Arab adversary

Under the British-installed king, Iraq was a major Western ally until a revolution by left-wing nationalists toppled the monarchy in 1958. With quiet encouragement from the US, Saddam Hussein rose to prominence in the late 1970s against leftist rivals, shifting Iraq somewhat from its pro-Soviet to a more non-aligned orientation. Apparently without regard to his establishment of the most totalitarian regime in the Middle East, the US joined France, Great Britain, and the Soviets in accepting Iraq's importance in the regional balance of power. All maintained a largely cooperative relationship with this exceptionally oppressive regime, much to the chagrin of human rights advocates. While US officials never called Iraq an ally, they saw it as a strategic asset with which they could cooperate throughout its dramatic military buildup in the 1980s.

For years, Middle East experts, human rights supporters, and many others called on the US to end its backing for Saddam Hussein's regime. They pointed to Iraq's 1980 invasion of Iran and the bloody eight-year war that followed, its brutal suppression of the country's Kurdish minority, its support for international terrorism, and its large-scale human rights violations. Perhaps most egregious was Iraq's use of chemical warfare against both Iranian troops and its own civilian Kurdish population during the 1980s – by far the largest use of such weapons since they were outlawed in 1925. The response of the world's nations was a major test as to whether international law was be treated as a serious matter, and the US, along with much of the world community, failed the test. US agricultural subsidies and other economic aid flowed into Iraq, and American officials looked the other way as much of this was laundered to purchase military equipment. The US sent an untold amount of indirect aid – largely through Kuwait and other Arab countries – which enabled Iraq to increase its war-making capacity.[27]

When a Senate Foreign Relations committee staff report in 1988 brought to light Saddam Hussein's widespread killings of Kurdish civilians in northern Iraq, Senator Claiborne Pell introduced the Prevention of Genocide Act to put pressure on the Iraqi government. However, the Reagan administration successfully moved to have the measure killed.

The Iraqi invasion of Kuwait, an important American client state with enormous oil reserves, in August 1990 finally led to a dramatic policy reversal by Washington. Invading Iran, seen as a dangerous challenge to American hegemony, had been cheered on, but the invasion of oil-rich Kuwait provided a new threat to American hegemony in the Persian Gulf region and was not to be tolerated. While the Arab League joined the rest of the international community in condemning this latest aggression, the US successfully pushed to block any peaceful means to get Iraq to withdraw from the newly occupied country. In addition, the US used what was apparently falsified satellite footage making it appear that Iraqi troops were massing near the Kuwaiti–Saudi border in order to trick the Saudis into allowing American and other foreign forces to enter their territory to defend them.[28]

Even after hundreds of thousands of US and other foreign troops entered the region, there were possibilities for a negotiated settlement. However, there was no American attempt to negotiate, with President Bush informing Saddam Hussein that his only choice was to capitulate without negotiation or be crushed by force. Indeed, it appears that the US wanted to go to war in order to destroy Iraq's military and industrial capacity[29] and to bolster its own dominance of the region.

In a military campaign dubbed "Operation Desert Storm," the US and its allies began bombing Iraq on January 16, 1991, one day after the United Nations-imposed deadline for Iraqi withdrawal from Kuwait. It was almost exclusively an air war until American ground troops entered the fighting in late February, liberating Kuwait and temporarily occupying a large swath of southern Iraq after slightly more than four days.

Two weeks earlier, Iraq had accepted a Soviet peace proposal in full and agreed to withdraw from Kuwait in compliance with UN Security Council resolution 660. The US, however, rejected the deal and pledged to continue prosecuting the war. Even as Iraqi forces finally began withdrawing from Kuwait, the US continued its assault on Iraqi forces, killing thousands of Iraqis in their vehicles on what became known as the "Highway of Death."

Though the United Nations had only authorized member states to do what was necessary to rid Iraqi forces from Kuwait, the US went well beyond the UN mandate in its determination to inflict a devastating blow to Iraq's infrastructure through what became, in a period of just six weeks, the heaviest bombing campaign in the history of war, targeting roads, bridges, factories, irrigation systems, power stations, water works, and government offices. Even Saddam Hussein's most strident critics in the Gulf were offended at the level of overkill, particularly what was inflicted upon Iraq's civilian population, unwilling conscripts, and the country's non-military infrastructure.[30]

According to a *Washington Post* report soon after the war,

> Many of the targets were chosen only secondarily to contribute to the military defeat of Iraq. ... Military planners hoped the bombing would amplify the economic and psychological impact of international sanctions on Iraqi society. ... Because of these goals, damage to civilian structures and interests, invariably described by briefers during the war as "collateral" and unintended, were sometimes neither. ... They deliberately did great harm to Iraq's ability to support itself as an industrial society.[31]

At the end of the war in March, the long-suppressed Kurds in the north and Shi'ites in the south launched a rebellion. They initially made major advances, only to be crushed in a counter-attack by Iraqi government forces. Despite

President Bush's call for the people of Iraq to rise up against the dictatorship, US forces – which at that time occupied a small section in the southeastern part of the country – did nothing to support the post-war rebellion and stood by while thousands of Iraqi Kurds, Shi'ites, and others were slaughtered. In the cease-fire agreement at the end of the war, the US made a conscious decision to exclude Iraqi helicopter gunships from the ban on Iraqi military air traffic, the very weapons that proved so decisive in crushing the rebellions. Thousands were slaughtered. It appears that the George H. W. Bush administration feared that a victory by Iraqi Kurds would encourage the ongoing Kurdish uprising in Turkey, a NATO ally.[32] The US also feared that a radical Shi'ite Arab entity – led by Iranian-supported factions, much like what in fact occurred 15 years later – would emerge in southern Iraq and have serious implications for American allies in the Gulf with restive Shi'ite populations. (After goading the Kurds into an armed uprising with the promise of military support during the 1970s, the US abandoned them precipitously in return for an Iraqi agreement with Iran that accepted the latter's claim regarding the Shatt al-Arab, a strategic waterway.[33])

The US blocked the lifting of the crippling UN economic sanctions initially imposed following the invasion of Kuwait even after Iraq's withdrawal. This had a devastating impact on the civilian population, following after the damage to the civilian infrastructure during the bombing, in which the US destroyed 18 out of 20 electrical power stations, disabling water pumping and sanitation systems, some of which were hit directly. The result was untreated sewage flowing into rivers that supplied drinking water. Since the sanctions prohibited the importation of many of the spare parts, allegedly because they could also be used as components of military systems, the Iraqis were unable to repair these facilities. As a result, there was a dramatic increase in typhoid, cholera and other illnesses that recently had been largely eliminated. Importation of ambulances and other emergency vehicles, and even their spare parts, were also among the items banned under the sanctions. Similarly, hospitals were unable to acquire spare parts for incubators, kidney dialysis machines and other equipment. Even materials such as food and medicines not covered by the ban became difficult to purchase due to the lack of funds. Severe malnutrition led to stunted physical and mental development of hundreds of thousands of Iraqi children. An August 1999 UNICEF report noted that the mortality rate for children under five had more than doubled since sanctions were imposed.[34] Estimates of the total number of Iraqis killed as a result of malnutrition and preventable diseases as a direct consequence of war damage and sanctions have ranged from a quarter million to over one million, the majority of whom were children.[35]

In an interview on the CBS news show "60 Minutes," Secretary of State Madeleine Albright was asked about the devastating impact sanctions were having on the children of Iraq, with host Lesley Stahl quoting the figure of half a million killed. Albright replied that "we think the price ... is worth it."[36]

Meanwhile, the US was engaging in periodic air strikes against Iraq, including a heavy four-day bombing campaign in December 1998. By the end of the decade, the US bombing of Iraq averaged more than one a week.

For most in the Washington establishment, simply keeping Iraq in a state of penury was enough. Once a mid-level power with a sizable armed force and industrial capacity willing and able to defy US demands, it now was reduced to the status of an impoverished, effectively deindustrialized state with no offensive military capability. Its long-range missiles, nuclear program, chemical and biological weapons, and related programs had all been eliminated by a rigorous UN-sponsored inspections regime. Its navy and air force were essentially non-existent and its army reduced by more than half. The most rigorous inspections regime in history oversaw Iraq's disarmament. Though withdrawn under orders of President Clinton just prior to the December 1998 bombing campaign and not allowed to return until late 2002, UN inspections documented that Iraq, despite periodic noncooperation with the inspectors, had achieved at least qualitative disarmament.[37]

However, in March 2003, the Bush administration – with support from congressional leaders of both parties – decided that containment was not enough. Instead, the US – with the support of Britain and small contingents from several other countries – launched an invasion and occupied Iraq, unleashing a bloody eight-year counter-insurgency war. US troops were not withdrawn until the end of 2011.

Credible estimates of civilian deaths from the war have ranged as high as 600,000. Nearly 4,500 US troops, over 10,000 soldiers and police of the new Iraqi government, and over 55,000 insurgents were also killed. Well over two million Iraqis fled into exile, including an estimated 40 per cent of the country's professional class. An additional two million have been internally displaced. The US fired virtually all civil servants and other state employees, resulting in government ministries becoming fiefdoms of sectarian parties, often with extreme and parochial agendas. The Iraqi armed forces, another bastion of secular nationalism and national unity, were eliminated and replaced by a hodgepodge of sectarian militias. Sectarian violence, virtually unknown in recent Iraqi history, has torn the country apart and terrorist attacks continue across the country.

The US originally justified the conquest on the ground that Iraq had reconstituted its chemical and biological weapons capability and its nuclear program, that it possessed long-range missiles, and that it was collaborating with Al-Qaeda. All such claims were based on flimsy evidence at most and were repeatedly questioned by foreign governments and independent security analysts. Indeed, all these accusations soon were proven false.

The actual reasons for the war appear to have been based upon a qualitative change in US policy under the George W. Bush administration. In the decades following World War II, US administrations – to varying degrees – saw American dominance as exercised though multiple independent centers of power. These included the United Nations and other inter-governmental organizations, with increasing emphasis in more recent years on the role of international financial institutions, such as the World Bank and the International Monetary Fund. International law was seen as a vehicle to facilitate the use of America's preeminent military and economic power in the interest of world order. While certain elements of international law could sometimes be stretched or quietly undercut – and occasionally blatantly disregarded – the prevailing view in Washington was that the United Nations system allowed for a relatively stable world order in which the US and its allies could usually accomplish their goals and was far less dangerous than a more anarchic system.

However, the US's emergence as the world's only remaining superpower seemed to mean that following the rules had become passé. US military spending was higher than that of the rest of the world combined, and American commercial and cultural influence far exceeded that of any other country. Consequently the view among leading policy makers in the Bush administration was that the US could now go it alone. The UN and international law came to be seen as a constraint and an anachronism. According to this world view, the US no longer had to play by the rules and had the right and the ability – indeed, the duty – to impose a global Pax Americana.

This attitude manifested itself in a number of other policy shifts during this period. Cases in point include the broad bipartisan consensus in Washington supporting Israeli colonization and incipient annexation of large segments of the occupied West Bank and Golan Heights, the abandonment of the referendum process in Moroccan-occupied Western Sahara, and efforts to sabotage the Millennium Development Goals and other aspects of the world body's agenda at the UN World Summit in September 2005.

This hubris manifested an intensified belief in American "exceptionalism" within and outside the Bush administration. In his introduction to the 2002 National Security Strategy, President Bush asserted that the US represents "a single sustainable model for national success."[38] In particular, according to the President, "I believe the United States is *the* beacon for freedom in the world. And I believe we have a responsibility to promote freedom that is as solemn as the responsibility is to protect the American people, because the two go hand-in-hand."[39] Historian Margaret Macmillan observed that, "Faith in their [Americans'] exceptionalism has sometimes led to a ... tendency to preach at other nations rather than listen to them, a tendency [to believe] that American motives are pure where those of others are not."[40] Journalist Eric Zuesse observed how Bush "made clear right at the start that the United States had to be accepted by other nations as being not merely the first among equals, but a role apart, which simply mustn't be judged like other countries."[41] Furthermore, notes Zuesse, Bush "gives every indication that he hates Man-made international law, and really believes he's serving God through his campaign to destroy and replace it by his standing *above* it."[42]

In an interview, Paul Wolfowitz emphasized that the alleged "weapons of mass destruction" were never actually the primary reason for war. Instead, he explained that the President saw himself in an epochal struggle against evil and wanted to reorder the Middle East.[43] This reflects a Manichean moralism that sees the world in simplistic terms of good versus evil. A revealing glimpse at the religious underpinning of the American leadership's view of America's destiny through the invasion of Iraq could be gleaned from the 2003 Christmas card of Vice-President Cheney and his wife, which contains the quote, "If a sparrow cannot fall to the ground without His notice, is it probable that an empire can rise without His aid?"[44] President Bush was even blunter in a conversation with Mahmoud Abbas in June of 2003, when he reportedly told the Palestinian prime minister that "God ... instructed me to strike at Saddam, which I did."[45]

Perhaps it is no accident that a number of the neo-conservative intellectuals who pushed for the invasion of Iraq were Trotskyists in their youth. Subsequently, as then, they have embraced a kind of a vanguard mentality, asserting that an ideal system destined by history sometimes needs to be imposed by force, which will surely be embraced by the vast majority of the population grateful for their liberation, while the minority who do not will have to be dealt with harshly. Whether the premise was religious or secular, however, the evidence seems strong that the American decision to invade Iraq was in great part driven by ideology.

The US had violated international legal norms regarding foreign intervention and the use of force against sovereign states on many past occasions. However, most of these cases were either through covert actions – as with CIA involvement in military coups (such as Iran in 1953 and Guatemala in 1954) – or through overt military interventions done under the cover of a regional security pact – such as the Organization of American States for the intervention in the Dominican Republic in 1965 or the Southeast Asia Treaty Organization during the Vietnam War.

The US-led invasion of Iraq was also significant in terms of its sheer brazenness. The vast majority of the world's governments, UN Secretary General Kofi Annan, and a broad consensus of international legal scholars saw it as a clear violation of the United Nations Charter.

The formal shift in US attitudes was codified in the *National Security Strategy of the United States* (NSS), adopted in September 2002. This argued that the US should strike preemptively at any country it believes is developing biological, chemical or nuclear weapons;[46] "America will act against such emerging threats before they are fully formed."[47] This underscores the basis of the Bush administration's post-invasion rationale that while Iraq may not have actually had any WMDs, offensive delivery systems or WMD programs, even just having the potential to develop such weapons sometime in the future was enough to justify the invasion.[48] The invasion of Iraq, therefore, was not a "preemptive" but rather a "preventive" war. The 2002 NSS blurs the distinction, arguing that since it is hard to know when or how terrorists might strike, it is therefore justifiable to attack any country which might be developing weapons potential that might someday be used against US interests. But there is reason to believe that the change in policy toward the use of force is even more radical than that, since administration officials began to justify the Iraq war as a means of spreading US-style liberal democracy to the Arab/Islamic world. In effect, the US had come to see invading and occupying sovereign nations as a legitimate means of social and political engineering.

There is little to support the idea that the invasion of Iraq was undertaken simply for the sake of oil company profits. Saddam Hussein was already selling his oil at a level satisfactory to Western buyers under the UN-supervised Oil for Food program, and his standing among fellow OPEC members was low. He could not have persuaded the cartel to adopt policies detrimental to US interests. The oil companies – which are most interested in stability in the region – were at best ambivalent about the invasion. In addition, even if one were to assume that the Bush administration was primarily interested in advancing the agenda of US corporate capitalism, even the more optimistic estimates of the overall costs of the invasion and occupation and the resulting damage to the economy made Wall Street as a whole quite nervous about the project, whatever the short-term benefits to Big Oil.

However, a case still could be made for economic factors playing a role in the decision to invade Iraq. The debt crisis and the resulting structural adjustment programs imposed on many developing countries by the International Monetary Fund, as well as similar policies made possible by the growing power of Western-dominated international financial institutions, has made it difficult for their governments to pursue economic or other policies opposed by the US, enabling Washington to impose legally and openly what in previous decades could be accomplished only through cruder forms of intervention. Neo-liberal global economics can also explain the end of the left-leaning nationalism that was once common in the Arab world, with Egypt, Algeria, Sudan, Yemen, and Syria abandoning their semi-socialist policies to embrace what are euphemistically referred to as "free-market reforms." These Arab states also exhibit a significant reduction in their anti-Western rhetoric, support for terrorists and radical insurgents, and other behaviors disturbing to Washington.

Ba'athist Iraq was the only Arab state to largely resist such trends. Combining a sizable educated population, large oil resources, and adequate water supplies, Iraq was able to maintain a truly independent foreign and domestic policy. Even 12 years of draconian sanctions – while severely limiting Iraq's ability to do much damage to US interests beyond its borders – could not overthrow the government or make it more cooperative with Washington's strategic and economic agenda, prompting the US to revert to cruder forms of intervention. This is not to imply that Saddam Hussein's rule was anything close to being a progressive model for development. Whatever the nature of his regime, however, Saddam was clearly failing to adhere to Washington's global script. Consequently, the US felt obliged to send a clear signal to any potentially recalcitrant regimes than such insubordination would not be tolerated. As a result, the Bush administration was determined to impose a new order whereby this important Middle Eastern country would have no choice but to play by US rules. Since simply appending a conquered nation to its conqueror's territory is not considered acceptable behavior anymore – US allies Morocco and Israel notwithstanding – a less formal system of control needed to be established. So Washington adopted a plan for Iraq that bore a striking resemblance to the British strategy in the Middle East following the collapse of the Ottoman Empire. Rather than formally annexing Iraq, Britain occupied the country just long enough to establish a kind of suzerainty. Iraq was made nominally independent within a few years, but Britain could effectively veto the establishment of any unfriendly government and could dominate the economy. Under Coalition Provisional Authority (CPA) chairman Paul Bremer, radical changes were imposed on the Iraqi economy closely mimicking the infamous structural adjustment programs shackled to indebted nations by the International Monetary Fund. These included:

- the widespread privatization of public enterprises, which – combined with allowing for 100 per cent foreign ownership of Iraqi companies – renders key sectors of the Iraqi economy prime targets of burgeoning American corporations,
- the imposition of a 15 per cent flat tax, which primarily benefits the wealthy and places a disproportionate burden on the poor,
- the virtual elimination of import tariffs, resulting in a flood of foreign goods into the country; since smaller Iraqi companies – weakened by more than a dozen years of sanctions – are unable to compete, hundreds of factories have had to shut down, adding to already-severe unemployment,
- 100 per cent repatriation of profits, which severely limits reinvestment in the Iraqi economy,
- a lowering of the minimum wage, increasing already widespread poverty, and
- leases on contracts for as long as 40 years, making it impossible for even a truly sovereign government to legally make alternative arrangements.

A poll taken in 2004 revealed that 65 per cent of Iraqis would prefer a largely state-controlled economy and government subsidies of basic services, while only 6.6 per cent would support a free-market system where private entrepreneurs have largely unrestricted access to the economy. Reflecting this sentiment, the original draft for the Iraqi constitution declared that "Social justice is the basis of building society," that Iraq's natural resources would be owned collectively by the Iraqi people, and that every Iraqi had the right to work, and that the government would be legally bound to provide employment opportunities to everyone. The underlying theme of the draft was that the state would be the collective instrument of the Iraqi people for achieving development. However, thanks to intense intervention by US ambassador Zalmay Khalizad, these provisions were superseded by an article stressing that "The state shall guarantee the reforming of the Iraqi economy according to modern economic bases, in a way that ensures complete investment of its resources, diversifying its sources and encouraging and developing the private sector."[49]

In addition, from power stations to telecommunications, US designs have replaced Iraqi and European systems, further incorporating Iraq into an American orbit. In many respects, US economic policy toward Iraq resembles a neo-mercantilism more than strict neo-liberalism.

Explaining the US invasion of Iraq in terms of imposing militarily what the IMF could not impose itself, however, may only be part of the story. Skeptics of claims that the Bush administration invaded Iraq simply for its oil correctly observe that the US is less dependent on Persian Gulf oil than are European or East Asian countries. However, controlling Iraq – the largest Arab country in the Gulf region, which contains the world's second-largest oil reserves and borders three of the world's five largest oil producers – and establishing 14 major military bases as originally planned would have given the US enormous leverage.

In the coming decades, in the event of a trade war with the European Union or a military rivalry with an ascendant China, effective control over Persian Gulf oil would provide a trump card for Washington to play to its advantage. The invasion of Iraq, then, may represent not just a frightening repudiation of the post-World War II international legal order embodied in the United Nations Charter but also a return to the nineteenth century great power politics of imperial conquest undertaken to control key economic resources.

In direct contravention of World Trade Organization regulations – which the US insists upon rigorously enforcing against other nations – occupation forces initially restricted investment and reconstruction efforts almost exclusively to countries which supported the invasion. Also, American contractors and their employees were given preference in lucrative reconstruction efforts over Iraqi companies and Iraqi nationals. Under the US occupation, Bremer's edicts denied Iraq the right to give preference to its own highly-skilled workforce in the reconstruction effort. Instead, Washington provided more than $50 billion in contracts – more than twice Iraq's GDP – to 150 US companies. The biggest beneficiary – with contracts totaling over $11 billion – was Halliburton, a firm which Vice-President Cheney had been president of and still was a major stockholder in.[50]

Though some in the Bush administration had advocated the complete privatization of the oil industry, American oil companies made clear that – given the likely nationalist backlash – such a blatant takeover would not work. Instead, they successfully argued that Iraq's national oil company should remain in place but be allowed to negotiate production sharing agreements, which enable private companies to reap enormous profits at the expense of the exporting governments. Such arrangements are common with African and other less developed oil exporters, but are not found elsewhere in the Arab world, in large part because the oil extraction infrastructure is already well-established and these agreements generally include terms of 25 to 40 years that lock in the provisions set at the time the contract was signed. While future Iraqi governments could change their laws, they would be unable to alter these oil contracts.

The 17 oil fields currently under production were allowed to remain under the nationalized Iraqi oil company, but all fields subsequently to be developed were to be opened to foreign companies under production sharing agreements. This would, in effect, grant private companies control of 64 per cent of Iraq's known reserves, and – if the estimated additional reserves are exploited – foreign companies could control up to 87 per cent of Iraq's oil.[51] Iraqi vice-President Adil Abdul-Mahdi acknowledged that "this is very promising to the American investors and to American enterprise, certainly to oil companies."[52]

After years of state control under Saddam's dictatorship, there is little doubt that some liberalization and restructuring of the economy was necessary. However, most Iraqis opposed such changes, and segments of the Fourth Geneva Convention and Hague Regulations regarding territories under foreign occupation prohibits occupying powers from substantially altering the economic system to their benefit. The results of a poll commissioned by the CPA asking Iraqis why they believed insurgents attack US-led Coalition forces, showed 78 per cent saying it was because "the Coalition is trying to steal Iraq's wealth," more than twice the percentage who agreed with President Bush's assertion that "they do not want democracy in Iraq."[53]

This widespread sentiment that the US was simply after their nation's wealth and putting the profits of well-connected American companies over the livelihoods of ordinary Iraqis fueled the very armed resistance. And that made any attempt at rebuilding – based on whatever economic model – virtually impossible. While certain Iraqi elites are certainly willing to be co-opted into the neo-liberal paradigm in return for a share of their spoils, it is doubtful that they will be able to hold on to power in the face of mass resistance. As a result, the US may have no more success imposing its free-market utopia on the Iraqis than the Soviets had in imposing their socialist utopia on the Afghans.

Iran: a regional challenger

Iran, formerly known as Persia, is the base of a civilization which had played a major role in the greater Middle East for more than 2,500 years. During much of the nineteenth and early twentieth centuries, however, the country retained only formal independence in the face of Russian and British intervention and economic domination. Following World War II, growing nationalistic forces in Iran's democratically-elected parliament found itself in conflict with the pro-Western Shah (emperor). Following the prime minister's nationalization of British oil interests and a feared alliance with leftist forces in 1953, the US organized a coup against the constitutional government of

Mohammed Mossadegh and supported the Shah as an increasingly repressive and autocratic client ruler. Though the US had supplanted Great Britain as the primary outside power in that oil-rich country, Gulf security remained primarily in British hands until Prime Minister Harold Wilson, recognizing Britain's reduced role as a world power, announced in 1969 that his country would withdraw most of its security commitments from areas east of the Suez Canal.

In the midst of strong anti-interventionist sentiment among the American public at the height of the Vietnam War, an overt large-scale military presence in the Persian Gulf did not seem politically feasible. However, the Nixon administration had experienced some success in curbing anti-Vietnam War protests through "Vietnamization." That is, by increasing the role of South Vietnamese conscripts on the ground and by escalating the American air war, American troop strength could be reduced, along with American casualties and draft rolls, even as violence against the Vietnamese escalated. Thus in 1971, the President expanded this concept under the rubric of the "Nixon Doctrine," which characterized his "surrogate strategy" on a global level. According to Nixon, "we shall furnish military and economic assistance when requested. ... But we shall look to the nation directly threatened to assume the primary responsibility of providing the manpower for its defense."[54]

The Persian Gulf emerged as the first testing ground for extending the regional *gendarme* concept beyond the American War in Vietnam. The Shah owed his throne to the US, had a lot of money to purchase weapons, and desired to feed his own meglomania, All of this made him a promising surrogate. Throughout the 1970s, the US sold over $20 billion in advanced weaponry to the Shah – with an additional $20 billion on order when he lost power – an enormous sum for that period. In addition, there were as many as 8,000 American advisors and trainers – mostly working for private defense contractors – in Iran in order to transform his armed forces into a sophisticated fighting force capable of counter-insurgency operations. This policy was successfully implemented when Iranian troops – with American and British support – intervened in support of the Sultan of Oman against a leftist rebellion in the Dhofar province in the mid 1970s. In 1979, however, Iran's Islamic revolution brought this policy crashing down, replacing the compliant Shah with a regime stridently rejecting client state status.

In response to this shocking failure of surrogate strategy, the Carter Doctrine was announced in 1980. The US, as President Jimmy Carter declared, would no longer rely on potentially unstable allies and their armed forces but would now intervene directly through a newly established Rapid Deployment Force, which later grew into the Central Command, for American military activities in the Middle East. Washington reached an agreement with the Saudis whereby, in exchange for selling them an integrated package of highly sophisticated weaponry, they would build and pay for an elaborate system of command and naval, and air facilities large enough to sustain US forces in intensive regional combat. For example, the controversial sale of sophisticated

AWACS airborne radar to Saudi Arabia in 1981 constituted a linchpin of an elaborate communications system comparable to that of NATO. According to a *Washington Post* report at that time – then denied by the Pentagon – this was to be part of a grand defense strategy for the Middle Eastern oil fields that included an ambitious plan to build bases, equipped and waiting for use by American forces, in Saudi Arabia.[55]

In the event of war, it was hoped that American forces would be deployed so fast and with such overwhelming force that they would suffer few casualties and that the fighting would end quickly. Consequently, disruptive anti-war protests would be minimal. This was of particular concern, since Congress had recently passed the War Powers Act, whereby the legislative branch could effectively veto a president's decision to send American troops into combat after 60 days. Though the exact scenario in which US forces would be deployed could not have been predicted at the time, the Carter Doctrine made possible the American military and political successes against Iraq a decade later.

The revolution that replaced the Shah, Washington's main pillar in the Persian Gulf region, with a zealously anti-imperialist regime struck a major blow to US power. But despite the revolution, the subsequent hostage crisis, and terminating diplomatic relations, the US still sought an opening to exercise influence in Iran.

Thus, from 1981 to 1986, the US clandestinely shipped arms to Iran's Islamic government. By helping to shore up the Iranian military in the war with Iraq, which Washington aided in major ways, these shipments served as one means to implement the US policy of promoting the mutual destruction of these two countries in order to bolster its own hegemony. In addition, part of the secret arms transfer was channeled to anti-Soviet Afghan *mujahidin* (pursuers of *jihad*) on Iran's eastern border. And a factor in some of the later arms transfers was hope for Iran's cooperation by using its influence to facilitate the release of American hostages held by radical Shi'ite groups in Lebanon.[56] More significantly, it appears that the primary motivation for the clandestine arms sales was to buy access to and hopefully gain influence in the Iranian military. The US also passed on names of suspected Iranian leftists to government authorities, resulting in the execution of hundreds of dissidents.

Despite this limited cooperation, the US generally sided with Iraq during the eight-year war that resulted when Saddam Hussein's forces invaded western Iran barely a year after the triumph of the Iranian revolution. While the US tolerated widespread attacks by Iraq against Iranian oil tankers during the war, its navy intervened in 1987 to protect Kuwaiti oil tankers and other Persian Gulf shipping – including Iraqi oil and other shipping – from Iranian retaliation. In what became known as the "Tanker War," these Kuwaiti ships were re-flagged as American ships, thereby giving the US the excuse to attack Iran should these ships be fired on. This expanded US military role led to a series of armed engagements between the US and Iran along the country's southern coast. Following one military encounter with Iranian forces in July

1988, an American missile fired from a Navy cruiser shot down an Iranian passenger airliner on a regularly scheduled flight over Iranian airspace, killing all 290 people aboard.[57]

After the death of revolutionary leader Ayatollah Ruhollah Khomeini in 1989, Iran began making gradual moves toward greater liberalization and political pluralism, substantially reducing its earlier support for radical Islamic movements beyond its borders. Ironically, however, the US increased its hostility toward the Iranian revolution over the next decade, greatly disappointing Iranian reformers who had hoped for rapprochement with the US. Despite the dramatic, if uneven, steps towards liberalization in Iran and some toning down of anti-Iranian rhetoric in the waning months of the Clinton administration, various sanctions and other anti-Iranian measures by the US grew harsher by the end of Clinton's presidency than those during the regime's most repressive and extremist period in the mid 1980s. In addition, the US still refused to re-establish diplomatic relations with this largest country in the Middle East.

There was some hope at first that the new Bush administration might be willing to mute this hostility. However, in his 2002 State of the Union address, President Bush linked the increasingly pluralistic Iran with the totalitarian regimes of Iraq and North Korea as part of an "axis of evil, arming to threaten the peace of the world" along with its "terrorist allies."[58] This was seen as a serious blow to Iranian moderates who had been fighting for greater political openness and better relations with the West.

Since the overthrow of Saddam Hussein's regime in Iraq in 2003, the US has turned its attention to Iran as the allegedly most dangerous challenge to US hegemony in the region, particularly in regard to its nuclear program. In subsequent years, hardline elements in Iran reconsolidated their control of the country, increasing internal repression and stepping away from the government's earlier and unsuccessful efforts at rapprochement with the West.

Unlike Iraq in 2003, Iran really does have a nuclear program. And while there is no evidence that it is anything but peaceful at this point, most observers agree that there is potential for the program to evolve later on in a military direction. Iran has had a nuclear program since 1957, when President Dwight Eisenhower signed the first of a series of nuclear cooperation agreements with the Shah. Over the next two decades, the United State not only provided Iran with technical assistance but also supplied it with its first experimental nuclear reactor, complete with enriched uranium and plutonium with fissile isotopes. Despite the refusal of the Shah to rule out the possibility of developing nuclear weapons, the Ford administration in 1975 approved the sale of up to eight nuclear reactors with fuel and, in 1976, agreed to the sale of lasers believed capable of enriching uranium. The *Washington Post* reported that an initially hesitant President Gerald Ford was assured by his advisors that Iran was only interested in the peaceful uses of nuclear energy. (Ironically, these advisors included Secretary of Defense Donald Rumsfeld; his chief of staff, Dick Cheney; and the director of non-proliferation at the Arms Control and Disarmament Agency, Paul Wolfowitz – all of whom, in their more recent presidential advisory roles, insisted on just the opposite.)[59]

Much of the concern expressed by US officials revolves around suggestions that Iran would use nuclear weapons for aggressive purposes. However, given the constant threats against them, a far more likely motivation for obtaining nuclear weapons capability – if they ever chose to do so – would be the perceived need for a nuclear deterrent to defend itself.

Iran might look at the experience of the two other members of the alleged "axis of evil:" Iraq, which had given up its nuclear program over a decade earlier and subsequently allowed IAEA inspectors back in the country to verify the absence such a program, was invaded and occupied by the US and its government overthrown. By contrast, no one dares to invade North Korea, which reneged on its agreement and resumed production of nuclear weapons. And its government remains in power. The Iranians may see a lesson in that. In addition, soon after coming to office, the Bush administration decided to unfreeze America's nuclear weapons production and launch a program to develop smaller tactical nuclear weapons, including those capable of penetrating underground bunkers such as those in which Iran is conducting part of its nuclear research at a time when it is the one under threat of a massive armed attack and already the regular target of cyberwarfare. In this connection, it is important to remember that the only country to actually use nuclear weapons in combat has been the US, in the 1945 destruction of two Japanese cities, which American political leaders still defend.

In the post-Cold War world, the US has demonstrated little tolerance for any regime that challenges its global domination. This is particularly true when there is the potential of establishing a credible deterrent that might undermine the ability of the US and Israel to act with impunity. The destruction of such regimes – either slowly through sanctions or more quickly through an invasion – serves as a warning to any other state that would even consider challenging American hegemony.

Notes

1 *Foreign Relations of the United States, 1945,* vol. VIII, cited in J. and G. Kolko, *The Limits of Power,* New York: Harper & Row, 1972, p. 45.
2 S. Spiegel, *The Other Arab-Israeli Conflict,* Chicago: University of Chicago Press, 1985, p. 51.
3 See for example National Security Council Memorandum 5801/1, "Statement by The National Security Council of Long-Range U.S. Policy Toward The Near East," January 24, 1958, *Foreign Relations of the United States,* 1958–60, vol. XII, Washington: US Government Printing Office, 1993, pp. 17–32.
4 J. Mearsheimer and S. Walt, *The Israel Lobby and U.S. Foreign Policy,* New York: Farrar, Straus and Giraux, 2007.
5 G. W. Bush, "Address to a Joint Session of Congress and the American People," United States Capitol, September 20, 2001, Washington: Office of the Press Secretary, 2001. URL: <http://www.whitehouse.gov/the-press-office/2011/09/08/address-president-joint-session-congress> (accessed November 9, 2012).

6 Cited in N. Chomsky, *9–11*, New York: Seven Stories Press, 2001.

7 J. LeCarre, "A War we Cannot Win," *The Nation*, November 19, 2001, pp. 15–17.

8 Interview with T. Barake of Al Arabiya by Hillary Rodham Clinton, Dubai, UAE, January 11, 2011. URL: <http://still4hill.com/2011/01/11/secretary-clintons-interview-with-taher-barake-of-al-arabiya/> (accessed November 9, 2012).

9 "US Urges Restraint in Egypt, Says Government is Stable," Reuters, January 25, 2011. URL: <http://www.reuters.com/article/2011/01/25/ozatp-egypt-protest-clinton-idAFJOE70O0KF20110125> (accessed November 9, 2012).

10 "White House Monitoring Egypt Situation Closely," Reuters, 26 January 2011. URL: <http://www.reuters.com/article/2011/01/26/ozatp-egypt-protest-whitehouse-idAFJO E70P0MC20110126> (accessed November 19, 2012).

11 Ibid.

12 S. Wilson and J. Warrick, "As Arabs Protest, U.S. Speaks Up," *The Washington Post*, January 27, 2011. URL: <http://www.washingtonpost.com/wpdyn/content/article/2011/01/26/AR2011012608075.html> (accessed November 9, 2012).

13 "Press Conference by the President," The White House, February 15, 2011.

14 "Mullen Reaffirms American-Bahraini Alliance," American Forces Press Service, February 25, 2011. URL: <http://www.militaryavenue.com/Articles/Mullen+Reaffirms+American-Bahrain. ... > (accessed January 1, 2013).

15 M. Landler and H. Cooper, "U.S. Trying to Pick Winners in New Mideast," *The New York Times*, February 24, 2011. URL: <http://www.nytimes.com/2011/02/25/world/middleeast/25diplomacy.html?page> (accessed November 9, 2012).

16 Defense Security Cooperation Agency, News Release: Bahrain – M1152A1B2H MMWVs and TOW-2A and TOW-2B Missiles, September 14, 2011. URL: <http://www.dsca.mil/PressReleases/36-b/2011/Bahrain_10–71.pdf> (accessed November 9, 2012).

17 "Yemen Unrest – Monday 21 March 2011," *The Guardian*, March 21, 2011. URL: <http://www.guardian.co.uk/world/blog/2011/mar/21/yemen-army-commanders-defect> (accessed November 9, 2012).

18 J. Yaphe, "Post-Revolutionary Transitions: A Conference Report," Event Report, Institute for National Strategic Studies, Center for Strategic Research, March 31, 2011. URL: <http://www.ndu.edu/inss/docUploaded/YAPHE_REVOLUTION_Event_Report.pdf> (accessed November 9, 2012).

19 "US Embassy Statement on April 27 Events," Embassy of the United States, Sana'a, Yemen, April 28, 2011. URL: <http://yemen.usembassy.gov/ues.html> (accessed November 9, 2012).

20 "House Appropriations Committee Funds U.S.–Israeli Cooperation," *Near East Report*, vol. 38, no. 18, August 14, 1995, p. 99, and S. Twing, "A Comprehensive Guide to U.S. Aid to Israel," *Washington Report on Middle East Affairs*, April 1996, p. 7.

21 Figures cited in E. Pound, "A Close Look at U.S. Aid to Israel Reveals Deals That Push Cost Above Publicly Quoted Figures," *The Wall Street Journal*, September 19, 1991, p. A16.

22 M. Wenger, "The Money Tree: US Aid to Israel," *Middle East Report*, May – August 1990, p. 12.

23 E Sheehan, *The Arabs, Israelis and Kissinger: A Secret History of American Diplomacy in the Middle East*, New York: Readers Digest Press, 1976, p. 200.

24 This came in a vote by the Palestine National Council meeting in Gaza on April 24. It was confirmed in a PNC meeting on December 18, 1998 in the presence of visiting US President Bill Clinton and was formally accepted by Israeli Prime Minister Benyamin Netanyahu.

25 Despite these restrictions, the Palestinian delegates – consisting primarily of respected West Bank intellectuals – were, in practice, able to operate separately from the Jordanian delegation and work in close coordination with the PLO.

26 Background briefings, US Department of State, Washington, DC, March 21, 1995.

27 A good summary of the quiet US support for Iraq can be found in an article on the media coverage of the scandal: R. Baker, "Iraqgate: The Big One that (Almost) Got Away," *Columbia Journalism Review*, March/April 1993. For a more detailed account, see M. Phythian and N. Passas, *Arming Iraq – How the U.S. and Britain Secretly Built Saddam's War Machine*, Boston: Northeastern University Press, 1996.

28 J. Heller, "Photos Don't Show Buildup," *St. Petersburg Times*, January 6, 1991, p. 1A.

29 In an interview with BizLaw Journal, Roger Fisher noted, "I believe President Bush wanted to defeat the army of Iraq militarily. He thought a war would do that, and I think he wanted a war." Fisher told of meeting with Kuwaiti leaders in exile prior to the war and offering suggestions for negotiating strategy, adding that, while seeming to react positively, they told him, "No, we can't afford to offend the United States and President Bush wants a military victory." (Interview with Brian Anderson, "'*Getting to Yes*' Twentieth Anniversary," March 7, 2001). I have heard similar stories from scores of diplomats, journalists and academics in the Middle East.

30 Based upon interviews of leading academics and government officials in GCC countries by the author in January 1992.

31 B. Gellman, "Allied Air War Struck Broadly in Iraq," *Washington Post*, June 23, 1991, p. 1.

32 D. Schorr, "Ten Days That Shook the White House," *Colombia Journalism Review*, July/August 1991, pp. 21–23.

33 The Shatt al-Arab is the 100-mile river formed from the convergence of the Tigris and Euphrates rivers that constitutes the southern end of the Iran–Iraq border. Iraqi resentment over this agreement, which resulted from pressure by Iran and the US, is one issue that precipitated Iraq's invasion of Iran four years later.

34 United Nations Children Fund, "Iraq Survey Shows 'Humanitarian Emergency,'" August 12, 1999 [Cf/doc/pr/1999/29]. See UNICEF Operation Newsline. URL: <http://www.unicef.org/newsline/99pr29.htm> (accessed November 11, 2012).

35 The higher estimates have been extrapolated from a 1995 report from researchers for the Food and Agriculture Organization and various reports from UNICEF. The lower estimates are from reputedly more scientific studies, including the 1999 report "Morbidity and Mortality Among Iraqi Children" by Columbia University's R. Garfield, and "Sanctions and Childhood Mortality in Iraq," a May 2000 article by M. Ali and I. Shah in *The Lancet*, the journal of the British Medical Society.

36 Madeleine Albright, CBS News, "60 Minutes," May 12, 1996.

37 S. Ritter, "The Case for Iraq's Qualitative Disarmament," *Arms Control Today*, June 2000. URL: <http://www.armscontrol.org/act/2000_06/iraqjun> (accessed November 10, 2012).

38 G. W. Bush, "Introduction," *The National Security Strategy*, The White House. URL: <http://georgewbush-whitehouse.archives.gov/nsc/nss/2006/>, URL: <http://georgewbush-whitehouse.archives.gov/nsc/nss/2006/intro.html> (accessed November 10, 2012).

39 B. Woodward, *Plan of Attack: The Definitive Account of the Decision to Invade Iraq*, New York: Simon and Schuster, 2004, p. 88.

40 Cited in D. Hiro, *Secrets and Lies: Operation "Iraqi Freedom" and After: A Prelude to the Fall of U.S. Power in the Middle East?* New York: Nation Books, 2002, p. 388.

41 E. Zuesse, *Iraq War: The Truth*, Whiting, VT: Delphic Press, 2004, p. 121.

42 Ibid., p. 118, emphasis in original.

43 "Deputy Secretary Wolfowitz Interview with Karen DeYoung, Washington Post," US Department of Defense, Office of the Assistant Secretary of Defense (Public Affairs), News Transcript, May 28, 2003. URL: <http://www.defense.gov/tran scripts/transcript.aspx?transcriptid=2676> (accessed March 6, 2013).

44 N. Kristof, "The God Gulf," *New York Times,* January 7, 2004. URL: <http:// www.nytimes.com/2004/01/07/opinion/the-god-gulf.html?ref=nicholasdkristof> (accessed November 10, 2012).

45 A. Regular, "'Road map is a life saver for us,' PM Abbas tells Hamas," *Haaretz,* June 24, 2003. URL: <http://www.haaretz.com/print-edition/news/road-map-is-a-life-saver-for-us-pm-abbas-tells-hamas-1.92200> (accessed May 14, 2013).

46 Bush, "Introduction."

47 Ibid.

48 Woodward, *Plan,* pp. 85–86.

49 H. Docena, "Iraq's Neoliberal Constitution," Silver City, NM & Washington, DC: Foreign Policy in Focus, September 2, 2005.

50 A. Juhasz, "Bush's Economic Invasion of Iraq," *Los Angeles Times*, August 14, 2005.

51 Ibid.

52 Adel Abdul Mahdi, speech before the National Press Club, Washington, DC; December 22, 2004.

53 Coalition Provisional Authority Poll, June 9–19, 2004, cited in Brookings Institution, "Iraq Index: Tracking Variables of Reconstruction and Security in Post-Saddam Iraq," September 26, 2005.

54 President R. Nixon, "Address to the Nation on the War in Vietnam," November 3, 1969, The American Presidency Project. URL: <http://www.presidency.ucsb. edu/ws/index.php?pid=2303> (Accessed May 14, 2013).

55 S. Armstrong, "Saudis' AWACS Just a Beginning of a New Strategy," *Washington Post*, November 1, 1981, p. 32.

56 Revelations about the clandestine arms transfers in 1985–86 became the basis of the Iran-Contra scandal, which plagued the Reagan administration during most of its second term.

57 There is rather startling contrast between the desperate American rationalizations for the attack – most of which were later disproven by press investigations – and the major propaganda campaign waged against the Soviet Union following its downing of a South Korean airliner in September 1983. Ironically, the Iranian airliner was on course over Iranian airspace at the time it was destroyed, whereas the Korean airliner was off course and flying over Soviet airspace near sensitive military installations.
In April 1990, the senior President Bush awarded the Legion of Merit award to the commander and the officer in charge of anti-aircraft warfare on the *Vincennes*, the warship that shot down the plane. Despite being responsible for the attack, they were praised for their "exceptionally meritorious conduct in the performance of outstanding service" in the Gulf and for "calm and professional atmosphere" during that period. M. Moore, "2 *Vincennes* Officers Get Medals," *The Washington Post*, April 23, 1990.

58 President G. W. Bush, State of the Union address, January 29, 2002, CNN Politics. URL: <http://articles.cnn.com/2002-01-29/politics/bush.speech.txt_1_firefighter-returns-terrorist-training-camps-interim-leader?_s=PM:ALLPOLITICS>.

59 D. Linzer, "Past Arguments Don't Square with Current Iran Policy," *Washington Post*, March 27, 2005; p. A15.

4 Israel

The limits of conventional and nuclear deterrence

Ghada Hashem Talhami

It is often argued that in terms of international political theory, Israel fits the model of a superpower bridgehead which transformed itself into the Center, that is, the dominant power in the Middle East. What is still a matter of contention, however, is whether it is still the guardian of Western – or imperial – interests in this region or has evolved into a semi-independent Center. In reality, it has developed its own web of alliances and relationships with the regional Peripheral states – and more precisely, with their centers.[1] Arab writers have always identified Israel – and even before its birth, the Jewish "national home" – as the beachhead of one of the world's great powers, dependent on Great Britain until 1948 and subsequently on the world's emerging superpower, the United States. Even though Israel owes its creation to the movement of religious Zionism, beginning with Rabbi Judah Alkali's 1839 work, *Derchai Noam* (Pleasant Paths), calling for the establishment of colonies in the Holy Land to facilitate the return of the Messiah, later Zionist leaders largely exemplified secular, ethnic nationalism and used pragmatic means to realize their dream of a Jewish state.

Zionist leaders managed eventually to steer the thinking of British and French architects of the Sykes-Picot Agreement and the Balfour Declaration (1916–17) in the direction of a Jewish-dominated and strategically valuable Palestine.[2] A symbiotic arrangement developed between the two. The British would deflect any criticism of recolonizing a former part of the Ottoman Empire by supporting Jewish aspirations to return to Palestine, using the newly-minted mandate system for cover, while the Jews structured their Zionist dreamland with full approval of the architects of the post-World War II settlement.

Israel's creation would not have been possible without the destruction of the Ottoman regional order which formerly imposed a long period of hegemony over the region based on a commonality of culture and religious faith.[3] It should be easy to classify Israel, then, as a bridgehead of an imperialist order, which was British at first. Eventually, the Jewish *Yishuv* (community) in Palestine placed itself under the American umbrella but not without a struggle between David Ben Gurion and Chaim Weizmann, who represented the British Zionist Organization.[4] Thus, harmonious interests succeeded in linking the Center of the new American imperialist order to the Periphery bridgehead nation in the region.

This relationship, however, is continuously undergoing severe mutations as Israel transitions itself from a client state to a regional hegemon in its own right, with its own peripheral allies. International political theorists caution against the applicability of theoretical analysis to this volatile region. They maintain that theories often fail to explain the origins of this area's wars or the limitations on seemingly powerful systems of deterrence. They point to the repeated failure of the region's military hegemon, here most frequently Israel, to obtain compliance from its enemies despite its resort to the use of overwhelming force. The balance of power theories, as well as those of deterrence, also proved inadequate as useful paradigms for explaining the region's recurrent wars. This may be explained by the intractability and multi-dimensional nature of the Arab–Israeli conflict or the changing power-alignment in the Persian Gulf sub-region.[5]

The role of Zionism

The creation and survival of the state of Israel have a great deal to do with the evolution of Zionist ideology. This belief system not only continues to function as a motivator and inspirational tool for Israel's territorial expansion and frequent defiance of the imperialist Center, it also casts a spiritual patina over what is essentially a patron–client relationship with its international sponsor. Insistence on a superior moral claim, which the dominated Palestinian population can never match, has also managed to complicate the theory of political realism as it is applied to the Middle East. This same moral claim overshadowed the Center–Periphery imperialist theory often utilized to illustrate the "harmony of interests." Nowhere is the pervasive spiritual claim of Zionism more apparent than in Israel's defense of its policy on Jerusalem. Israel's claim to East Jerusalem during the post-1967 period and its continued attempt to deny residency rights to its Arab population have always been in complete defiance of the Fourth Geneva Convention (1949) and several United Nations resolutions opposed to the annexation of this city. Yet Israel always justifies its actions on the basis of "moral entitlement" which it considers stronger than that of the Palestinians.[6] Israel, in general, justifies its existence and most of its policies which often run counter to acceptable international norms of behavior by invoking rights which are unrelated to international law or UN consensus but are recognizable only to the Israelis themselves and their ideological supporters. The Palestinians, by contrast, base all of their claims to nationhood and statehood on generally acceptable principles such as the right of self-determination and on Article 2(4) and Article 51 of the UN Charter, which – aside from actions carried out by the Security Council – outlaw all use of force except in the case of individual or collective self-defense against an armed attack. The Israelis go to the extent of justifying the creation of their state by resorting to Biblical claims, utilizing demographic arguments and invoking the right to use overwhelming force against civilian populations by recalling their experience with Nazi Germany.[7] Israel's latest justification for converting itself into a totally Jewish state, for example, is based on its fear of the "Arab demographic threat," a concept derived from the works of Israeli demographer Sergio de la Pergula and geostrategist Arnon Sofer, a confidant of Prime Minister Ariel Sharon.[8]

The impact of historical memory

Israel's persistence in demanding to be held to a unique standard of morality befitting its special reading of recent Jewish history has great implications for its foreign policy. It is not only the claim to perpetual victimhood which fuels this moral stance; it is also the manner in which Zionism over the years was able to construct a distinct identity, which American historian Staughton Lynd has called "a blood and soil" history. But as Israel found itself enmeshed in wars since its founding in 1948, younger scholars attempted to produce what journalist and historian Benny Morris in the 1980s called "new history." These writers attempted to steer the nation away from its special brand of ethno-history. Among those expressing alarm at inculcating young Israelis with the official narrative on such matters as the origins of the state, Palestinian refugees, and Jordan's collusion with the Jewish *Yishuv* are historians, sociologists and journalists such as Simha Flapan, Ilan Pappé, Avi Shlaim, Baruch Kimmerling and Tom Segev, as well as Misrahi critic Ella Shohat. Even Benny Morris counted himself within this company before he recanted his earlier deconstruction of the national narrative of the 1948 War. For instance, the old historians described the process of settling Palestine as "colonization," which created a progressive world for all. The new historians viewed it as "colonialism" since the land was not vacant and the process of settlement resulted in a dominant and a subordinate community. Challenges arose concerning the term "*Eretz Yisrael*" (Land of Israel), which underwent many changes throughout the centuries.

The development of a school of national history was attributed to historian and one-time minister of culture and education Ben Zion Dinur. He was also one of the moving spirits behind the construction of Yad Vashem, the Holocaust Museum. According to this national view, the Holocaust experience eliminated any choice for Jews between assimilating in their native communities and choosing Jewish statehood in Palestine. It is this collective memory of European persecution which drove the Haganah, the core militia of the future Israeli Defense Forces (IDF) to adopt a policy of expelling Palestinians from their land in order to maximize the Jewish state's territorial control during the 1948 War. Known as Plan Dalet (*Tochnit Dalet*), this official directive turned out to be an effective strategy for emptying captured land of its original inhabitants.[9] Even though Morris eventually justified these policies as means of securing the survival of the young state, other historians, like Pappé, challenged the national myth of Israel's near extinction at the hands of the Arab armies who came, purportedly at least, to rescue the Palestinians. Sociologist Kimmerling pointed to the conscious choice of religious terms like *"Aliyah"* (ascent) when referring to Zionist migration plans in order to adjust the demographic imbalance between Arabs and Jews before 1948. He also pointed to the term *"Eretz Yisrael,"* which evoked the idea of the continued dominant Jewish presence in Palestine over the centuries, contradicting the historical record.[10] The debates, therefore, illustrate not only a growing lack of certainty over defining Israel's *raison d'être* but also the rigidity of state policies towards the Palestinians. Israel's official national history illustrates the inadequacy of political theory in explaining local and superpower efforts to adjust to the permanent Middle East power vacuum favoring Israel.

The militarization of the state

Israel's road to military superiority over its neighbors is often portrayed as a long and arduous journey. In reality, the Jewish *Yishuv* in Palestine was militarized early, when it fought the British and the Palestinians simultaneously. Israel, additionally, never distinguished its foreign from its defense policies, with the prime minister also simultaneously holding the defense portfolio. As early as the 1920s, the *Yishuv* sought military protection for its settlements which frequently served as the main absorption centers for newly-arrived refugees. The Haganah was the first militia to perform this task, eventually graduating to the status of the core group within the IDF after 1948. Even the settlements' youths were trained in agricultural methods and military warfare as they were enrolled in an organization known as *Nahhal*. The Haganah had an elite striking unit, the *Palmach*, while other political factions had their own underground formations as exemplified by the *Irgun Zvai Leumi* (national military organization of Israel), headed by Mehachem Begin, and the Stern gang, led by a group headed by Yitzhak Shamir. The unification of all these militias under the Haganah's banner finally cemented Ben Gurion's leadership as the head of the new state. Other military structures were already in place. The air force dates back to 1947 when the so-called Air Service, or *Sherut-Avir*, was outfitted with 11 single-engine aircrafts. By the end of the 1948 War, Israel possessed over 100 planes, and by the 1980s, its land army ranked third after that of the US and the USSR in military capability.

The standing army made up 30 per cent of the ground forces, while the rest were reservists who served only one month each year. By 1994, Israel's ground forces were divided into 42 armored brigades, 21 infantry brigades and six territorial brigades.[11] By 2010, the size of its military personnel, including reservists, rose to 676,500. By contrast, Egypt's military forces numbered 957,500 men, making them the largest armed force in the Arab world. Syria's military, however, numbered 639,000, while Iran mustered a military force of 833,000. The size of Israel's military force is compensated for by the efficiency and combat readiness of its air force. This branch of the military numbered 461 aircraft by 2011, as compared to 461 for Egypt, 310 for Iran and 555 for

Syria.[12] Israel enjoys a qualitative edge over its Arab neighbors in terms of weapons and skill which extends beyond its superior airpower. The Arab states, by contrast, suffer from domestic political weakness and inter-Arab friction, leading some to enter into secret alliances with their Jewish neighbor. Israel relies heavily on its air force due to its pronounced qualitative edge over its enemies in this area. It also depends on an early warning system which compensates for its lack of territorial depth, a situation somewhat ameliorated after the 1967 War. Since the greatest concentration of Israeli civilian population and industrial installations is located within a coastal area nine by 13 miles wide, Israelis always expressed vulnerability to attacks from the east. Even with the addition of ballistic missiles and conventional weapons, and despite extending their control to Sinai until 1973 and still to the Golan Heights and the West Bank, Israelis often point to their strategic vulnerability.[13] Israel has constantly upgraded its missile defense system since it acquired a nuclear capability in the late 1950s. In addition, its navy obtained two Dolphin design submarines fitted with nuclear cruise missiles from Germany in 2004.[14] The submarines are considered Israel's second line of defense in the eventuality of an attack by Iran and the destruction of the state's nuclear asset.

Israel's emphasis on its military security, which influences its regional foreign policy, began early. Ben Gurion's role as the country's first prime minister impressed upon him the need to enhance its defenses. He believed that the IDF had a unique responsibility to defend the nation, and that the needs of the state had to be integrated with this special institution. He was also convinced that the Arab states were determined to destroy Israel, especially in light of their rejection in 1947 of UN General Assembly Resolution 181, which called for partitioning Palestine into a Jewish and an Arab State. Israel's strategy was to defend the settlements, but without fixing the state's borders in advance, a strategy which was intended to minimize its civilian losses. This translated into an emphasis on offense, with the intent of achieving rapid victory over an enemy pictured as numbering in the millions and fully capable of withstanding unlimited human losses. The army's strategy which emerged during the 1948 War and later identified as instructions to local commanders known as Plan Dalet, called for capturing Palestinian territory and emptying it of its native population. Ben Gurion also advocated converting the nascent air force into a "shock force" to destroy the Arabs' air defenses before they knew hostilities were starting, while fully aware that this might lead to serious diplomatic problems. He was convinced that the Arabs, whom he termed "possibly protégés of Hitler" were bent on Israel's destruction.[15]

To offset the numerical inferiority of the IDF, Ben Gurion advocated relying on an early warning system. Preventive attack was thought to be the only way of enabling the air force to operate as advance shock troops, especially when followed by ground forces. He believed that such tactics could paralyze the enemy's retaliatory capability.

Israel gained unprecedented protection when it extended its control to the Sinai Peninsula, the Golan Heights and the West Bank in 1967. Military observation stations at the southern end of Sinai permitted the luxury of a 20-minute warning alert as soon as Egyptian planes took off from Cairo. The Camp David Agreement of 1978 drastically reduced this warning period to two minutes after the Israelis withdrew from Sinai. The annexation of the Golan Heights in 1980 let it be known that there was no intention of returning this territory to Syria, and this helped alleviate some of the sense of vulnerability the Israelis have felt since the 1973 War.[16] Israel continuously uses the argument of strategic defense to justify annexation of the Golan Heights, although control of the sources of the Jordan River may have provided a greater incentive.[17]

Claims of perpetual Arab hostility

Israel's obsession with security inevitably led to the incorporation of preventive strikes into its defense strategy. But just as this was explained as resulting from lack of territorial depth before 1967, it was also argued that strikes were justified by the constant state of war and the Arabs' unwillingness to make peace. Official propaganda, which seeped into most American standard historical works, echoed these views. In reality, it was always Israel which turned down the idea of an unconditional peace with the Arabs. The first missed opportunity was the Lausanne Conference of 1949 when Israel resisted pressure by the UN Conciliation Commission for Palestine (CCP) to allow the return of the Palestinian refugees, estimated to number three-quarters of a million people. It also rejected the idea of offering compensation for lost properties as required by UN Resolution 194, even though its admission to the UN was conditional on accepting this. The Israelis claimed that compensating the refugees would be a huge economic undertaking and that the returning refugees would never become economically viable due to the loss of their properties. The fact that the Israelis at the time were negotiating a huge reparations package with West Germany never persuaded them to do the same for Palestinians.

Several members of the Arab League (AL) failed in their attempts to press the Palestinians' claims, largely due to the resistance of American Secretary of State Dean Acheson, who rejected the idea of symmetry between Israeli and Nazi guilt. He also turned back efforts to equate Palestinian compensatory claims with those of Arab Iraqi Jews, whose emigration to Palestine was considered by Zionists as essential for the "ingathering" of all Jews. Efforts by AL members, led by Syria, to boycott German goods in retaliation tapered off by 1953. The issue of the Palestinian Right of Return was shelved until the Madrid Peace Conference of 1992.[18]

In subsequent years, Israel continued to blame failure to reach a peace agreement on its neighbors. A great deal was made of Egypt's rejection of an Israeli peace offer following the 1967 War, when AL members, led by

President Gamal Abdul Nasser, declared the "three no's" formula: no peace with Israel, no recognition of Israel, and no negotiations with this state. Israel's peace offer at that point – to give back Sinai in return for freer passage through the Suez Canal and the Gulf of Aqaba – fell short of Arab minimal expectations, as it refused to consider withdrawal from the West Bank, offering only autonomy to the civilian population. The fate of East Jerusalem was declared as non-negotiable and Israel clung to the Gaza Strip while making plans to empty it of its Arab residents.[19] A more credible Arab peace initiative was made in March 2002, when the AL offered Israel full diplomatic relations by its members and those of the Organization of Islamic Conference (OIC) in exchange for ending the occupation of Arab lands and returning to the 1967 frontiers based on UN Security Council Resolution 242. This plan also called for the establishment of an independent Palestinian state, with East Jerusalem as its capital.[20]

The nuclear option and Israel's policy of deterrence

Israel's determination to acquire a nuclear capability ahead of its neighbors eventually became the main pillar of its policy of deterrence. The US originally was greatly alarmed by this development, fearing a full arms race in the region and the potential for Soviet involvement. In the end, Israel's acquisition of this technology proved to be a successful case of a small state defying a superpower.

Since the early days of the state, Ben Gurion believed that the Arabs would never yield to conventional Jewish weapons and that neither would the Jews be able to withstand repeated armed engagements with their numerically-superior neighbors. He envisaged a future in which the inevitable forces of change would improve the Arabs' military performance with the help of the Soviets, resulting in Arab political unification. He was quoted as saying to victorious IDF officers in November 1948 that Israel had won not because its army achieved miracles, but because the Arabs' performance was incredibly bad. He believed that Jewish scientific advancements, which in his view contributed to the Allied victory in World War II, would enable Israel to acquire a nuclear bomb. He felt that, in order to survive, his state was engaged in a race against time and that nuclear weapons offered the only solution to the numerical imbalance between Arabs and Jews. He not only worried about the Arabs' rise to comparable military status, but he also calculated that the US would soon impose non-proliferation on Arabs and Israelis alike.

Israel's nuclear ambitions were heightened by Egypt's missile program, which was developed by German scientists. Israel shared its anxieties with France with which it shared the humiliation of the Suez War in 1956. Their victory in that war was undone by threats from the US and the USSR. French Premier Guy Mollet, thus, gave Israel nuclear technology willingly, which he dubbed "the royal gift," while France itself was seeking admission to the nuclear club. Although Israeli statesman Shimon Peres claimed total credit for concluding the French deal due to his French Socialist contacts, the latter had equally as compelling an incentive to collaborate with Israel. But when de Gaulle came to power in 1958, he stopped short of supplying the plutonium separation plant for Israel's Dimona reactor, which Israel eventually obtained directly from French supplier Saint Gobain Nucléaire. Israel also supplied the Gaullist government with American computer technology – which the US provided to the Weizmann Institute but denied to France – necessary for estimating the measurements of the French bomb.

By 1959, the conversion of the Dimona reactor in the Negev Desert into an atomic plant was completed, enabling it to produce a few atomic bombs capable of destroying major Egyptian targets like the Aswan High Dam. Soon after that, Israel developed nuclear missiles capable of reaching Soviet targets as well. In response to their Suez War experience, the Israelis wanted to display a deterrent against any future Soviet attacks. Even when special American envoy Avrell Harriman assured Israeli Prime Minister Levy Eshkol in 1965 that "Kennedy had cured Khruschev & Company of using the threat of nuclear war," the Israelis never overcame their fears.[21]

Israel attempted to develop its atomic program in complete secrecy. But President John F. Kennedy knew of the Israeli project as early as 1961, when he sought clarifications about the Dimona reactor. American aerial photographs provided evidence of the reactor, which Israel continued to describe as a textile factory. Prime Minister Ben Gurion finally admitted the truth in 1960 and was forced to allow inspection tours by representatives of the US Atomic Energy Commission in 1961 and 1962. Kennedy decided to hold up the delivery of a shipment of Hawk anti-aircraft missiles, the first such weapons purchased by Israel, pending clarifications. Following a report that 16 countries would attain nuclear status by the 1970s, he was already apprehensive about atomic proliferation. Kennedy demanded an explanation from Shimon Peres in a White House meeting on April 2, 1963. Peres, then the director general of the Defense Ministry, was taken by surprise and reportedly promised that Israel would not become the first country to introduce nuclear weapons in the Middle East, and Kennedy succumbed to this studied stroke of ambiguity. Although Prime Minister Eshkol (1963–69) later castigated Peres for the manner in which he yielded to Kennedy's pressure, this ambiguity became the essence of Israel's nuclear posture. The nature of Peres's verbal dexterity – parroted again and again over years – was later revealed in an interview on a German television station in 1991. Peres admitted that this was an intentional choice of words in order to avoid lying to the American president. In subsequent years, America's silent approval grew deeper; it had missed its chance of preventing nuclear proliferation in the Middle East.[22]

Kennedy also offered American guarantees to protect Israel's 1949 borders and secure the scrapping of Egypt's missile program in exchange for the freezing of Israel's nuclear plans. When this failed, his displeasure with Ben Gurion's atomic ambitions contributed to the latter relinquishing his positions as prime minister and minister of defense during the summer of

1963. Nasser, however, made his acceptance of the American offer conditional on Israel's willingness to hold up its end of the proposed bargain.[23] Ben Gurion went on to form a new party, Rafi, which became known in Israel as "the atomic party."[24]

Kennedy's assassination lifted the pressure off Israel's back. President Lyndon B. Johnson proved to be more understanding and was greatly occupied with the Vietnam War. By June 1968, he opted to end the embargo on weapons to Israel and Jordan. Eshkol claimed in an interview with the Israeli daily *Davar* on January 24, 1969 that he was virtually given a veto over the US arms sales to Jordan.[25] The US did not specify any conditions before delivering these weapons, although American officials at the National Security Council (NSC) and other agencies recommended forcing Israel either to end its occupation of Arab lands or to sign the NPT, which it eventually refused to do, promising again never to be the first to "introduce" such weapons into the region. This position was later clarified by Yitzhak Rabin when he was an ambassador to Washington as merely a promise never to test these weapons. But any discussions of a quid pro quo ended when Johnson abruptly authorized the weapons' delivery after both major political parties, as well as the US Senate, endorsed the sale of the F4s to Israel.[26]

Nixon became greatly alarmed when he received a secret memo on July 19, 1969 from the NSC's adviser, Henry Kissinger, informing him that Israel had already developed the means to deliver its atomic weapons by acquiring 12 surface-to-surface missiles from France. Israel was also planning to produce around 30 more missiles, designed to deliver nuclear warheads, by the end of 1970. The memo explained that even secret or undeclared possession of nuclear weapons would heighten danger. Kissinger felt that if this information was leaked out, the Soviets might extend nuclear pledges to their Arab allies.

Kissinger and other NSC members felt that, since the US was no longer able to halt the possession of these weapons, it should at least conceal any knowledge of Israel's nuclear status. As a result, NSC members called for pressuring Israel to sign the NPT, which would not force it to suspend its program but would allow the US to engage it in discussions concerning compliance. Finally, it was suggested that in case Israel's nuclear program was revealed, the US could say it had tried to deflect it from this path but failed.[27]

The Reagan administration, which was the first to authorize a major arms deal, the Airborne Warning and Control System aircraft (AWACS), to Saudi Arabia in 1981, moved quickly to assuage Israel's fears. But a more important development soon impinged on the sphere of US–Israeli relations, namely Israel's bombing of the Iraqi nuclear reactor. This was met with official public displeasure since Iraq was already a member of the International Atomic Energy Agency (IAEA) and a signatory of the NPT. The US decided to suspend delivery of F-16 aircrafts which were intended to counterbalance the AWACS.[28] Reagan sent a note to Prime Minister Menachem Begin, protesting the use of American military equipment in the raid, only to be met with the following response: "If anybody should think that one sovereign country should consult another sovereign country about a specific military operation in order to defend its citizens, that would be absurd."[29]

Another crisis developed when Israel formally annexed the Golan Heights in December 1981. This resulted in rupturing a recent Israeli–US strategic cooperation agreement targeting the Soviets. During this same period, Israel's possession of a large arsenal of atomic weapons was made public through the revelations of Israeli nuclear technician Mordechai Vanunu, but the US continued to turn a blind eye.[30]

Rabin's idea of not declaring possession of any nuclear weapons in order to avoid provoking the Soviets, the so-called "bomb in the basement" option, came unraveled with news of Israeli testing of a nuclear bomb over South Africa. On September 22, 1979, the US satellite Vela unexpectedly entered South African skies, accidentally picking up a mysterious signal near Cape Town. CBS radio journalist Dan Raviv first uncovered this story while in Tel Aviv and then flew to Rome to avoid the reach of Israeli censors. On February 22, 1980, he announced the news of an Israeli explosion of a nuclear bomb in the Atlantic Ocean off South Africa with help from that country's regime. Suspicions of Israeli–South African collaboration in developing nuclear weapons had circulated since 1977 but had not been corroborated. However, it was well known that Israel had assisted South Africa in developing a delivery capability and that Israeli scientists were working at the University of Witwatersrand. In return, Israel received cheaply-processed South African U235, the radioactive form of uranium needed for weapons manufacture.[31]

Yigal Allon's policy of conventional deterrence

Israel's quest for nuclear weapons did not go unchallenged within the political establishment. Yigal Allon offered a counterplan to Ben Gurion's nuclear program and was already critical of the latter's acquiescence in the partition plan since he considered the existence of an Arab entity within Palestine a potential threat. He came up with the strategy of preventive conventional force to assure Israel's survival. Allon's idea was based on the early identification of any *casus belli,* or justification for war, followed by quick military action. He favored launching "first strikes" at dangerous enemy positions even before any hostile action against Israel had materialized. Among several *casus belli* he listed was a renewal of the closing of the Straits of Tiran, open since the Suez War. He also stated his preference for extending Israel's control to the Jordan Valley by provoking a war with Jordan, which acquired it during the 1948 War. Although the nuclear program was never abandoned, the IDF did adopt his preventive attack theory vis-à-vis the West Bank and applied it to front-line Arab villages as early as the attack on Qibya in 1953. Israel hoped that these attacks would alleviate its territorial vulnerability, especially in places where its width barely exceeded ten miles.

Allon rejected the nuclear program because he felt it was dangerous and unnecessary, providing the Arabs an excuse to go nuclear. He argued that Israel could never achieve a state of mutual nuclear deterrence with the "irrational Arabs." Ben Gurion himself was not averse to a West Bank land grab, especially in the eventuality of King Hussein's removal from power. But his minister of defense, Eshkol, never accepted Allon's plan as an alternative to the nuclear strategy. A "first strike" policy, he and Ben Gurion argued, would provoke the "irrational Arabs" when Israel still lacked a "second strike" capability during the 1950s.

Thus, conventional force was used against the West Bank village of Sumu' in 1966 as punishment for a raid by Syrian-based guerrillas of the Palestine Liberation Organization (PLO). The Rabin-led attack almost brought the end of King Hussein's rule as his outraged Palestinian subjects protested his failure to defend the front-line villages of the West Bank. Egypt's involvement in Yemen at the time prevented it from viewing this raid as a *casus belli*. But Israel's use of its conventional deterrence against Syria the following year provoked Egypt into preparing for war. Nasser staged several reconnaissance flights over Dimona to demonstrate his ability to defend his Syrian allies. The last of these occurred on May 17, 1967, causing Israel to call up its military reserves. Opponents of the conventional deterrence theory seemed to be vindicated since the Egyptians presumably could not have done this without Soviet backing.[32] Fear of a Soviet, rather than an Arab, attack on Dimona was always Israel's and America's nightmare.

The Egyptian response to Israel's policy of nuclear deterrence

Knowledge of Israel's nuclear plans reached the Arab world as early as 1964. Thus, the Arab window of opportunity for the destruction of Israel's nuclear capability lasted from 1965 until the 1967 War. An article on March 12, 1966 in the semi-official Egyptian daily, *al-Jumhuriyya*, suggested the possibility of an Arab preventive attack. At the same time, the CIA revealed in a document which found its way to the State Department that even low-level Israeli commanders were openly discussing the probability of unleashing a nuclear attack against Egypt. Specifically, the Egyptian heartland along the Nile would be targeted and the Aswan High Dam demolished, with the expectation that one nuclear device, if perfectly positioned, could cause a 400 foot wave to rush down the narrow Nile Valley. Several warnings to Israel were published in the Arab press following the Arab summit meeting of 1966.

Israeli officials such as Defense Minister Rabin argued that only pledges of Soviet support could have emboldened Nasser to call for the removal of UN troops from Sinai. Others felt that the Egyptian president was just creating a "controlled crisis" but had no intention of carrying out a preemptive attack. He was assumed to be strengthening his bargaining position, hoping that the Americans would rush to diffuse the crisis.

Many Egyptians expected an Israeli attack in the form of a conventional "first strike" across the border. It was thought that this would provide an opportunity to bomb Dimona and to capture the port of Eilat while the enemy remained stuck in Sinai. It was assumed that Nasser would then move against Israel's heartland via Jordan, supported by Syrian troops and fast approaching Iraqis. What added to Israeli tension were calls for military action by PLO and Arab journalists – closely monitored in Tel Aviv – pressing for attacking Dimona before Israel became fully nuclearized. Muhammad Hassanein Heikal, Nasser's adviser, issued similar calls on the pages of *al-Ahram*.

Nasser expected that an Israeli attack would provide several retaliatory options, but he did not envisage the speed, intensity, and scale of the attack on June, 6. However, the Aswan High Dam was not targeted, since Israel was still a few years shy of testing its atomic weapons. And Israel was unable to unleash its atomic arsenal against PLO guerrilla attacks from Syria in subsequent years, since they operated well below the nuclear threshold. The irrelevance of its nuclear strategy in campaigns against guerrillas, such as the war against Hezbollah in 2006, was to challenge Israel's war theories severely.[33]

Sadat's response to the Israeli nuclear reality

Following Nasser's death in 1970, Egyptian officials and the media showed remarkable restraint with regard to Israel's nuclear program. This was surprising in light of revelations that Israel threatened to resort to its nuclear option during the 1973 War if the US did not replenish its conventional weapons, referring to Israel's initial defeat in apocalyptic terms such as "the destruction of the second temple."[34]

Anwar Sadat missed another opportunity to demand Israel's acceptance of the NPT as the price for signing the Camp David peace treaty. He apparently never pushed the idea during the Camp David negotiations, fearing the collapse of the peace talks. He knew of Begin's vehement opposition to such a deal, although Egyptian Prime Minister Mustafa Khalil and other Foreign Ministry officials brought up the idea.[35] During the Sadat and Mubarak years, nuclear issues remained largely confined to Egyptian scholarly and scientific publications. In 1995, *al-Siyaseh al-Duwaliyyah,* published by *al-Ahram*'s Center for Political and Strategic Studies, put out a special issue on nuclear weapons.[36] The journal focused on Egypt's compliance with the NPT and Israel's stockpiling of nuclear weapons. Huda Abd al-Nasser, the deceased president's scholarly daughter and guardian of his legacy, contributed to another publication of *al-Ahram* Center in 2000 on the history of Egypt's nuclear program. The study referred to Egypt's Nuclear Commission, founded in 1957, which was centered on theoretical research. Apparently, Egypt froze its nuclear program in its tracks by agreeing to scrap what would have constituted an essential delivery system, meaning its entire missile research program. By 1979–80, discussions in the Egyptian People's Assembly determined that any nuclear program should be confined to the production of hydroelectricity.

Egypt was among the first states to sign the NPT in 1970 but did not ratify it until February 1981. There were no attempts to extract Israeli concessions or seek future nuclear cooperation with the great powers. When the debate began in parliament, the government expressed the hope that Israel would still decide to sign the treaty in the wake of the Camp David Agreement. To reassure the legislators, Kamal Hussein Ali, Egypt's foreign minister, said that unless Israel explodes atomic weapons on its own soil, there would be no hard evidence of its possession of such weapons in the eyes of the international community. He reminded the legislators that Israel did not use these weapons during the 1973 War. Finally, in desperation, Sadat ratified the treaty without parliamentary approval after six days of parliamentary debate. He admitted that by doing so he was hoping to gain the friendship and cooperation of the US which was seriously opposed to proliferation. Even after Vanunu's revelations regarding Israel's nuclear arsenal in 1986, Cairo remained silent on the subject. But Mubarak did become one of the most outspoken advocates of nuclear disarmament in the Middle East.[37]

The American position on Israel's nuclear capability

As William Quandt's seminal study, *Peace Process,* shows, Israel's military superiority and technological advantage allowing it to stand up to any Arab coalition resulted from American military assistance. Each American administration since Kennedy has implicitly accepted Israel's nuclear status, subject to some conditions. These included the prohibition against openly declaring its nuclear weapons and using them only as "the ultimate deterrent" – and never on the battlefield. In turn, the US has committed itself to supplying whatever conventional weapons are needed in order to make resorting to nuclear warfare unnecessary.[38]

The US did not stop here, but continued to increase its military assistance to Israel in order to boost its arsenal of conventional weapons. A new threshold was reached during the George W. Bush administration in 2007, when the annual military grant to Israel was increased to $3 billion, or half the US military assistance program worldwide. An informal formula has also become part of the annual congressional legislation dealing with these matters, requiring proof that any arms sale to a Middle East country "will not adversely affect Israel's qualitative military edge" over its enemies. The formula was reiterated to Israeli defense officials in 2009, according to cables released by WikiLeaks.[39]

The manner in which US military assistance is delivered to Israel is also designed to grant it maximum advantage unavailable to other allies such as Egypt and Saudi Arabia. As John Mearsheimer and Stephen Walt explained, Israel receives its entire grant at the beginning of each fiscal year, and this is placed in an interest-bearing account in the US Federal Reserve Bank. By contrast, all other aid recipients receive their funding in quarterly installments and are expected to buy their weapons in the US. Israel is allowed to use around 25 per cent of its grant to buy from its own military industries. This prevents the US from monitoring where the money is spent, and it often finds its way to illegal Israeli settlements in the occupied West Bank. In addition, the US gives Israel access to its intelligence, something not allowed to its NATO allies.[40] Israel's stockpile of biological and chemical weapons, on the other hand, is never deemed dangerous enough to warrant American inspection or pressure, unlike the cases of Iraq and Libya in the past.[41]

Israel's nuclear deterrence and its limitations

Israel's use of its conventional deterrent and the world's tacit acknowledgment of its nuclear status following the 1967 War failed to guarantee its future victories on the battlefield. Even though Egypt demonstrated its ability to cross the Suez Canal and attack Israel in 1973, its initial military success in the field was soon reversed. There is much evidence, however, that Egypt, Israel and the US colluded in affecting the outcome of that war.[42]

Israel's Lebanon adventure

Even though the Sadat regime benefited economically from its American alliance, it failed to gain as much as it anticipated in its subsequent foray into the thicket of direct contacts with Israel despite the unusual involvement of an American president in those negotiations. The Sinai was returned to Egypt, just as Sadat had promised, but only as a demilitarized territory. The Egyptian military was placed in mothballs while Israel continued to punish its other regional antagonists at will. Notably, the absence of a threat of Egyptian military intervention facilitated Israel's invasion of Lebanon in 1982. A punishing blow was administered to the PLO there, enabling Israel to pursue its long-term interest in gaining control of the sources of the Litani River. Invading its neighbor to the north also made possible another Israeli dream dating back to 1955, which called for the creation of a "Jewish-Christian front in the Arab ocean." At the time, Foreign Minister Moshe Sharett was hotly opposed to a Ben Gurion–Dayan plan to "buy" a Maronite officer who would be willing to cooperate with the invasion of his own land. Sharett recorded in his diary that this would get Israel bogged down in a mad adventure that will only bring it disgrace.[43]

Secret visits by leading Israeli generals to Maronite leaders began in 1977 involving Rabin and Pierre Gemayel, the founder of the Phalangist Party. Although the latter lectured Rabin during their first meeting in a missile boat off the Maronite stronghold of Junieh, referring to the Palestinian presence in Lebanon as being Israel's fault, the alliance moved forward. The Israeli intervention in Lebanon's second civil war saw the introduction of Syrian troops into Lebanon as Syria attempted to impose some kind of order along its western flank. The resultant Israeli invasion of Lebanon and the siege of Beirut, did not accomplish all of Israel's objectives. Instead, Palestinian resistance, negotiations with President Reagan's envoy Philip Habib, and the unexpected fallout from the massacres of several hundred Palestinians at the Sabra and Shatila refugee camps, catapulted the Palestinian cause to international prominence. All of a sudden, the prophecy of Israeli IDF chief of intelligence, Major General Yehoshua Saguy, that "whoever reaches Beirut ... will be touching upon the basic problem of 1948, and whoever tries to remove the Palestinians from Lebanon will necessarily be asked what the solution to their problem is," suddenly came true.[44] In an effort to lift the spirit of his besieged fighters in Beirut, Arafat was fond of reminding them of Nasser's words during the Egyptian–Israeli War of Attrition in the late 1960s. Nasser would be happy, Arafat reported, if the PLO managed to keep at least one Israeli brigade pinned down. Arafat added that now the PLO was keeping 100,000 Israeli troops occupied. Nevertheless, the PLO's resistance in West Beirut led an angered wartime president, Bashir Gemayel, to shout to Arafat over the phone that if the Palestinian leader wished to make West Beirut his Stalingrad, he should do it in his own country.[45]

The Israelis occupied Beirut and then prepared to leave after concluding a peace treaty with President Amin Gemayel in May 1983, only to see this revoked due to combined pressure by Syria's Hafiz Assad and a Lebanese leftist coalition.[46] Demoralized by the fallout from the camp massacres and by the failure of the American intervention due to Shi'ite suicide attacks, the Israelis withdrew to southern Lebanon. By 1985, they established autonomous control over a large swath of land, calling it a "security zone." Having succeeded in pushing out the PLO's forces, the Israelis now faced the Lebanese guerrilla movement known as Amal, and by 1987, its more lethal successor and rival, Hezbollah.[47] The Israelis maintained control over this southern area from 1978 until 2000, which expanded by 1985 to include 10 per cent of Lebanon.

One reason Syria sabotaged the Israeli–Lebanese treaty in 1983 was Israel's refusal to link its withdrawal to its evacuation of the Golan Heights. Hezbollah backed Syria on this demand and the struggle continued. By 1989, the civil war in Lebanon was formally ended with the signing of the Taif Agreement, leaving Hezbollah in charge of defending the south. But the war between Lebanese guerrillas and the IDF raged on.

Repeating their tactics against the civilian population in Gaza, the Israelis hoped to alienate Lebanese civilians against Hezbollah. But the guerrilla organization became embedded within the civilian population. When Ehud Barak was elected prime minister in 1999, he was able to carry out his promised unilateral evacuation from southern Lebanon in 2000, without achieving any of Israel's original goals. In commenting on the ferocity of Hezbollah's resistance, Rabin said in 1987 that Israel must bear some responsibility for "letting the genie out of the bottle."[48]

The Israeli withdrawal from the southern zone did not result in a peaceful border, and the Israelis continued to be alarmed at the resulting power vacuum and Hezbollah's rush to fill it. Gun duels across the border increased and Israel continued its policy of targeted assassinations (as in Gaza previously), resulting in the killing of Sheikh Ragheb Harb, the young Hezbollah leader, in 1985. By that time, Abbas Musawi has emerged as the most significant of the generation of scholar-soldiers leading this movement following his return from Najaf and establishing a *hawza* (Shi'ite seminary) in Baalbak, in the Beqqa Valley. Imad Mughniyah, the bright star of the movement and the head of its external security organization, was also assassinated in 2008.

Beirut's impoverished suburbs, including Dhahiya, came under the new leadership of Hassan Nasrallah, and a new infrastructure was built, with emphasis on volunteerism, self-help, and sacrifice. Hezbollah did not conduct any revenge killings against the population of the south after Israel's withdrawal. But skirmishes with Israeli troops were on the rise, especially when the latter were spotted near the Shabaa Farms, which had been seized from Lebanon and attached to the Golan Heights.[49]

The Second Lebanon War of 2006 was triggered by similar conditions along Israel's northern undemarcated border. The war was also due to Israel's mistaken sense that the murder of Lebanese Prime Minister Rafik Hariri the previous year, and the resulting forced pullout of Syrian troops, provided another opportunity to eliminate Hezbollah altogether. At the same time, Israel was provoked by news of Hezbollah's acquisition of a "first strike" capacity to utilize its own familiar preemptive strategy. Hezbollah began using newly-supplied Iranian weapons such as Zelzal 2 ('earthquake') and rockets with a range of 20 kilometers and attacked Israel's Merkava tanks. Noor guided missiles were used to target ships, resulting in the disabling of the INS *Hanit* in Lebanese waters. Israel retaliated with air attacks and artillery bombardment, eschewing land engagements in order to minimize its casualties.

Hezbollah's civilian infrastructure was also targeted, disrupting Lebanon's communication system. Among Israel's major targets was the Dhahiya suburb, which was suspected of housing most of Hezbollah's commanders. The degree of destruction suffered by the civilian population was massive, causing most of the Shi'ite population to leave their homes. But despite this, Israel's declared objective of ending Hezbollah's entrenchment in the south and restoring the regular Lebanese army to this area was never achieved. Israeli Brigadier General Guy Zur, who fought in this war, described Hezbollah as "by far the greatest guerrilla group in the world."[50] The newly enunciated Dhahiya doctrine emphasized the use of aerial bombardment of densely-populated areas as a suitable deterrent. The Israelis tried this again in their attack on Gaza in 2007, but also with negligible results. The amount of destruction unleashed on these areas failed to detach people from their leadership or to prevent the rebuilding of damaged infrastructure and the resumption of fighting. Yet Israel continues to underestimate the peril of guerrilla fighters who challenge the iron and firepower of a sophisticated army.

Iranian allies turn into determined foes

The emergence of an Islamic regime in Iran in the late 1970s and its transformation into the center of worldwide Shi'ite resurgence was bound to attract Israel's attention. Iran rejected Israel's friendship on several fronts, such as by arming Hezbollah in Lebanon, turning Israel's embassy in Tehran over to the PLO, and opposing the American-brokered Oslo Agreement of 1993. These policies antagonized the US as well, especially when the Iranians criticized Israel's oppression of the Palestinians in the West Bank and Gaza. As Geoffrey Kemp, a member of the Nixon Center, summed the matter up, any sustained criticism of Israel will not be tolerated. Ever since the Iranian hostage crisis of 1979–81, Iran has acquired a sullied image in the American Congress, where Israel's interests are ardently defended. This view developed long before Iran was known to be enriching uranium.[51]

But Israel's determination to put an end to Iran's potential future development of nuclear weapons has succeeded in obscuring a history of economic and strategic cooperation between the two countries. It is well known that Shah Muhammad Reza Pahlavi always maintained warm relations with the Jewish state, exchanging arms for oil. Since both were major US clients at the time, with the Shah anointed as the "policeman of the Gulf," there was no reason for friction between them. Even the beginnings of Iran's atomic experiments under the auspices of the Atoms for Peace program in the 1970s did not alarm the Israelis. But since the Shah had always aspired to a leadership role within the Arab and Muslim world, he could ill afford to embrace Israel publicly. Therefore, the Shah did not support Israel during the 1973 War, and was critical of Israel's occupation policies in the West Bank and Gaza. His government voted for the "Zionism is racism" UN resolution in 1975 and went along with the majority of Arab states who opposed the presence of American troops in the Persian Gulf region[52]

Iran's balancing act under the Shah between its Arab co-religionists and the Jewish state, nevertheless, did not preclude doing business with Israel or occasionally seeking its help. According to a 1980 article in the Israeli leftist daily *Davar* by Uri Lubriani, a former ambassador to Iran, Allon was always ready to help Iran.[53] Allon was said to be the frequent guest of Iran's deputy prime minister, Nassrallah Nassiri, the head of Savak, Iran's secret intelligence service. Nasseri, who was later executed by the Islamic regime, maintained exclusive control over all contacts with visiting Israelis. Most of these visits concerned Israeli assistance in bringing Savak up to the standards of Israel's Mossad.

The Shah sought Israel's help in improving his country's image in the US following revelations of the regime's wide use of torture. Israel's services were particularly needed in order to win the support of the pro-Israel lobby and the American media. Not surprisingly, when relations soured after the fall of the Shah, several Israeli military and intelligence experts were calling for an American invasion of Iran. The Israelis were publicly lamenting the cancellation of most Iranian contracts, amounting to $225 million in 1979. Most of these were with the Sultam enterprises in Yaken'am, which produced artillery. Sultam was a subsidiary of Koor, owned by Israel's semi-official labor federation, the Histadrut. The cancellation resulted in the immediate loss of 2,000 jobs in Israel.[54]

The Israel lobby in the US continued to obstruct a fair assessment of Iranian–US relations in the post-Pahlavi period. Ranking expert on Iran, James A. Bill, attributed this to the US obsession with its two major allies in the region, Israel and Saudi Arabia. When the administration of George W. Bush attempted to reevaluate this relationship prior to the attacks of September 11, 2001, the American–Israel Public Affairs Committee (AIPAC) lined up 70 members of Congress who signed a petition calling for continuing economic sanctions against Iran. Other high-powered groups, such as the Atlantic Council on Iran, couched their recommendations for ending the sanctions in language referencing Israeli interests as the defining security issue for the US.[55] An American international energy consultant, Thomas Stauffer, complained during that same period that the American public never realized that a "gaping hole" existed in the embargo against shipments of weapons to Iran. He explained that this hole was used by the Israelis to sell their own weapons to Iran at 400 per cent markup.[56] An agreement was signed in Paris by Israel and Iran in 1980, assuring the latter of Israeli shipments of arms in exchange for the safe exit of tens of thousands of Iranian Jews.[57]

When Iran decided to develop its nuclear capability (with the potential of eventual weaponization), presumably in reaction to Iraq's use of chemical weapons against its Kurdish population, Israel finally met the most serious challenge to its nuclear hegemony over the Middle East. And as President Barak Obama was attempting to steer his country towards a diplomatic solution, he was finding it difficult to prevent Israeli Prime Minister Benjamin Netanyahu from addressing the American public over his head. The debate raged on in the US, with hawkish experts like Matthew Kroenig arguing in favor of a quick preventive attack on Iran's nuclear installations. He claimed that this option was the only step that would persuade Israel against acting on its own.[58]

Israel and Turkey: the transformation of a military alliance

Israel's longstanding strategy of cultivating close relations with the non-Arab Outer Circle of the region was rejected in recent years not only by Iran, but also by Turkey. Arab relations with the Republic of Turkey have always been tense, mainly due to Ankara's association with western security plans during the Cold War. These included the Baghdad Pact – later renamed the Central Treaty Organization (CENTO) – in 1955. Until 1964, Turkish–Israeli relations were harmonious as a result of the former's alliance with the US. The first sign of Turkish disillusionment with the US resulted from President Johnson's threat to break off relations with Turkey if the latter invaded Cyprus. Several Arab countries, along with Israel, supported the Turkish position at the UN,

but Egypt, Syria and Lebanon dissented. The Cyprus crisis, thus, demonstrated the predisposition of several Arab and Islamic states to extend support
and motivated Turkey to become a de facto member of the OIC in 1975. The
economic crisis of 1979–81 also pushed Turkey to cement its relations with
Arab countries. The Turkish economy was reeling under the impact of the
rising cost of heating fuel and oil following the fall of the Shah of Iran.
Energy costs in that year exceeded the total value of Turkish exports by 30
per cent, resulting in a 16 per cent unemployment rate and the depletion of
foreign reserves.[59]

General Kenan Evren initiated contacts with Saudi Arabia in 1980, and
Turkey was granted $75 million in aid and also oil at discretionary prices. But
Turkey came under Saudi pressure to abandon its ties to Israel. This coincided
with Israel's annexation of East Jerusalem on July 30, 1980, a move which
elicited Turkish consternation. Eventually Turkey downgraded its consulate in
Jerusalem due to a motion of censure in the Turkish parliament protesting its
continued alliance with Israel. This step launched the slow road to the diplomatic recognition of the PLO. Yet, the Turks were unwilling to sever their
relations with Israel.[60] The Turkish–Israeli alliance was believed to be on the
brink of collapse since it lacked what Stephen Walt called the glue of such
relationships, namely a set of shared values. Advocates of the Israeli alliance
were always Turkey's generals and civil bureaucrats who wanted to shore up
the country's secular system. This collided with the public's affinity to the
Palestinians, particularly over the issue of Jerusalem. Another reason for disillusionment with Israel was the Israel lobby's support for the Armenian
Genocide Resolution in Congress, House Resolution 106, in 2007, whereas in
the past, it always supported Turkey's interests.

But a major gulf between the two allies developed as a result of the threat
of partitioning Iraq during the 1990s, which would have culminated in establishing an independent Kurdish state. The Israelis were supportive of this,
since they had a long history of clandestine relations with Iraqi Kurds.
Clearly, neither Turkey nor Iran favored such an outcome.[61] Israel's long
established "periphery" policy of relying on its strong bonds with the US to
maintain its hegemonic position in the Middle East, therefore, could not
withstand the impact of the changing ideological realities of its erstwhile
allies, Turkey and Iran. Even this non-Arab Outer Circle proved unpredict-
able once Iran emerged as the first revolutionary Islamist state whose new
center devoted itself to destroying the hegemony of the Center and Turkey
rediscovered its Islamic identity and roots. Dubbed "the new Ottomanism,"
Turkey's transformation as a result of the rise of Islamist parties such as the
AKP calls for an enlarged role for Ankara in the Middle East.

The Syrian crisis of 2011–12

The Syrian uprising of 2011 has affected not only Syria's regional position but
also Turkey's tilt to the Arab world, which previously resulted in weakening

its Israeli alliance. As Turkey became a conduit for arms to Syria's opposition forces, Israel saw the uprising as an opportunity to eliminate Syria's Ba'ath regime and in the process weaken Iran and Hezbollah – and split Hamas from them as well. By bringing down the strongest remaining Arab nationalist government, Israel hopes to secure itself in the Arab centers which are effectively allied with it, and to facilitate the rise of a new Iranian regime in Tehran, reprising the role of the Shah as the center of the Periphery serving as a major pillar of American strategy. Netanyahu is calling for the elimination of these regimes, describing Syria, Iran and Hezbollah as the "axis of evil," inspiring Patrick Seale to write of Tel Aviv's eagerness to bring down "the whole axis which has dented its supremacy in the Levant."[62]

What to do about the Palestinians

Few can argue that Israel's existential vulnerability does not result from its failure to reach an accommodation with the Palestinians. No other international conflict in recent memory has undergone the same number of attempted peace settlements as the Israeli–Palestinian conflict. The Oslo Peace Accords of 1993 bore little fruit for the Palestinian side since they left such issues as East Jerusalem, the Palestinian right of return, future borders, and Palestinian statehood to an unspecified time in the future. Following this major peace effort, the PLO was allowed to establish subordinate governmental structures initially in Gaza and Jericho, with promises of wider control on good behavior. This could not alter the dynamics of the post-1967 Israeli occupation. In effect, the PLO agreed to accept whatever terms its former enemy – as determined by its good nature or enlightened self-interest, perhaps nudged by Washington – would agree to in the future. One may argue that by raising the expectations of the Palestinians, Oslo was a doomed experiment for them, although not so for Israel. This was due to several factors, such as the presence of a militarized settler regime with full control over its own transportation and water infrastructure.

The settler regime had unusual beginnings. Once Israel began the occupation in 1967, Prime Minister Eshkol and his government maintained a low profile, rarely touring the newly acquired territories, particularly East Jerusalem, lest the Soviets call for a General Assembly vote demanding an immediate pull-out. But the Justice Ministry began to issue directives on how to unify the two Jerusalems, East and West, without exciting international public opinion. This involved directing diplomatic missions abroad to emphasize Israel's commitment to the protection of freedom of worship for Muslims and Christians. The act of annexing East Jerusalem was to be described initially as "diplomatic fusion." But the boundaries of the city were to be expanded, and 27 square miles were eventually added to the formerly Jordanian-controlled section while excluding Arab populated villages and neighborhoods. This was in order to build Jewish housing developments beyond the Green Line, Israel's undeclared pre-1967 frontier.

The settlements went off to a galloping start as Israel countered criticism by explaining its actions as merely municipal or administrative in nature, and by protesting the label "occupation." Although building settlements on occupied land was the underlying premise of "*aliyah*" in the past, the Israelis ran into serious international problems after 1967. Some Israeli legal experts, like Yehuda Blum, argued that the West Bank was not occupied territory, since it had no sovereign and was taken from Jordan, whose claims of sovereignty were generally unrecognized. But Eshkol faced vehement opposition from Theodore Meron, the legal adviser to the Foreign Ministry, who maintained that the settlements were in clear violation of the Fourth Geneva Convention of 1949. He also counseled strongly that if Israel chose to maintain these settlements, it must limit their use to temporary military personnel. He advised specifically against putting settlements in the Golan Heights, where Syrian sovereignty was unassailable. But Eshkol's government never accepted his advice and proceeded to build "facts on the ground" in order to face its critics, primarily the US, with a *fait accompli.*

The Israelis also examined several ideas about the densely-populated refugee camps in Gaza, charging Ada Sereni, an Italian immigrant, with the task of ascertaining the willingness of the camp residents to move to other areas outside of historic Palestine. When her efforts came to naught, other ideas emerged, such as one by Ezra Danin, a prominent secret agent, who suggested moving the Palestinian camp dwellers to West Germany, where there was a need for migrant workers. Some leaders thought in terms of creating an IDF-controlled Palestinian state, suggesting that it should be named "Ishmael."[63] Eshkol said to visiting French philosopher Jean Paul Sartre that "we have nothing to give and nothing to concede" on the matter of the return of the refugees.[64]

The Israelis also refused to call the areas under their control "occupied," insisting instead on the euphemism "liberated territories," later changed to "administrative territories" upon the suggestion of the legal adviser to the military government.[65] Even though the Palestinian National Authority (PNA), which took over after Oslo, renounced the right to armed struggle, and despite the work of mixed committees which studied the refugee issue during the Madrid Peace Conference of 1992, no recommendations were accepted. The one serious attempt to deal with this question was provided by Shlomo Gazit, retired Israeli chief of intelligence. While agreeing that the return of the refugees was their right according to UN instruments, he came up with the novel idea of linking this to the creation of an independent Palestinian state, which would adopt its own Law of Return, similar to Israel's. But Gazit, like almost all Jewish Israelis, rejected allowing the refugees to return to their original towns and villages within the Green Line.

For the Palestinians who did not wish to relocate to the future Palestinian state, Gazit suggested Palestinian citizenship for those who continued to reside in other Arab states. In 1995, Mahmoud Abbas, then the second highest PNA official after Arafat, engaged in secret talks with Yossi Beilen, a member of the dovish Israeli party Meretz, resulting in a recommendation for settling the refugees within the boundaries of the projected Palestinian state. But even this plan failed to assuage the fears of Israeli hawks such as Sharon, who expressed concern over placing concentrations of refugees so close to Israel. Additionally, a majority of Israelis continue to reject the Palestinians' right of return or even to apologize for the injustice which they suffered.[66]

Israeli preoccupation with security proved the main reason for the evisceration of peace plans contemplated after 1967. Changes in the alignment of regional forces following the American invasion of Iraq in 2003 provided the George W. Bush administration yet another opportunity for peace making. The PNA had failed to extract any Israeli concessions during the Clinton-sponsored Camp David II negotiations in 2000. Illegal settlements continued to rise, especially in Greater Jerusalem. Clinton, on his part, conducted the entire talks in close consultation with Prime Minister Ehud Barak, with whom he shared a strong antipathy to Arafat. Finally, the outbreak of the Aqsa *intifada* of 2000, judged to be the logical outcome of the failure of the Camp David II talks, moved the US to launch another peace initiative. This led to the Roadmap to Peace, accepted by both Arafat and Sharon.[67] Sponsored by the US, UN, EU and the Russian Federation, the Roadmap, nevertheless, avoided laying out the perimeters of the projected Palestinian state. The plan called for freezing settlement building in the West Bank and Gaza. It adopted a phased approach, demanding that each side contribute its share of concessions. What torpedoed the map, however, was the intervention of President Bush, who addressed a letter to Prime Minister Sharon in 2004 expressing the view that the settlements were by now population centers and that consequently Israel's future borders could not follow the 1949 armistice lines.[68]

The PNA's continued cooperation with Israeli security personnel in the West Bank further undermined any popular legitimacy it had retained. Indeed, whatever legitimacy it had possessed at the start flowed from the Oslo Accords, creating a rift between it and Hamas in Gaza. It was also becoming quite evident that repeated calls to recharge the peace process were simply a distraction while Israel continued to expand its settlements and spread its control over the resources and means of communications of the West Bank. The American and Israeli window of opportunity was said to result from the rift between the PNA and Hamas.

But Gaza was another matter. The separation between the two Palestinian entities provided a justification for Israel's resistance to more peace talks, on the pretext that there was no viable "peace partner" with whom to negotiate. Hamas, which adhered to the ideology of Islamic resistance, was subjected to harsh economic blockades, an assassination campaign targeting most of its leaders, and repeated aerial attacks before it began to respond with Iranian-supplied missile barrages aimed at southern Israeli towns. Mubarak's regime in Egypt became an Israeli partner in enforcing a siege around Gaza, and a signatory to an elaborate Israeli security plan in 2005, known as the

Philadelphi Agreement. This was followed by attempts to control the Rafah crossing point to Egypt, resulting in the Agreement of Movement and Access (AMA), which provided for observers from the EU. The commercial entry point of Kerem Shalom (Kerem Salem) was also fortified by the Israelis.

After Gaza severed its relations with the PNA, it was subjected to an Israeli "shock and awe" campaign called Operation Cast Lead, which was intended to repair some of the damage to Israel's deterrence doctrine suffered during the 2006 attack on Lebanon. Israel now replicated the use of the Dhahiya doctrine, aiming again at inflicting maximum punishment on a civilian population in order to incite it to rebellion. The policy did indeed restore the effectiveness of Israel's conventional deterrence, but at the enormous cost of renewed international sympathy for the Palestinians. This was clearly a case of winning the war but losing the peace.

Conclusion

Israel succeeded over the years in leveraging its position as a favored US ally in the Middle East into that of a regional superpower of substantial proportions. Its policy has always been to maximize its territorial control over Palestinian lands, water resources and communications while attempting to thin out the indigenous Christian and Muslim population. Israel's Law of the Return, which was extended to encompass many Russians and Ethiopians with little claim to Jewishness (although they could be expected to develop a Jewish/Israeli identity), had the long-term objective of converting as much as possible of the territory under its control into an ethnic Jewish state. But its total rejection of a pluralistic state of Arabs and Jews has led to ignoring several opportunities to exchange land for peace. The only option left was to place its faith in increased militarization, even to the extent of being the first state in the region to develop nuclear weapons. This encouraged early leaders, like Ben Gurion and Peres, to threaten to bomb the Aswan High Dam if Egypt menaced the atomic reactor at Dimona. Israel finally succeeded in crushing the forces of Arab secular nationalism during the height of the Cold War, when the Soviet Union seemed to be on the brink of mounting a serious attack to abort its nuclear weapons production. The arms race in the Middle East, which turned nuclear in 1959, left the Arabs in the dust as Nasser, for whatever reasons, missed his chance to neutralize Israel's atomic ambitions during the two years preceding the 1967 War.

But Israel's US allies have let it be known that nuclear weapons could be used only as a deterrent, and never on the battlefield. This prompted Israeli military planners such as Allon to insist on refining the country's conventional deterrence policy, which was put to great effect against any combination of Arab and regional enemies. Part of this strategy called for entering into formal and informal alliances with the non-Arab countries making up the region's Outer Circle in order to neutralize the impact of Arab confrontation states such as Syria and Iraq. But even this strategy proved to be short-lived as both Iran and Turkey underwent significant ideological transformations which, in the case of Turkey, led to seeking economic support from Arab and Islamic countries. Another former ally, the Shah of Iran, made way for a revolutionary regime in Tehran that would base much of its legitimacy on leading a pan-Islamic struggle against Zionism and Israeli and American hegemony.

Israeli military planners, who regularly occupy the higher rungs of power, have failed to understand the effectiveness of Islamic resistance movements, such as Hamas and Hezbollah. In the post-Cold War years, new Islamic alignments seem to be challenging the former strategic consensus of the Reagan years, which presupposed the existence of a community of interests between Iran, Turkey and Saudi Arabia. Neither do the Israelis seem to appreciate the impact of the Jerusalem issue on Arab and Islamic public opinion in countries where democratic politics calls for popular validation of foreign policy. The Syrian crisis of 2011, however, created serious rifts between Syria and Turkey and between Turkey and Iran and opened a new opportunity for Israel to call for the destruction of the Syrian Ba'ath regime.

One of the most unexpected developments of the post-1967 strategic order in the Middle East has been the return of popular resistance movements. As the Oslo Accords seem to be losing their effectiveness, and as the Israelis persist in the belief that Palestinians have been cured of their obsession with armed struggle, Israelis have been sideblinded by other regional events. One of these is the inevitability of the rise of challengers to their atomic hegemony. The other is the return to a more structured form of guerrilla resistance, notably in the case of Hezbollah. Israeli lack of realism also extends to its blind faith in the permanence of the American alliance. The decline of the Soviet Union, which emboldened the US to introduce its own troops into the Persian Gulf region, though supposedly an auspicious development for Israel, has also eroded its value as the bulwark against Soviet attacks in the region. Thus, Israeli's role as a significant US ally may eventually shrink.

Notes

1 J. Galtung, "A Structural Theory of Imperialism," *Journal of Peace Research*, 1971, vol. 8, 81–117.
2 G. Mahler, *Israel: Government and Politics in a Maturing State*, New York: Harcourt Brace Jovanovich, 1990, pp. 9–13.
3 L. Fawcett, "Alliances, Cooperation and Regionalism in the Middle East," in L. Fawcett, ed., *International Relations of the Middle East*, London: Oxford: Oxford University Press, 2005, pp. 180–81.
4 C. Smith, *Palestine and the Arab-Israeli Dilemma*, 2nd ed., New York: St. Martin's Press, 1992, pp. 117–18.
5 J. Stein, "War and Security in the Middle East," in Fawcett, *International Relations*, pp. 206–7.

6 M. Hastings, "A Deaf and Defiant Israel is Gambling with its Future," *Financial Times,* March 27, 2010, p. 9.

7 J. Massad, "The Rights of Israel," *Kanaan-The-e-Bulletin*, vol. 11, no. 2569, 2011. URL: <http://www.english.aljazeera.net/indpeth> (accessed May 14, 2011).

8 A. Ghanem, *Palestinian Politics after Arafat: A Failed National Movement*, Bloomington: Indiana University Press, 2010, pp. 23–24.

9 G. Talhami, "New Historians and Revisionist Scholars," in C. Rubenberg, ed., *The Encyclopedia of the Israeli-Palestinian Conflict*, vol 2, Boulder, CO: Lynne Rienner, 2010, pp. 987–94.

10 Talhami, "New Historians."

11 G. Talhami, "Israeli Warfare since 1967," in J. Powell, ed., *Weapons and Warfare*, Pasadena, CA: Salem Press, 2010, pp. 759–64.

12 T. Buck, "Uncertain Horizons," *Financial Times*, February, 24 2011, p. 7.

13 The Jaffee Center Study Group, *The West Bank and Gaza: Israel's Options for Peace*, Jerusalem: Jerusalem Post Press, 1989, pp. 103–4.

14 Talhami, "Israeli Warfare," in Powell, *Weapons*, pp. 259–64.

15 A. Bar-Or, "The Evolution of the Army's Role in Israeli Strategic Planning: A Documentary Record," *Israel Studies*, 1996, vol. 1, 98–121.

16 Mahler, *Israel*, pp. 212–15.

17 W. Quandt, *Peace Process: American Diplomacy and the Arab-Israeli Conflict since 1967*, Washington, DC: The Brookings Institute, 1993, p. 339.

18 G. Talhami, *Palestinian Refugees: Pawns to Political Actors*, New York: Nova Science Publishers, 2003, pp. 173–97.

19 T. Segev, *1967: Israel, the War and the Year that Transformed the Middle East*, New York: Henry Holt, 2005, pp. 562–65.

20 "Arab Peace Initiatives," *Chicago Tribune,* December 19, 2008, p. 33.

21 S. Aronson, *Israel's Nuclear Programme, the Six Day War and Its Ramifications*, London: King's College Mediterranean Studies Programme, n.d., pp. 14–19, 24–25, 30, 38.

22 Y. Melman, "Let the world worry," *Haaretz,* December 13, 2006. URL: <http://www.haaretz.com/print-edition/features/let-the-world-worry-1.207039> (accessed December 13, 2007).

23 M. Bar-Zohar, *Ben Gurion,* New York: Delacorte Press, 1978, p. 1525.

24 Segev, *1967*, pp. 264, 524–25, 543.

25 Quandt, *Peace Process*, p. 523 (note 28).

26 Ibid., pp. 57–58.

27 "Nixon Archives," 1969. Nixon Presidential Library and Museum. URL: <http://nixon.archives.gov/virtuallibrary/documenys/mr/071969.israel.pdf> (accessed October 23, 2009).

28 Quandt, *Peace Process*, p. 339.

29 S. Tillman, *The United States in the Middle East: Interests and Obstacles*, Bloomington: Indiana University Press, 1982, pp. 38–39.

30 Quandt, *Peace Process*, p. 577 (note 46).

31 I. Shahak, ed., *Israel's Global War: Weapons for Repression*, Belmont, MA: AAUG, 1982, pp. 49–51.

32 Aronson, "Israel's Nuclear Programme," pp. 43–55.

33 Ibid.

34 G. Talhami, *Palestine in the Egyptian Press: From al-Ahram to al-Ahali*, Lanham, MD.: Lexington Books, 2007, pp. 328–30.

35 W. Quandt, private communication.

36 Special Issue on Nuclear Weapons (Arabic), *Al-Siyasah al-Duwalliyah*, 1995, vol. 31 passim.

37 Talhami, *Palestine*, pp. 331–33.

38 Aronson, "Israel's Nuclear Programme," pp. 85–86.
39 W. Pincus, "United States Needs to Reevaluate its Assistance to Israel," *Washington Post,* October 17, 2012. URL: <http: http://www.washingtonpost. com/world/national-security/united-states-needs-to-reevaluate-its-assistance-to- israel/2011/10/15/gIQAK5XksL_story.html> (accessed November 10, 2012).
40 J. Mearsheimer and S. Walt, "The Israel Lobby," *London Review of Books,* 23 March 2006. URL: <http://ksgnotes1.harvard.edu/Research/wpaper.nsf/rwp/RWP-o11> (accessed March 23, 2006).
41 T. Stauffer *et al.*, "The End of Dual Containment: Iraq, Iran & Smart Sanctions," *Middle East Policy,* 2001, vol. 8, 84–85.
42 Talhami, *Palestine,* pp. 331–3.
43 Z. Schiff and E. Ya'ari, *Israel's Lebanon War,* New York: Simon and Schuster, 1984, pp. 13–14.
44 Ibid., p. 201.
45 Ibid., pp. 208, 218–19.
46 G. Talhami, *Syria and the Palestinians: The Clash of Nationalisms,* Gainesville: University Press of Florida, 2001, p. 151.
47 See J. Goodzari, *Syria and Iran: Diplomatic Alliance and Power Politics in the Middle East,* London: I. B. Tauris, 2006, p. 145.
48 A. Norton, *Hezbollah: A Short History,* Princeton, NJ: Princeton University Press, 2007, p. 33.
49 Ibid., pp. 33–7.
50 Ibid., pp. 45, 87–93.
51 See R. Roth *et al.*, "Symposium: U.S. Policy Toward Iran: Time for a Change," *Middle East Policy,* 2002, vol. 8, 12–13.
52 P. Mishra, "Iran-Israel History Suggests Different Future," *Outlook,* March 11, 2012. URL: <http://www.outlook.com.owa/?ae=Item&t=IPM.Note&id> (accessed March 12, 2012).
53 U. Lubrani, "Yigal Allon in the Palace of the Shah," in I. Rabonovich and Y. Reinharz, eds, *Israel in the Middle East: Documents and Readings on Society, Politics, and Foreign Relations, Pre-1948 to the Present,* 2nd ed., Lebanon, N.H.: Brandeis University Press, published by University Press of New England, 2008, pp. 357–62, originally published in Hebrew as "Allon bearmon hashah" in *Davar,* 20 April 1980, pp. 3–4.
54 Shahak, *Israel's Global War,* pp. 32–9.
55 J. Bill, "The Politics of Hegemony: The United States and Iran," *Middle East Policy,* 2001, vol. 8, 95.
56 Stauffer *et al.*, "The End," pp. 84–85.
57 Mishra, "Iran-Israel History."
58 M. Kroenig, "Time to Attack Iran: Why a Strike is the Least Bad Option," *Foreign Affairs,* 2002, vol. 91, 76–86.
59 H. Yavuz and M. Khan, "Turkish Foreign Policy Toward the Arab–Israeli Conflict: Duality and the Development," *Arab Studies Quarterly,* Fall 1992, vol. 14, 78–9.
60 Ibid., 73–86.
61 G. Bacik, "The Limits of an Alliance: Turkish-Israeli Relations Revisited," *Arab Studies Quarterly,* 2001, vol. 23, 54–60.
62 P. Seale, "The Destruction of Syria," *The Washington Report on the Middle East,* September 2012, pp. 7, 11,
63 Segev, *1967,* pp. 514, 531–33, 542, 575.
64 Ibid., pp. 525.
65 Ibid., p. 543.
66 Talhami, *Palestinian Refugees,* pp. 163, 169–73.

67 J. Baker, "A Roadmap to Nowhere," *Bitterlemons*, May 5, 2008. URL: <http://www.bitterlemons.org/previous/bl050508ed17.html#pal2> (accessed October 15, 2012).

68 "Exchange of letters between PM Sharon and President Bush," April 14, 2004, Israeli Ministry of Foreign Affairs. URL: <http://www.mfa.gov.il/MFA/Peace+Process/Reference+Documents/Exchange+of+letters+Sharon-Bush+14-Apr-2004.htm> (accessed March 7, 2013).

Part III

Potential counterbalancing forces

5 Post-revolutionary Iran

Resisting global and regional hegemony

Mojtaba Mahdavi

The Middle East was in the forefront of human progress during much of world history but – along with other parts of Asia and Africa – fell into the role of underdeveloped Periphery with the rise of the modern World System, in which a fundamental gap in power and wealth divided a group of Center countries in Europe and areas of European settlement from the rest. Iran in particular was the seat of some of the world's most powerful empires, starting with that of the Achaemenids under Cyrus the Great and later sporadically resuming its imperial role under the Parthians, Sassanians, and Safavids to rival the Romans, Byzantines, and Ottomans. According to the historian Marshal Hodgson, in the Islamic civilization the Persian language "had more than purely literary consequence: it served to carry a new overall cultural orientation within Islamdom" and came closer than any possible rival – notably "the relatively parochial French or Latin" – during the 1500s to acquiring the status of a worldwide medium of communication.[1]

However, the world has changed and the Middle East today – including Iran – is "highly dependent on the avatars of the world's geopolitics."[2] Is World System theory capable of explaining these changes in global politics? It seems that no single grand theory can problematize the rise and fall of empires, civilizations and power centers. Nonetheless, an essential component of World System theory, meaning the Center–Periphery and/or hegemony–rivalry continuum, seems satisfactory. The Center–Periphery inequality is, Johan Galtung argues, a major form of structural violence in the current World System. In his words:

> The world consists of Center and Periphery nations; and each nation, in turn, has its centers and periphery. Hence our concern is with the mechanism underlying this discrepancy, particularly between the center in the Center, and the periphery in the Periphery.[3]

There is – as Galtung further explains – disharmony of interest between the periphery in the Periphery and the periphery in the Center but there is greater harmony of interest between the "bridgeheads" at the center in the Periphery, or the elites that constitute the center in a Periphery, and the center in the

Center. "Bridgeheads" have more in common with the center in the Center than with the periphery in the Periphery.[4]

We suggest here that there is an unequal relationship between the Center and the Periphery reinforced by the World System. However, states in the Periphery maintain some degrees of autonomy to exercise their leadership in response to the internal forces of their societies. In other words, both international and internal forces/constraints shape the institution of the state and its behavior and policies. A triangular relationship among the global structure of power, regional states and social forces/movements shapes the international politics of the Middle East. Put simply, the interaction among the trilogy of the global economic and political system, the institution of the individual state and the dynamics of civil society in each country determine the international politics of the region.[5] Two relentless forces of global structure and state–society relations shape state behavior. Regional and international relations of the state are formed by interactions between the World System from without and civil society/social movements from within. More specifically, we subscribe to the following theoretical outlook: first, a realist approach to the study of international relations of the Middle East is useful – complementing Galtung's imperialist approach – in that it stresses the centrality of the institution of the state, its national security, and "the relations of global system to regional actors." However, realism "deploys too narrow a concept of the state, and ignores both state–society and transnational factors. It may, as the study of revolutions and social movements shows, obscure the underlying dynamics of change."[6]

Second, contrary to the state-centrism of realism, "Foreign Policy Analysis takes us inside the society and the decision-making process, but in so doing it loses its focus on the state itself."[7] It also undermines the persistent force of the World System but overemphasizes culture and value system in shaping the state behavior.

Third, the role of ideas, political ideologies and cultural values is evident. A constructivist account of international relations holds that culture, norms and shared values shape the perceptions and policies of the state in global politics. Nonetheless, culturalist explanations often serve the hegemonic global order to rationalize the superiority of the West and the subordination/ inferiority of the rest.[8] This chapter keeps a clear distance from "regional narcissism,"[9] meaning the exaggeration of the unique nature of the Middle East culture, history, society and politics. The Middle East is one among other regions of the World System. It is too naive to attribute state behavior to a timeless, eternal and essentialist concept of Islamic mindset. State behavior is shaped by the interaction of many socio-economic and political factors in the contemporary World System. Moreover, one needs to maintain some degree of "scepticism about the weight of history" in explaining the national, regional and international policies of the Middle Eastern states. The "past, remote or more recent, cannot on its own explain the present." It is in fact, "contemporary forces which make use of the past: they select and use those elements of the past, national, regional, or religious, which suit their present purposes."[10] In other words, "ideologies, nationalist or religious, that do most to invoke the past are themselves modern creations, selected, when not invented, fetishes of the age."[11] The regional and global relations of post-revolutionary Iran provided a case in point where relentless forces of global structure and state–society relations, or interactions between the World System from without and civil society/social movements from within, have shaped state behavior.

We aim to shed light on the trajectory of post-revolutionary Iran's regional and global politics under changing leadership. Although the constitution and the governmental system have remained in place since 1979, it is useful to think in terms of four distinct periods of leadership, which we term separately as "republics." We will closely analyze the development of Iran's foreign policy under the leadership of Ayatollah Khomeini (first republic: 1979–89) and then the administrations of President Rafsanjani (the second republic: 1989–97), President Khatami (the third republic: 1997–2005), and President Ahmadinejad (the fourth republic: 2005–13). As will be shown, Iran's foreign policy has gone through various stages, each posing various challenges. These challenges were related to the geopolitical realities of pre-Cold War, post-Cold War, and post-9/11 developments, and Iran adopted specific measures to counter or cope with each of them.

The focus will be exclusively on policies involving the US, the EU, the Arab states of the Persian Gulf, Hezbollah, and Syria. We also will shed some light on Iran's nuclear policy and the impact of the pro-democracy Green Movement and the discourse about "the Shi'ite Crescent" and the Arab Spring on Iran's global and regional influence/policy. These policy cases have been carefully chosen because each highlights an aspect of Iran's post-revolutionary foreign policy strategies, which are multidimensional and complex in nature. A number of general observations will be made regarding Iran's unique approach in order to support the following specific arguments: that there is a pattern of continuity and change in foreign policy making; that there is a reciprocal relationship between domestic developments and foreign policy strategies; that the foreign policy agenda is characterized by an ongoing fluidity and dynamism; and that Iran has taken both ideological and pragmatic approaches.

The Khomeini era (1979–89): idealism and revolutionary ideology

Ayatollah Khomeini transformed Iran's last monarchy into the Islamic Republic. However, the regime he founded was a complex mixture of Islamic clericalism and secular republicanism. He created a hybrid regime that simultaneously has combined elements of totalitarian, author-itarian, and democratic politics, with each of these principles coming to the fore during successive periods – termed "republics" here – since 1979.[12] The First Republic (1979–89) of the Khomeinist state was essentially a "one-man show" dictated by Ayatollah Khomeini.[13] Nonetheless, in the post-Khomeini era, with no charisma in politics, no war, and growing domestic opposition, disagreements over socio-political issues divided the Khomeinist forces. The post-Khomeini state went through three different political periods: the second republic (1989–97), the third republic (1997–2005), and the fourth republic (2005–13). Each republic presented a different face of Khomeinism.

The ideological discourse that informed Iran's foreign policy under the leadership of Ayatollah Khomeini was called "Khomeini's way" or *khat-e-imam*, represented by popular slogans of the time, such as "exporting the revolution" and "Neither East, Nor West." This vision was idealistically grounded in the view that foreign policy should be based on Islamic values and principles. Khomeini attributed major problems of the Muslim world, including Iran's, to the world's dominant powers in general and the US in particular. The imperial arrogant West, or *estekbar*, was seen as a source of corruption, political turmoil, and instability throughout the globe.

It is not surprising that "Khomeini's way" and his mission extended beyond the borders of the Muslim world to take on global dimensions. This mission was driven by the Islamic principles that advanced Khomeini's "universalist" agenda in the sense that Islam became the panacea for addressing the ills of the world. For example, in a 1989 letter to the then Soviet leader Michael Gorbachev, Khomeini announced the bankruptcy of Western and Eastern ideologies and called upon the Communist leader to adhere to Islamic principles for "the well-being and salvation" of his nation.[14] Khomeini wrote: "Islam is not peculiar to a country, to several countries, to a group of people or countries, or even the Muslims. Islam has come for humanity. ... Islam wishes to bring all of humanity under the umbrella of justice."[15] Such statements reflected the revolutionary nature of Iran's policies during Khomeini's era, which alienated regional neighbors and provoked paranoia among them. Iran's policy of exporting the revolution was hostile towards the conservative Arab monarchies of the Persian Gulf states. As a result, Iran's Arab neighbors took defensive measures to impede Iran's ambition to export its revolution. As Shireen Hunter contends, "Iran's Islamic universalist pretensions and its revolutionary and antimonarchy discourse, a discourse influenced by left-leaning Third Worldist views that considered the Arab reaction, together with imperialism and international Zionism, as forming a triangle of evil."[16]

It can therefore be argued that Iran's regional ambitions under Khomeini's leadership were focused on altering the "balance of power in favor of Islamist and radical forces."[17] Iran had Syria's blessing for this effort, and Syria – with its secular Arab nationalist Ba'athist ideology and a leadership dominated by members of a heterodox Shi'ite sect, the Alawites – was "the first state in the region" to support Iran during its war with Iraq.[18] Syria was worried about the effect that a possible victory for Iraq would have on "the intra-Arab balance" and calculated that Iraq's defeat and the replacement of its government with a pro-Syrian Ba'athist regime would create conditions that would give it a strategic advantage in the Middle East.[19]

Iran's regional revisionist policy constituted in focused on its influence and increasing its presence on the Israeli borders with both Syria and Lebanon, where Shi'ite Muslims made up major parts of the population. This reaffirmed the Islamic Republic's initial promise to give the Shi'ite-Alawite Syrians and the Lebanese Shi'ites political, military, and economic support. Iran and its Revolutionary Guard were thus influential forces in the creation of Hezbollah in 1985. This is evident in the following remarks made by the former Iranian Minister of the Interior, Ali Akbar Mohtashemi:

> Hezbollah is part of the Iranian rulership … a central component of the Iranian military and security establishment; the ties between Iran and Hezbollah are far greater than those between a revolutionary regime with a revolutionary party outside its borders.[20]

Nonetheless, the Iranian involvement with Hezbollah did not make it "merely an instrument of the Iranian leadership's desire to spread the revolution."[21] To argue that Hezbollah was simply an extension of Iran's power in Lebanon "would be just as absurd as to conclude that the Maronite militias, which received $150 million from Israel during Yitzhak Rabin's government in 1974–77, were nothing other than instruments of Israeli policy."[22] Hezbollah enjoyed a deep social base in the Shi'ite community in Lebanon and welcomed support from, and strategic alliance with, post-revolutionary Iran. For Iran's policymakers, "Lebanon was the ideal locus for realizing the supranational pretensions of the Iranian revolution,"[23] putting Iran in the forefront of the struggle against Zionism and furthering its plan to empower Shi'ite communities to support its interests.

The Arab monarchies of the Persian Gulf reacted to Iran's perceived threat by financially supporting Iraq during the Iran–Iraq war (1980–88). In 1981, they created the Gulf Cooperation Council (GCC) as "a protective mechanism" against the spread of Iran's influence in the region.[24]

During this period, Iran's radical and revolutionary policy was evident in the American hostage crisis, which has been called the "most explicit rejection of the pillars of international society … and the institutions of international law" in recent times.[25] During this crisis, Khomeini openly supported the occupation of the American embassy and used it to solidify his internal position as the undisputed leader of post-revolutionary Iran. In so doing, he encouraged "a period of radicalization," in which he opposed the leftist and liberal factions of the Revolution, specifically liberal/nationalist Prime Minister Mehdi Bazargan.[26] In general, the seizure of the US embassy was a manifestation of Khomeini's universal Islamic ideology in that it symbolized "the 'total' victory of the Islamic Revolution, kindling flames of hope in the hearts of the enchained nations."[27]

The Rafsanjani era (1989–97): pragmatism and reconstruction

Ayatollah Khomeini died in 1989, but he marked his legacy on the regime. Before his death he issued a juristic ruling, or *fatwa,* against Salman Rushdie's novel *Satanic Verses.* The *fatwa* created much tension between Iran and the West and lasted into the post-Khomeini era. Moreover, in the summer of 1988, a year before his death, he made a difficult decision to save the Islamic Republic. He reluctantly accepted the ceasefire in the eight-year Iran–Iraq War, as it no longer served the interests of the state. Despite his fiery talk against imperialism and the disbelieving (*kafir*) enemy, as the founding father of the republic Khomeini had no choice but, to use his own phrase, to drink from "the poisonous chalice." "The poisonous chalice" of the peace with Saddam Hussein with no clear victory, however, enabled the regime to survive, although Khomeini's death brought some shifts in Iran's regional and global policies.

The second republic (1989–97) under President Hashemi Rafsanjani routinized the revolutionary charisma and institutionalized the office of the *Faqih* (jurisprudent) under the leadership of Ayatollah Ali Khamenei. Iran in the 1990s was experiencing a growing socio-ideological disenchantment. Civil society managed to challenge the repressive intentions of the state. For conservatives, the harsh truth to accept was the emergence of a growing gap between their socio-cultural values and those of the youth, the post-revolutionary generation. The state had failed to create the man/woman or the society Ayatollah Khomeini had envisioned. With almost two-thirds of its population under 30, Iranian youth remained a powerful social force. Post-secondary education, internet and satellite televisions made the youth well-informed about national and global issues. However, they were socioculturally disenchanted, politically disappointed, and economically dissatisfied. Pressures from civil society – especially the middle class, women and the youth – and the escalated elite factionalism forced the regime to open up public space and allow a limited degree of socio-political liberalization. This domestic crisis also brought some shifts in Iran's foreign policy.

Rafsanjani's presidency coincided with the end of the Iran–Iraq war and marked an era in which Iran was urgently pursuing policies that addressed its "practical needs" for post-war economic and social reconstruction.[28] The exhaustive eight-year war "forced the Iranian regime to realize the limits of its power" and to modify a number of its major policies.[29] To this end, Rafsanjani de-emphasized Khomeini's idealistic approach to focus on national interests, which impacted on the country's internal and external policies in a number of ways. For example, he realized that Khomeini's ideological commitment to exporting the revolution would not help post-war Iran to recover economically. His statement that "we cannot build dams with slogans" expressed his intent to preserve and maximize the country's national interests.[30]

In order to achieve his objective of reconstructing (*sazandegi*) Iran's economy and "cop[ing] with the new world order formed with the demise of the

Soviet Union and the supremacy of the US," Rafsanjani adhered to a pragmatic approach to foreign policy.[31] This involved rereading and softening the once cherished slogan of "neither East nor West" and adopting a regional "good neighbor policy" that Rafsanjani contended was based on "respect for territorial integrity as well as social and religious values of other peoples."[32] As he wanted the Persian Gulf to "become like an area around a home, like a common farmland," his regional policies were non-confrontational and invited the cooperation of Arab countries.[33] Rafsanjani was particularly concerned about mending Iran's relationship with Saudi Arabia, which had been characterized by hostility during Khomeini's era, with Iranian pilgrims staging frequent political demonstrations on Saudi soil during the annual pilgrimage or *Hajj*. The Iranian regime under Khomeini had utilized the *Hajj* as a vehicle to export the Islamic Revolution, to wage an attack against "so-called American Islam, and to propagate its anti-US and anti-Israeli views by staging political rallies and protests."[34] When Rafsanjani ascended to the presidency, he put an end to the demonstrations.

During this period, Iran's relationship with Shi'ite groups in the region, especially Hezbollah, was heavily influenced by Rafsanjani's pragmatic foreign policy. Hezbollah's ideology is based on the theory of Governance of the Religious Jurist (*Velayat-e-Faqih*), which Khomeini elaborated upon in his famous tract on Islamic government. According to this theory, the authority of the *Faqih* has no limits and his wisdom derives from God and the Prophet Muhammad's family.[35] At the beginning of the 1990s, Hezbollah leaders (e.g., Ayatollah Mohammed-Hussein Fadlallah) were promoting the ideal of an Islamic Republic in Lebanon, which they defined as a state ruled by Islamic law.

However, the political landscape of post-Khomeini Iran, the new thinking in its foreign policy and Rafsanjani's pragmatism led to a shift in Hezbollah's political outlook. Sheikh Subhi al-Tufayli, Sayyid Abbas al-Musawi, and Sayyid Husayn al-Musawi were at the center of a major debate on its future in Lebanon. They asserted that it was not in Hezbollah's interest to wage *jihad* (striving; the Islamic equivalent of the Christian "just war") against the West, given that Iran was calling for a truce. Instead, they advocated rapprochement and favored integration into mainstream Lebanese politics. Rafsanjani identified and supported their position.[36] Moreover, "Hezbollah did not abandon the ideal of an Islamic state, [but] it was now argued that, given Lebanon's demographics, the establishment of an Iranian-style system of government was unfeasible."[37]

The aftermath of Khomeini's death also resulted in a heightened level of cooperation between Iran and Syria in Lebanon. At this time, Syria was occupied with containing the Maronite resistance led by General Michel Aoun, who had the blessings of Iraq. It sought Iran's help in squashing the resistance, and the consequent alliance with Iran empowered Syria to oppose Saudi Arabia and the Arab League, which were both seeking to "mediate the crisis at the expense of Syria's exclusive role in Lebanon."[38] Iraq's support for Aoun therefore solidified the Tehran-Damascus relationship. Iran organized an anti-Aoun coalition in Tehran, which included Mahdi Shamsaddin of the Shi'ite Higher Council and Palestinian radicals such as Abu Musa and Ahmed Jebril, among others.[39]

Further, Iraq's invasion of Kuwait in August of 1990 and the start of the Persian Gulf War boded well for Iran and its relationship with Persian Gulf states since Iraq replaced Iran as the "threat to the security and integrity of [the region]."[40] Both Iran's decision to condemn the Iraqi invasion and its subsequent policy of neutrality during the war signified its willingness to forge closer ties with Arab states and the West. This stance was particularly favorable, as it provided Iran with an opportunity to strengthen its relations with European states, including two permanent members of the UN Security Council – Russia and France. As a result, Europe felt "a general sense of optimism about Iran's political direction after the accession" of Rafsanjani.[41] Europe's economy made it a valuable partner for Iran, as the partnership clearly distinguished between European countries and the United States. The US imposition of sanctions on Iran (e.g. passage of the 1996 Iran-Libya Sanctions Act) had increased hostility between the two countries, causing Iran to welcome Europe's support.[42] However, Iran-EU relations remained uneasy. In 1992, the EU initiated a "critical dialogue" with Iran over a host of issues, such as Khomeini's *fatwa* against Salman Rushdie, Iran's human rights record, and its policy vis-à-vis Israel, terrorism, and nuclear proliferation. In 1997, EU-Iran relations deteriorated when a German court issued a verdict against Iranian officials for their involvement in the assassination of Iranian opposition leaders in Germany. This was a turning point for the EU-Iran relations: the verdict put an end to the policy of "critical dialogue," and all European countries withdrew their ambassadors from Tehran. "Relations seemed beyond repair, at least from the EU vantage point."[43] In the last year of President Rafsanjani in office, Iran's foreign relations were in a deep crisis, one striking indication of which being that no European ambassador remained in Iran. The Islamic Republic needed a new face and new policy towards detente.

The Khatami era (1997–2005): detente and dialogue

By the late 1990s, the catastrophe in Iran's foreign relations, and the domestic socio-cultural and economic crisis had intensified factional politics within the elite, providing much opportunity for the unexpected victory of the reformist presidential candidate, Mohammad Khatami, on May 23, 1997. Khatami became the candidate standing for change, and received the protest vote, making him a "Cinderella candidate"[44] and eventually an "accidental president"[45] of the Islamic Republic. In the aftermath of his landslide victory, President Khatami maintained Rafsanjani's pragmatic approach but shifted its emphasis to what came to be called a "reformist agenda." The reformist approach was based on two central pillars: political reforms in the domestic arena – which included strengthening civil society as well as facilitating an open press, freedom of speech – and the rule of law.[46] It sought a condition of dialogue and détente that would normalize Iran's relationship with other countries. To this end, Khatami put forth two key initiatives: (1) the principle of a "Reduction of Tensions" (*Tashanoj Zodaei*) and (2) a "Dialogue of Civilizations" (*Goftogoye Tamadonha*). Both of these were intended to enhance Iran's stance regionally and internationally and had significant connotations for the kinds of policies Iran adopted during Khatami's era. Khatami expressed his regret for the 1979 US hostage crisis. In a 1998 interview with CNN, he went so far as to state that he admired the fundamental sociopolitical and moral principles and values on which the US was built. However, this statement was expressed in such an adulatory manner that even proud Americans tended to find it excessive.[47]

While Khatami embarked upon his mission to stabilize Iran's relationship with the world, Iran implemented a policy of generous economic and political support for Islamist groups in the region, notably Hamas and Hezbollah. This policy was supported by the supreme leader, Khamenei, and reflected the complex and multipolar character of decision-making in Tehran.[48] Khatami's policy towards Lebanon and Hezbollah was consistent with his policy of détente and dialogue. "As Hezbollah became a major player in Lebanese politics and achieved electoral successes, politics in Iran also became more animated" under President Khatami.[49] In 1996, he visited Lebanon and met with representatives of all communities, including political rivals of Hezbollah among the Maronite Christians and the Sunni Muslims, as well as the Shi'ite Amal Party. His speech during a 2003 visit to Lebanon demonstrated passion for peace and pluralism: "Lebanon is the nation of love and justice and consciousness. It is here that the earth takes on a celestial form as the love of Jesus melds with the wisdom of Muhammad and the Justice of Ali."[50]

Further, the Iranian-Syrian relationship was strengthened during this period due to the Turkish-Israeli strategic partnership in the mid-1990s during the 1991 Madrid Conference and the 1993 Oslo Process. As these developments had undermined Syria's position in the region and added to its insecurity, Damascus saw Iran as a strategic partner that could reinforce its position in the Middle East. Hafez al-Assad's visit to Tehran in 1997 and Khatami's visit to Syria in 1999 signified the heightened level of cooperation between the two states.[51]

Although Ayatollah Khomeini sought to reduce the US military presence in the region, his policies failed to achieve that result. Khatami's policy on the Persian Gulf states was a departure from Khomeini's radical ideology of "exporting the revolution." As Shahram Chubin explains, Khatami believed that good relations with the Persian Gulf states would lead the US to leave the region because this would remove the threat to its interests. Khatami's policy in the Persian Gulf therefore aimed "to consolidate a system of regional security through bilateral confidence-building measures that might, eventually, lead to institutionalize regional security arrangements and make the presence of US forces superfluous."[52]

During the 1997 presidential election campaign, Khatami made it clear that he would pursue a policy of détente. "In the field of foreign policy," Khatami argued, "we would like to announce that we are in favor of relations with all countries which respect our independence, dignity and interests."[53] Once elected president, his first attempt was to improve Iran's relations with both Europe and neighboring countries. Iran was still recovering from the prolonged eight-year war with Iraq, and its economy was suffering due to a lack of investment in various industries, which had increased the unemployment rate. Opening Iran up to foreign investment was seen a means to solve its economic problems. Shortly after he became president, Khatami therefore pursued policies that would improve Iranian-European relations and gain economic help from Europe. But when Khatami assumed the presidency in 1997, no European ambassador was stationed in Iran. A major step was taken when Foreign Minister Kamal Kharrazi assured European countries that Khatami's government would not uphold the 1989 *fatwa* against Salman Rushdie.[54] Europeans then reopened their embassies in Tehran. In welcoming Khatami's action, the European Union declared that this "increases the possibility that closer cooperation can be discussed in renewed dialogue."[55]

Contrary to the United States' approach, the European Union engaged in a "critical dialogue" with the Iranian government, demanding greater respect for political and human rights. For the most part, Iran's response was positive. As a result, for the first time since 1979 the UN Human Rights Commission – in opposition to the United States – declined to put Iran among the countries that violated human rights. Moreover, Khatami realized that Iran could not normalize relations with the Persian Gulf sheikhdoms as long as it did not harmonize its relations with Saudi Arabia. Khatami successfully established amicable relations with Saudi Arabia, which nullified the dispute between Iran and the United Arab Emirates over Abu Musa and the Lesser and Greater Tunb islands. Only a few months after the 1997 election, in December of that year, the eighth Summit of the Islamic Conference Organization convened in Tehran, a success for Khatami's policy of ending an era of Iran's isolation.

Shortly after his election, in an interview with CNN, Khatami praised American civilization, expressed his appreciation for American democracy and its link with religion, paid respect to the American people, acknowledged the legitimacy of the American government, condemned all forms of terrorism, and even expressed his regret for the 1979 American hostage crisis.[56] Nonetheless, Khatami criticized American foreign policy for the "mode of relationship" it pursues with nations such as Iran; he also condemned American foreign policy for its dependence on Israel and vice versa. In his words,

> ... a bulky wall of mistrust [exists] between us and the American administration, a mistrust rooted in improper behavior by the American governments. As an example of this type of behavior, I should refer to the admitted involvement of the American government in the 1953 *coup*

d'etat which toppled Mosaddeq's government, immediately followed by a $45m loan to strengthen the coup government. I should also refer to the capitulation law [i.e., the status of forces agreement that Khomeini condemned during the 1960s] imposed by the American government on Iran.[57]

President Khatami pursued a policy of indirect dialogue with the US, through non-governmental contacts, although Ayatollah Khamenei saw this as "even more harmful than" restoring formal ties.[58] In his address to the UN General Assembly in September 1998, Khatami emphasized that all civilizations need to understand and to engage in dialogue with one another, and the United Nations Organization followed this up by declaring 2001 the Year of Dialogue between Civilizations. Khatami's speech "raised hopes for détente" with the US.[59] Washington's response to Khatami's initiatives was positive, and it toned down the anti-Iranian rhetoric and took some small positive steps. On June 17, 1998, US Secretary of State Madeleine Albright responded by announcing that:

> ... we are ready to explore further ways to build mutual confidence and avoid misunderstandings. The Islamic Republic should consider parallel steps. ... As the wall of mistrust comes down, we can develop with the Islamic Republic, when it is ready, a road map leading to normal relations.[60]

The Iranian president's speech opened up a series of exchange activities in sports, academe, and the arts. After half a century, for the first time Madeleine Albright admitted that the United States had "orchestrated the overthrow of Iran's popular Prime Minister, Mohammad Mosaddeq"[61] in the 1953 coup. Such longtime members of the US foreign policy establishment as Zbigniew Brzezinski, Brent Scowcroft, and Richard Murphy called for an end to the "duel containment" of Iraq and Iran.[62] With the support of the US, Iran received over $500 million in loans from the World Bank. The US met with Iranian officials at the UN to discuss the Afghanistan issue, added the Iranian opposition group People's Mojahedin Organization (MKO) to the list of terrorist organizations, and removed Iran's name from the list of major drug-producing states.[63]

In the beginning, the administration of President George W. Bush did not alter the Clinton administration's opening to Iran. Post-9/11, Iran was instrumental in removing the Taliban government and establishing a pro-American regime in Afghanistan. Not only did Iran continue its support for the anti-Taliban Northern Alliance, but, as Americans admitted, it was "extremely helpful in getting Karzai in as the president."[64]

The 2002 "axis of evil" speech of President Bush, in spite of choosing his words to attack "non-elected" sections of the Iranian state, proved counterproductive. The speech was instrumental in launching an anti-American united front, which united Khamenei and his hardliner-conservative allies, the pragmatist-conservatives headed by Hashemi Rafsanjani, the reformist

President Khatami and the reformists. The hardliners were quick to cite national security when attacking the reform institutions and the reformers. The speech contributed in several ways to the rise of Iran's hardliners to power. According to Ervand Abrahamian,

> Although billed as supporting "Iranian citizens who risked intimidation and death on behalf of liberty, human rights, and democracy," the speech had the exact opposite consequences. It created a mood of the past, especially of the 1953 coup. ... It emboldened conservatives with the argument that the notion of "dialogue" is naive, and that "homeland security" is the most vital issue of the day. It persuaded some reformers to tone down their public demands; others to put their hopes on the back burner waiting for better days. It also energized exiles – especially Pahlavi royalists – who dread reform and hope that ultraconservative obstinacy will bring about a revolution.[65]

President Bush's speech raised much speculation about a US plan for regime change in Iran. Resorting to the "ethnic card" in Iran, an American intelligence officer suggested that "poking ethnic issues could bring down the whole regime in a spectacular fashion."[66] Even prominent American scholars such as Bernard Lewis implicitly claimed that when Iranians saw Americans invading Iraq they would urge them to "come this way please"[67] – that is, "liberate us too." Washington began to repeat its charges that Iran was opposing the Arab-Israeli peace process, engaging in international terrorism, violating democratic and human rights, and developing nuclear weapons. Of these four charges, the last has remained the most significant one, raising the level of tension and hostility between the two states.

As Abrahamian rightly observes, from the American point of view two issues of democratic and human rights as well as Iran's involvement in terror were more "polemical and peripheral" in nature. The US remained silent and indifferent during Iran's reign of terror during the 1980s and never raised public objections over assassinations of exiled Iranian opposition leaders. Ironically, America's reaction to Iran's violations of human rights began post-1997, when Iran's behavior had dramatically improved thanks to the election of President Khatami. Similarly, there is not much hard evidence supporting Iran's involvement in anti-American terrorist activities. With the exception of Iran's support for Lebanon's Hezbollah, and insignificant aid to Hamas and Islamic jihad, Iran's role in the Arab-Israeli peace process has been marginal.[68]

The international situation following 9/11 thus put an end to Iran's efforts to normalize foreign relations. Khatami's "dialogue among civilizations" lost its momentum following Bush's "axis of evil" speech, which placed Iran among rogue states. It then became obvious that, contrary to the hopes raised by the reformists, Khatami's discourse and foreign policies could not provide the Islamic Republic with security and stability. Likewise, for the hardliners, Khatami's discourse no longer served as a safety valve for protecting the entire regime from international pressures. The strategy of regime change implemented in neighboring Afghanistan and Iraq, together with escalating tensions over Iran's nuclear program, created a renewed concern with national security and helped the hardliners consolidate their power by splitting the reformists and marginalizing their agenda for democratic transition. American foreign policy under the neoconservative-dominated Bush administration contributed to the rise of Iran's neoconservatives as a mirror image. Bush rejected Khatami's proposal in May 2003 for a comprehensive compromise with the US. The American neoconservatives believed that they were winning the war in Iraq and that Iran would be the next target. The Bush administration declined the proposal, and the State Department even reprimanded the Swiss ambassador for conveying the Iranian proposal.

The structure of international power has profoundly contributed to the radicalization of Iran's domestic and foreign policies in three interrelated ways: First, the post-9/11 world order – Bush's discourse and policy of "regime change" and "axis of evil" – weakened Iran's reformists and empowered the hardliners. Second, the conservative hardliners were quick to take advantage of global politics to pursue Iran's revisionist regional and international policies. Because of US military actions, Iran's most dangerous enemies in the East, the Taliban in Afghanistan, and Saddam Hussein of Iraq to the West, made way for pro-Iranian regimes and movements, including, in the case of Afghanistan, the Karzai government, the Northern Alliance and the former governor of Herat, Ismail Khan. In Iraq, Iran has successfully established close ties with the Shi'ite community – notably, the Islamic Dawa Party, the Supreme Council for the Islamic Revolution in Iraq, a radical cleric Muqtada al-Sadr, and the United Iraqi Alliance of Ayatollah Sistani – as well as both major Kurdish parties, the PUK (Patriotic Union of Kurdistan) and the KDP (Kurdistan Democratic Party). Furthermore, the difficulty Americans faced in Iraq was part of the reason why the conservative hardliners in Iran felt confident enough to take unprecedented risks in the 2005 presidential elections. Third, as will be discussed later, the impact of world politics in radicalizing Iran's nuclear policy was profound. Iran under Khatami continued to talk to the UK, France, and Germany (the EU3) and suspended its nuclear enrichment for two years (2003–5). But the effort never led the US, as Iran expected, to abandon its regime change policy and lift economic sanctions. Only in December 2007 did the US National Intelligence Estimate (NIE) announce that Iran had suspended its nuclear weapons program in 2003. But Iran's hardliners had already seized the moment to radicalize nuclear policy, defeat the reformists and elect a hardliner, Mahmoud Ahmadinejad, as president, in 2005.

The Ahmadinejad era (2005–13): rhetoric and radicalism

The 2005 presidential election marked the beginning of a new era in the Islamic Republic of Iran: an era of neoconservative Khomeinism, which was consolidated in June 2009 with Ahmadinejad's disputed re-election. He was promoted by the office of the *Faqih*, the state-security apparatus, and Iran's neoconservatives – a group of young members of Islamic Revolutionary Guards Corps cultivated in the post-war period. Iran's neoconservatives aspire to revive the social base of the regime among the urban and rural Poor, which became eroded in the post-Khomeini era. The president of the fourth republic speaks about distributive social justice, promises to fight Iran's new class of mafia-like rentiers, the clerical noble-sons (*agha-zadeh ha*), and assures the Poor that he will bring the "oil money to their table." Ahmadi-nejad's slogans may sounds like progressive social radicalism rather than regressive conservatism. However, the reality is that his social conservatism and neoliberal socio-economic policies have been costumed with his populist discourse and rhetoric of social justice. Moreover, the irony is that neo-conservative Khomeinists are blessed by the state rents and shadow economy run by the revolutionary foundations controlled by the office of the *Faqih*.[69]

Like the Shah's regime, the Islamic Republic remains a rentier state and derives its major financial power, not from citizen's tax, but mainly from pet-rodollars and oil resources. The regime has used this power, making the state a domain dominated by particular rent-seeking interests and imposing certain policies and importing certain goods to buy loyalty and organize antidemo-cratic groups. The rentier state has produced, to use Milovan Djilas's classic concept, a "new class" of *agha-zadeh ha*, which continues to enjoy its privi-leged position in the political domain. Ahmadinejad's populist discourse and his rhetoric of social justice are instrumental in serving his pragmatist purpose, i.e., to replace the old oligarchy with a new one and to establish a populist, centralized state backed by the lower classes and sponsored by petrodollars. For this reason, his government has spent the oil revenue with the intention of absorbing popular votes for the 2009 presidential election and the 2012 par-liamentary elections.[70] It has also been accused of having distributed $720 million interests of *saham-e edalat* (justice shares) among some particular sections of the society shortly before the controversial 2009 presidential election.[71]

It is widely believed that with the rise of Iran's neoconservatives to power the Islamic Republic's social base may be shifting from a *mulla* – merchant coalition – to the predominance of revolutionary security and military forces. For the first time, a Khomeinist (ex)military man and – since the short administration of Abu al-Hasan Banisadr (1980–81) – not a Khomeinist reli-gious scholar is the president of the Republic. The conservatives, in spite of their internal conflicts, have gained complete control, and the absolute rule of the supreme leader, Khamenei, in internal, regional and global matters seems at hand.

Iran's pragmatic approach to foreign policy was severely undermined in the aftermath of 9/11 when George Bush applied the term "axis of evil" to Iran, Iraq, and North Korea. Iranian hardliners – conservatives, or principlists (*osul gerayan*) – exploited America's foreign policy. What followed was the rise of "a security state" in which most members of the regime took on a hardline stance in order to criticize Khatami's foreign policy measures for being weak, naive, and ultimately ill-suited to serve Iran's external interests. As a result, Iran's 2005 presidential election ended with hardline conservative forces seizing power. Ahmadinejad's cabinet consisted of "military, intelligence, security and prison administration" backgrounds.[72] The subsequent domestic policies advocated by Ahmadinejad had a strong anti-American stance, which was to be advanced at the expense of undermining freedom of the press and weakening civil society. It is thus plausible to assert that Bush's policy "contributed to the domestic triumph of radicalism and resurgence of an anti-Western foreign policy stance" that made Ahmadinejad the winner.[73]

The two key US responses to 9/11 – the invasion of Afghanistan and then of Iraq – were major watersheds in the Middle Eastern political landscape. They had a profound impact on security concerns of the countries in the region, including Iran, which embarked on establishing new roles.[74] In 2004, it was geographically surrounded by American troops occupying Afghanistan and Iraq and the US military presence in the Arab monarchies to the south and the former Soviet republics to the north.

When Ahmadinejad took office in this climate of insecurity, he hoped to establish a "balance between 'regionalism' and 'globalism'."[75] During his first term, Iran's international objective was to further solidify its economic and political relations with the EU. The success of this effort was evident when Iran became "a willing supplier of energy to Europe and welcome[d] European investment."[76] Concurrently, Iran aimed to undermine America's offensive policies, which became increasingly more vocal and threatening because of Iran's controversial nuclear program and the economic and military aid it provided to Shi'ite groups. Strengthening its ties with Europe also gave Iran a means to "avoid [having to face] a US-EU united front."[77] Although the US and the EU shared general policy positions in regard to Iran's nuclear endeavors, Iran increased its efforts to strengthen its relationship with EU members.[78] The EU in return adopted a rather mixed policy approach towards Iran. On the one hand, it criticized the nuclear program, at least on the surface, and offered economic and political incentives to refrain from developing nuclear weapons. On the other hand, the EU members, apart from the UK, welcomed the policy of countering American hegemony in the region as "a staunch critic of US interventionism in the Middle East."[79]

In the aftermath of the US occupation of Iraq, the Shi'ite groups there received Iran's moral, military, and economic aid. Iran's regional influence reached the point that "the entire fate of the US efforts to stabilize Iraq and a peaceful transition to power rested on Iranian intentions."[80] Some of these groups, such as the Mahdi Army and the Dawa Party, grew politically and competed in the country's national election.[81] Consequently, the Arab states of the Persian Gulf grew increasingly concerned. As Hunter points out, the relationship between Iran and the Arab states has "historically been [and continues to be] characterised by competition, deep-rooted mutual suspicions and misgivings."[82] The Arab states interpret Iran's involvement in regional developments and its sympathy with liberation movements and/or Shi'ite groups as part of its persistent drive to achieve supremacy in the region (a desire that pre-dates the 1979 Revolution) and the ongoing ideological and Shi'ite-oriented nature of the Islamic Republic.

Iran also sought to reinforce its partnership with Syria to advance their shared effort to undermine US presence in Iraq. Iran gave its full support to Syria in the aftermath of US political pressure on the latter to assume accountability for its alleged involvement in the assassination of Lebanese Prime Minister Rafiq Hariri. The result of that was a joint effort by Iran and Hezbollah "to rebuff pressure against the Syrian regime."[83] Iran supported Syria, and in return, Syria gave Hezbollah arms and economic support, demonstrating the existence of a triangular alliance to resist the activities of US and its Arab allies. Iran's partnership with Syria and Hezbollah has subsequently grown stronger. For example *Al-Ahram Weekly* reports that Iran's investment in Syria reached an estimated $3 billion by the end of 2008.[84]

Iran's generous financial and military support to Hezbollah has also increased significantly in the aftermath of 9/11 and the 2003 invasion of Iraq. This helped Hezbollah to successfully resist the Israelis in the 2006 war, which makes it apparent that Ahmadinejad's government has had the backing of the supreme leader, Ayatollah Khamenei, and has restored Khomeini's foreign policy agenda and shares Khomeini's revolutionary ideological strategies, including the aspiration to facilitate the "popular mobilization and the spread of revolution outside of Iran's borders."[85]

Nuclear Iran? Regional and global impact

Iran's nuclear program, begun under the Shah's regime in the early 1970s, was interrupted by the Revolution and war and was revived only in the early 1990s. The international power structure contributed greatly to the revival. All US intelligence agencies have declared that the weapons component of the program was dropped in 2003 and has not been resumed. The US is not the world's single hegemon, although some observers thought for a while that it had attained that status. However, the US is by far more powerful militarily than any other country and continues to play a central role in world politics. US policy in the Middle East rests on three pillars: the priority of stability over democracy for allied regimes like that of, say, the Saudis – previously – Mubarak of Egypt, or the Shah of Iran; the security, survival and regional superiority of Israel; and the free flow of oil – except sometimes in the case of regimes that resist the Center. US policy vis-à-vis Iran is no exception to this. The current policy of the West, including the US, towards the nuclear issue provides a case in point. A nuclear-armed Iran – or to some extent even one with a level of nuclear technology that would allow it to weaponize at a later date, the so-called "Japanese option" – would shift the balance of power in the region. It would end Israel's nuclear monopoly that allows it to act with a large degree of impunity. It would probably foster a nuclear arms race with other countries in the region and encounter the hostility of the five permanent members of the UN Security Council. Despite all the virulent rhetoric (such as the prediction that the regime ruling Jerusalem will eventually vanish from the pages of time, repeatedly mistranslated in the Western media as a threat to "wipe Israel off the map"), the Islamic Republic knows that a nuclear attack against Israel or the US would be suicidal. A nuclear-armed Iran would not constitute an existential threat to the West or Israel. Instead, it would counterbalance the dominant nuclear regime. Hence, putting aside the rhetoric, it seems that stability/status quo of the hegemonic position of Israel and the US in the region remains the driving force for US and Israeli policy towards Iran, and many Israelis feel that without the absolute security provided by their nuclear weapons monopoly the Zionist project would decline in the face of decreased immigration and increased emigration.

The rationale for Iran's nuclear policy is threefold: First, Iran is a major regional power and seeks to be on the cutting edge of science, specifically nuclear technology. This is a matter of national prestige. Second, Iran is the home of the world's third largest oil reserves – not including less desirable or less easily extracted oil in Canada and Venezuela – and the second largest gas reserves. Yet, thanks to the targeted economic sanctions by the West, the oil and gas industry has not developed, and the country is currently importing a great deal of refined oil. Iran sees nuclear power as an alternative source of energy. Third, according to Abrahamian, like Japan, Iran is interested in a "full nuclear cycle," not for making bombs but for the "option of having it." Iran is not the only country to pursue this right; there are about 30 countries in the world that hold to the "Japanese option." The goal is to protect national security, and the rationale is deterrence.[86] On a legal level, the Non-Proliferation Treaty recognizes that the development of nuclear energy for peaceful purposes is an "inalienable right."

Three major factors contribute to Iran's national security concern: First, there is the eight-year Iran–Iraq war (1980–88), started by Iraq – following provocative talk about exporting the Islamic Revolution – and backed by Western countries and their Arab client regimes. Since war and peace were "imposed" on Iran, the authorities planned to ensure the very survival of the state, pushing for the revival of the nuclear program. Second, Iran is surrounded by nuclear powers, including Russia, Pakistan, India, China, and Israel, not to mention the US itself, given the existence of American bases in many neighboring countries, e.g. Azerbaijan, Turkey, Iraq, Afghanistan, Saudi Arabia and elsewhere in the Persian Gulf and in former Soviet republics such as Georgia and Uzbekistan. Third, Bush's "axis of evil" speech in 2002, the quick American invasion of non-nuclear Iraq, the hesitancy to invade a nuclear North Korea, and the continued policy and/or discourse of regime change have contributed to the radicalization of Iran's nuclear position. The recent case of military intervention in Libya to overthrow Gaddafi evoked the compelling conclusion that had he continued to develop his own deterrent rather than dismantling his nuclear program in 2003 the Libyan leader would have been insulated from such outside action.

Neither Iranian nor American politics is monolithic. In both countries the authorities share common concerns about national security, yet differ in approaches. In the US, liberals, conventional conservatives and neoconservatives are divided on how to deal with the question of Iran. The "regime change" idea is pursued mainly by the neoconservatives, many of whose leading spokespeople belong to think-tanks such as The American Enterprise Institute and the Project for the New American Century and were securely established in the Pentagon and to a lesser degree in the White House during the younger Bush's administration. Unlike their fellow conventional conservatives, they do not distinguish between factions inside Iranian politics and are determined to undo the loss of an important client regime in the 1979 Revolution.

Similarly, Iranian authorities, in spite of their common concern for the survival of the revolutionary regime, are divided on how to pursue this goal. For the reformists, the strategy of "regime change" in general, and the American opposition to Iran's nuclear program in particular, have no military solution and must be confronted at once with democracy at home and diplomacy abroad. Security and democracy are interconnected, and democratization will ensure the security and survival of the state. They worked with Europe, Russia and Japan to undermine US efforts to isolate Iran, slowed down military programs in return for good relations with Europe, allowed more inspections, and signed an additional protocol to assure the UN that Iran's nuclear program is peaceful.

By contrast, for the conservative hardliners, the nuclear issue, like the American hostage crisis and the Iran–Iraq war, serves as a pretext to dismantle reforms and reverse the democratic wave. Liberalization and democratization, the hardliners believe, provide Americans with the best opportunity to overthrow the Islamic Republic. Not all the reformists have been strong enough to counter the anti-American rhetoric: some have been "won over," some have practiced "self-censorship," some "put the issue of reform on the back burner," and only a few continue to fight for both democracy and national integrity.[87]

Kenneth Waltz, a renowned scholar of the neorealist approach (which emphasizes that the constant pursuit of power is dictated by the nature of the international system, unlike traditional realists, who attribute it to the malevolence of human nature), recently argued that "Iran should get the bomb" because "nuclear balancing means stability."[88] A nuclear Iran would contest Israel's nuclear monopoly in the Middle East, bringing nuclear balance of power that would stabilize the region. Waltz correctly argues that, "despite a widespread belief to the contrary, Iranian policy is made not by 'mad mullahs' but by perfectly sane ayatollahs who want to survive just like any other leaders."[89] Moreover, he contests the fear of an arms race in the region should Iran get a bomb:

Should Iran become the second Middle Eastern nuclear power since 1945, it would hardly signal the start of a landslide. When Israel acquired the bomb in the 1960s, it was at war with many of its neighbors. Its nuclear arms were a much bigger threat to the Arab world than Iran's program is today. If an atomic Israel did not trigger an arms race then, there is no reason a nuclear Iran should now.[90]

Waltz's realist approach is matched by his ethical concern, as he advises the US and its allies to pursue diplomacy with the Iranian state and lift economic sanction, let alone war and military intervention:

The United States and its allies need not take such pains to prevent the Iranians from developing a nuclear weapon. Diplomacy between Iran and the major powers should continue, because open lines of communication will make the Western countries feel better able to live with a nuclear Iran. But the current sanctions on Iran can be dropped: they primarily harm ordinary Iranians, with little purpose.[91]

Waltz's position on this matter is compelling for a region in which one state – Israel – already has nuclear weapons and cannot realistically be expected to give them up. An Iranian nuclear capacity could create a counterbalance – a "balance of terror" – that would prevent either of the rivals from acting from impunity, as has been the case with Israel. In a better world, the appropriate compromise would be a nuclear-free zone for the Middle East (allowing for a balance of power at a less dangerous level, with only conventional weapons), but only a utopian would think of that as a real alternative at the moment – and might actually be more feasible in response to a future Israeli–Iranian nuclear balance of terror. The US and other Centers nations could impose such a nuclear-free region if they were determined to do so, but the overwhelming influence of pro-Israeli forces in the US today makes this almost unimaginable in the foreseeable future.

The Green Movement and realpolitik

Iran's pro-democracy Green Movement, formed in the aftermath of the disputed presidential election of June 12, 2009 provides a clear example of a revolt of part of the periphery against the center in the Periphery, although in this case the center in the Periphery has broken its ties with the Center and is challenging its hegemony.

The post-election revolt demonstrated a serious political conflict between the reformist elite and the conservatives. However, the revolt was much deeper and broader than an intra-elite conflict. It was truly a *social movement*, a revolt of periphery against center. This needs clarification: first, the Green Movement is largely, but not exclusively, a middle class movement. This is evident in the slogans, discourse, and methods of participation. However, this is still a movement of the periphery, as the middle class and even the upper middle class are deprived of political and economic power. Second, it is true that the regime still enjoys a degree of support from the Poor in the rural and urban areas. Nevertheless, the Poor are no longer the main social base of the regime. As mentioned earlier, the Islamic Republic is ruled by a new class of oligarchs consisting of the security apparatus, the high-ranking clerics, and top merchants supported by the state. Third, Iran's more than four million wageworkers – excluding the salaried middle class[92] – have remained relatively ineffective in recent pro-democracy movement. This is largely due to the state's strict control over all labor organizations and the reformists' inability to communicate with the working class. However, the current economic crisis and the failure of Ahmadinejad's populist socio-economic policies have disappointed the middle class Poor and the working class. The Poor may not have yet actively participated in the movement, but it is no longer the backbone of the regime. Fourth, although significant in number and well educated, the youth and women remain a part of the periphery in Iran's political structure. It is estimated that a million young men and a million young women attend universities. The under 30s constitute almost two-thirds of Iran's 75 million people and have remained the most vulnerable to unemployment, inflation, and economic instability. They are disappointed with the socio-economic and cultural policies of the state and constitute the backbone of the Green Movement.[93]

The response of the center of the Center to this movement has a profound impact on both periphery and center in the Periphery. More specifically, international politics continues to play a significant role in the future success or failure of the current pro-democracy Green Movement. On the one hand, the main casualty in the event of an American and/or Israeli military collision with Iran would be the latter's democratic movement, while, ironically, the US and Israel would enhance popular support for the current regime.

The Iranian youth are disenchanted with socio-cultural policies and dissatisfied with the economic situation. Yet they are looking for an Iranian solution to such Iranian problems. The US "would be making a huge mistake if it concluded that these young Iranians are automatic allies of the West."[94] On the other hand, a real challenge for a legitimate democratic opposition is to balance the national interest with international opportunities by learning how to fight for democracy and national sovereignty while working within boundaries imposed by the World System.

Democratization in Iran encounters three conflicting interests/priorities of three different parties. The main concern of the Islamic Republic is survival, while the priority of the global hegemon is to maintain its own hegemony. And the key demands of most Iranians are good governance, social justice, and representative government, i.e., a pragmatic definition of democracy. Hence, the Green Movement is caught between a rock and a hard place – between an authoritarian repressive local regime and a hegemonic global order guided by realpolitik.

Iran and the "Shi'ite Crescent": the clash of cultures or geopolitics?

The "Shi'ite Crescent" is a politically motivated concept coined by King Abdullah II of Jordan in December 2004. King Abdullah of Saudi Arabia reinforced this notion, and then-President Mubarak of Egypt even claimed that Shi'ite communities in the Arab world are more loyal to Iran than to their own countries. He argued, for example, that "Iran has an influence over Shia who makes up 65 per cent of Iraq's population."[95] The alleged Shi'ite Crescent comprises Iran, Iraq, Syria, Hezbollah in Lebanon, and Hamas in the Gaza Strip – all of whom challenged the interest of the status quo axis made up of the US, Israel, and conservative Arab regimes. This implies that Iran plays a central role in the Shi'ite Crescent mobilizing Shi'ite communities and exploiting their socio-political grievances along sectarian fault-lines to secure its own regional dominance.

The discourse of a Shi'ite Crescent and the consequent "Shiaphobia" seem problematic for a number of reasons. First, Hamas is not a Shi'ite movement, and Iran is not the single advocate of Hamas in the region. Hamas is a Sunni organization, an outgrowth of the Palestinian Muslim Brotherhood, and receives significant financial support from Saudi Arabia and Qatar. Moreover it now has distanced itself from Syria and Iran by siding with the Syrian Sunni Islamist opposition, Turkey, Egypt, and other conservative Arab (and Sunni-dominated) countries. This partial defection from alliance with Iran is not based on a cultural and religious fault-line (Sunni–Shi'ite divide). Instead, it is clearly a political and strategic choice in the context of changing geopolitics of the region. Like other political actors, Hamas and Iran shift their political alliances over time based on their political interests.

Second, members of the Alawite subsect of the Shi'ites dominate the Syrian regime but its adherents constitute no more than 13 per cent of the population, while several factors make the "sectarian" explanation of the Iranian–Syrian alliance problematic. With influences of Christianity and various other beliefs that could under different circumstances put them outside the pale of Islam incorporated among their doctrines, the Alawites represent such an unorthodox form of Shi'ism that only recently – whether representing greater ecumenicalism or simply political opportunism – has this group been accepted by mainline Shi'ite scholars as a part of their own branch of Islam. And while the Assads rely on a network of Alawite families and a broader Alawite population that fear a future radical Sunni regime that might be motivated by both religious intolerance and retribution against them for supporting the current rulers, the Ba'athist ideology of the Syrian government ironically represents secularism and the idea of one Arab nation without sectarian distinction. Finally, there is much reason to believe that Damascus would have dropped its alliance with Tehran and made peace with Israel long ago had it been able to recover the Golan Heights peacefully.

Third, the Iraqi case is equally problematic, as it simply overlooks divisions among the Shi'ites and Sunnis, and the alliance between Shi'ite Arabs and

Sunni Kurds in post-Saddam Iraq. It ignores the US role in the country and underestimates the Turkish and Saudi factors in the ongoing crisis in Iraq.[96] The Shi'ite Prime Minister, Nouri al-Maleki, and the Shi'ite cleric Muqtada al-Sadr hardly would sit at the same table. Moreover, President Jalal Talibani, a Kurdish Sunni Muslim, is a friend of Iran, while Ayad Allawi, the leader of the opposition and the opponent of Iran's role in Iraq, is a Shi'ite Muslim. Interestingly, the Saudi regime, the champion of Sunni Islam in the region, supports Ayad Allawi, a secular Shi'ite! Besides, despite Iran's advice, Muqtada al-Sadr joined a supra-sectarian coalition with Ayad Allawi to defend Iraq's national interests. Iraqi Shi'ites are not proxies of the Iranian regime; they are first Iraqis and then Shi'ites. Take the following case, for example: In early and late October 2012, the Iraqi Shi'ite government ordered two Iranian cargo planes heading to Syria to land in Baghdad to ensure that they were not carrying weapons to Syria.[97] One wonders about the reality of the alleged Shi'ite Crescent when the Shi'ite Iraqi government searches two cargo planes of the Shi'ite Iranian government to ensure that the Syrian Shi'ite government dose not receive weapons to fight Sunni rebels. The simple point is that political interests and geopolitics most often prevail over abstract religious fault-lines. Furthermore, there has been conflict among the Sunni organizations in Iraq, for example between "Awakening Councils" and al-Qaeda of Mesopotamia. The American invasion, in sum, has profoundly contributed to sectarian politics in Iraq, and Iran has clearly gained more influence in the region. Iran has pursued a policy of engagement with Iraq to strengthen economic and political ties to prevent another war with Iraq.

Fourth, both Pakistan, a Sunni majority state with some 30 million Shi'ites, and India, a secular state with some 15 million Shi'ites are completely ignored in this analysis. There is not much hard evidence supporting Iran's interference in the internal affairs of Shi'ite communities in Pakistan and India to expand its influence in South Asia. Likewise, the Shi'ites in these countries have not picked Iran's interests over their national interests.

Fifth, the Lebanese Hezbollah arguably is the strongest component of the so-called Crescent in the Arab world, and yet the usual discourse misrepresents some facts about the nature and aims of this organization: Iran did play a central role in the creation of Hezbollah, but it was not a coincidence that the organization rose in response to the Israeli invasion of Lebanon in 1982. The ongoing alliance between Hezbollah and Iran is a reality. However, as Hassan-Yari observes,

> It appears that the Hezbollah's interest is limited in scope and mainly to the Lebanese national territory and rhetorically to the Gaza Strip. Sunni and Shia Arabs see Hezbollah as the only credible military force that resisted and defeated Israel's military power. The unprecedented growing sympathy for Hezbollah among Arabs worries the rulers of Sunni Arab countries who are often seen as docile tyrants incapable of saying no to Americans and Israelis. In other words, in the absence of strong Arab

regimes the paramilitary organizations like Hezbollah fill the vacuum, by default.[98]

Six, it is interesting that Bahrain, a country with 75 per cent Shi'ite population but ruled by an autocratic Sunni minority elite, is not included in the Shi'ite Crescent. Bahrain is excluded because its regime is a conservative Arab one allied with the West and the home to the US Fifth Fleet in the region. Likewise, Shi'ite communities in other conservative Arab countries, particularly in Saudi Arabia, are marginalized and do not enjoy full religious, cultural, and socio-political rights. Hence, "by insisting on the fabricated idea of Shia Crescent, the Arab rulers deepen the suspicions in their own societies and encourage sectarianism."[99] The Shi'ites in Bahrain and Saudi Arabia are not proxies of the Iranian regime. Like Saudi Arabia, Iran is a major regional power, aiming to expand its regional influence. This might include supporting Shi'ite communities in the region. However, the point is that the Arab client regimes use the overstated threat of Iran to silence the local legitimate demands for political reform in their countries. In the past few years, Human Rights Watch has harshly criticized Saudi Arabia and Bahrain for torture of their Shi'ite citizens and blatantly discriminatory policies against Shi'ites.[100]

Last but not least, the discourse about the Shi'ite Crescent implies that the religious mind provides the superior explanatory factor for the Muslim politics. It undermines the complex network of economic and political factors in international relations. It reduces the political into some constructed religious fault-lines and reinforces the Orientalist discourse. We argue that religion and cultural values are often politicized to serve the interests of global and regional power. In many cases geopolitical interests overshadow religious values. Realpolitik bypasses and trumps cultural fault-lines.[101] Post-revolutionary Iran is a case in point: Iran and Iraq, the two greatest Shi'ite-majority countries fought over eight years (1980–88). Iran never challenged Russia over the violation of basic rights of the Chechen Muslims, nor did it defend the rights of Muslims in East China. Iran has overlooked, to say the least, a systemic killing of several thousands of Muslims in the current crisis in Syria. In the territorial dispute between Armenia and Azerbaijan over Nagorno-Karabakh in the 1990s, Iran sided with Armenia, not with the Shi'ites in Azerbaijan. And the Shi'ite political authorities in Iran killed, imprisoned, and suppressed the ordinary Shi'ite population of their own country during the 2009 pro-democracy movement. Hence like other states, the Islamic Republic most often picks its immediate political interests over some abstract shared cultural and religious values.

Iran, in sum, has evidently expanded its regional influence in the post 9/11 period, particularly in the post-Saddam era. The cardinal question is whether and how the concept of Shi'ite Crescent is capable of explaining the complex picture of politics in the region. We argue that this concept overemphasizes sectarianism and religious fault-lines (the Sunni–Shi'ite divide). It oversimplifies the nature of conflicts and cooperation. It overlooks the intention of the political elites who coined and constructed this concept. It singles out Iran as the unique and immediate threat in order to avert attention from other matters. Like Saudi Arabia, Turkey and other regional powers, Iran has used religion, ideology and ethnicity to maximize its political interests. However, the big elephant in the room is that the discourse about the Shi'ite Crescent is used as an excuse to ignore the legitimate socio-political rights of the "forgotten Muslims," or the "Arab Shias."[102] It serves as an ideological tool to suppress the Shi'ite communities under the rule of Arab client regimes.

Iran and the Arab Spring: declining or increasing influence?

Iran's foreign policy has been relatively popular among the common people (i.e., periphery in the Periphery) of the Middle East – particularly in Palestine, Lebanon, and Egypt – because it openly opposes Zionism and client regimes (the center in the Periphery) and US foreign policy in the region and supports the Palestinian cause. "This is so despite the fact that the mainstream Arab media and politicians portray Iran as a non-Arab, Shia threat to the Sunni Arab world."[103] However, "the majority [in the predominantly Sunni Arab world] is critical of the role of Iran in Iraq" and sees Iraq under Shi'ite leadership as a "battleground for the US and Iran to settle their differences."[104]

The June 2009 Green Movement in Iran changed popular perception of Iran's foreign policy in the region. As Dr Elaheh Rostami-Povey's field research demonstrates, "the secular left, nationalists and Islamists" in the region have raised questions about the brutality of the Islamic Republic in suppressing peaceful demonstrations and "feel they cannot trust a regime that is not accountable to its own people." Nonetheless, they are also sceptical of the support of the West, Israel and the conservative Arab regimes for Iran's pro-democracy movement and are "wondering whether this is an attempt to destabilize Iran." For this reason, the popular support in the region for the pro-democracy movement in Iran is "limited." Likewise, Iran's pro-democracy movement has not actively supported "the movements in the region on the ground that the anti-imperialist and anti-Zionist position is monopolized by the [Iranian] state."[105] Thus Iran's revolutionary Islamism has begun to lose its credibility and popularity among Muslims in recent years. "In the eyes of many people in the region, Turkey – a secular state [if now with an Islamic face], supporting Palestinians – is replacing Iran."[106] Moreover, Turkey under the Justice and Development Party (AKP) is seen as a modern and moderate Islamic alternative to radical Islamism and to autocratic secular nationalism. During and after the Arab Spring in 2011, many began to sympathize with the Turkish model rather than with Iran's revolutionary Islamism. Furthermore, while Turkey clearly supports opposition forces in Syria, Iran's regional policy in support of Bashar al-Assad in the ongoing uprising undermined Iran's popularity.

Syria has become a battleground for two different forces in the region. On the one hand, the West, the conservative Arab states (particularly Saudi Arabia and Qatar), Turkey under the AKP, a post-revolutionary Egypt under

Muslim Brotherhood leadership, and, interestingly, Hamas are siding with the revolutionary opposition. On the other hand, Russia, China, Iraq, Hezbollah and Iran support the Assad regime. As Vali Nasr argues, "Washington has seen the developments in Syria as a humiliating strategic defeat for Iran." While Iran remains a significant player in the Syrian crisis, the West and its allies have excluded it from any diplomatic role in the matter. The Obama administration fears that such involvement "would throw Tehran a lifeline and set back talks on Iran's nuclear program." However, while Iran is unable to desert Assad, saving him seems not to be possible either. Iranian political elites are deeply divided on whether to terminate their "unwavering support." Iran would certainly like to participate in diplomatic discussions in order to look after the interests of Syrian Shi'ites, including Alawites, and especially in order to rebuild its "damaged prestige in the Arab world" for the post-Assad era.[107]

Iran's policy towards the Arab Spring deserves a closer examination. First, Iran saw the uprisings as an opportunity to expand its political influence in the region, marginalize US influence, advance its anti-Zionist policy, and develop strong ties with Islamists who would replace the pro-Western dictatorships. Second, Iran sought to win over the rising Islamist parties in these countries. Khamenei compared the Arab uprisings to the 1979 Islamic Revolution and used a new narrative of "Islamic Awakening" to underline the Islamic character of these movements. Iran's foreign policy makers probably knew that the Arab Spring – as in the case of the Iranian Revolution more than three decades earlier – was not exclusively Islamist, but rather drew participants – both Muslims and Christians – from the secular left, liberals, and nationalists, as well as religious forces (who, however, would win big victories in most of the free elections that were being demanded). There was nothing inherently Islamist in the Arab Spring. However, Iran's regional policy aimed to exploit subsequent developments. Third, an alliance with Tunisia and Egypt would provide an asset to minimize the pressures of economic sanctions against Iran and maximize support for Syria. Hence, Iran gave a warm welcome to the first president of post-revolutionary Egypt, Mohamed Morsi, in his visit to Tehran to participate in the 16th Non-Alignment Movement (NAM) summit in August 2012.

However, Morsi's opening address disappointed Iran. He clearly distanced himself from Iran's position on Syria, sided with the West and its allies, and asked Assad to step down from office. Moreover, he opened his speech with words that seemed to draw attention to the original issue dividing Muslims into sects 14 centuries ago and add salt to an old wound with greetings not just to the Prophet Mohammad but also to the four "Rightly Guided Caliphs" accepted by Sunni Muslims, as though to challenge the Shi'ite rejection of the legitimacy of the first three of these. This was probably a message both to Shi'ite Iran and to fellow Sunnis, particularly the Saudis and to the Salafis of the Nour Party in Egypt, that post-revolutionary Egypt would not accept Iran's regional hegemony. Morsi also used the concept of Arab Spring and ignored Khamenei's alternative narrative of Islamic

Awakening. The post-Arab Spring governments have many common interests with post-revolutionary Iran, but they engage in regional rivalry and are not automatically its natural allies.

Conclusion

Under the Shah's regime, Iran was a close ally of the West, acting as its major regional policeman in the Persian Gulf. Together with Saudi Arabia, Iran stood as one of the twin pillars of US influence in the region. Fitting into the Israeli "periphery doctrine" – of allying with non-Arab states in what this volume has called the "Outer Circle" of the region – it was a close ally of Israel. It was an active member of the Western security alliance in the region (CENTO) and carried out proxy intervention in Oman on behalf the West. By contrast, the 1979 Revolution brought a dramatic shift, and in the subsequent era Iran emerged as the main regional revisionist power, challenging US and Israeli hegemony and clashing with centers in the Periphery allied with the center in the Center. The rise of Iran as a major regional power, with alleged nuclear ambitions and the specter of a "Shi'ite Crescent" feared by US-aligned Arab autocrats has created new political fault-lines throughout the Middle East. This struggle has extended into political competition between Iran and the US/Israel/Saudi Arabia tacit alliance in the proxy settings of Lebanon, Palestine, Iraq and Syria. Although the pro-democracy Green Movement in 2009 brought a serious crisis of legitimacy to the regime, the Islamic Republic has remained secure and continues with its strategic aims, threatening a possible conflagration with the United States and/or Israel.

A triangular relationship among the global structure of power, the state, and social forces/movements shapes the regional and international politics of post-revolutionary Iran. Two relentless forces of global structure and state–society relations shape Iran's policies. Regional and international relations of the state are formed by interactions between the global political system from without and civil society/social movements from within. Moreover, while the role of ideas, political ideologies and cultural values in international relations is evident, it would be naive to attribute the behavior of the Iranian state to an abstract, timeless, and essentialist Islamic mindset. The state's foreign policy is shaped by many socio-economic and political factors in the contemporary world.

I have evaluated the pattern of Iran's foreign policy strategies in the first republic under the leadership of Ayatollah Khomeini and its aftermath under Supreme Leader Khamenei, as manifested in what are identified here as the second, third, and fourth republics under presidents Rafsanjani, Khatami, and Ahmadinejad, respectively. Following the 1979 Revolution, Iran sought to reassess and redesign its foreign policy agenda in a fashion that deeply reflected the ambitions of its ideological mastermind, Ayatollah Khomeini, who embarked on a policy agenda that was starkly confrontational toward both the West and the East. For Khomeini, Islam was the panacea for the ills of the world, and its application to international relations had the potential to address the "toothless" aspirations of both communism and liberal capitalism.

Although Khomeini's agenda with regard to the West was chiefly ideologically driven, his foreign policies nonetheless had aspects of compromise and fluidity. Kenneth Waltz aptly contends that all revolutions are ultimately "socialized to the international system."[108] Khomeini's Iran was no exception when he: (1) unconditionally accepted the 1988 UN Security Council Resolution 598, which called for ending the war with Iraq, because he realized that Iran might lose the war due to the support that the US and other Western countries were giving to Iraq, and (2) agreed to an arms deal with the US and Israel in an ironic turn during the Iran–Iraq war, which he justified on the ground that the country "needed arms to defend itself against Iraqi aggression."[109] It could, therefore, be argued that Khomeini laid the groundwork for Iran to adopt a foreign policy position that was both fluid and dynamic. As the ideological doctrine that became his legacy informed subsequent policy-making processes, he can be seen as the political as well as the spiritual "tutor" of post-revolutionary Iran's foreign policy makers. "The important cautionary point is that the fluidity of Iranian revolutionary politics is such that today's idealists may be tomorrow's realists and vice versa."[110]

Post-1979 Iran's foreign policy arena has illustrated both continuity and change. Khomeini's slogan – or policy – of "exporting revolution" serves as a case in point. Rafsanjani and Khatami moved away from this policy and advocated non-confrontational policies that responded to the new realities of the post-Cold War global and regional order. However, Ahmadinejad somehow returned to the confrontational approach towards the US, reviving Khomeini's famous slogan of "America cannot do a damn thing to us," (*Amrika hich ghalati nemitavanad bekonad*). The controversy over Iran's nuclear policy and its alleged regional ambitions, as well as its policy towards Israel and the US presence in the region suggests that "the post-Khomeini regime's legitimacy is almost entirely based on the Revolution and the system founded by Ayatollah Khomeini; it cannot negate Khomeini's principles without negating itself."[111] Ahmadinejad's foreign policy does not signify a radical discontinuity with Khomeini's era, but rather, is just "a re-packaging and/or re-ordering of Iran's foreign priorities given the dictates of certain national security interests."[112]

There is a dialectical interaction between domestic and foreign policy. The regional and global policies of four republics of the post-revolutionary regime reflected the domestic polices of the political elites and the dynamic of social forces in different periods. Rafsanjani took a non-confrontational approach to the rest of the world in order to reconstruct Iran economically and socio-politically after the Iran–Iraq war ended. Khatami pursued a partnership with the EU in order to address Iran's economic ills and adopted a moderate foreign policy approach based on "reduction of tensions" with the West in aiming to strengthen the rule of law and promote the freedom of the press as well as the advancement of civil society. As Chubin notes, during Khatami's era foreign policy was a "means to address domestic political problems."[113] Furthermore, President Khatami's idea of "Dialogue among Civilizations" gained recognition by the UN, declaring the year 2001 the official year of Dialogue between Civilizations. Khatami's UN speech "raised hopes for a détente" with the US.[114]

But President Bush's "axis of evil" speech in 2002 raised much speculation about a US plan for regime change in Iran. The speech shocked the reformists and contributed to the rise of Iran's neoconservatives in a number of ways. According to Ervand Abrahamian, the speech "created a mood of the past, especially of the 1953 coup," forced the hardliners to raise the flag of national security, persuaded some reformers "to put their hopes on the back burner waiting for better days," and energized "Pahlavi royalists – who dread reform and hope that ultraconservative obstinacy will bring about a revolution."[115] The World System in general and Bush policies in particular contributed to the ascendency of Ahmadinejad. This demonstrated that there is an undeniable relationship between foreign events and domestic political patterns, which inform each other in a reciprocal manner.

In the aftermath of the 2001 American invasion of Afghanistan and 2003 invasion of Iraq, the Middle Eastern states sought to reassert their political and strategic roles in the region. These events made Iran particularly insecure, as it was geographically surrounded by American troops and pro-American Arab states in the Persian Gulf. It was shown that although Iran had relatively friendlier relationships with the Arab states during the Rafsanjani and Khatami eras, these states continued to remain suspicious of Iran. As a result, they favored the continual presence of the US in the region to counter Iran's quest for regional supremacy and its desire to control the "destiny of the Persian Gulf sub-region," which had been continuous "feature[s] of Iranian foreign policy" since the Revolution.[116] The relationship between Ahmadinejad's Iran and the Arab states manifests another dimension of the way domestic developments inform foreign policy strategies and vice versa.

The concept of "exporting the revolution" acquired new dimensions during Ahmadinejad's first term in office and became more focused on regional dominance and counterbalancing US hegemony. Syria played a crucial role in the achievement of this ambition, as it was one of the few regional states which had maintained a relatively stable and friendly relationship with Iran since the Revolution. Syria's position was thus a blessing for Iran, as the region was filled with governments that saw post-1979 Iran and its ideals of revolution as a threat to their national or regime security. Hence, in the current crisis, Iran continues to defend the Assad regime, even at the cost of losing its popularity among the masses in the Arab world, undermining its previously amicable relations with Turkey and missing opportunities for a rapprochement with Egypt, Libya, and Tunisia and expanding its sphere of influence into North Africa.

The "tug of war" between Iran and the US has not ceased since the Revolution. Iran's approach to the US at times has been both confrontational (e.g. under Khomeini and Ahmadinejad) and non-confrontational (e.g. under Khatami and Rafsanjani). The foreign policy of each country in relation to the other has resembled a strategic chess game in that "wherever Iran goes, it faces the United States [and vice versa]."[117] In sum, post-revolutionary Iran has redefined and reasserted its foreign policy in response to geopolitical considerations, international developments, and the realities of pre-Cold War, post-Cold War, and post-9/11 orders. This is a testament to the complex and multidimensional aspects of Iran's post-1979 foreign policies, which have been ideologically driven, contextually contingent both on religious ideologies and on pragmatic political developments, and geopolitically motivated.

Notes

I would like to thank Navid Pourmokhtari for his help with this chapter.

1 M. Hodgson, *The Venture of Islam: Conscience and History in a World Civilization*, vol. 2: *The Expansion of Islam in the Middle Periods*, p. 293, and vol. 3: *The Gunpowder Empires and Modern Times*, Chicago and London: University of Chicago Press, 1974, p. 47.
2 M. Castells, *The Information Age – Economy, Society and Culture*, vol. 1, *The Rise of the Network Society*, Oxford: Blackwell, 1996, p. 146.
3 J. Galtung, "A Structural Theory of Imperialism," *Journal of Peace Research*, 1971, vol. 8, 81–117 (303).
4 Ibid.
5 F. Halliday, *The Middle East in International Relations*, Cambridge: Cambridge University Press, 2005, pp. 303ff.
6 Ibid., p. 304.
7 Ibid.
8 See M. Mahdavi and W. Knight, eds, *Towards the Dignity of Difference? Neither "End of History" nor "Clash of Civilizations"*, Farnham, Surrey, UK: Ashgate Publishing, 2012.
9 Halliday, *The Middle East in International Relations*, p. 319.
10 Ibid., p. 322.
11 Ibid.
12 See H. Chehabi, "The Political Regime of the Islamic Republic of Iran in Comparative Perspective," *Government and Opposition*, 2000, vol. 36, 48–70. It is worth noting that Mehdi Bazargan's short-lived interim government and Abol-Hassan Banisadr's short-lived presidency were not included in this category.
13 M. Moslem, *Factional Politics in Post-Khomeini Iran*, Syracuse, NY: Syracuse University Press, 2002, p. 143.
14 R. Ramazani, "Reflection on Iran's foreign policy: Spiritual pragmatism," *Iranian Review*, 2010, vol. 1, 56.
15 R. Khomeini, as cited in Ramazani, "Reflection on Iran's foreign policy," 56.
16 S. Hunter, *Iran's Foreign Policy in the Post-Soviet Era*, Santa Barbara, CA: Praeger, 2010, pp. 191–92.
17 A. Ehteshami and R. Hinnebusch, *Syria and Iran: Middle Powers in a Penetrated Regional System*, London and New York: Routledge, 1997, p. 42.
18 I. Salamey and Z. Othman, "Shia revival and welayat al-faqih in the making of Iranian foreign policy," *Politics, Religion, and Ideology*, 2011, vol. 12, 208.

19 Hunter, *Iran's Foreign Policy*, p. 207.
20 Cited in Salamey and Othman, "Shia revival," 209.
21 H. Chehabi, "Iran and Lebanon in the Revolutionary Decade," in H. E. Chehabi (ed.), *Distant Relations: Iran and Lebanon in the Last 500 Years*, London: I. B. Tauris, 2006, p. 229.
22 Ibid.
23 Ibid.
24 R. Ramazani, "Iran's foreign policy: Contending orientations," *Middle East Journal*, 1989, vol. 43, 210.
25 A. Adib-Moghaddam, "Islamic utopian romanticism and the foreign policy culture of Iran," in *Critique: Critical Middle Eastern Studies*, 2005, vol. 14, 280. It is worth noting that the rule of immunity for diplomats is indeed one of the oldest and one of the least violated parts of international law. However, we should keep in mind that aggression and genocide, inter alia are more severe violations of contemporary international law. Ironically, it is only recently that international law tried to ban aggression and genocide.
26 Ibid.
27 M. Ebtekar, as cited in Adib-Moghaddam, "Islamic utopian romanticism," 281.
28 Ramazani, "Reflection on Iran's foreign policy," 58.
29 S. Maloney and R. Takeyh, "Pathway to Coexistence: A New U.S. Policy toward Iran," in R. Hass *et al.*, *Restoring the Balance: A Middle East Strategy for the Next President*, Washington, DC: The Brookings Institution, 2008, p. 64.
30 Ramazani, "Reflection on Iran's foreign policy," 59.
31 Salamey and Othman, "Shia revival," 202.
32 See R. Ramazani, "Iran's foreign policy: Both north and south," *Middle East Journal*, 1992, vol. 46, 394.
33 Ibid.
34 Hunter, *Iran's Foreign Policy*, p. 192.
35 M. Dehshiri and M. Majidi, "Iran's foreign policy in post-revolution era: A holistic approach," *The Iranian Journal of International Affairs*, 2009, vol. 21, 101–14.
36 N. Hamzeh, "Lebanon's Hezbollah: From Islamic revolution to parliamentary accommodation," *Third World Quarterly*, 1993, vol. 14, 321–37.
37 H. Chehabi, "Iran and Lebanon after Khomeini," in Chehabi, ed., *Distant Relations*, p. 297.
38 Ehteshami and Hinnebusch, *Syria and Iran*, p. 135.
39 Ibid.
40 E. Rakel, "Iranian foreign policy since the Islamic revolution: 1979–2006," *Perspectives on Global Development and Technology*, 2007, vol. 6, 172.
41 A. Drenou, "Iran: Caught Between European Union – United States Rivalry?" (Ch. 5), in A. Ehteshami, and M. Zweiri, *Iran's Foreign Policy: From Khatami to Ahmadinejad*, Reading, Berkshire, UK: Ithaca Press, 2008, p. 79.
42 F. Soltani, and R. Amiri, "Foreign Policy of Iran after Islamic revolution," *Canadian Centre of Science and Education*, 2010, vol. 3, 202.
43 W. Posch, "Iran and the European Union," in Robin Wright, ed., *The Iran Primer: Power, Politics, and U.S. Policy*, Washington, DC: United States Institute of Peace Press, 2010, p. 190.
44 M. Milani, "Reform and Resistance in the Islamic Republic of Iran," in J. Esposito and R. Ramazani (eds), *Iran at the Crossroads*, New York: Palgrave Macmillan, 2001, p. 29.
45 S. Bakhash, "Iran's Remarkable Election," in L. Diamond, M. Plattner, and D. Brumberg (eds), *Islam and Democracy in the Middle East*, Baltimore: Johns Hopkins University Press, 2003, p. 119.
46 Soltani, and Amiri, "Foreign Policy," 202.
47 K. Pollack, as cited in Hunter, *Iran's Foreign Policy*, p. 192.
48 Rakel, "Iranian foreign policy since the Islamic revolution."

49 H. Chehabi, "Iran and Lebanon after Khomeini," in Chehabi, ed., *Distant Relations,* p. 301.
50 Quoted in Chehabi, "Iran and Lebanon," p. 306.
51 Hunter, *Iran's Foreign Policy.*
52 S. Chubin, *Iran's Nuclear Ambitions,* Washington, DC: Carnegie Endowment for International Peace, 2006, p. 30.
53 BBC, May 13, 1997, quoted in Ansari, *Iran, Islam, and Democracy,* p. 131.
54 L. Andersen, *Iran-EU-USA Relations: Seen through the Rushdie Affair,* London and New York: I. B. Tauris Publishers, 2001.
55 Ibid., p. 292.
56 "Interview with President Khatami," CNN, January 8, 1998. In this interview, Khatami called the 1979 American hostage crisis a "tragedy" and "excessive."
57 BBC, January 9, 1998, quoted in Ansari, *Iran, Islam and Democracy,* p. 135.
58 Barraclough as cited in Rakel, "Iranian foreign policy since the Islamic revolution," p. 179. S. Barraclough?
59 E. Abrahamian, "Empire Strikes Back: Iran in U.S. Sights," in B. Cummings et al., (eds) *Inventing the Axis of Evil: The Truth about North Korea, Iran, and Syria,* New York: The New Press, 2004, p. 93.
60 Office of the Spokesman, June 18, 1998, US Department of State; quoted in G. Sick, "The Future of Iran–US Relations," *Global Dialogue,* vol. 3, Spring/Summer 2001. URL: <http://www.worlddialogue.org/content.php?id=148> (accessed March 8, 2013).
61 "CNN Insight: U.S. Comes Clean About The Coup In Iran." URL: <http://tran scripts.cnn.com/TRANSCRIPTS/0004/19/i_ins.00.html> (accessed October 26, 2012).
62 Abrahamian, "Empire Strikes Back," p. 95.
63 G. Sick, "The Clouded Mirror: The United States and Iran, 1979–99," in Esposito and Ramazani, *Iran at the Crossroads,* p. 201.
64 G. Sick, "The Axis of Evil: Origins and Policy Implications," *Middle East Economic Survey,* vol. 45, 14 (April 8, 2002), quoted in Abrahamian, "Empire Strikes Back," p. 96.
65 Abrahamian, "Empire Strikes Back," p. 94.
66 S. Behn, "Pentagon Officials Meet with Regime Foe," *Washington Times,* June 4, 2003, quoted in Abrahamian, "Empire Strikes Back," p. 103.
67 B. Lewis, "Time for Toppling," *Wall Street Journal,* September 28, 2002; and interview with Professor Bernard Lewis, C-SPAN, December 30, 2001, quoted in Abrahamian, "Empire Strikes Back," p. 103.
68 For further discussions, see Abrahamian, "Empire Strikes Back," pp. 102–8.
69 Ahmadinejad's colleagues such as Sadeq Mahsouli, former minister of Social Welfare, and Mohammad-Reza Rahimi, Vice-President, among others, are members of the new oligarchy. The former is a billionaire real-estate broker and the latter also is a billionaire benefiting from exclusive political rents.
70 Regarding the 2012 parliamentary election, see Ahmad Janati, "Jarayan-e Enherafi baraye Entekhabat-e Majles Tarh Darad," BBC Persian, May 24, 2011. URL: <http://www.bbc.co.uk/persian/rolling_news/2011/05/110524_l03_janati_election. shtml> (accessed June 15, 2011).
71 M. Mofateh, "Paygiri-e Tozi-e Gheire Ghanooni Pool Tavasot-e Dolate Ghabl az Entekhabat 88," BBC Persian, May 25, 2011. URL: <http://www.bbc.co.uk/per sian/iran/2011/05/110525_l39_majlis_investigation_presidential_election.shtm> (accessed June 15, 2011).
72 K. Ehsani, "Iran: The populist threat to democracy," URL: <https://www.merip. org/mer/mer241/iran-populist-threat-democracy> (accessed February 7, 2013).
73 Salamey and Othman, "Shia revival," 203.
74 K. Barzegar, "Regionalism in Iran's foreign policy," *Iranian Review,* February 7, 2010. URL: <http://www.iranreview.org/content/Documents/Regionalism_in_Iran_s_ Foreign_Policy.htm> (accessed 26 October 2012).

75 Ibid.
76 Drenou, "Iran Caught Between European Union" as cited in Ehteshami and Zweiri, *Iran's Foreign Policy, 2008, p. 84.*
77 Rakel, "Iranian foreign policy since the Islamic revolution," 182.
78 Ibid.
79 Drenou as cited in Ehteshami and Zweiri, *Iran's Foreign Policy*, p. 84.
80 Salamey and Othman, "Shia revival," 203.
81 Ibid.
82 Hunter, *Iran's Foreign Policy*, p. 185.
83 Salamey and Othman, "Shia revival," 209.
84 See Hunter, *Iran's foreign policy.*
85 Salamey and Othman, "Shia revival," 203.
86 D. Barsamian et al., *Targeting Iran*, San Francisco: City Light Bookstore, 2007.
87 Abrahamian, "Empire Strikes Back," pp. 140–47.
88 K. Waltz, "Why Iran Should Get the Bomb: Nuclear Balancing Would Mean Stability," *Foreign Affairs*, 2012, vol. 91, 1–5.
89 Ibid., 4.
90 Ibid., 5.
91 Ibid.
92 H. Moghissi and S. Rahnema, "The Working Class and the Islamic State in Iran." In Stephanie Cronin, ed., *Reformers and Revolutionaries in Modern Iran: New Perspectives on the Iranian Left*, London and New York: Routledge Curzon, 2004, pp. 280–81.
93 See M. Mahdavi, "The Civil Society Approach to Democratization in Iran: The Case for Bringing it Back in Carefully," in Ramin Jahanbegloo, ed., *Civil Society and Democracy in Iran*, Lanham, MD: Lexington books, 2011, pp. 79–93. Also, see M. Mahdavi, "Post-Islamist Trends in Postrevolutionary Iran," *Comparative Studies of South Asia, Africa and the Middle East*, 2011, vol. 31, 94–109.
94 T. Ash, "Soldiers of the Hidden Imam," *The New York Review of Books*, November 3, 2005. URL: <http://www.nybooks.com/articles/archives/2005/nov/03/soldiers-of-the-hidden-imam/?pagination=false> (accessed October 26, 2012).
95 H. Mubarak, interview with the *Al-Arabia* television station, April 2006, quoted in H. Hassan-Yari, "Clashology within Islam: Not Civilizational, but Political," in Mahdavi and Knight, eds, *Towards the Dignity of Difference?*, p. 76.
96 See Hassan-Yari, "Clashology," pp. 75–76.
97 "Iraq searches Syrian-bound Iranian plane," Associated Press, October 28, 2012. URL: <http://www.foxnews.com/world/2012/10/28/iraq-searching-for-weapons-on-iranian-planes-heading-to-syria> (accessed October 28, 2012).
98 Ibid., p. 76.
99 Ibid.
100 "Denied Dignity: Systematic Discrimination and Hostility toward Saudi Shia Citizens," Human Rights Watch, September 3, 2009, URL: <http://www.hrw.org/en/reports/2009/09/03/denied-dignity-0> (accessed October 28, 2012); and "Torture Redux: The Revival of Physical Coercion during Interrogations in Bahrain," *Human Rights Watch*, URL: <http://www.hrw.org/node/88201> (accessed October 28, 2012).
101 See Mahdavi and Knight, *Towards the Dignity of Difference?*
102 G. Fuller and R. Francke, *The Arab Shia: The Forgotten Muslims*, New York: Palgrave Macmillan, 2000.
103 E. Rostami-Povey, "Iran's regional influence," in E. Hooglund and L. Stenberg, eds., *Navigating Contemporary Iran: Challenging Economic, Social and Political Perceptions*, London: Routledge, 2012, p. 190.
104 Ibid.
105 Ibid., pp. 190–91.

106 Ibid. p. 191.
107 V. Nasr, "Syria After the Fall," *The New York Times*, July 28, 2012. URL: <http://www.nytimes.com/2012/07/29/opinion/sunday/after-syrias-assad-falls-the-us-must-work-with-iran.html?_r=1> (accessed October 26, 2012).
108 K. Waltz, *Theory of International Politics*, Reading, MA: Addison-Wesley, 1979, cited in Ramazani, "Reflection on Iran's foreign policy," 57.
109 Ramazani, "Reflection on Iran's foreign policy," 58. Also see T. Parsi, *Treacherous Alliance: The Secret Dealings of Israel, Iran and the United States*, New Haven: Yale University Press, 2007.
110 See Ehteshami and Zweiri, *Iran's Foreign Policy,* p. 28.
111 Ehteshami and Hinnebusch, *Syria and Iran*, p. 55.
112 K. Afrasiabi, and A. Maleki, "Iran's foreign policy after 11 September," *The Brown Journal of World Affairs*, 2003, vol. 9, 257.
113 S. Chubin as cited in Rakel, "Iranian foreign policy since the Islamic revolution," 178.
114 Abrahamian, "Empire Strikes Back," p. 93.
115 Ibid., p. 94.
116 Ehteshami and Hinnebusch, *Syria and Iran*, p. 28.
117 H. Rowhani, as cited in Chubin, *Iran's nuclear ambitions*, p. 117.

6   Egypt

The continuing storm?

Karen Aboul Kheir

The iconic images of Tahrir Square in the 18 days that followed January 25, 2011 resonated throughout the region and beyond. The "Arab Spring" may have kicked off in Tunisia, but it was from Egypt that the process of contagion throughout the region began in earnest. This evoked once more Egypt's historical role as trend setter and regional leader. Not since the successful crossing of the Suez Canal during the 1973 war with Israel had Egyptians genuinely experienced such pride and joy in their achievements. This time their concerns were principally domestic: ending decades of oppressive and corrupt rule that had diminished all aspects of society and politics in Egypt, as well as its regional and international stature.

Just as the peaceful occupation of public spaces became a model for protest movements in several Arab countries, the Arab world followed closely how Egypt would handle its post-Mubarak transition. The choices Egypt made would have a profound regional impact, and its success in establishing a democratic, more equitable system would strengthen and inspire similar transitions in other Arab countries. The rise to power of the Muslim Brothers was viewed with trepidation by many inside Egypt as well as in other Arab countries. Would their policies change the very nature of state and society in Egypt? Would it embolden Islamist groups of various orientations in other Arab countries?

The images of Tahrir resonated outside the Arab world as well. In Spain, England and the US, protestors took to occupying public spaces to object to social inequality and the unresponsiveness of political elites to the concerns of their electorates. World System theorist Immanuel Wallerstein noted the threads linking the protests and revolts that swept so many parts of the world in 2011.[1]

The financial crisis of 2008 had brought the world capitalist system to a state of structural crisis and disequilibrium that was no longer tolerable. The system, he argued, could no longer cope with the stresses of inequality within it, which were manifesting themselves in severe and unprecedented social and political polarization and discontent.

Having been integrated into the global economy, Egypt was no exception to this situation. According to official figures for the year 2010, the poorest 40 per cent of Egyptians shared only 22 per cent of GDP, whereas the richest 20 per cent monopolized 40 per cent.[2] The millions of Egyptians that poured out into public squares all over Egypt were by and large protesting against this state of inequality and the system of governance that fostered it to benefit a narrow and corrupt elite.

There were ramifications to this crisis of the world capitalist system on the geo-political level as well. As the global economy bifurcated, with the US, Europe and Japan falling into a period of almost no economic growth, fiscal crisis and unsustainable levels of sovereign debt, the transfer of influence and power to other rising countries, such as China and Brazil, accelerated. The US was no longer able to dominate the international system created "in its image" in the wake of World War II, nor manipulate the institutions of global governance, such as the United Nations and its Security Council or the World Trade Organization. The fragmentation of power on the world scene was reflected in the inability of these organizations to achieve consensus on how to deal with crises that increasingly assumed global proportions.

Events in Egypt and the Middle East were not divorced from this new "world disorder." The post-colonial regional "map" that came into being following World War II was also put in jeopardy by the wave of protests that swept the Arab world. The "Arab Spring" represented, in the words of Rami Khouri,[3] a "Big Bang" moment for states, regimes, nations and citizens of the Arab world. Authoritarian regimes in Tunisia, Egypt and Libya were upset, their rulers ousted. The unity and territorial integrity of several states were threatened, most clearly in the case of Syria, where peaceful protest, met with brutal repression, threatened to escalate into civil war.

The "Arab Spring" further complicated a regional balance of power that was already changing. Rising non-Arab regional powers – Turkey and Iran – posed a growing challenge to Israel's position as the regional hegemon. Traditionally close ties between Turkey and Israel became strained. The small Emirate of Qatar was carving out for itself a new position by mediating various regional crises from Lebanon to Sudan. Iran aspired to spread its influence in the Arab world through alliances with the Syrian regime, Hezbollah in Lebanon and Hamas in Gaza. It was accused by Saudi Arabia of fostering domestic unrest in several Arab countries through Shi'ite minorities, and the Kingdom pushed Arab countries into an escalating state of confrontation with Iran. Egypt was remarkably conspicuous by its absence. Its regional efforts remained almost exclusively linked to Palestinian–Israeli issues, it sided with the hostile US–Saudi stance towards Iran, and viewed Turkey's rise with suspicion and resentment.

The turmoil which swept the region in 2011 and 2012 presented a challenge to these rising powers. Turkey's "zero problems" foreign policy collapsed in disarray. Iran struggled with tenacity to ensure the survival of its ally, the Assad regime in Syria. Fearful that the wave of unrest could spread further, Saudi Arabia moved to increase cooperation between the region's monarchies in order to bolster their hold on power. It did not hesitate to swiftly dispatch armed forces to its small neighbor Bahrain to crush popular protest there. The inability of the US to prevent the fall of its longtime ally Husni Mubarak signaled its decreasing influence, and to many eyes this posed a threat to the survival of US–Israeli regional hegemony. Changes in Egypt cast uncertainty on the future of US–Israeli–Egyptian coordination, as well as Egypt's "strategic commitment" to peace with Israel. Israel felt increasingly isolated as the Arab regimes that had long acquiesced to a US-led regional order toppled all around it.

Moreover, the deteriorating security conditions in Egypt following the fall of the Mubarak regime threatened to turn Sinai once more into a flashpoint for conflict. The smuggling of all forms of arms and contraband to Sinai flourished. The pipeline carrying gas to Israel and Jordan was attacked and put out of service more than a dozen times within a year. Israelis feared for their security, while Egyptians feared this state of affairs would be taken as a pretext to introduce some form of international security arrangements there. The Egyptian state's hold on Sinai seemed ever more precarious in August 2012, when a virtually unknown militant group murdered 16 Egyptian soldiers, before hijacking armed vehicles and heading across the borders into Israel, where they were promptly killed.

The newly elected Egyptian president, Muhammad Morsi, moved swiftly. He consolidated his power by removing the aged members of the Supreme Council of the Armed Forces, and putting a younger group of military commanders in charge of restoring order in Sinai. While moving a larger military contingent into the border area than the peace accords permit, Egypt's new Minister of Defense took care to contact Israeli leaders to assure them this did not imply any hostile intentions towards them. But the massive social, economic and political problems in Sinai, were the outcome of decades of mismanagement as well as of the securitization of governance in Egypt as a whole. Setting this right will require a lot more than a bigger army presence and promises of a better future. The situation is further complicated by Sinai's proximity to Gaza, under the rule of Hamas. The possible triggers of conflict, terrorist attacks and other threats to regional security remain numerous.

The wave of change sweeping the region constituted a bold challenge to the idea held by many that "only through a strategic re-imagining of the Middle East and the outside world's role in it," to be undertaken obviously by the said "outside world," can any real change be brought about in the Middle East.[4] The region that for so long had seemed immune to forces of democratization and regional integration was now swept by winds of change emanating from within. Political leaders and strategic analysts in the US and elsewhere were caught off guard, surprised not only by the scale of protests and the speed with which they spread but also by their own limited ability to influence events. Taking a stand on "the right side of history" by declaring support for Egypt's young revolutionaries was not so much a moral choice for Washington as it was a necessary adaptation to changing facts on the ground.

Despite its repeated declarations on the need to respect the human rights of protestors in Bahrain, the US could do little to prevent the naked use of force against civilians there on the part of its close allies, as much as it preferred the situation to be handled differently. NATO's intervention in Libya, as limited and relatively painless to Western powers as it was, might more realistically be regarded as the West's "last hurrah" in the region rather than as a prelude to further military involvement. There was precious little appetite among these countries to commit to any intervention in Syria, despite escalating humanitarian concerns. The US will continue for some time as an important player in Middle East politics and will attempt to shape the outcome of current developments to suit its interests, but as its economic strength and ability to lead diminish in a world of multiple poles of power, the role of regional actors will gain prominence and influence.

Veteran Egyptian diplomat Aly Maher expressed what most Egyptians hoped their country's role would be in this complex regional context: "A democratic Egypt cannot continue business as usual in its relations with the rest of the world." While Egypt should comply with every agreement, treaty and convention it had signed, as well as keep its friends, allies and partners, he argued that "no cooperation or foreign relationship should infringe on its sovereign and independent decisions.[5]

Many Arabs, and certainly most Egyptians, looked forward to a more proactive Egyptian role around which Arab countries could coalesce to redress the growing influence of non-Arab regional players.

Historical overview: Egypt's regional status

Muhammad Ali Pasha, the Ottoman commander who ruled over Egypt throughout most of the first half of the nineteenth century, has been credited with laying the foundations of the modern Egyptian state and setting the example for projecting its power into the Arabian Peninsula, Africa and the Levant. But as Khaled Fahmy's study of Muhammad Ali's reign points out, his aim was not an independent Egypt as such, but rather to establish hereditary rule for his family in the Ottoman Empire's most wealthy province while maintaining nominal allegiance to Istanbul as his legitimizing framework.[6] Fahmy tellingly quotes Muhammad Abdou, Egypt's famous nineteenth-century reforming cleric, who argued that Muhammad Ali's innovations were meant first and foremost to benefit his army and thereby enhance the strength of his dictatorial rule, as well as extend the territories under his control. He sent Egyptians to study medicine, Abdou admitted, but these doctors were not deployed throughout the country to treat the Egyptian people. They acted only in the service of the army.[7]

Muhammad Ali exploited British–French rivalry, as well as the progressive weakness of the Ottoman Empire, which lacked the capability to forcibly remove him from office, and therefore was forced to acknowledge his rule over Egypt. His regional "project" – which, at its height in the 1830s led him to send his armies through Syria and deep into Anatolia with an eye on assuming power in Istanbul itself – ended when the European great powers perceived it as destabilizing the international balance of power.

Regardless of his intentions, Muhammad Ali's innovations laid a foundation on which later rulers continued to build a modern state. Discrimination against Egyptians in his army at the hand of foreigners who monopolized the higher ranks also helped to forge a distinct national identity. In the coming decades, the military would play an important role in the quest for Egypt's independence. Following the 1952 Revolution, led by the "Free Officers," it would dominate domestic politics.

During the 1950s and 1960s, Egypt again pursued an active regional and international role, thanks to the strengthening of its centralized state under President Gamal Abdel Nasser and his skill in exploiting the bipolar international configuration of power. This regional project had a wide constituency both within Egypt and outside it, drawing on the aspirations of Egyptians, Arabs and other African nations for liberation, independence and modernity. Domestically, Nasser's project allowed a wider social spectrum to achieve a better standard of living for themselves and their children, but it did not extend to allowing active political participation by the citizenry. Relying on Nasser's political charisma, and the regime's extensive propaganda and single-party machinery, Egyptians were mobilized to support government policies, not invited to question them. This project ended through a confluence of domestic and international factors that culminated in an overwhelming defeat by attacking Israeli forces in 1967 and the subsequent occupation of Sinai. But despite this devastating defeat, the 1950s and 1960s are regarded by many in Egypt – and elsewhere – as the "Golden Era" of the country's regional influence.

Until his death in 1970, Nasser worked rigorously to rebuild Egypt's decimated army. His successor Anwar Sadat brought Egypt's regional and international standing to new heights following the Egyptian army's successful crossing of the Suez Canal into Sinai in 1973. Although Egyptian forces were not able to liberate all of the occupied Sinai, the crossing was greeted with great jubilation throughout the Arab world. However, Sadat's choice to complete the liberation of Sinai through direct US-sponsored negotiation with Israel caused Egypt to become isolated in the Arab world. The commitment he undertook that the 1973 war would be the last war in which Egypt participated was viewed as outright abandonment of Palestinian and Arab rights and as providing great strategic value to Israel. As Kissinger is reputed to have quipped, there can be no war with Israel without Egypt, but no peace without Syria. The Egyptian–Israeli peace treaty became a cornerstone for US plans to create a new Middle East into which Israel was firmly integrated and over which the US and Israel enjoyed indisputable hegemony. It was not however, instrumental in achieving a just and lasting regional peace.

During the three decades of Mubarak's rule, the regime's primary objective became the preservation of stability on both domestic and regional levels. In its regional relations, Egypt closely towed the line of US policy, maintaining cooperation with Israel and other "moderate" US allies, however unwelcome to the Egyptian people this may have been. In return for their endorsement of his hold on power, Mubarak avoided any independent foreign policy stances. Stability soon turned into stagnation, and Egypt's domestic conditions and regional and international stature suffered as a result.

Egypt's regional influence, or soft power, was never solely a function of the existence of a strong state. During the nineteenth and early twentieth centuries, Egypt enjoyed a vibrant cultural and political environment, in which ideas from the "developed" countries of Europe and from the far corners of the Islamic Ottoman Empire took hold and flourished. Country nationalism, Pan-Islamism and Pan-Arabism all had their advocates and supporters in Egypt. Egypt was the first Arab country to have a parliament, political parties, a university, a constitution, etc. Egyptian teachers, judges, lawyers and journalists historically played a central role in establishing governmental, legal, and educational and journalistic institutions throughout the Arab world.

However, stagnation and repression under Mubarak took their toll on Egypt's soft power as well. As Arab oil-producing countries amassed enormous wealth, the regional balance of "soft power" changed. The free movement of labor and capital across borders associated with globalization meant Egyptians had lost their comparative advantage in the regional labor market to cheaper Asian workers on the one hand and to executives with more global experience on the other. The deterioration of the strength and capabilities of the Egyptian state under the Mubarak regime was directly linked to the country's diminishing regional influence.

The erosion of state capacity during the Mubarak years

Many Egyptian and Arab analysts would beg to differ with the conclusion of a study by US experts that "Egypt's change in government was not the result of the country reaching a tipping point" but that the proximate cause was the demonstration effect of the ouster of the Tunisian president.[8]

Scholars had been chronicling the mounting crisis of regime capability and legitimacy well before 2011. While none could predict when Egypt would reach a "tipping point," they drew a compelling picture of how domestic, regional and extra-regional actors and forces interacted to produce this crisis. The difference between the two interpretations is significant, for if pressure for change in Egypt had not reached a "tipping point," restoration of the old regime, with some modifications, would be possible. If, on the other hand, the popular eruption indicates the complete bankruptcy of the system, attempts to revive old policies and practices will result only in more protests and upheaval.

The crisis of the post-colonial state in the Arab world explains both the events in Egypt and why upheaval spread so quickly throughout the region. It also explains why the "transition" period in many Arab countries is so difficult, almost chaotic. In the words of Rami Khouri, these societies are undergoing "a very complex set of nation-building and nation-defining dynamics compressed into a ridiculously short time."[9] In Egypt, with millennia of history as an established state, it is not the shape of its borders or its territorial unity that is being challenged, but its domestic power configuration and mode of governance. The basic outlines of the crisis of the Egyptian regime have long been in plain sight. These include: the failure to produce and implement a vision for economic and social development, the central role of military and security institutions, the concentration of power in the hands of an increasingly narrow elite, erosion of legitimacy and increasing reliance on repression, the blocking of all avenues of peaceful change from below, and the refusal of the ruling elite to undertake reform from above.

The late Egyptian intellectual, Muhammad el Sayed Sa'eed, described the grand historical context in which the repressive, autocratic political systems in Egypt, and throughout the Arab world, developed.[10] Due to deep-seated animosity in Arab society to the entire heritage of the French and British colonial powers, the post-colonial state-building process in Arab countries was heavily influenced by the Italian, German and Soviet models. Moreover, the large number of intellectuals who during the 1940s and 1950s sought to realize an "Arab enlightenment" and the revival of a glorious past perceived the achievement of these goals as possible only through the establishment of a strong centralized state.

The centrality of the army and various security apparatuses within the structure of most Arab regimes also has historical roots, according to Sa'eed. In many cases, such as in Egypt and Syria, control of military force provided the means to win successive political, factional and sectarian struggles. Power came to rest in the hands of those individuals best able to use these instruments of force against individuals or groups unwilling to profess unquestioning and complete loyalty. They guarded their position of power jealously through intricate internal security systems.

The threat from Israel compounded the need for such a security-oriented approach to governance. Israel followed a policy of strong retaliation against any country from which any acts of resistance to its occupation were carried out. Regimes fearful of being dragged into a military confrontation for which they were unprepared, or those essentially unwilling to participate in this conflict, imposed systems of close surveillance and strict controls on their societies to prevent such attacks from taking place. The escalation of regional tensions with Israel and the subsequent Israeli occupation of more Arab territories resulted in a great expansion in the size and strength of Arab armies. This made further regime change through a military coup basically unfeasible.

In order to ensure social compliance, Arab regimes required more than brutal force. They therefore subordinated the requirements of economic development to their own political ends, guaranteeing their citizens employment and a wide array of social and economic benefits. While essentially inefficient, this system was maintained for a long time through foreign assistance and borrowing, creating huge levels of external debt and a growing budget deficit. In his study of how Egyptian governments during Mubarak's years attempted to deal with a growing fiscal deficit and decreasing revenues, Samer Soliman outlined how the regime increasingly came to rely on rentier income.[11] With the failure to undergo successful economic development, a large chunk of the Egyptian regime's revenues came from the remittances of Egyptians working abroad, especially in the Arab Gulf countries, the sale of oil and gas, and income from the Suez Canal. The source of revenue it could influence most however was foreign aid, which is why soliciting aid became one of Mubarak's major activities.

The manner in which the regime reordered its spending pattern to deal with decreasing revenues illustrated its priorities, and explained the increasing deterioration of the cohesion and efficiency of the state institutions. In order to compensate for reducing its outlays to the armed forces, it granted the military establishment greater financial autonomy. Through extensive invest-ments in various areas of civil production, the army could generate resources on its own, and dispense them as it saw fit. While reducing its spending on subsidies that benefitted the Poor, it spent more on the police, domestic security and the state-controlled media propaganda machine.

Allocations to local government also shrank. Governorates were required to rely on their own resources, but they lacked the legal power to levy taxes. Instead, they were allowed to create special funds derived from various muni-cipal fees and charges, as well as from "donations" from local businessmen. This was by no means an exercise in decentralization. It was in fact a prelude to the fragmentation of the state's huge bureaucratic edifice. High levels of corruption ensued, and there was an absence of any form of oversight of the funds collected and allocated by institutions of local government.

The Egyptian regime in effect became a predator, setting income generation above all other considerations even if it wreaked havoc on the state institu-tions as well as the economy. According to Soliman, the Egyptian state was unsuccessful in increasing its revenues through further taxation because its citizens did not recognize it as legitimate. There was a complete absence of duly-elected representative political institutions, and the regime shirked the responsibility and cost of creating an efficient bureaucracy to deal with the management and generation of taxes.[12]

In explaining the deteriorating performance in the Egyptian bureaucracy, Abdel Khalek Farouq noted the complete delinking of pay, bonuses and performance in the government sector, as well as the absence of any mechanism linking compensation to rising prices and inflation.[13] Overtime, bonuses and incentives became merely a means to compensate for deteriorat-ing real income. Government pay in key sectors like education and health was in no way adequate or in proportion to the effort, duties and responsibilities required of teachers and physicians. Farouq's findings in respect to government pay to employees in the local government sector confirm Soliman's conclusions regarding the fragmentation of government structures. He notes the extremely low levels of compensations these people, who represent more than 64 per cent of total government employees, received. This unleashed an overwhelming tide of administrative and financial corruption, rendering local officials almost completely beyond oversight or control.

Decreasing pay for the majority of government workers was at the same time accompanied by high levels of inequality among employees. This increased the sense of resentment and injustice. The regime was able to sustain such unequal distribution in large part through the lack of oversight of the government's budget. According to Farouq, it had become the custom for the budget to be presented with certain stipulations that allowed the government to reassign more than a third of the allocations approved by parliament. Moreover, many items were represented as one "bloc," with no itemization. These included not only expenditures of the armed forces but also those of the two chambers of parliament, the central bureau of accounting, and the higher council of the press. In other words, the regime had ample room to compensate those who were supposed to oversee its actions and expenditures.

Furthermore, the Mubarak regime increasingly resorted to repression to consolidate its hold on power. Basma Abdel Aziz's pioneering study on the use of violence by the Egyptian police against the civilian population, first published in 2009, chronicles how brutal force was no longer an instrument used only against the regime's political opponents, but also used against ordinary citizens not involved in political or labor agitation. As early as 1986, a large group of lawyers staged a strike in response to what they claimed was persistent mistreatment at the hands of the police.[14] The police were routinely used to break up labor strikes. In the wake of attempted assassinations of senior police officers in 1987, the use of brutal force against ordinary citizens grew even more widespread.

Abdel Aziz notes a qualitative change in the attitude of the regime towards society at this point. Society now, from the regime's perspective, consisted of three distinct "groups": friends, i.e., those trusted with leadership positions and allowed to share in the spoils of power; enemies, defined as those who oppose its policies and practices and therefore become the target of heavy-handed repression; and finally the "silent majority" of the population, who went about eking out their existence, unconcerned with politics – and with whom the regime was equally unconcerned.[15]

But as regime capabilities deteriorated and the state provided less and less in social services, the life of such ordinary Egyptians grew increasingly difficult. The regime began to perceive them as a threat to its survival, a potential enemy that must be consistently cowed in order to preempt any action they might take. The use of excessive force against the ordinary people became a systematic and widespread practice as never before in Egypt's modern history. In turn, their attitude towards the police force changed. As one example,[16]

Abdel Aziz recorded seven instances of assaults by civilians on the police during a two-month period in 2009, including attacks on police stations. These incidents, which took place not only in the Delta but also in Sinai and Upper Egypt demonstrated a serious breach in the relationship between society and law enforcement agencies and a serious erosion of the regime's legitimacy. The chasm between regime and society became pronounced, to the extent that Muhammad el Sayed Sa'eed tellingly concluded in 2005 that "The very state seemed to be suspended in mid-air."[17]

In an effort to widen its social base, and to bolster itself with fresh economic and human resources, the regime tried to co-opt elements of the rising capitalist class. This group had benefitted enormously from privatization, the expanding housing market, foreign aid to promote exports, and other economic policies. This growing private sector openly exploited loopholes and cut many corners to maximize its profits. Few of those employed in this private sector enjoyed health insurance, pensions or other rights stipulated by labor laws. Employees of government agencies in charge of overseeing compliance with these rules were among the least well paid in the Egyptian government.[18] Widespread corruption allowed businesses to shirk their responsibilities. Labor unions were government-controlled. Once businessmen became part of the ruling elite, they were also able to pass laws to protect their monopolies and unfair business practices.

Soliman points out the impact this had on creating multiple centers of power within the ruling elite.[19] There was on one hand the "old guard" – the aging traditional figures holding high governmental, military and security positions – and on the other hand there was a new "market oriented" elite who used its new political power to further an essentially neo-liberal economic vision. This in no way increased the regime's popularity. These wealthy figures, holding ministerial positions or active in the ruling National Democratic Party, were perceived by the majority of Egyptians to be exploiting political power for economic gain and receiving unfair advantages. They were also perceived as the primary group backing a transfer of power to Mubarak's son, Gamal, which was violently opposed by most Egyptians and not looked on favorably by the old guard.

Raison de nation, raison d'état, or *raison de regime*?

Ensuring the survival of the Mubarak regime also became the primary driver of Egypt's foreign policy, whereas lofty rhetoric of pan-Arabism and patriotism all but disappeared from its foreign policy discourse.

During the heyday of Arab Nationalism in the 1950s and 1960s, Nasser justified Egypt's foreign policy positions as responding to the interests of the entire Arab nation. Although Egypt's attempts at creating "united" Arab states, notably the attempt to "unite" with Syria, failed, Nasser's ability to influence the Arab "Street" did not materially diminish. Traditional monarchies in Saudi Arabia and Jordan feared his influence on their own officer corps and on the stability of their regime. The Arab cold war between "revolutionary" and "reactionary" regimes was reflected in a proxy war between Egypt and Saudi Arabia conducted on the battlefield of Yemen. Nasser justified Egypt's involvement in Yemen in terms of supporting the rights of the Yemeni people to move beyond the shackles of an extremely primitive political system in order to achieve modernity and progress. He had a vision of Egypt's national security that extended beyond its borders and included guarding the entrance to the Red Sea.

Under Nasser Egypt adopted an extremely active foreign policy in Africa, supporting liberation movements throughout the continent, including South Africa. Nelson Mandela was one of many African freedom fighters who came to Cairo seeking support and aid during this time. This policy created extensive good will towards Egypt, helping it to secure the cooperation of countries in the Nile Basin, the source of the waters on which Egypt is almost completely dependent. Egypt's catastrophic manipulation into the 1967 war initiated by Israel was related to this extended vision of national security, as well as to pan-Arab solidarity. In this context, threats to Syria's national security necessitated action on Egypt's part. Its defeat in this war effectively ended the use of *raison de nation* as a driver of Egypt's foreign policy.

Nasser's successor, Anwar Sadat made the restoration of the occupied Sinai the overwhelming priority of his foreign policy. Although the October 1973 war was undertaken in coordination with Syria, the Egyptian and Syrian leaders soon parted ways over Sadat's willingness to overturn a decades-old Arab policy of refusing direct negotiations with Israel. In his pursuit of the liberation of Egypt's occupied land, Sadat reversed almost all of this country's external alliances. Breaking with the Soviets, he declared that "99 per cent of the cards" needed to establish peace in the region were in the hands of the US. Egypt dramatically improved its relations with what was previously considered the "reactionary" camp, now known as the "moderate" camp, such as Saudi Arabia and Jordan. His trip to Jerusalem and the signing of the Camp David peace accords with Israel left Egypt effectively isolated in the Arab world, with even the headquarters of the Arab League moved out of Cairo. Sadat was adamant in maintaining that his country had suffered enough for the Arab cause, and that it was time for it to put its own interests – *raison d'état* – first.

In response to its peace with Israel, large amounts of foreign aid poured into Egypt, along with unprecedented quantities of imported consumer goods. In his series of books asking "Whatever happened to the Egyptians?" prominent Egyptian economist Galal Amin described the negative social and economic consequences of what was described as an "open door" policy.[20] This flood of foreign aid brought no material benefits to Egypt's economy, he argued, and instead exacerbated the plight of Egypt's Poor, vastly increasing the social and economic divide between a narrow elite and the majority of Egypt's population. Shortly after Sadat's assassination, the last section of Sinai under Israeli control was returned to Egypt. Although many questioned the high price in loss of Arab solidarity, and what many perceived as restrictions on Egypt's sovereignty over the Sinai, the fact remains that Sadat's foreign policy did ultimately achieve a major objective of the Egyptian people.

During Mubarak's early years, he acted to restore Egypt's relations with the Arab world. Moreover, along with several other Arab countries, Egypt participated in the US-led war to expel Saddam Hussein's invading forces from Kuwait. In return for this, Egypt's dire fiscal straits were relieved by the cancellation of a substantial sum of military debt to the US. Any hopes of creating an Arab security system harnessing Egypt's and Syria's military capabilities were however dashed as Saudi Arabia and other Gulf countries elected to maintain US forces on their soil to secure their defense.

In his analysis of Egyptian foreign policy during the Mubarak years, Ali Dessouki stressed the primacy of economics.[21] According to him, "Mubarak recognized that Egypt's success in obtaining aid and tackling its enormous debt problem was related to establishing its importance as a leader in the Arab world and the global south." At the same time, he argues that Mubarak's success in protecting his country from the waves of instability prevailing in the region came at the cost of, "according to his critics, a retreat from Egypt's regional role." While Dessouki acknowledges that there were increasing calls for a more active Egypt, he argued that its foreign policy elite seemed divided between the desire to perform an assertive regional role and wariness of its costs.

Egypt's foreign policy during the Mubarak years appeared increasingly geared towards protecting regime, not state, interests. The regime relied on foreign aid and loans to maintain its hold on power. Galal Amin has pointed to a lack of evidence that the impact of this money was anything but detrimental both economically and socially. During the last decade of Mubarak's rule, gaining US support for bringing his son to power appeared to be a major driver of Egypt's foreign policy. The gap between public opinion and foreign policy behavior became wider and wider, especially in relation to the regime's policy towards the Palestinians in Gaza. Israeli military assaults and the embargo imposed on the sector were met with little resistance or condemnation from Egypt. While Mubarak was said to devote a great deal of his time and effort to resolving the "Palestinian issue," other regional players, such as Turkey, began to take a much more proactive stance. In comparison, Mubarak's policies appeared less and less acceptable to the Arab and Egyptian public.

In a biting criticism of foreign policy in the Mubarak years, Egyptian regional affairs analyst Jamil Matar declared that "Egypt for the last four decades ... has lived under the rule of a minority that decided it was not in its own interest ... to propel Egypt to become the pivotal regional state."[22] According to Matar, Egypt abandoned its leading regional role by deciding it would not participate in any meaningful way in the interactions of the Arab regional system. At the same time, it withdrew itself from the African scene, with catastrophic implications for its foreign policy. Egypt today is suffering the consequences; in the Nile Basin region it faces direct and serious threats to its sources of water. In the Arab Gulf region efforts are underway to establish a missile shield defense system, and from Iraq and Syria in the east to Sudan and Yemen in the south, Egypt is surrounded by the threat of sectarian and other civil conflicts. Matar also warns of the impact of this elite stance on state capacity. He argues that when those in charge of Egypt's foreign policy decline to formulate and pursue an effective and pivotal role on the regional level, this leads to the deterioration or stagnation of the foundations of both its soft and hard power.

Egypt's regional relations under Mubarak

Mubarak and his small coterie jealously guarded the making and conduct of foreign policy. The professional diplomatic corps was effectively sidelined on major "files." Negotiations with the Nile Basin countries were conducted by the Ministry of Irrigation from a technical point of view, with representatives from the Ministry of Foreign Affairs present essentially as observers. Any political negotiations or contacts were conducted through National Security channels. The Palestinian file was entirely in the hands of Omar Suleiman, head of Egyptian intelligence.

This narrow approach to foreign policy evoked severe criticisms by veteran Egyptian diplomats, such as former Minister of State for Foreign Affairs and former UN Secretary General, Boutros Boutros-Ghali. Particularly in reference to Africa, he repeatedly stressed the need for enhanced relations on political and economic levels to increase Egypt's leverage in matters related to its vital national interests regarding the Nile. According to Boutros-Ghali, Mubarak was assured by some of his compliant bureaucrats that "all was well," and therefore dismissed several proposals to that effect as unnecessary.[23]

Egypt's relations with close Arab allies, such as Saudi Arabia and the Arab Gulf countries, were conducted on an extremely personal basis between leaders. A former Egyptian ambassador to a small Gulf country recounted having been completely sidelined on even the basic logistics of a visit by Mubarak. Upon arrival at the airport, Mubarak drove off with his host, with the entire cortege oblivious to where they were heading and where Mubarak would be staying. All forms of financial assistance, gifts, and the like were handled personally by the two heads of state. Egypt's regional alliances under Mubarak were clearly aligned with US policies in the region. He was markedly hostile to Bashar el Assad for personal as well as political reasons and viewed Hezbollah in Lebanon as an irresponsible and subversive agent of Iran. Mubarak aligned Egypt with the anti-Iran regional axis, including Saudi Arabia, the Gulf states, and Jordan. During the Israeli war on Lebanon in 2006, he put the blame for the devastation resulting from the Israeli attack squarely on Hezbollah's shoulders.

Mubarak's hostile attitude towards Iran was widely criticized by Egyptian intellectuals, as well as by some former diplomats, as excessive and unproductive in terms of the country's national interest. While Egypt had its differences with Iran, many believed that country to be a major regional player with which Egypt should engage. Iran, in their view, should not be classified as an enemy, while Israel, who repeatedly committed atrocities against Palestinians, and had been in several wars with Egypt, was treated as a "partner." Egyptians were particularly outraged by the Israeli officials' habit of visiting Egypt just before they assaulted another Arab country. Notably, Begin visited Sadat on the eve of the attack on Iraq's nuclear reactor, while Israeli Foreign Minister Tzipi Livni did the same as the attack on Gaza was looming in late 2008. Whether or not Egypt was forewarned in these cases, it appeared complicit in the eyes of many in Egypt and the Arab world.

Except for its efforts in Palestinian–Israeli negotiations and attempts to broker reconciliation between the feuding Palestinian factions, Fatah and Hamas, Cairo undertook little initiative in mediating Arab crises. It was a markedly ineffective provider of good offices to resolve the conflict in Sudan, despite the importance of this southern neighbor to its own national security. In Sudan, Yemen, Lebanon and elsewhere, new regional players such as Qatar began to assume a much higher profile, which Mubarak resented. His personal animosity towards the Emir of Qatar, as well as strains in the bilateral relationship, grew increasingly apparent.

The withdrawal of Egypt from the Arab scene was directly linked to its alliance with the US. In return for maintaining its peace agreement with Israel and assisting US efforts to "settle" the Palestinian–Israeli conflict and create a "stable" Middle East in which Israel could be fully integrated as well as enjoying military superiority, Egypt received substantial US aid. Starting in 1979, it became the second-largest recipient of US aid, surpassed only by Israel. However, the amount of American aid it received declined from $2.1 billion in the fiscal year 1998, to $1.5 billion in 2010. This came as a result of gradual reduction in economic aid. By comparison, in July 2009, the Bush administration signed a ten-year memorandum of understanding with Israel to increase military assistance from $2.4 billion in 2008 to more than $3 billion by 2018. Egypt received no corresponding increase in military aid.[24]

Reflecting US priorities, $1.3 billion of the $1.55 billion it allocates to Egypt annually is in the form of military aid, a figure that has remained constant since 1987. All US foreign military funding must be spent on American hardware and associated services and training. By most US and Egyptian accounts, relations between the two countries have centered on close contacts between their respective military and intelligence establishments. Especially during the Bush years, relations with Mubarak became strained over increasing US pressure for democratization. In a famous address delivered at the American University in Cairo, Secretary of State Condoleezza Rice expressed regret that for decades the US had prioritized stability over demo-cratization in the Middle East while achieving neither but announced that it now had a vision of a New or Broader Middle East emphasizing domestic political reform. Such "meddling" in domestic affairs was not welcomed by Mubarak. Nevertheless, bilateral military and security cooperation continued.

According to a report for the Congressional Research Service, US official attitudes toward Egypt's political system in the years leading up to 2011 ranged from "passionate opposition to a perceived brutal regime" to "passive acceptance of a stable government that is largely supportive of US policy goals in the Middle East, especially Arab–Israeli peace."[25] US proponents of strong bilateral ties argued that Egypt is the key to maintaining a strong American military presence in the oil-rich Persian Gulf, as well as to projecting US power into South and Central Asia. The US navy sends about a dozen vessels through the Suez Canal each month, with expedited passage for its nuclear ships, a process which normally takes weeks for other foreign navies. Egypt also provides overflight rights to US aircraft.

The Mubarak regime engaged in crucial security cooperation with Israel. Securing the border with Gaza, through which Israel feared weapons were being smuggled to Hamas, was a US priority. Between 2007 and 2011, the US provided Egypt with $116.34 million in financial aid to bolster border security and to combat smuggling. Under Mubarak, Egypt distrusted Hamas, worrying about a possible mass influx of Palestinians into the Sinai and the possibility of Hamas sleeper cells there being activated to carry out attacks on Israel.

Bilateral cooperation through intelligence channels dramatically increased in the context of the US "war on terror." Egypt provided valuable information regarding Islamist militants and their activities. It also participated in the US forced rendition program, with suspects sent for interrogation by Egyptian intelligence, whose personnel were later alleged to have used torture to extract confessions. Egyptian intelligence also is reported to have provided the Bush administration with information regarding Iraq's alleged possession of chemical and biological weapons to bolster its case for the invasion of Iraq.

The issue of democratization was a source of contention in Egypt's relations with the US. For the last few years Congress has debated whether US aid to Egypt should be conditioned on improvement in its human rights record, democracy and religious freedoms, as well as in efforts to control its border with Gaza. A portion of US economic aid, managed by AID, has been spent on democracy promotion. The Egyptian government, which claims the right to maintain complete control over the allocation of all foreign funding, stipulated that funding must come through official government channels and be dispensed only to NGOs registered with the Ministry of Social Affairs.

Advocacy NGOs were particularly suspect and "subversive" in the eyes of the Mubarak regime. It argued that their exposure of human rights violations tarnished "Egypt's reputation" in the eyes of the world, which was a direct threat to the regime's efforts to raise foreign aid and loans. The activities of these organizations were also a threat to the prevailing regime discourse that isolated "legitimate" economic and social demands on the part of Egyptians from "unacceptable" demands for civic and political rights. Many of these NGOs defended peasants, workers and other marginalized groups whose rights had been violated. In so doing, they endangered the traditional patriarchal "halo" which protected the regime and its leading figures from criticism. These groups challenged regime hegemony and the supremacy of the loosely defined concept of "national interest" as a justification for undemocratic practices and human rights abuses against its citizens.[26] They regarded the regime as corrupt and arbitrary, accusing it of formulating anti-democratic laws used in an arbitrary fashion to help regime supporters and undermine its opponents.

Egypt's Supreme Council of the Armed Forces takes the reins of power

Egyptian protestors who celebrated the overthrow of Mubarak on February 11, 2011 had no plans for the aftermath. They joyfully cleaned up and repainted Tahrir Square, entrusting the Supreme Council of the Armed Forces (SCAF), headed by Field Marshal Muhammad Tantawi, to manage the transition. There was little in the Council's history or makeup to recommend it for such a task. Conservative and authoritarian in accordance with their military training, appointed and maintained in office for extended periods at Mubarak's pleasure, and deeply complicit in the cronyism and corruption of his regime, the aging members of SCAF had little sympathy for the cause of change. Despite their declarations of respect for the "revolution's martyrs," Egypt's new military rulers were suspicious of and hostile to the young "revolutionaries" who had sparked the wider popular protests that ousted Mubarak. There were repeated attempts by individuals close to military circles to discredit these young people, accusing them of seeking to undermine the Egyptian state and destabilize society in the pursuit of "foreign agendas." Military security forces during this transitional period repeatedly used brutal force against demonstrators, killing some and injuring many, as well as making numerous arrests. Protestors had to organize "million man" marches into Tahrir Square on successive Fridays to force their rulers to put Mubarak on trial and to move forward on establishing a new political order.

There is little doubt that SCAF did its best to resist any fundamental change, notably to the military's privileged position. It was encouraged by the fragmentation of the forces calling for change: a protest movement that had neither a cohesive structure nor a clear vision of how to realize its goals. SCAF's inept management, whether intentional or not, left Egyptians exhausted by the lack of security, worsening economic conditions and severe shortages of basic necessities. The military rulers turned to the sole large organization with effective presence on the ground, the Muslim Brothers, to provide them with a social base of support. The illogical sequencing of political transition – first parliamentary and then presidential elections, to be followed by drafting a new constitution – was a product of the pragmatic alliance between these two forces. They in fact had much in common. Both ascribed to a conservative and authoritarian outlook, and both had an interest in sidelining newly emerged political forces.

Neither was the Obama administration, which had been surprised by the uprisings, anxious to see radical change in Egypt. Leading figures, such as Vice President Joseph Biden and Secretary of State Hillary Clinton, initially expressed support for Mubarak and confidence that the regime could withstand the crisis. When it became apparent that protests would not cease until Mubarak left office, the US began to press for an "orderly transfer of power." The preferred candidate to succeed Mubarak was Omar Suleiman, head of the Intelligence Service, with whom the Americans were well acquainted. Events overtook that option, and the administration hoped SCAF would be successful in quickly restoring order, and preventing any major changes in Egypt's foreign policy.

It cannot be said that SCAF was fortunate in its management of the transitional period on either the domestic or the international level. It lacked the necessary skills and experience. Moreover, domestic and international issues became increasingly entangled, making the navigation of a complex regional scene even more difficult.

Veteran diplomat Nabil El Araby was chosen by SCAF as Egypt's first post-revolutionary foreign minister. El Araby quickly began to formulate a more independent foreign policy. He made a major departure from its previous stances by declaring that Iran was not Egypt's enemy, a move not welcomed by the US, Saudi Arabia, the Gulf Arab states, or Israel. The Egyptian government was forced to speedily dispatch officials to the Gulf region to assure these countries that it had not reversed its commitment to their security. El Araby's tenure at the foreign office was extremely short. He soon left to assume the position of Arab League Secretary General following an unusual crisis on that front. In a challenge to Egypt's traditional privilege to hold this post, Qatar put forth its own candidate and withdrew the nomination only when Egypt presented El Araby's name as its candidate. This was generally perceived as a deliberate maneuver on the part of the Gulf states to remove him from the Ministry of Foreign Affairs.

During the following months, Egypt's foreign ministry as well as its military rulers maintained a low regional and international profile. Egypt took little action with respect to developments in Libya, Yemen, Bahrain or Syria, with the exception of a brief visit to Libya by Field Marshal Tantawi following the fall of Gaddafi. Reports indicated that he was not very warmly received.

Despite this low profile, SCAF confronted crises involving three of Egypt's traditional partners: Israel, the US, and Saudi Arabia. The first crisis with Israel involved the killing of several Egyptian soldiers on the Israeli border. This provoked outrage among Egyptian protestors. Although Israel rendered a very uncharacteristic apology, demonstrations surrounding the Israeli embassy in Cairo got out of hand in what was portrayed as an attempt to sack embassy offices. Egyptian security used harsh measures to disband the demonstration, and arrests were made. Israeli diplomats were subsequently evacuated from Cairo until different arrangements could be made to secure the Embassy.

Repeated acts of sabotage against the pipeline carrying Egyptian natural gas to Israel disrupted supplies and further strained relations between the two countries. Domestic opposition to the agreement to sell gas to Israel had been mounting in Egypt for several years. Allegations of corruption and unwarranted personal gain regarding this deal were leveled at one of Mubarak's close friends. The price was deemed too low, and many felt that Egypt should not be selling its gas for so little when its own population was suffering severe shortages. The crisis escalated when Israel was about to demand compensation from Egypt for the repeated interruption of services. At that point, an Egyptian court dissolved the contract on the grounds that payments had not been made on time. Egypt stressed the commercial nature of this issue, but in Israel it was perceived in strictly political terms as a portent of the emergence of a less compliant neighbor. Israel had tried hard to get Washington to prevent the overthrow of Mubarak. It felt increasingly isolated and threatened, expecting that democratically elected leaders in Egypt and elsewhere in the Arab world would demonstrate less tolerance of its behavior.

The ruling military council also became involved in a highly public standoff with Washington after Egyptian security forces searched the offices of several American and European pro-democracy NGOs and seized documents, computers and other materials. The pretext was that these organizations, which had been operating in Egypt for many years, had not received proper official authorization. The case was turned over to the courts, amid a wave of accusations linking such NGOs and individuals associated with them to subversive activities. Foreign employees were, for a period, not allowed to leave the country, and some took refuge in the American embassy to avoid arrest. This order was later rescinded, as there appeared to be no legal grounds to support it. The entire issue was fundamentally an ill-managed political confrontation, reflecting SCAF's distrust of NGOs and resentment of Western support for democracy promotion activities attempting to bypass government controls by directly funding civil society organizations. It has also been suggested this was part of a bigger "behind the scenes" confrontation between SCAF and the US, involving differences of opinion on the appropriate speed and direction of political change.

The crisis in relations with Saudi Arabia during this period centered around an Egyptian human rights lawyer who was arrested upon arrival in Saudi Arabia on a visit to Islamic holy places. He had been involved in a number of legal actions aimed at defending the rights of Egyptians employed in the country. Reports that he was arrested attempting to bring in a large cache of illegal drugs were met with disbelief in Egypt. Angry crowds gathered around Saudi Arabia's embassy in Cairo and its consulate in Suez to protest what they perceived as inadequate support from Egyptian diplomats for the accused individual. In unprecedented behavior, the crowds shouted insults against the Saudi royal family and scrawled them on the embassy's walls. The Kingdom withdrew its ambassador from Cairo, citing safety concerns. A visit by an Egyptian delegation, including the Speaker of Parliament was hastily arranged to mend fences. But the incident revealed simmering resentments regarding the treatment of Egyptians working in the Arab Gulf countries, especially Saudi Arabia. It also reflected awareness by Egyptians that Saudi Arabia did not welcome change in Egypt. Indeed, while it had promised financial assistance for the transition, no funds had actually been made available at this point.

SCAF was clearly unsuccessful in picking up the strands of the Mubarak regime's external ties. It did not have better luck with its domestic alliances, and its relationship with the Muslim Brothers soon fell apart. The Muslim Brothers – along with more extreme Salafi Islamist groups – gained an overwhelming majority in parliament, thereby changing the balance of power. Having first reneged on their agreement with other political forces not to seek a large majority in parliament and then on their promise to allow members from other political groups to hold key positions in parliamentary committees, the Muslim Brothers now moved to consolidate their hold on power by running a candidate in the presidential elections. When their candidate of choice, engineer Khairat el Shater – recently released after a long prison term – was disqualified on the basis of legal technicalities, the organization quickly nominated Morsi, an engineering professor and head of its political arm, the Party of Liberty and Justice. The Muslim Brothers were confident that their political experience and sophisticated organizational capabilities would ensure the success of their candidate.

The success of the Muslim Brother candidate owed much to the miscalculations of other political forces, including SCAF. The latter, as well as the establishment of the old regime, chose to back Ahmad Shafiq, the last prime minister appointed by Mubarak. Although able to win almost half the votes in the second round of presidential elections (in June 2012), both his links to Mubarak, and the obvious disdain with which he treated the protestors in Tahrir while he was in office pushed many voters to the Muslim Brothers' side. Had this group chosen to back, for example, former Secretary General of the Arab League, and former Foreign Minister Amr Mousa, the outcome might have been different. Mousa enjoyed recognition and a certain credibility for his outspoken criticisms of Israel and presented himself as having been somewhat removed from Mubarak's inner circle.

The opposition and pro-revolution forces also made their own miscalculations. Had its two most prominent candidates, Abdel Moniemn Aboul Fottouh, a longtime Islamist activist, and Hamdeen Sabahi, a former member of parliament with a Nasserite political orientation, pooled their resources and run on the same ticket, they would have clinched the election in the first round. Their combined votes easily exceeded all other contenders. While the two candidates had different orientations, there were enough common objectives that could have ensured a clear break with the past. The various candidates supporting a more inclusive, democratic system were unable to overcome the divisive impact of personal differences and political ambition. Morsi, the candidate of the Muslim Brothers, became Egypt's first president to come to office through competitive elections. He won by a bare majority, but almost half of those eligible to vote indicated their dissatisfaction with both candidates by failing to show up at the polls.

Just before the second round of presidential elections, Egypt's military rulers somewhat desperately tried to maintain their hold on power. Parliament had been dissolved by a court ruling related to irregularities in the election rules. SCAF issued a Supplementary Constitutional Declaration giving it control over the legislative powers of the dissolved parliament, as well as over all military matters and the declaration of war. This effectively created a second center of power, parallel to the presidency. But SCAF had few allies left, with the exception of some "older" liberal forces who endorsed its moves in fear of the Muslim Brothers' and Salafis' monopoly over the drafting of Egypt's new constitution. Upon his election, Morsi attempted to challenge this situation by inviting the disbanded parliament to reconvene. This threatened a confrontation with the judiciary. The parliament only met once before adjourning for a long recess. Open confrontation was avoided for the time being.

However, Morsi was soon able to consolidate his hold on power and to undermine SCAF. The opportunity presented itself following an attack by an unknown group on Egyptian soldiers in Sinai two months after his election. Morsi first removed key figures, such as the head of the Intelligence Service and the head of the Presidential Guard, as well as some senior ranks of the police force, from office. He also "requested" that Field Marshal Tantawi, head of SCAF, replace the head of military police. Not long afterward, Morsi announced that Tantawi and other SCAF members were retired from office. He appointed a new minister of defense and new heads to all military branches. The ease with which the latter move was implemented indicates prior consultation with younger ranks of officers. Indeed, Tantawi and other members of SCAF were not popular in the army. Their long tenure had prevented the promotion of younger officers. The economic privileges they enjoyed did not extend to others beyond the top military circle. SCAF's inept handling of the events in Sinai served as a professional affront to serious officers.

In short, Morsi was able to forge an agreement with the military, which also included official honors for the retiring figures. This was interpreted by many as a reassurance that the military and its former, or present, leaders would not be held to account on charges related to their management of the transitional period. It would be extremely premature, however, to argue that this move brought the military under civilian control. No actions were taken with regard to civilian oversight of the military budget, nor was there any discussion of the extensive economic enterprises under the military's sole control.

Egypt under the rule of the Muslim Brothers

Egypt's newly elected president, Muhammad Morsi gave his first major address on international and regional issues in Tehran at the Non-Aligned

Movement Summit in late August 2012. He was the first Egyptian president to visit Iran since the revolution of 1979. Great controversy had surrounded his decision to attend the conference to hand over its chairmanship, which Egypt had held for the three previous years, to Iran. The US and Israel had expressed their opposition to the visit, and it was greeted with disapproval by the Arab states of the Gulf. Morsi clearly wished to signal a new and bold Egyptian role but was also mindful of domestic as well as international opposition to closer ties with Iran. He compromised; he would visit Iran for only a few hours to attend the ceremonial inauguration of the conference on the way back from his first official visit to China.

Those hoping for a major departure in Egypt's foreign relations, or a speedy improvement of relations with Iran were disappointed. While Morsi praised the founders of the Non-Aligned Movement – including, for his first time as president, a reference to the late Gamal Abdul Nasser – and its aspirations to resist the hegemony of great powers, his speech put Egypt's stance in the same corner they had been in under Mubarak: supporting the positions of the US and Saudi Arabia. Although expressing – in a nod to his Iranian hosts – his support for the right of all nations to the peaceful use of nuclear energy, he did not condemn the severe economic sanctions imposed on that state. Ironically, he instead condemned the economic boycott imposed for several decades on Cuba. More importantly, Morsi took a strong stand on Syria, declaring that the Assad regime had lost all claims to legitimacy and must end, and expressing strong support for the cause of Syrian rebels. He said the world had a moral responsibility to halt the bloodshed in that country and that outside forces needed to intervene to do so. Morsi had previously proposed the cooperation of Egypt, Saudi Arabia, Turkey and Iran in the pursuit of a solution insuring a peaceful transfer of power in Syria. His clear denunciation of the Syrian regime, Iran's closest ally, could not be considered conducive to enlisting Iranian cooperation in this respect. If Egypt was to act as mediator, many observers noted, it should have avoided taking sides in such a forceful manner.[27]

It was noteworthy that Morsi in no way evoked notions of pan-Arab solidarity or Arab national security with respect to the Syrian crisis. He also went out of his way to highlight his Sunni Islamic affiliation. In addition to the traditional salutations to the prophet Muhammad and his family, customarily used at the beginning of speeches in Islamist discourse, Morsi mentioned a few Islamic historic figures who are the subject of Sunni/Shi'ite controversy. They are revered by Sunni factions, but subject to criticism and attack in some strands of Shi'ite discourse. This was a clear concession to the domestic opponents of his visit, that is, the Salafi movements in Egypt, as well as to Saudi Arabia. It indicates a worrisome inclination of Morsi to follow Saudi Arabia's lead in cloaking its geo-political rivalry with Iran in terms of a Sunni–Shi'ite confrontation. Morsi had on a previous occasion made a brief reference to Egypt's role in "upholding Sunni Islam."

Although Morsi visited Saudi Arabia twice in the short period following his election – the first in a private pilgrimage to the holy sites, during which he was received by the King, and the second to attend the Islamic Summit held in Mecca – relations were not particularly warm. There have been historic animosities between the Saudi regime and the Muslim Brothers, and the former does not appear to have overcome its old suspicions. Morsi was careful to reiterate on several occasions that Egypt had no designs on "exporting" its revolution, nor was it intending to interfere in any way in the domestic affairs of its neighbors. These declarations were clearly aimed at reassuring Saudi Arabia and the other Arab Gulf countries, which employ large numbers of Egyptian expatriates. Out of fear of "contagion," new restrictions were put in place limiting the ability of Egyptians to obtain visas to visit or work in Gulf countries.

It was not Saudi Arabia, but rather Qatar, that emerged as the new regime's benefactor. Qatar's ruler made a short visit to Cairo during which he made a $2 billion "deposit" in Egypt's Central Bank to offset the dangerous dwindling of Egypt's foreign currency reserves. Qatar, it must be noted, was a strong supporter of opposition forces in Libya and is currently, in cooperation with Saudi Arabia and Turkey, providing material and military support to the "Free Army" opposing the regime in Syria. It has historically been a refuge to Muslim Brothers escaping repression in Egypt. Sheikh Yousef al Qaradawi is one of the major Islamic figures who have for many years made Qatar their home.

Although Morsi clearly intends to pursue an active foreign policy, he does not appear to be pursuing a coherent new vision. His first state visit was to attend the African Union Summit in Ethiopia, consistent with the centrality of Egypt's national interests with regard to the Nile, but he made no clear proposals on how Egypt's differences with the other Nile Basin countries could be resolved. In the same vein, he made grand declarations concerning Egypt becoming "China's gateway to Africa" and expanding economic cooperation and the transfer of technology, but no specific projects or plans appeared to be in place. His visits to Europe to sign various economic agreements bring to mind Mubarak's frequent travel to that part of the world.

While much was made of Morsi visiting China before Egypt's traditional ally, the US, there did not appear to be a shortage of consultations and cooperation with the latter. For example, the US State Department implied its awareness that changes in Egypt's top military echelons were going to take place. Some reports indicated that Secretary Clinton had broached the subject with Tantawi on her visit to Cairo soon after Morsi's election. Various political factions in Egypt were critical of the close ties between the Obama administration and the Muslim Brothers. Seeking to undermine the latter's credibility, Ahmad Shafiq, the defeated candidate for president, repeatedly implied the Americans had supported Morsi's election.

In September 2012, Morsi confronted the first test of his ability to handle foreign policy crises on the anniversary of the 9/11 attacks. The trailer of an obscure film including material that denigrated the prophet Muhammad was widely shared through the internet. This outraged Muslims all around the world, especially among Salafi groups. Egypt was among the first countries in which anti-American demonstrations erupted, demanding that the US take action against those who produced the film and that it pass laws prohibiting the production or distribution of similar material in the future. Protestors marched on the American Embassy in Cairo, breaching its perimeter. Whereas these events did not end tragically, as did similar protests in Libya, where the US Ambassador and three embassy staff members were killed in an armed attack on a consulate, they were deemed no less worrisome. The Obama administration was not pleased that President Morsi – who was on an official visit to Europe at the time – did not immediately and strongly condemn the attack. US commentators noted that President Morsi, in his first statements regarding these events, focused far more on the right of Muslims to be outraged by such insults to their religion. There were also concerns that Egyptian security forces had been lax in protecting embassy premises. The American media reported an angry phone call to Morsi from Obama, after which security was tightened around the embassy in Cairo, which suspended its services to the public. Egyptian security forces eventually cleared the area surrounding the embassy and the nearby Tahrir Square of all protestors, resorting to the use of tear gas and making numerous arrests.

These events highlighted the difficulties in managing bilateral relations in a period of domestic and regional fluidity. Under attack from domestic political opponents for his "soft" stance on the Arab Spring and support for Islamist governments in the Middle East, Obama declared that he did not consider Egypt an ally, although it was not an enemy. The White House later clarified that the President meant that Egypt was not a formal ally in the legal sense, but the implied rebuke to Egypt's government was nevertheless clear. In Egypt, President Morsi was also trying to balance domestic and foreign policy considerations. With an eye on upcoming parliamentary elections, and fearful of allowing the Salafis to take the lead on sensitive religious issues, Morsi's first reaction was to affirm his Islamic credentials. US reactions soon brought home that he had to take into consideration the implications of his statements in terms of international relations as well. Prominent figures from the Muslim Brothers also went to great lengths to express their condemnation of the attacks, although they continued to call for the US to take action to ensure that Islam and its religious symbols would not be subjected to such disrespect.

The full impact of the transnational Islamist orientation espoused by the Muslim Brothers on Egypt's foreign policy remains to be seen. Will official foreign policy reflect the ideas of the Muslim Brothers, or will President Morsi put some distance between his administration's policies and theirs? This question is particularly important with respect to Egypt's policies on the Palestinian issue. What impact will the historically close ties between the Muslim Brothers and Hamas have regarding the situation in Sinai and relations with Israel? In the period following the fall of Mubarak, Egypt brokered an agreement between various Palestinian factions to form a Palestinian coalition government. This was interpreted as an easing of Mubarak's hostility towards Hamas. Egypt also successfully brokered the return of a kidnapped Israeli soldier who had been held in Gaza for several years. But security analysts worried that the easing of restrictions at the crossing points between Egypt and Gaza may facilitate the movement of militants into Egypt.

Following the attacks on Egyptian soldiers in Sinai, President Morsi did not oppose the military's decision to destroy the famous "tunnels" running under the Egyptian border with Gaza that had served as the primary route for providing the Gaza population's everyday needs. There were suspicions that the tunnels were also used to smuggle weapons and move illegal immigrants and militants, as well as for various other activities. In view of the urgent need to impose Egypt's control on Sinai, the existence of these tunnels could no longer be tolerated. Hamas cooperated with Egyptian authorities, eager to establish that it was in no way responsible for and in no way endorsed the attack on Egyptian soldiers. But Hamas leaders soon began to express concern regarding the closure of the tunnels, calling for Egypt to provide an alternative avenue for supplying Gazans' basic needs.

There is no doubt that Morsi will have to avoid the appearance of coordinating closely with Israel or appearing to condone its actions against Palestinians. While relations between the two countries are unlikely to be "friendly," there is no reason to assume, at this point, that they will completely disintegrate either. As mentioned earlier, Egypt took pains to reassure Israel that its actions in Sinai did not indicate hostility. Egypt, Israel and the US have a common interest in maintaining peace and security in Sinai. Trying to force overt multilateral cooperation in this respect would likely be met with resistance from Morsi, who would not want to be remembered as the president who allowed foreign troops back onto Egyptian soil, or agreed to compromise Egypt's sovereignty over its own land. In the absence of a major disruption, it is likely that US-brokered cooperation between Egypt and Israel can continue on a more suitably low profile.

In terms of its domestic political and economic orientation, the new regime does not appear to hold a fundamentally different program from that of its predecessor. After the Muslim Brothers majority in parliament vehemently opposed signing a loan agreement with the IMF on both religious and political grounds, the new government installed by Morsi proceeded to negotiate an even bigger IMF loan. Muslim Brothers spokesmen were quick to describe this move as one of extreme necessity, and therefore defensible in both religious and political terms. The Muslim Brothers' economic program, and Morsi's speeches, emphasize the role of the private sector, the importance of encouraging foreign investment and increasing external trade. Many of the leading figures in the organization are businessmen, with significant interests and ties in Arab Gulf countries as well as Turkey, among other places. While recognizing the need to provide more jobs to reduce youth unemployment, there are no clear plans outlined in the program on how that could be achieved. Moreover, Morsi has made various promises to increase government employees' wages and pensions and to provide special pensions for various other groups in need. Without a clear plan to increase state revenues, this will mean more deficit spending, an unlikely solution to Egypt's economic problems.

President Morsi's political tactics to win supporters and neutralize enemies are also familiar. The cabinet he appointed after a long delay shared many of the hallmarks of previous governments, overwhelmingly made up of technocrats and even some bureaucrats, with a few key positions, such as the Ministry of Information (overseeing the media), allocated to the party faithful. The Shura Council – the second chamber of parliament, in which the Muslim Brothers and the Salafis hold a majority – speedily exercised the rights granted to it under the previous regime to dismiss almost all editors-in-chief of nationally owned newspapers and magazines and appoint new ones. There were various other attempts to muzzle the highly critical media. Charges were brought against a few journalists for "insulting the head of state," a term consistently used against regime opponents since the early twentieth century.

A perfect storm? Or more to come?

In his analysis of the events starting in January 2011, Ezzedin Choukri Fishere asks whether this was Egypt's "perfect storm" or if we can expect similar ones to follow?[28] He likens the upheaval to a perfect storm, i.e., one that resulted from the confluence of a number of disparate events and continued on its own course until its force dissipated. The storm of the January revolution has now more or less calmed, but have the various conditions that gave rise to it in the first place changed? His answer is that some have and some have not. The general mood of humiliation and failure that pervaded Egypt has, in Fishere's view, lightened. The atrophied political system has regained some vitality through the incorporation of new forces and wider opportunities for participation as well as a sense that elections now matter. On the other hand, not much has changed in terms of relieving social and economic injustice, the failure of state institutions to perform their most basic tasks, and the prevalence of traditional and authoritarian world views in all governing institutions. The latter have not managed to treat Egyptian citizens with any greater degree of respect, although Egyptian citizens now view and treat state institutions with a great deal less respect. In sum, conditions are ripe for producing a new storm.

Egypt faces many challenges in overcoming its present weakened condition. A new and innovative approach must be found to reduce severe social inequality, while achieving growth and providing job opportunities to the millions of unemployed and disaffected young Egyptians. The entire security apparatus must be reconstructed according to a new orientation in which human rights and professional competence are well ingrained and fully respected.

There are important issues to be confronted with regard to military–civilian relations and protecting civil liberties, not to mention navigating a way through the current regional and international disorder. So far, the Muslim Brothers, who achieved a majority in parliamentary elections as well as winning the presidency, do not appear to possess such a vision. Their world view, policies and practices make them more a part of the old regime than a force for change. It will be up to the various social and political forces in Egypt seeking change to organize themselves and work on developing a new and alternative vision. As with all other countries, maintaining an active international role for Egypt requires that it first establish a solid domestic base.

In Fishere's view, the January revolution resulted from the confluence of a number of disparate events, which came together to produce the conditions of a perfect storm. But many of these conditions remain unchanged, and therefore Egypt should expect more turbulence ahead. Events would soon support this analysis. In November and December 2012, what has been labeled the "crisis of the constitution" brought Egyptians into the streets in protest of regime policies, and more worrisomely, brought various political and social factions into direct confrontation.

There were many dimensions to this crisis, but it essentially reflected the need for a new political and constitutional framework able to encompass the growing complexity of Egyptian society. It also reflected the persistence of Mubarak-era blurring of the line between state institutions and the regime. Morsi perceived the Constitutional Court as an extension of that regime, and in order to remove what he regarded as a threat to his powers, took steps that undermined the foundations of the judiciary as an independent institution.

To regime supporters, the draft constitution and the referendum provided a way to move forward, out of Egypt's prolonged transitional period. But its opponents perceived it as a power grab by the Muslim Brothers. There were serious reservations related to human rights and social justice, as well as to the powers the draft awarded the president and the ambiguous language that would create future problems. The line dividing opponents and supporters did not necessarily correlate with the Islamist/secular divide. There were Islamist groups that opposed the draft for very different reasons. The Islamist overtones of the draft were meant to guarantee political support, allowing the regime to present itself as representing the majority.

Morsi's insistence on proceeding with a referendum does not bode well for future stability. Much of the judiciary refused to oversee it, while lawyers, journalists, a wide spectrum of political forces, and perhaps hundreds of thousands of ordinary citizens – notably from the Christian minority – expressed serious objections to it. While the phrase "Egyptians broke the barrier of fear" – in reference to January 2011 – may sound hackneyed, it is nevertheless true. Without benefit of ideological guidance or political affiliation, they are standing up for their rights. The fragmented political forces aspiring to a better system of governance are developing strength and experience. It is highly unlikely they will tolerate what they perceive as unjust or repressive practices.

The severe trust deficit and the limited competence of government in Egypt at this point make addressing its fundamental problems all the more difficult. In addition to dealing with a sizeable budgetary deficit and high level of debt, a new and innovative approach must be found to reduce severe social inequality, achieve growth and provide jobs for the millions of unemployed and disaffected Egyptians. The entire security apparatus must be reconstructed according to a new orientation in which human rights and professional competence are well ingrained and respected. There are important issues to be confronted with regard to military–civilian relations and protecting civil liberties, not to mention navigating a way through the current regional and international disorder. So far, the Muslim Brothers who achieved a majority in parliamentary elections as well as succeeding in putting their candidate into the presidential office do not appear to possess the necessary skills to tackle these tasks. It will be up to the various social and political forces in Egypt seeking change to organize themselves and work on developing a new and alternative vision. As with all other countries, maintaining an active international role for Egypt requires that it first establish a solid domestic base.

Notes

1 I. Wallerstein, "The world class struggle: the geography of protest," *Agence Global*, June 1, 2012. URL: <www.agenceglobal.com/index.php?show==articale+tid=2809> (accessed August 15, 2012).
2 S. Radwan, "al tahadi al-Iktisadi ba'd al-thawrat al'arabiyah," *Al-Siyassa al-Dawliya*, 2012, 188, 66–69.
3 R. Khouri, "The arab big bang," *The Jordan Times*, December 22, 2011. URL: <http://jordantimes.com/the-arab-big-bang> (accessed September 24, 2012).
4 S. Kinzer, *Reset Middle East: Old Friends and New Alliances*, London: I. B. Taurus, 2010, p. 7.
5 A. el Sayed, "Egypt's political situation and foreign relations," paper presented to the International Conference on North Africa and the Middle East: Challenges and Opportunities, Aarhus University (Denmark), May 27–28, 2011. URL: <http://cir.au.dk/fileadmin/site_files/filer_statskundskab/subsites/cir/pdf-filer/Egypts_Political_Situation_and_Foreign_Relations_Maher_1_.pdf> (accessed September 25, 2012).
6 K. Fahmy, *Kol Regal al-Pasha: Muhammad Ali wa Gaishah wa Bena' Misr al-Haditha*, 2nd ed., translated by S. Younis, Cairo: Dar Al-Shorouk, 2011, pp. 76–86.
7 Ibid., p. 39.
8 J. Alterman, "Egypt in Transition: Insights and options for US policy", Center for Strategic and International Studies, January 2012. URL: <http://csis.org/publication/egypt-transition-insights-and-options-us-policy> (accessed September 24, 2012).
9 R. Khouri, "Speedy state-building, messy not dangerous," *Agence Global*, April 18, 2012. URL: <www.agenceglobal.com/index.php?show=articale+tid=2778> (accessed August 15, 2012).
10 M. el Sayed Sa'eed, *al-Intiqal al-Dimuqrati al-Mohtagaz fi Misr*, Cairo: Merit, 2006, pp. 30–33.
11 S. Soliman, *The Autumn of Dictatorship, Fiscal Crisis and Political Change under Mubarak*, Stanford, CA: Stanford University Press, 2011, pp. 163–70.

12 Ibid., pp. 97–98.
13 A. Farouq, *Jazur al-Fasad al-Idari fi Misr*, Cairo: Dar al Shorouk, 2008, pp. 365–67.
14 Ibid., p. 172–78.
15 B. Abdel Aziz, *Ighra' al-Sulta al-Mutlaqa*, Cairo: Sefsafa, 2011, pp. 49–57.
16 Ibid., p. 94.
17 el Sayed Sa'eed, *al-Intiqal al-Dimuqrati*, p. 9.
18 Farouq, *Jazur al-Fasad*, pp. 369–70.
19 Soliman, *Autumn*, pp. 171–73.
20 See, among other works by the same author, G. Amin, *Whatever Else Happened to the Egyptians?* Cairo: The American University in Cairo Press, 2004.
21 A. Dessouki, "Regional Leadership: Balancing Off Costs and Dividends in the Foreign Policy of Egypt," in B. Korany and A. Dessouki, eds, *The Foreign Policy of Arab States: The Challenge of Globzalization*, Cairo: The American University in Cairo Press, 2008, pp. 167–92.
22 J. Matar, "Markazyet Misr Laysat Sbadeyah," *Al-Shorouk*, April 16, 2012, p. 9.
23 Interview with the author, Cairo, January 2012.
24 J. Sharp, "Egypt: Background and U.S. Relations," Congressional Research Service, January 28, 2011, pp. 17–20. URL: <http://www.cfr.org/egypt/congressional-research-service-egypt-background-us-relations/p23949> (accessed September 25, 2012).
25 Ibid.
26 N. Pratt, "Hegemony and Counter-hegemony in Egypt: Advocacy NGOs, Civil Society and the State" (Ch. 4), in Sarah ben Nefissa *et al.*, eds, *NGOs and Governance in the Arab World*, Cairo: The American University in Cairo Press, 2005, pp. 123–50.
27 N. Mos'ad, "Algham fi Khitab Morsi Betahran", *Al-Shorouk*, August 31, 2012, p. 10.
28 E. Fishere, *Fi 'Ain al-Asefah*, Al Doha: Bloomsbury-Qatar Foundation Publishing, 2012, pp. 13–18.

7 Turkey under the AKP

Axis change or pragmatic activism?

Tozun Bahcheli

Elected to a third consecutive term in June 2012 with a comfortable majority, Turkey's Justice and Development Party (*Adalet ve Kalkinma Partisi* – AKP), led by Prime Minister Recep Tayyip Erdogan, now has held power for more than ten years. It has ushered in political stability, improved the country's democratic credentials and achieved impressive economic growth. It has also raised Turkey's regional and global profile and influence.

These advances stand in contrast to the tribulations that Turkey experienced during the previous decade. Coalition governments then shuffled in and out of office on average once every 18 months during the 1990s, making it virtually impossible to achieve a consensus on key issues facing the country. In one memorable year, 1995, three politicians – representing separate political parties – assumed the office of foreign minister. Without effective stewardship, Turkey nearly stumbled into war with Greece the following year over the issue of a tiny Aegean islet. Even more troublesome for ordinary Turks was the sorry state of the economy, which appeared to lurch from one crisis to another. A major economic crisis in 1994 sparked exceedingly high inflation rates and unemployment, causing great hardship. Before the damage from this was patched up, another major crisis struck in 2001, throwing nearly a million Turks out of work within weeks. In the parliamentary elections the following year, the AKP skilfully capitalized on the shortcomings of the incumbent three-party coalition and formed the first one-party-majority government in Turkey in over a decade after winning more than three-quarters of the parliamentary seats on November 5, 2002.

The leading members of the AKP, Erdogan, Abdullah Gul, and Bulent Arinc, had been members of two earlier Islamist parties, the Refah Party ("welfare party" – RP) and its successor, the Fazilet Party ("virtue party" – FP), both of which had been banned for allegedly violating Turkey's principle of secularism. Following the banning of Fazilet, a group of its younger members led by Erdogan, a businessman and popular former mayor of Istanbul, and Gul, an economist and member of parliament since 1991, decided to split from it and found a new Islamist party, the AKP, to contest the 2002 parliamentary elections. This new party was clearly differentiated from its predecessors. Adroitly downplaying the AKP's Islamist roots, Erdogan and Gul positioned it as a moderate, reformist, business-oriented party of the center-right. AKP leaders objected to descriptions in the Western media portraying the party as "Islamist," "Islamic," or "moderately Islamist" and have insisted on characterizing it as a conservative democratic one. And the AKP pointedly "pledged the party's support for secularism, democracy and Turkey's traditional pro-Western foreign policy, particularly the goal of EU membership."[1]

These reassuring goals were essential not only to soothe Turkey's Western partners but also to assuage the fears of its secular establishment – consisting of the military, the judiciary, and, to a lesser extent, the foreign policy establishment – that the party would not threaten the country's secular order. But the powerful secularists remained deeply suspicious of the party's agenda, and so, in fashioning its foreign policy, the AKP felt obliged to pay a great deal of attention to domestic political considerations to ensure that it would not suffer the same fate as other Islamist parties. This was especially the case during the party's first term in office.

The Davutoglu doctrine, the lure of EU membership, and the Cyprus issue

Although he had no prior experience in world affairs, Erdogan wasted no time in taking charge of Turkey's foreign policy agenda. He appointed Ahmet Davutoglu, a professor of international relations, as his chief foreign policy adviser soon after the AKP electoral victory in 2002. Gul became foreign minister in March 2003 and, until he assumed the largely-ceremonial presidency in August 2007, was one of the key architects of the AKP's foreign policy. In the meantime, Davutoglu wielded increasingly larger influence and Erdogan affirmed his importance by appointing him as foreign minister in May 2009.

Before he became a key member of the AKP's foreign policy team, Davutoglu published his seminal book *Strategic Depth, Turkey's International Position*, in 2001. He argued that Turkey had failed to utilize its multiple geopolitical and historical assets and articulated a vision of a more ambitious and multi-dimensional foreign policy. According to Davutoglu, strategic depth is derived from geographical and historical depth. In his view, Turkey is richly endowed, thanks to its location "right at the centre of Afro-Eurasia. We have territories in Asia and in Europe and we are a neighbour to Africa through the Eastern Mediterranean."[2]

In applying his "strategic depth" doctrine, Davutoglu prescribed a policy of engaging neighbors to foster greater security and economic interdependence. In addition, he argued for high-level political exchanges and an active pursuit of peace. Davutoglu contended that Turkey had squandered opportunities to realize its global mission in the past due to its conflicts with neighbors, and he coined the famous catchphrase, "zero problems with neighbors," to serve as a policy guide. Unlike the previous Turkish governments led by secular parties that eschewed references to Turkey's Ottoman experience, Davutoglu boldly stated that, as the natural heir of the Ottoman Empire, Turkey should utilize the historical and cultural links with the lands that were once part of that realm. This policy orientation received the greatest attention on account of the AKP government's energetic engagement with the country's Arab neighbors. However, when it first assumed office, its leaders were singularly focused on one overriding goal, namely securing Turkey's membership in the European Union.

A few days after his party swept to power, Erdogan wasted no time before visiting European capitals to underscore his party's commitment to pursuing EU membership and to secure a date for the start of accession talks. During its first two years in office, the AKP government adopted an ambitious legislative agenda and achieved an impressive number of reforms in order to improve the country's prospects of admission to the EU. It removed several barriers to freedom of expression, introduced broadcasts in Kurdish and other "minority" languages, and took steps to subordinate the formerly powerful military to civilian control.

That a party with Islamist roots became the ardent champion of EU membership is remarkably ironic. The leading members of the AKP had previously held senior positions in the banned Islamist parties that had adamantly opposed this. As leader of the RP, Necmettin Erbakan had denounced the EU as a Christian club that always treated Turkey poorly; and just a few years before the AKP took office, Gul (at that time an RP member of parliament) had declared that "a key aim of the RP was to protect Turkey's values against the EU."[3] Yet by 2002 there was no more eloquent advocate of the cause of EU membership than Gul.

In reversing their earlier views on the EU membership issue, Gul, Erdogan, and other AKP leaders appear to have undergone a genuine conversion, based on their reassessment of where Turkey's best future prospects lay, both politically and economically. But it must also be noted that their sharp turn toward the pursuit of EU membership was a political master-stroke that at once opportunely confounded their critics, averted a clash with the Turkish secular establishment, and arguably even helped shield the AKP against future military intervention. As the (self-appointed) guardians of secularism, the military leaders were suspicious of the AKP, but they also favored EU membership in the belief that it would safeguard the secular order. For secularists generally, EU membership constituted the ultimate realization of the Kemalist mission to make Turkey an integral part of the West. Indeed, except from some marginal groups, practically all segments of Turkish society supported EU membership. Longing for better times and smarting from the effects of the severe economic crisis of 2001, three-quarters of the Turkish public expressed support for EU membership when the AKP took the helm.[4] Whatever may have been the mix of motives that propelled the AKP towards the pursuit of EU membership, the decision to do so was a profoundly consequential step. Though it was not fully realized, the AKP's European agenda would lead to some key policy choices, not least those related to the settlement of the Cyprus issue that had long complicated Turkey's relations with the US and Europe.

For several decades practically all Turkish politicians paid lip service to the defense of Turkish Cypriot rights as a national imperative. Governments in Ankara, while formally obliged to respond to periodic UN-led initiatives to broker a settlement, for the most part were content to leave the issue alone and to preserve the post-1974 status quo, which amounted to a policy of maintaining the division of Cyprus (with the Turkish-populated North Cyprus separating from the internationally recognized, overwhelmingly ethnically Greek Cypriot state). By 2002, however, a new factor would cast doubt on the status quo: namely, the looming prospect that Cyprus (i.e., the Greek part) would gain membership in the EU. For several months preceding the Turkish parliamentary elections in November 2002, Greek and Turkish Cypriot leaders met regularly with a team representing UN Secretary-General Kofi Annan in anticipation of a new and, this time urgent, UN initiative to settle the dispute prior to the island's EU membership. It was against this background that the AKP was confronted with the Cyprus issue. Eight days after its electoral victory, Annan submitted the "Annan plan" (as it became popularly known) for a settlement that provided for the reunification of Cyprus as a federation.

Given the AKP's European aspirations, it was clear to its leaders that accession of a still-divided Cyprus would, at a minimum, seriously complicate Turkey's own accession bid and perhaps even derail it completely. No sooner had the Secretary-General presented his draft plan than Northern Cyprus President Rauf Denktash declared it unacceptable, citing among other reasons the plan's lack of recognition of Turkish Cypriot sovereignty. For decades, Denktash had been able to count on virtually automatic support from the Turkish government for his policies and pronouncements. But this time the only response from Ankara was a deafening silence, and when the AKP issued its policy statement on Cyprus it declared at the outset that the UN plan was negotiable. The AKP thus implicitly accepted Brussels' linkage between Turkey's EU aspirations and Turkish support of UN efforts to achieve a settlement. Erdogan boldly declared on January 2, 2003: "I am not in favour of the continuation of the policy that has been maintained in Cyprus over the past 30–40 years. ... We will do whatever falls on us. This is not Denktash's private matter."[5]

Though weakened by the AKP's repudiation, Denktash remained a force to be reckoned with because of his public standing as a patriot and senior statesman, and his deep connections with Turkey's secular establishment. In the ensuing clash of wills, the AKP government ultimately prevailed, and Denktash felt obliged to quit as chief Turkish Cypriot negotiator. Mehmet Ali Talat, his pro-settlement successor, mounted a well-organized campaign and, as the AKP had hoped, delivered a solid (65 per cent) vote when the Annan plan was put to a referendum in April 2004. However, the even more decisive no vote of the Greek Cypriots (76 per cent) meant that the Turkish Cypriots' approval was in vain: Cyprus entered the EU still divided and with the Turkish Cypriots excluded.

The AKP government played a helpful role in the Cyprus negotiations by taking an unequivocal stand in support of the Annan plan at the risk of confronting powerful constituencies at home. But troubles with Brussels over Cyprus emerged even before Ankara officially started accession negotiations in October 2005. In a bid to encourage Turkish Cypriots to support the Annan plan, EU emissaries had made promises to end the economic embargo that impeded economic development in North Cyprus. However, by admitting the Greek Cypriot-controlled Republic of Cyprus as a member, the EU enabled the Greek Cypriots to use their newfound leverage to scuttle efforts to end Turkish Cypriot isolation. Ankara retaliated against this obstruction by refusing to open its ports and airport to the vessels and aircraft of the Republic of Cyprus, as required by the customs union agreements that Turkey signed as a precondition to commence EU accession negotiations. When reminded by Turkish officials of their promises to end the isolation of Turkish Cypriots, EU representatives argued that this was a *political* commitment – as opposed to a legally binding agreement – that Brussels was unable to carry out while insisting that Turkey fulfill its *legal* obligation and open its ports to the Republic of Cyprus. Ankara rejected this argument, and in any case, it would be politically risky for it to comply with EU demands without a *quid pro quo* that would relieve Turkish Cypriot political and economic isolation. In the meantime, the Greek Cypriot government had used its veto powers to block several of the chapters of the *acquis communitaire* (the body of law that has emerged in the EU) that Turkey needed to complete to advance its accession to the Union.

Both Turks and Europeans know well that the Cyprus issue is by no means the only, or even the most important, obstacle in Turkey's path to EU membership. European governments and publics have long harbored reservations about admitting Turkey on the grounds that "it is too big, too poor, Muslim and non-European." Whether the stated qualms stand up to close scrutiny is arguable, particularly in view of Turkey's recent strong economic performance, but Turkey has to contend with increasing resistance by some of the key EU members and their public's opposition to its membership. In particular, when he was president of France, Nicholas Sarkozy joined Greek Cyprus to block some of the negotiating chapters. Sarkozy and German Chancellor Angela Merkel have opposed Turkish membership, arguing instead for the alternative of a "privileged partnership," which Ankara has flatly rejected.

Turkish diplomacy, soft power and economic factors

With EU–Turkish relations practically stalled almost from the start of accession negotiations, the AKP government pursued an energetic policy of engaging the countries in its neighborhood and beyond. "Strategic depth," as envisioned by Davutoglu and embraced by Erdogan, aimed at cultivating relationships, providing the principal focus of Turkish diplomacy. Emboldened by early diplomatic achievements, the AKP increasingly saw itself playing a global role as well. Its global ambitions are exemplified by its decision to open 22 new embassies and encouragement of Turkish investments in Africa, as well as such initiatives as Erdogan's visit to Somalia in August 2012 to challenge the international community to pay attention to the dire needs of that helpless country. In a speech he delivered at a conference in London on November 23, 2011, Davutoglu boasted of Turkey's credentials as a global power, pointing out that "we are either a member of, or strategic partner or observer" in "all international organisations," ranging from NATO, the UN, the G20, the Alliance of Civilizations, and hopefully the EU to the Organization of the Islamic Conference, and the founder of the Turkish-speaking States Council (including former Soviet republics) – even an observer in ASEAN and a dialogue partner of the GCC, the Arab League, and the African Union.[6] Under Davutoglu's influence, Turkish diplomacy did not try merely to achieve "zero problems with neighbors" but also to bring about peaceful settlements of problems between them and to calm sectarian tensions within countries. A partial list of disputes that Turkey tried to resolve includes those between Syria and Israel, Hamas and Fatah, Syria and Saudi Arabia, Iran and the West, Pakistan and Afghanistan, Russia and Georgia, and Serbia and Bosnia-Hercegovina, as well as those among the main factions in Lebanon. In a column on August 19, 2010, *The Economist* saluted Davutoglu's diplomatic endeavors under the heading "The Great Mediator" and humorously reported "that Botswana had sought his help in fixing a territorial dispute with Namibia."[7]

Past governments had emphasized Turkey's considerable hard power attributes, most prominently its military, the second biggest in NATO. To a greater degree than its predecessors, the AKP emphasized Turkey's soft power assets by using cultural and educational cooperation, public diplomacy, visa liberalization, development aid, and – not the least – investment and trade.

A variety of actors and agencies, some of which are official, have been increasingly active in projecting Turkey's soft power in neighboring countries. The importance the AKP has assigned to these efforts is indicated by the increasing resources it has assigned to key agencies such as the Turkish International Cooperation and Development Agency (TIKA), which distributes development aid, mostly to poor Muslim countries. TIKA disbursements grew more than nine-fold in seven years – from $85 million in 2002 to $780 million in 2008.[8] The government has also been active in cultural and religious diplomacy. According to Kerem Oktem, the Yunus Emre Cultural Centers have been engaged in promoting Turkish language and culture since 2007 – "first in the Balkans and more recently in the Middle East."[9] The Presidency for Religious Affairs, answerable to the Prime Minister, has provided a variety of "religious services ... for Muslim communities in the Balkans, Central Asia and the Caucasus."[10]

The AKP has encouraged educational links between Turkey and the outside world, but some Turkish educational activities have operated independently. Of these, the most important by far are the "Gulen" schools associated with the influential Turkish religious scholar Fethullah Gulen. The schools promote conservative values, but their teaching is not overtly religious. All have a reputation for rigorous instruction and have often been favored by elites. It is estimated that about 1,000 schools are associated with the Gulen movement operating in more than 100 countries.[11]

Civil society includes countless business associations, lobby groups, and religiously-oriented social networks[12] engaged in enhancing Turkey's visibility and weight in its neighborhood and globally. None of these has attracted as much regional attention as the new phenomenon of popular culture spread through Turkish soap operas in the Balkans, the Caucasus, Central Asia and especially the Middle East. It is estimated that one particular episode of the series called *Gumus* (*Noor* in Arabic) had 70–80 million Arab viewers. The popularity of Turkish television and the removal of visa requirements for visitors from many Arab countries resulted in a surge of tourists. Against a background of warming relations between Turkey and its Arab neighbors, the state-run Turkish Radio and Television Corporation (TRT) launched a new Arabic-language channel, *TRT al Turkiya,* in April 2010. During the ceremony marking the introduction of the new channel, Prime Minister Erdogan declared effusively that it had a potential 350 million viewers.

Together with its Arab-friendly policies and the myriad soft power engagements, Turkey and its leadership have achieved unprecedented popularity in the Arab Middle East. A poll in the Arab world conducted by the University of Maryland in 2010 found that Erdogan was the "most admired world leader."[13] He received a hero's welcome when he visited Egypt, Tunisia, and Libya in the aftermath of the uprisings that overthrew authoritarian rulers. Turkey's success in reconciling Islam with a democratic secular system raised hopes, primarily in Washington and other Western capitals, that the newly liberated Arab countries would adopt the "Turkish model." Turkish leaders have been reticent about promoting their country as a model, choosing "instead ... to portray Turkey more as an 'inspiration' for those struggling to transform the region."[14] Some of the leaders in the newly liberated Arab countries did indicate an interest in the "Turkish model" and spoke warmly of Turkish achievements, but these pronouncements were primarily intended to reassure Western countries that they are modern and not fanatical. There is scant interest at the leadership level in Egypt, Tunisia, and Libya in following the Turkish path of political development. During his triumphant visit to Egypt in September 2011, Erdogan unwittingly evoked objections from senior members of the Muslim Brotherhood by extolling the virtues of a secular system and recommending this for Egypt.[15]

A large part of Turkey's appeal in its neighborhood is related to its economic achievements. Under AKP rule, Turkey's economy has performed remarkably well. During the party's first eight years in power, Turkey's GDP went from $231 billion to $736 billion,[16] and the per capita income of Turks nearly tripled. "From 2002 through 2007, the Turkish economy grew by an average of over 6 per cent a year. Exports have tripled ... Foreign direct investment (FDI), which amounted to $684 million in 1990, increased exponentially to $9.1 billion in 2010."[17] Thanks in part to the reforms in its banking sector in the aftermath of the economic crisis in 2001, Turkey has weathered the effects of the 2008 recession better than many others, including those in the Eurozone. While European economies have stagnated and Turkish exports to the EU countries have declined, Turkey has greatly expanded its trade with the Middle East and the Caucasus.

Highly competitive Turkish businesses have increased their exports throughout the neighborhood. And while Turkey solicits investments from the Gulf states, Turkish investment in the Arab countries has grown "six-fold to more than $30 billion in a decade,"[18] and Turkish firms won "almost $20 billion worth of contracts on some of the Gulf's largest construction schemes."[19] Turkey relied on loans from the IMF to keep its economy afloat in the past. But, in a reversal of roles, it became a donor, agreeing in 2012 to provide $2 billion in credits to Egypt.[20]

"Zero problems with neighbors" in the Middle East

Among a string of new Turkish diplomatic initiatives in the Middle East, the most remarkable was the warming of relations with Syria. These two neighbors had a troubled relationship for many years. Two issues were particularly acrimonious: Turkey's increasing use of the waters of the Euphrates that limited the volume available downstream and Syrian support for the Kurdistan Workers' Party (PKK). Led by Abdullah Ocalan, the militant group was allowed by the Hafez Assad regime to use Syria as a safe heaven and repeatedly launched attacks against Turkey from bases there. But in 1998, in the face of Turkish threats of military action, Assad expelled Ocalan and banned the PKK from operating in Syria. Unable to find a safe haven after numerous attempts, the PKK leader was captured by Turkish agents in Kenya, in February 1999 and brought to Turkey, where he was put on trial and jailed.

Damascus now welcomed new Turkish initiatives. Better relations with Turkey offered Syria the prospect of escaping isolation at a time when it felt especially vulnerable, for in the aftermath of the US invasion of Iraq it now faced great pressure from Washington over its role in both Iraq and Lebanon. In any case, the two neighbors shared an interest in containing Kurdish nationalism. In addition, both opposed the invasion and feared the spillover that might result from Iraq's disintegration.

In a gesture appreciated by the Syrian government, Turkish President Ahmet Necdet Sezer attended the funeral of Hafiz Assad in 2002. The Turkish parliament's decision the following year against allowing US troops to invade Iraq through Turkish territory elevated Turkey's standing in Syria and the rest of the Arab world. High-level visits ushered in a remarkable warming of political relations and greatly expanded bilateral trade. A Turkish parliamentary delegation visited Syria in April 2003. These overtures set the stage for the historic visit to Turkey of Syrian President Bashar Assad the following year. Other high-level visits followed. In 2004, Erdogan flew to Damascus to sign a free trade agreement. A year later, President Sezer disregarded US pressure and went on a state visit to Damascus, and Assad traveled to Turkey in 2007. On one occasion, underscoring the warming of their countries' relations, Assad and his wife Asma joined Erdogan and his wife Emine on a vacation in Turkey.

The AKP's "zero problems" policy did not aim at just improving political relations. It also involved a drive to expand Turkey's economic opportunities in the region. From a modest $729 million in 2000, Turkey's trade with Syria increased to $2.74 billion in 2008.[21] Although this represented a small part of Turkey's total trade, the new export opportunities seized in Syria and other Middle Eastern neighbors significantly boosted the Turkish economy.

The blossoming trade with Syria resulted from extraordinary progress in political relations. In accordance with a treaty signed in 2009, the two countries abolished visa requirements for each other's nationals, thereby greatly increasing travel. The treaty also led to the first ministerial meeting of the Turkey–Syria High-Level Strategic Cooperation Council (modeled on the earlier Council for Turkey and Iraq) in October 2009. Indicating growing trust between Ankara and Damascus, Turkey even served as mediator in peace negotiations between Syria and Israel until they were terminated after the latter's invasion of Gaza in December 2008.

While Turkish–Syrian relations flourished until 2011, the once-close Turkish–Israeli relations deteriorated with the invasion of Gaza. In a bid to advance the Palestinian–Israeli peace process, Turkey had conferred a rare honor on both Israel's President Shimon Peres and Palestinian Authority President Mahmoud Abbas by inviting them to address the Turkish parliament during their state visits in 2007.

Turkey hosted Prime Minister Ehud Olmert only few days before he sent forces to Gaza. In his meetings with Erdogan, Olmert encouraged Turkey's ongoing endeavor to facilitate peace between Israel and Syria. Then when the invasion occurred so soon afterward, Erdogan felt betrayed, and Turkish mediation essentially ended. Turkey's irritation was compounded by Israel's excesses during the invasion. Public sentiment overwhelmingly sympathized with the Palestinians. In any case, few in the AKP were keen on the idea of close relations with the Jewish state.

Turkey had voted against the partition plan for Palestine in 1947 but recognized the Jewish state in 1949. For many years, it was the only Muslim country to have diplomatic relations with Israel. Turkish–Israeli relations subsequently weathered periodic strains, mostly over Israeli actions in the occupied Palestinian territories. However, they rarely reached breaking point until the Israeli assault on the Gaza flotilla in 2008 that resulted in the killing of nine Turks. As a gesture to the Palestinians, Turkey accepted the

PLO's request to open an office in the Turkish capital in 1979, before the US and the European countries recognized it as the sole legitimate representative of the Palestinian people. There were some later irritations in the Turkish–Israeli relationship, as when former Turkish Prime Minister (later President) Turgut Ozal attempted to improve relations with Arab states. However, beginning in the mid-1990s, Turkey and Israel took extraordinary steps to advance their relations, much to the consternation of the Palestinians, Turkey's other Arab neighbors, and Iran.

The two governments entered into a host of agreements on such matters as educational exchanges, tourism, environmental cooperation and free trade. But the "core of the relationship was military-strategic."[22] From Ankara's perspective, the enhanced Turkish–Israeli partnership increased pressure on Syria in the context of its support for the PKK. The Military Training and Cooperation Agreement, signed in 1996, "outlined a range of joint training and intelligence-sharing activities, including Israeli access to the Konya airbase and Turkish airspace for training purposes, Israeli modernization of the Turkish air force, and Israeli provision of military technology to Turkey."[23] These agreements expanded bilateral trade and conferred a significant boost to the Israeli defense industry which welcomed the new export opportunities.

Ankara's perennially frustrated attempts to obtain military supplies from the US in the face of opposition by Greek and Armenian lobbies provided a major reason for seeking Israeli military hardware and technology. Additionally, the Turkish government believed that an enhanced relationship with Israel would gain support from the Israel lobby in dissuading Congress from acceding to the Armenian diaspora's campaign to apply the label "genocide" to the massive killing of Ottoman Armenians during World War I.

While Turkish–Israeli relations flourished, Ankara also sought to boost its support of the Palestinians in various ways. These included channeling modest, though growing, aid to them through the Turkish International Cooperation and Development Agency (TIKA); endorsing the project sponsored by the Turkish Chambers of Commerce (TOBB) to set up an industrial zone on the border between Israel and Gaza in the hope of generating employment for many Palestinians; offering a training program for Palestinian diplomats; and opening the Ottoman archives containing land registration records in Jerusalem, thereby presumably aiding Palestinian efforts to counter illegal Israeli expropriations of Palestinian properties.[24]

But the most contentious Turkish action concerning the Palestine issue occurred soon after Hamas won the Palestinian legislative elections in 2006. The AKP government then invited its leader, Khaled Meshal, to Ankara for talks. Unlike Israel and the United States, who protested the visit, Turkey argued in favor of diplomatic engagement with Hamas and against the economic blockade and isolation of Gaza. Responding to Israel's criticism, then Foreign Minister Abdullah Gul argued that Ankara "advised Hamas to disarm, become more moderate, and enter into diplomatic negotiations with Israel."[25] A Turkish columnist opined that without Turkey reaching out and relieving its diplomatic isolation, Hamas would have had to turn to "the Iran-Syria-Hezbollah axis."[26] Ankara also tried unsuccessfully to persuade Hamas and the Fatah-controlled Palestinian Authority in the West Bank to overcome their differences and speak with one voice.

Israeli irritation over the Hamas leader's visit to Turkey proved to be a minor setback to the relationship, but Turkish–Israeli relations were more seriously tested in the aftermath of Israel's invasion of Gaza on December 27, 2008 that resulted in heavy Palestinian casualties. As protesting Turks in various cities condemned Israeli actions, Erdogan castigated Israel for maintaining an embargo against Gaza. As he put it "In Gaza, people seem to live in an open prison. In fact, all Palestine looks like an open prison."[27] Soon afterwards, at a panel in Davos where both he and Israeli President Shimon Peres spoke, Erdogan accused Israel of war crimes, telling Peres "When it comes to killing, you know very well how to kill."[28]

In October 2009, Turkey withdrew its invitation to Israel to participate in a multinational military exercise. Relations deteriorated further when Deputy Foreign Minister Danny Ayalon publicly humiliated Turkish Ambassador Ahmet Oguz Celikkol. Ayalon told the Israeli media covering the meeting with the Turkish Ambassador: "Pay attention that he is sitting in a lower chair … that there is only an Israeli flag on the table and that we are not smiling."[29] Ankara promptly demanded and received an official apology. Relations between the two countries reached their lowest point when Israeli forces boarded a Turkish vessel en route to deliver humanitarian supplies to Gaza while it sailed in international waters. In the ensuing brawl, eight Turkish citizens and one Turkish-American were killed. An angry Turkish government demanded an apology and compensation for the victims, as well as an international investigation of the incident and the lifting of the Israeli blockade of Gaza. Unhappy about Israel's refusal to comply, Turkey expelled the Israeli ambassador on September 1, 2011, cut all military ties with Israel and reduced its diplomatic relations to the level of second secretary. On the other hand, trade relations between the two countries have not been interrupted. Nevertheless, recent agreements between the Greek Cypriot government and Israel to exploit the natural gas deposits discovered in the eastern Mediterranean and to cooperate on exporting gas upset Turkey and added yet another squabble to Turkish–Israeli relations. The Turkish public overwhelmingly support Palestinians in their struggle against Israel, and Erdogan left no doubt about his position when he accused Israel of being a "terrorist state" during renewed hostilities in November 2012.[30]

The setbacks in Turkish–Israeli relations aroused considerable anxiety in Washington, raising questions in official US circles about whether Turkey was going through an axis shift in its foreign policy. Against a background of improved ties with all Arab neighbors and a near-breakdown of its formerly close ties to Israel, Turkey under the AKP appeared to move close to Iran. For nearly two decades before the AKP attained power, Turkish–Iranian relations were uneasy. This was a period when the fiercely secular Turkish military wielded great influence over national policy. Turkish governments accused Iran of backing anti-secular forces in Turkey and suspected it of involvement in several attempts to assassinate prominent secularists, as well as assisting the PKK.[31] In any case, as two of the region's most powerful countries, these neighbors have competed for influence in the Caucasus, Central Asia, and the Middle East.

It was to be expected that in keeping with its "zero problems with neighbors" the AKP government would seek to improve ties with Iran. Although some of their interests diverge, they have had common causes as well. Notwithstanding Ankara's occasional accusations of Iranian aid to the PKK, both countries are apprehensive about Kurdish nationalism and have opposed Kurdish independence in northern Iraq out of fear that their own Kurdish minorities would be emboldened and demand autonomy if not outright independence. They have collaborated against Kurdish separatist fighters in northern Iraq who launch attacks against their respective countries. Moreover, they take exception to the "attempt by the West to intervene in the Middle East, which both regard as being a Muslim sphere of interest."[32] Beyond these commonalities is the all-important energy relationship: hydrocarbon-rich Iran is the second largest exporter of natural gas as well as of substantial amounts of oil to energy-poor Turkey. Iranian oil and gas has helped Turkey reduce its reliance on Russian hydrocarbons. The volume of trade between the two countries has increased "more than tenfold from $1.25 billion in 2002 to $16.05 billion in 2011,"[33] but the vast amounts of energy that Iran exports to Turkey accounts for most of this.

In keeping with its quest to engage neighbors and solve regional problems, the AKP government sought to defuse tensions between the West and Iran over the latter's uranium enrichment program. Accordingly Erdogan and Davutoglu invested considerable diplomatic capital to find a formula that would be acceptable to both Iran and the International Atomic Energy Agency (IAEA) and thereby alleviate Western fears over Iran's nuclear intentions.

Although they have not stated this in public, Turkish leaders are against Iran's acquisition of nuclear weapons.[34] However, they believe that diplomatic engagement rather than military action against Iran is the only credible approach to dealing with the issue. This stance is not unlike that of several European powers, but Iran sees them as beholden to Washington. By contrast, Turkey under the AKP appeared to Tehran to be an acceptable intermediary. Erdogan castigated the West for its hypocrisy in remaining silent about Israel's nuclear arsenal while agitating over Iran's peaceful nuclear enrichment activities. The Turkish government also spoke against increased economic sanctions against Iran.

Following a deadlock in negotiations between Iran and the permanent members of the UN Security Council plus Germany (P5 plus 1) and, with initial encouragement by the Obama administration, Turkey and Brazil together petitioned Iran in early 2010 to accept an offer to exchange its low-enriched uranium for fuel rods. Iran had rejected this offer earlier but now relented.

However, before Turkey and Brazil could savor what appeared like a diplomatic breakthrough, the US and its allies rejected the deal, arguing that "that would have left enough low-enriched uranium in Iran's hands for the production of a nuclear device."[35] When the UN Security Council voted to apply additional sanctions on Iran in June 2010, Turkey and Brazil voted against them. In Washington, the AKP government's action was seen as an unprecedented rejection by its NATO ally and renewed fears that Turkey under the AKP was moving away from the West in favor of its Eastern neighbors.

However, later developments have shown these fears to be unwarranted. In a move welcomed by Washington but heavily criticized by Tehran, Ankara decided at the NATO summit in Lisbon in November 2010 to allow the stationing of an anti-missile system on its soil that Iran believes to be aimed at it. Ankara insisted that there be no mention of Iran as a threat and, in a reference to Israel, that the data collected by radar would not be shared with non-NATO members. During a visit to Iran in March 2012, Erdogan tried to reassure his hosts by saying "If NATO does not comply with Turkey's conditions, we can ask them to dismantle the system."[36]

On another front, the clash of interests over the Assad regime in Syria has the potential to inflict further damage to Turkish–Iranian relations. While Iran has provided the Syrian regime with financial aid and arms, Turkey has been a principal backer of the Syrian opposition and has allowed Syrian rebels to receive arms and training on Turkish soil. In a sign of deteriorating relations, in December 2012, Turkey's Interior Minister Naim Sahin accused Iran of allowing its territory to be used to launch attacks against Turkey.[37] Notwithstanding these strains, the record of the AKP government is in keeping with the traditional Turkish policy of carefully managing its relations with its powerful neighbor.

In contrast to its finely-tuned approach to Iran, Turkey's dealings with post-Saddam Iraq have seemed hard-headed and have taken some unanticipated turns. Like such other neighbors of Iran and Iraq as Syria, Turkey has opposed Iraq's breakup in the aftermath of the US invasion and occupation. As expected, Turkey's political and military establishment viewed the rise of a de facto Kurdish state in Iraq with alarm, fearing that it would inflame nationalist sentiment among Turkish Kurds and destabilize the country. Accordingly, the Turkish government expressed its "vociferous" opposition to Kurdish aspirations to achieve independence, and even warned against a federal system that would grant autonomy to Iraqi Kurds. Within a few years, however, Ankara was obliged to quietly draw back from its declaration that establishing an ethnic federation in Iraq was unacceptable and would constitute a "red line." Affirming their intention to remain a part of Iraq, and comforted with their alliance with the US occupation forces, Kurdish leaders confidently disregarded Ankara's demand.

While Iraqi Kurds proceeded to consolidate their gains, the AKP government faced an immediate, though familiar, threat from Kurdish insurgents at home. On June 1, 2004, having evidently decided that the government had no intention of granting full cultural and political rights to the Kurds, the PKK terminated the ceasefire that it had observed since 2002 and resumed its war against the Turkish state. The AKP government's problem was compounded by the fact that many PKK attacks on Turkish targets were originating from bases in northern Iraq in territory controlled by the Kurdish Regional Government (KRG).

Neither the nominal Iraqi government in Baghdad nor the US government was prepared to take measures to prevent such incursions, the former because it was run by a Shi'ite-Kurdish coalition whose actual control did not extend to Iraqi Kurdistan and the latter because its armed forces were fully occupied with fighting a fierce insurgency in Iraq's Arab provinces. With PKK attacks from northern Iraq unhindered by any government, a frustrated Erdogan was reduced to engaging in occasional angry rhetoric with KRG president Barzani, accusing his government of not just tolerating but of providing the PKK fighters with logistical support. In turn, Barzani protested that the key to solving the PKK problem rested with Ankara's willingness to achieve a political settlement of its Kurdish problem, thereby putting the onus on Turkey.

Paradoxically, while Ankara studiously avoided official contact with the KRG for nearly five years, Turkish businesses have engaged in lucrative multibillion-dollar trade with the Kurdish region. Three-quarters of Turkish–Iraqi trade, reported to total $10–12 billion in 2012, is between Turkey and the KRG,[38] and an estimated 55–60 per cent of the companies doing business in the Kurdish region are Turkish. By 2008, the Turkish government reversed its policy vis-à-vis Iraqi Kurds and began to deal with the KRG directly rather than work, as in the past, through the Baghdad government. With its position due to be weakened following the departure of US troops, the Kurdish leadership welcomed the change of Turkish policy, and high-level visits soon followed as economic ties deepened further.

However, while Turkish–KRG ties improved greatly, Turkish ties with the Baghdad government led by Nuri al-Maliki deteriorated. Erdogan's government openly backed the secular Iraqiyya Party leader, Ayad Allawi, in the elections of March 2010. But following uncertain results, it was al-Maliki who cobbled a government together the following December. Relations between Baghdad and Ankara went from bad to worse after that, with Erdogan's government accusing the Iraqi prime minister of pursuing a sectarian agenda while al-Maliki accused the Turkish leader of interfering in Iraq's domestic affairs and called Turkey a "hostile state." The strains between the two governments worsened when Turkey refused to extradite fugitive Iraqi Vice President Tareq al-Hashemi (a Sunni Arab), whose death sentence at home on charges of having run death squads was widely interpreted as part of a sectarian power struggle.

Ankara–Baghdad relations have undergone further strain with the remarkable warming of ties between Turkey and the KRG. Casting aside its former policy of dealing with it through Baghdad, Turkey has reached agreement with Massoud Barzani's government to import oil from the Kurdish region without involving Iraq's central government and has discussed ambitious plans to increase such imports through a new pipeline. Ironically, this policy reversal appears to be empowering the Kurdish de facto state in northern Iraq, a course that Ankara would have considered unthinkable in earlier years. But domestic considerations have been uppermost in Ankara's new course: Turkey needs to diversify its sources of energy, and the once-derided Barzani increasingly appears as a useful ally in fighting the PKK.

On the other hand, Turkey's actions could hurt its trade relations with Baghdad. The Maliki government expressed its displeasure by banning the Turkish Petroleum Corporation from an oil exploration project in Basra in November 2012. It also refused permission to Turkish Energy Minister Taner Yildiz to fly to Erbil, the Kurdish region's capital, for an oil and gas conference in December 2012. Overshadowing the serious decline in the Ankara–Baghdad relations is the Turkish resentment of al-Maliki's close relations with Iran and his support for Syria's Assad regime that Turkey is helping to overthrow.

Turkey has struggled to cope with changes in the political landscape of the Middle East in the aftermath of the "Arab Spring." The biggest challenge by far has been the uprising and ensuing civil war in Syria. Syria was the centerpiece of Turkey's diplomacy in the Middle East, and Erdogan's government assumed that it had considerable leverage over President Bashar Assad. And yet, when the Syrian regime started to use violent measures against civilian protesters, Ankara was unsuccessful in its bid to restrain him. Similarly, the many hours that Foreign Minister Davutoglu spent with the Syrian leader recommending reforms to end the escalating violence were to no avail. As the civil war accelerated and more than 200,000 Syrians refugees poured into Turkey, the AKP government condemned the Assad regime and began to assist the opposition. Turkey has been left to agonize about the danger of long-lasting instability along its 560-mile border and has been particularly distressed about spillover effects if Syrian Kurds achieve autonomy in post-Assad Syria and complicate Turkey's efforts to contain Kurdish separatism at home. To make matters worse for Turkey, as previously noted, its Syrian policies have damaged its relations with Iraq and Iran as well as Russia.

The Balkans, the Caucasus, Russia, and the eastern Mediterranean

The considerable fluidity and drama of the AKP government's diplomacy in the Middle East contrasts with its experience in other neighboring regions. Nevertheless, while the Erdogan government has been far more preoccupied in the Middle East, it also bolstered Turkey's relations with the Caucasus and especially the Balkans, where its presence increased significantly. Once parts of the Ottoman Empire, these regions have provided considerable opportunities for applying Davutoglu's policy. And these are places where Turkey faces little competition, either from other countries in the region or from outside powers, making them "a safe and 'low cost' area" for it to pursue "its 'strategic depth' and 'zero problem' policies."[39]

In some respects the AKP's Balkan policies continue those of its predecessors since the end of the Cold War. Turkey's approach to the region is partly explainable by Turkey's cultural affinity with the Muslim communities in a region dominated by countries with Christian majorities. The spectacle of Serb victimization of Bosnian Muslims (hereafter Bosniaks) and Kosovars during the Balkan wars greatly disturbed Turkish public opinion and was a major factor that propelled Turkey's participation in NATO's military campaigns against Serbia during the 1990s. Also, Turkish governments took into consideration "the domestic pressure of a large number of Turks, themselves descendants of Muslims who fled the Balkans from the late nineteenth century onwards."[40] Moreover, as with the commercial dimension of the "zero problems with neighbors" in the Middle East, Turkey's policy in the Balkans has been economically driven, allowing Turkish businesses to engage in profitable economic activities.

It is understandable that, as in the former Ottoman lands in the Middle East, Davutoglu's regular effusive references to the Ottoman legacy would provoke negative responses. This is apparent at the popular level in the Balkan countries, given the bitter memories of Ottoman rule in most of the region. But it has not been a problem at the level of policy makers.[41]

In accordance with his quest to project Turkey's "soft power," Davutoglu has contributed to peaceful relations and reconciliation of states that were on opposite sides during the Balkan wars of the 1990s. One of Turkey's notable diplomatic achievements was the meeting of the presidents of Bosnia-Herzegovina, Croatia, and Serbia in Istanbul in April 2010, which affirmed "Serbia's respect for the territorial integrity of Bosnia-Herzegovina."[42] This represented a milestone in Serbia's relations with independent Bosnia. In the following year, Davutoglu reportedly "helped negotiate ... the language of a Serbian apology for the atrocities in Srebrenica."[43] Yet another significant act of reconciliation occurred soon afterwards. In a ceremony of great symbolism attended by Erdogan and French Foreign Minister Bernard Kouchner in 2010, Serbia's President Boris Tadic also participated in the commemoration for the Bosniak victims of Srebrenica. Not the least of Turkey's Balkan achievements has been the establishment of close relations with Serbia that would have been unthinkable during the 1990s. The two countries have greatly bolstered their economic relations, and, in 2010, they even abolished visa requirements for each other's citizens.

In pursuing a policy of active engagement in the Balkans, Turkey under the AKP has benefited from a "power vacuum" in the region, seizing a geopolitical "window of opportunity."[44] By contrast, on account of Russia's presence and deep-rooted interests, Turkey has found it a lot harder to make inroads in the Caucasus. Russia is one of Turkey's biggest trading partners, with a total trade of $38 billion in 2008[45] most of which is in Russia's favor on account of the huge volume of oil and gas that Turkey imports from its neighbor. Russia's Gazprom provides more than 60 per cent of Turkey's natural gas, while a third of its oil and much of its coal also comes from Russia[46]

Trade and deepening economic links have been instrumental in warming Turkish–Russian relations since the end of the Cold War, beginning even before the AKP came to power in 2002. Millions of Russian tourists holiday in Turkey every year. Bilateral relations have improved substantially in pursuit of common interests since then, but conflicting goals also have generated friction. The two countries compete for influence in the Caucasus and, to a lesser extent, among the Turkic republics in Central Asia. Turkey's goal to become an energy hub and its plans to circumvent and compete with Russian pipelines have impinged on Russian interests. More recently, the two countries' clash over the future of the Assad regime has threatened to damage their relationship.

On the whole, Turkish governments have appreciated the limits of their leverage with Russia and have been reticent about undermining relations. The AKP government followed this approach as much as its predecessors. Thus, when Russia invaded Georgia in 2008 in retaliation for the latter's attack on South Ossetia, Ankara "issued only cursory criticism and confined itself to urging respect for Georgia's territorial integrity."[47] In another indication of its reluctance to provoke Russia, the Turkish government observed strict limits, as required by the Montreux Convention of 1936, in allowing US vessels to cross the Turkish Straits to provide aid to Georgia in the aftermath of the Russia–Georgia fighting.[48]

In the wake of the Soviet Union's dissolution and replacement by 15 separate independent states, there was much speculation that the Turkic republics of Central Asia, namely Turkmenistan, Kirgizstan, Uzbekistan, and Kazakhstan, would establish close ties with Ankara on account of their linguistic and cultural links with one another. However, beyond agreeing to cultivate trade and economic relations with Turkey, these countries have assigned a greater importance to preserving strong economic and political links with Russia.

Of the Turkic states, only neighboring Azerbaijan has established close political and economic relations with Turkey. Locked in a seemingly unwinnable struggle with Russian-backed Armenia over the future of the Nagorno-Karabagh enclave and the occupation of a swath of its territory by Armenian forces, Azerbaijan has eagerly sought Turkish help. However, beyond providing indirect military assistance to its Turkic neighbor in the form of supplies and training, and in view of Russia's military presence in Armenia, Turkey has refrained from injecting itself into the Azeri–Armenian military confrontation. It has no interest in the escalation of the conflict over Karabagh.

On the other hand, Turkish–Azeri collaboration over Azerbaijan's hydrocarbon resources is of great importance to both. Turkey imports considerable supplies of Azeri oil and natural gas. The Baku-Tblisi-Ceyhan pipeline, commissioned in 2006 and built with strong US support, carries Azeri oil to the Turkey's Mediterranean coast for export to Western markets. Added to the existing Kirkuk-Ceyhan oil pipeline that carries Iraqi oil to Turkey, it gave a substantial boost to plans to make the country an energy hub. Turkey has approved plans to construct another pipeline to carry Russian and Kazakh oil from Turkey's Black Sea port of Samsun to Ceyhan in the south. There are pipelines, too, that carry Russian, Azeri, and Iranian gas to Turkey. Plans have been made since 2002 for the Nabucco pipeline project, backed by Washington, to carry Caspian oil from Turkey to central Europe while bypassing Russian-controlled pipelines. If the obstacles to realizing this project could be overcome, it would reduce Europe's dependence on Russian energy and further enhance Turkey's role.

In one of the most challenging diplomatic initiatives, the AKP government attempted to normalize relations with Armenia and end acrimony over Yerevan's insistence that Turkey should acknowledge the genocide against the Armenians during World War I. A promising initiative that started with the visit of President Gul to Armenia in 2008 on the occasion of a soccer match yielded two protocols the following year. These called for establishing diplomatic relations and opening the Turkish-Armenian border, which Turkey closed in solidarity with Azerbaijan over the Karabagh issue. But what appeared to be a worthy objective in line with the "zero problems with neighbors" policy floundered in the face of Azerbaijani protests over Ankara's willingness to take such a step while Armenia continued to occupy Azeri territory. There were also strong domestic objections from nationalist quarters at home. In retreat, Erdogan felt obliged to declare that parliamentary acceptance of the protocols would be linked to resolving the Karabagh issue. The protocols fared no better in Armenia, where the government also retreated in the face of strong objections by the opposition and from the Armenian diaspora to key provisions, including one calling for a joint Armenian-Turkish historical commission to investigate the events of 1915 rather than for Turkey's acknowledgement of genocide.

As in the Caucasus, the "zero problems with neighbors" policy achieved mixed results in the eastern Mediterranean. The AKP government had acted boldly by reversing the decades-old policy supporting the division of Cyprus and encouraged Turkish Cypriots to vote in 2004 in favor of the Annan plan that called for reunification. But when the EU accepted Cyprus' accession despite Greek Cypriot rejection of the UN plan, Ankara felt betrayed. By admitting the Greek-Cypriot controlled Republic of Cyprus as a member, the EU effectively created a major impediment to Turkish accession. As Ankara feared, the Greek Cypriot government proceeded to use its veto on several chapters of the *acquis*, thereby helping stall Turkey's accession.

Turkey supported the resumption of negotiations between Greek and Turkish Cypriot leaders in 2008, but it has not shown its previous eagerness. Recent disagreements over huge offshore gas deposits discovered in 2011 further endanger relations between Turkey and the Greek Cypriots. Increasing cooperation by the latter with Israel in exploiting this resource has led Ankara to accuse the Greek Cypriot government of impinging on its exclusive economic zone, and it has warned that energy companies participating in exploration activities would be barred from joining any new oil and gas exploration in Turkey.

While continued acrimony characterizes Turkey's relations with Greek Cyprus, the once crisis-prone relations between Greece and Turkey have improved considerably since the beginning of their rapprochement in 1999. Disagreements over the Aegean continental shelf, the exclusive economic zone, and the territorial sea had repeatedly brought the two neighbors to the brink of war, most recently in 1996. Although none of the core disputes in the Aegean has been resolved, Erdogan's government has continued efforts to reduce the possibility of confrontation and thereby to achieve stability in bilateral relations. The AKP's decision to reverse Turkish policy on Cyprus and support the Annan plan eased Ankara's relations with Athens. For nearly a decade and a half, a sense of calm has prevailed in Greek–Turkish relations, and neither country has shown any inclination to disturb the current state of affairs.

Turkish relations with the US and Europe

Relations between Ankara and Washington experienced a major setback soon after the AKP came to power when the Turkish parliament rejected a motion to allow US forces to use Turkish territory for launching their impending invasion of Iraq. Soon, however, it was Ankara's turn to be distraught, as the invasion spawned an alliance between Iraqi Kurds and the US and, as previously noted, strengthened the de facto Kurdish state in northern Iraq. This presented Turkey with a major security problem, and, from Ankara's vantage point, the US displayed scant sensitivity about important Turkish interests. When it launched the first Gulf war more than a decade earlier, the US demonstrated that it was oblivious to Turkey's security concerns when it enabled a self-governing Kurdish entity to emerge in Iraq's north. That same war also cost Turkey dearly in economic terms by putting an end to its formerly lucrative trade with Iraq, previously one of its biggest trading partners.

Disenchantment with the US has grown even more conspicuous among the Turkish public. A Pew Global Attitudes Project Survey in 2007 reported that a great majority of Turks held a strikingly negative opinion of the country, with only nine per cent expressing a positive view, a drop of 21 points from the already low level the organization found five years earlier.[49]

The Turkish public's view of the US improved modestly after Barack Obama's election as president. Obama visited Turkey within a few months of assuming office in a bid to repair previous damage to the relationship. In his address to the Turkish parliament he described Turkish–US relations as a "model partnership," replacing the term "strategic partnership" used by previous administrations. His hosts interpreted this to mean that the US wanted to elevate the level of cooperation. Obama also established close personal rapport with Erdogan that "mitigated strains in 2010 caused by differences over Iran, Turkish–Israeli tensions, and the reintroduction of a Congressional resolution on the 'Armenian genocide' issue, which had long bedeviled the relationship."[50]

Both the US and Turkey realize that the nature of their relationship has changed since the end of the Cold War, and Washington understands that it can no longer take its partner for granted. The AKP has shown that it will take independent action in pursuit of interests that do not always align with those of its ally, as both governments sought to overcome the damage caused by the invasion of Iraq. While taking issue with Ankara over its relationship with Hamas, deteriorating relations with Israel, warm relations with the Assad regime prior to the uprising, and seeming closeness to Iran, the Obama administration has pursued a nuanced policy in its relations with Turkey and has recognized its increased economic and diplomatic clout, particularly in the Middle East. Like his predecessor, Obama has appreciated Turkey's contribution to the US-led International Security Assistance Force (ISAF) in Afghanistan. The US President sees Turkey as a "critical partner" in dealing with his administration's "three most urgent strategic issues – Afghanistan, Iraq, and Iran."[51] Moreover, both Obama and his immediate predecessor clearly have seen the AKPs Islamist roots and its greater focus on the Islamic world as "an advantage."[52]

The Obama administration looks favorably at Turkish activism in the Middle East. In spite of differences over such issues as relations with Israel, it sees Turkey as a useful partner in containing Syria's instability and "as a counterweight to Iranian influence in the region."[53] Moreover, Washington hopes the Turkish "model" will inspire political parties and movements that have become empowered since the outbreak of the "Arab Spring." For its part, like its predecessors, the AKP government appreciates the numerous areas of overlap between Turkey's interests and those of its NATO ally. These include measures enabling Turkey to become an energy hub to reduce its (and Europe's) dependence on Russian energy, checking Russia's power in the Black Sea region and in the Caucasus and Central Asia, and promoting Turkey's membership in the EU, as well as enhancing stability in the Middle East.

While Turkey's ties with the US have improved, its faltering EU membership prospects have kept relations with Europe awkward and acrimonious. It has barely progressed on its membership course. Since negotiations began in 2005, only one of the 33 "chapters" required for accession has been completed, with 18 others blocked, mostly by Greek Cyprus and France. While it complains of obstacles, the AKP government has done little since 2005 to continue the reforms undertaken to satisfy membership criteria. In its report of October 10, 2010, "the normally cautious European Commission made clear that in several areas Turkey not only was failing to make sufficient progress towards EU standards but was regressing, particularly in terms of democratization, political accountability, independence of the judiciary and freedom of expression."[54]

The Turkish response to the Commission's blunt observations was uncompromising. There appear to be divisions within the senior ranks of the AKP about pursuing EU membership. Erdogan's periodic denunciations of the organization suggest that he has lost interest in joining it. On the other hand, President Gul continues to believe in the need to strive for membership.[55]

Even though Turkey's accession prospects have diminished, neither the Turkish government nor the EU has shown any desire to end the membership course. Turkey has benefited greatly in economic terms from the process, which has led it to encourage "an unprecedented inflow of foreign investments and, through reassuring the financial markets, helping to stabilize interest and exchange rates and fuelling the credit boom that has driven the domestic demand that has produced the impressive growth figures of the last decade."[56] Europe is vital to Turkey's economy in other respects as well, considering that 38 per cent of its exports go there[57] and that three-quarters of its tourists are European.

Realpolitik, ideology, and domestic factors

Some writers have cited the origins of the AKP in political Islam, and the expanded engagement of Erdogan's government with the Muslim Middle East, together with worsening relations with Israel, as evidence of the "Islamization" of Turkish foreign policy. "Islamic" inclinations could indeed account for Turkish actions in several instances. Davutoglu's extraordinary visit to Burma in August 2012, accompanied by Erdogan's wife Emine, to draw international attention to the severe discrimination against the Rohingya Muslims, provides one such example. Erdogan's visit to Somalia in August 2012 to mobilize the international community to help Somalis conceivably had more to do with helping a desperate Muslim people than with showing solidarity with a struggling African state. Whatever the motives, these initiatives were positively viewed by the international community.

However, while he has shown sensitivity to discrimination experienced by Muslims in various parts of the world, the Turkish Prime Minister exposed himself to charges of hypocrisy on account of his relations with Sudan's President Omar al-Bashir.[58] Erdogan visited Sudan in 2006. In November 2009, responding to Western criticisms when Bashir was invited to the Organization of Islamic Conference summit in Istanbul, he declared that he saw no evidence of genocide and asserted that no Muslim could commit that crime.[59]

Erdogan and Davutoglu have often taken the lead in addressing issues that resonate in the Arab and Muslim world, most prominently in relation to the Palestinians. AKP leaders appear more sensitive to the challenges faced by Muslim societies than were their predecessors and have vied for a leadership position in the Islamic world. Nevertheless, the party's ten-year record hardly demonstrates that an "axis shift" has shifted Turkey's position to an Islamic-oriented one. While it has bolstered relations with many Muslim countries, Erdogan's government has shown remarkable diligence in improving ties with such Christian-majority countries as Russia, the Ukraine, Georgia, Greece, and virtually all the Balkan states. Even in the case of countries with which ties have seen no improvement, the AKP has shown a willingness to reverse old policies, as in negotiating path-breaking protocols with Armenia and supporting the Annan plan for Cyprus.

Recent improvements in relations with the US, as well as the collapsed rapprochement with Assad's Syria that also has strained ties with his Iranian ally, point to the failure of the AKP to make a radical break with Turkey's post-1945 foreign policies. Such developments have helped alleviate anxieties in some Western quarters that Turkey – even if it has lost hope for membership in the EU – is turning its back on its long-time allies in favor of closer relations with Iran and perhaps even Russia. While one cannot discount the influence of Islamic identity – whose saliency could grow in the future – in shaping Turkey's foreign policy, the AKP's record demonstrates pragmatic activism.

The AKP's greater activism in the Middle East has occurred in the context of declining US influence in the wake of its military withdrawal from Iraq and its inability to achieve progress in settling the Palestinian–Israeli dispute. Turkey has taken advantage of the limitations of the region's other major powers, namely Iran and Egypt. Although Iran has benefited from the emergence of a Shi'ite-dominated post-Saddam Iraq and continued alliance with Syria, influence over Hezbollah and Hamas, the hostility of most Arab regimes (and much of the public) has constrained its clout. As Turkey fostered closer relations with Saudi Arabia, the Gulf Arab states have been content to see Turkey play a greater role in the region to help contain Iran. Moreover, the passive regional role of Egypt under ex-President Hosni Mubarak made it easier for Turkey to forge new links in the region. In the Balkans, too, Turkey has taken advantage of geopolitical opportunities and expanded its influence without attracting the type of international attention resulting from its Middle Eastern engagements.

One of Turkey's major incentives to forge new alliances in the Middle East relates directly to its Kurdish problem. Few challenges have preoccupied the country as much as the demand from its Kurdish citizens for far-reaching reforms, including the right to state-funded education in the Kurdish language, and, more controversially, creating federal arrangements to allow Kurdish autonomy in the southeast. While they have struggled to contain the PKK-led Kurdish insurgency at home, Turkish governments have long sought to enlist cooperation from Iraq, Iran and Syria to contain Kurdish nationalism. The increasing threat of Kurdish separatism resulting from the emergence of a de facto Kurdish state in northern Iraq brought with it a commonality of interest and significant cooperation with Iran and Syria. However, by 2007–8, Washington's decision to share "actionable intelligence" with Ankara on the PKK, together with the more conciliatory approach of Iraqi Kurdistan, paved the way for a remarkable improvement in Turkish relations with it. In the wake of deteriorating relations with Damascus, Tehran, and Baghdad, some commentators have observed that, ironically, the Iraqi Kurds are Ankara's only friends in the region.

Other domestic factors, both political and economic, have helped shape Turkish foreign policy as much as have global and regional considerations.

One notable achievement of the AKP has been reducing the military's influence and bringing it under civilian control. With the generals unable to dictate security priorities, the AKP was able to soften its approach to various neighbors once considered Turkey's adversaries, thus improving relations with Syria, Iran, and the Iraqi Kurds.

Although Turkey's democracy lags behind that of many in the West, its standards have improved since the AKP came to power. Much more than in the past, the government has to pay greater attention to public sentiment. In keeping with popular sensitivity, most Turks have endorsed the AKP's support for the Palestinians and denunciations of Israel. On the other hand, when Erdogan and Davutoglu appeared to beat the drums of war against the Assad regime, strong opposition from the Turkish public obliged them to temper their rhetoric in order to calm fears of military intervention.

After several years of diplomatic accomplishments for Turkey, the recent uprisings in the Arab world have created new problems for it. With considerable justification, some writers argue that Turkish responses during the "Arab Spring" have been muddled and inconsistent, while others say that the upheavals reveal the limitations of the AKP's "zero problems" policy and of Turkey's capacity to influence such developments. Erdogan called upon Mubarak to resign soon after the outbreak of the Egyptian uprising but did not hesitate to congratulate Iran's President Mahmoud Ahmadinejad on his success in the 2009 elections that most Western observers accused of being fraudulent. Also, in view of the substantial Turkish investments in Libya, Erdogan initially hesitated on the issue of endorsing UN sanctions and NATO military intervention there but eventually joined the action.

In the case of Syria, there are considerable grounds on which the AKP's approach can be faulted. It may be argued that Erdogan and Davutoglu were naive both in putting much faith in Turkey's relationship with Assad's regime prior to 2011 and then in supporting rebels whose political goals are less than clear and may even prove inimical to Turkish interests. Also, some critics argue that the AKP government may have overestimated the influence that growing regional and global engagements would yield. Other critics argue that Turkey's decision to downgrade its relations with Israel has undercut its diplomatic capacity in the region. As some observers have pointed out, it was Egyptian President Mohammed Morsi rather than Erdogan who secured the ceasefire between Israel and Hamas in November 2012.

Regardless of setbacks, the AKP's foreign policy record during its first decade in power includes impressive accomplishments. Not the least of its successes has been in setting its external relations on solid domestic foundations. The policies that fuelled strong economic growth have enabled Ankara to establish multiple economic and trade partnerships abroad and to integrate the Turkish economy into the globalized world. The country's political stability during this period provides another key asset for the AKP. Furthermore, by popularizing the idea of peaceful relations with neighbors and distancing

Turkey from the overbearing influence of the US, the AKP has generated extensive support at home.

The contrast between the 1990s, when Turkey struggled with multiple foreign policy challenges, and the past decade of accomplishments and a growing sense of confidence could not be starker. Since the AKP came to power, it has confounded those who argued that it is driven by ideological considerations, and it has demonstrated a capacity to pragmatically fine-tune its policies in its evolving relationship with both the US and nearby countries. Few doubt that it has grown more influential in its neighborhood and is poised to play a greater role globally.

Notes

1 G. Jenkins, "Muslim Democrats in Turkey?" *Survival*, 2003, vol. 45, 54.
2 A. Davutoglu, "Turkey-US relations: A Model Partnership, Global and Regional Dimensions," Speech delivered at the 28th Annual Conference on US-Turkish Relations Organized by ATC-DEIK, Washington, DC, June 2, 2009. URL: <http://www.mfa.gov.tr/minster_s-speechat-the-28th-annual-conference-on-us-turkish-relations.en.mfa> (accessed November 10, 2012).
3 A. Gul, interview, December 23, 1994 (Ankara), quoted in P. Robins, "Confusion at Home, Confusion Abroad: Turkey Between Copenhagen and Iraq" *International Affairs*, 2003, vol.79, 553.
4 A. Carkoglu and K. Kirisci, *Turkiye Dis Politikasi Arastirmasi*, (Survey of Turkish Foreign Policy), Istanbul: Bogazici University, 2002.
5 "Turkish Cypriot Leader Is Criticized by Ankara," *New York Times*, January 3, 2003. URL: <http://www.nytimes.com/2003/01/03/world/turkish-cypriot-leader-is-criticized-by-ankara.html> (accessed December 3, 2012).
6 Speech entitled "Vision 2023: Turkey's Foreign Policy Objectives'"delivered by H. E. Ahmet Davutoglu, Minister of Foreign Affairs of the Republic of Turkey at the Turkey Investor Conference: The road to 2023 organized by Goldman Sachs (London, November 22, 2011). URL: <http://www.mfa.gov.tr/speech-entitled–vision-2023–turkey_s-foreign-policy-objectives–delivered-by-h_e–ahmet-davutoglu–minister-of-foreign-af.en.mfa> (accessed November 12, 2012).
7 "The Great Mediator," *The Economist*, August 19, 2010. URL: <http://www.economist.com/node/16847136> (accessed November 9, 2012).
8 R. Nurdun, *Turkish International Cooperation and Development Agency* (TIKA), 2010. URL: <http://www.ecocci.com/DC/PDF/19.04.201017_34Presentation%20of%20TIKA.pdf> (accessed December 8, 2012).
9 K. Oktem, "Projecting Power: Non-Conventional Policy Actors in Turkey's International Relations" (Ch. 6), in K. Oktem, A. Kadıoglu, and M. Karli, eds, *Another Empire: A Decade of Turkey's Foreign Policy Under the Justice and Development Party*, Istanbul: Bilgi University Press, 2012, p. 87.
10 Ibid., p. 88.
11 Ibid., p. 93.
12 Ibid., p. 91.
13 B. Gosh, "Erdogan's Moment," *Time*, November 28, 2011. URL: <http://www.time.com/time/magazine/article/0,9171,2099674,00.html> (accessed December 9, 2012).
14 B. Aliriza and B. Aras, *U.S.–Turkish Relations: A Review at the Beginning of the Third Decade of the Post-Cold War Era*, Center for Strategic and International Studies, November 2012. URL: <http://csis.org/publication/us-turkish-relations> (accessed November 20, 2012).

15 "Islamists Criticize Turkish Premier's 'Secular Remarks'," *The Wall Street Journal*, September 15, 2011. URL: <http://online.wsj.com/article/SB100014240531 11904491704576570670264116178.html> (accessed December 9, 2012).

16 "U.S.–Turkey Relations: A New Partnership," *Council on Foreign Relations*, Independent Task Force Report 69, May 2012, 18.

17 Ibid.

18 T. Reid, "Turkey's eastern trading bet pays off," *Financial Times*, August 29, 2012. URL: <http://www.ft.com/intl/cms/s/0/94646ab6-f1c5–11e1-bda3–00144feab dc0.html#axzz2EboHlQZT> (accessed November 9, 2012).

19 Ibid.

20 "Turkey to provide Egypt with $2 billion in finance," *Reuters*, September 15, 2012. URL <http://www.reuters.com/article/2012/09/15/us-egypt-turkey-finance-idUSBRE88E0BQ20120915> (accessed December 3, 2012).

21 O. Oktav, "Regionalism or Shift of Axis? Turkish–Syrian–Iranian Relations" (Ch. 4) in Oktav, ed., *Turkey in the 21st Century: Quest for a New Foreign Policy*, Farnham, Surrey and Burlington VT: Ashgate, 2011, p. 79.

22 N. Tocci, and J. Walker, "From Confrontation to Engagement: Turkey and the Middle East" (Ch. 3) in R. H. Linden *et al.*, eds, *Turkey and Its Neighbors: Foreign Relations in Transition*, Boulder, CO and London: Lynne Reiner, 2012, p. 41.

23 Ibid.

24 Linden, *Turkey*, p. 43; B. Aras, *Turkey and the Palestinian Question*, SETA-Foundation for Political and Economic and Social Research, January 2009, p. 5. URL: <http://setadc.org/pdfs/SETA_Policy_Brief_No_27_Palestinian_Question_Bulent_Aras.pdf> (accessed December 3, 2012).

25 T. Akyol, "Hamas ve Turkiye," *Milliyet*, February 18, 2006, cited in Aras, *Turkey*, p.6.

26 Y. Congar, "Mesal, Esad, Bush, Erdogan," *Milliyet*, July 3, 2006, cited in Aras, *Turkey*, p. 6.

27 Aras, *Turkey*, p. 8.

28 P. Turgut, "Behind the Turkish Prime Minister's Outburst at Davos," *Time*, January 30, 2009. URL: <http://www.time.com/time/world/article/0,8599,1875981,00. html> (accessed November 19, 2012).

29 B. Sobelman, "Q & A: Israel's diplomatic row with Turkey," *Los Angeles Times*, January 19, 2010. URL: <http://articles.latimes.com/2010/jan/19/world/la-fg-israel-qa19–2010jan19> (accessed November 19, 2012).

30 "Turkey's Erdogan calls Israel a terrorist state," *Reuters*, November 19, 2012. URL: <http://www.reuters.com/article/2012/11/19/us-palestinians-israel-turkey-idUSBRE8AI0FH20121119> (accessed November 24, 2012).

31 K. Akkoyunlu, "Turkey's Iranian Conundrum: A Delicate Balancing Act," (Ch. 11), in Oktem, Kadioglu, and Karli, *Another Empire*, p. 264.

32 G. Jenkins, *Occasional Allies, Enduring Rivals: Turkey's Relations with Iran*, Central Asia-Caucasus Institute Silk Road Studies Program, May 2012, p. 9.

33 Ibid., p. 6.

34 H. Pope "Pax Ottomana," *Foreign Affairs*, 2010, vol. 89, 9.

35 Jenkins, *Occasional Allies*, p. 38.

36 "Erdogan in Iran, says NATO radar could be dismantled if needed," *Today's Zaman*, March 30, 2012. URL: <http://www.todayszaman.com/news-275856-erdo gan-in-iran-says-nato-radar-could-be-dismantled-if-needed.html> (accessed November 23, 2012).

37 A. Bozkurt, "Turkish Minister Sahin Slams Iran for Providing Support to PKK/ KCK," URL: <http://www.todayszaman.com/news-302004-turkish-minister-sahin-slams-iran-for-providing-support-to-pkkck.html> (accessed December 23, 2012).

38 S. Kerr, "Turkey: Economics and Energy Interests Ease Old Cross-Border Tensions," *Financial Times*, December 9, 2012. URL: <http://www.ft.com/intl/cms/s/

0/3cbf092a-2f1d-11e2-b88b-00144feabdc0.html#axzz2GCwg9cNd> (accessed December 12, 2012).

39 O. Anastasakis, "Turkey's Assertive Presence in Southeast Europe: Between Identity Politics and Elite Pragmatism" (Ch. 8), in Oktem, Kadioglu, and Karli, *Another Empire*, p. 187.

40 Ibid., p. 186.

41 Ibid., pp. 205–6.

42 I. Ruma, "Turkish Foreign Policy toward the Balkans: Overestimated Change within Underestimated Continuity" (Ch.7) in Oktav, *Turkey*, p. 144.

43 J. Traub, "Turkey Rules," *New York Times*, January 20, 2011. URL: <http://www. nytimes.com/2011/01/23/magazine/23davutoglu-t.html?pagewanted=all&_r=0> (accessed December 3, 2012).

44 Athanastakis, " Turkey's Assertive Presence," p. 187.

45 H. Kramer, *AKP's "New" Foreign Policy Between Vision and Pragmatism*, German Institute for International and Security Affairs, Working Paper, FG 2, June 1, 2010, p. 20. URL: <http://www.swpberlin.org/fileadmin/contents/products/ arbeitspapiere/Krm_WP_Neu_ks.pdf> (accessed October 10, 2010).

46 Ibid.

47 A. Evin *et al.*, *Getting to Zero: Turkey, Its Neighbors and the West*, Transatlantic Academy, Washington, DC, August 15, 2010, p. 15. URL: <http://www.transatlan ticacademy.org/publications/getting-zero-turkey-its-neighbors-and-west> (accessed November 22, 2012).

48 Ibid.

49 "Why Turks Feel Threatened by the US," *World Public Opinion*, September 5, 2007. URL: <http://www.worldpublicopinion.org/pipa/articles/brmiddleeastnafri cara/393.php> (accessed November 22, 2012).

50 Aliriza and Aras, *U.S.–Turkish Relations*.

51 Tocci and Walker, "From Confrontation to Engagement," p. 45.

52 Aliriza and Aras, *U.S.-Turkish Relations*.

53 M. Abramowitz, "Turkey's Foreign Policy Decoded," paper delivered at the Heinrich Boll Foundation Conference in Istanbul, December 3, 2011. URL: <http://tcf.org/blogs/botc/2011/12/turkey2019s-foreign-policy-decoded> (accessed November 22, 2012).

54 G. Jenkins, "Breaking Anchor: Turkey's Disappearing EU Accession Process," *Turkey Analyst*, vol. 5, 21, November 7, 2012. URL: <http://www.silkroadstudies. org/new/inside/turkey/2012/121107A.html> (accessed December 19, 2012).

55 D. Dombey, "Gul urges Turkey to stay on EU path," *Financial Times*, November 13, 2012. URL: <http://www.ft.com/intl/cms/s/0/de9173b2–2da8–11e2–8ece-001 44feabdc0.html#axzz2EboHlQZT> (accessed December 6, 2012).

56 Jenkins, "Breaking Anchor."

57 D. Dombey, "Politics Threatens Turkey's Trade Links," *Financial Times*, December 6, 2012. URL: <http://www.ft.com/intl/cms/s/0/08dd9a2c-3fb2–11e2-b2ce-00144 feabdc0.html#axzz2EboHlQZT> (accessed December 6, 2012).

58 M. Abramowitz, "Erdogan's Hypocrisy in Sudan," *The National Interest*, July 23, 2012. URL: <http://nationalinterest.org/commentary/erdogans-hypocrisy-sudan- 7228> (accessed November 22, 2012).

59 "Sudanese President Bashir's Visit to Turkey in Limbo," *Hurriyet Daily News*, August 11, 2009. URL: <http://www.hurriyetdailynews.com/default.aspx?pageid= 438&n=a-muslim-can-never-commit-genocide-erdogan-defends-bashir-2009-11-08> (accessed November 24, 2012).

8 "Identity politics"

Europe, the EU and the Arab Spring

Philip Marfleet and Fran Cetti

Europe had already turned inward when the Arab uprisings began in January 2011. Leaders of the European Union faced economic recession and increased social tension when events in Tunisia and Egypt abruptly presented them with new challenges. As their multiple crises deepened, EU politicians reacted more and more nervously to political change in the Arab states. For 20 years their approach to the Middle East had been shaped by three strategic aims: to promote neoliberal policies for economic change, to inhibit growth of Islamist movements and to control migration to Europe. This chapter examines their growing anxiety over the spirit of Tahrir and its implications for Europe's "Mediterranean neighborhood." It asks whether the uprisings have prompted a new neighborliness – or reinforced old prejudices and policies of exclusion.

For many people of the Arab world Europe is both closer and more distant than ever before. The paradox lies in European reactions to the Arab uprisings – a mixture of admiration and anxiety. Within days of the fall of President Mubarak in February 2011, Catherine Ashton – the senior official for foreign affairs in the EU – declared that events unfolding in North Africa were of "historic proportions."[1] Her headline comments were laudatory: change promised better lives for people of the region, offering respect for human rights, pluralism, rule of law and social justice. The EU "must not be a passive spectator," declared Ashton, and must support wholeheartedly "the wish of people in our neighbourhood to enjoy the same freedoms that we take as our right."[2] The EU would launch a new and embracing policy for the Mediterranean, she said: a "Partnership for Democracy and Shared Prosperity." Her statement on behalf of the Union contained a series of warnings, however. The EU would pursue an "incentive-based approach" to its partners in the region: it would offer "more for more," so that faster economic and political reform would win more support from Europe.[3] By the same token, changes seen as unwelcome in Europe would prompt a less positive response – and of these the most important was associated with what Ashton called the challenge of "mobility." She warned governments, NGOs, and social movements in North Africa and the Middle East that more effective law enforcement on borders, migration, and asylum was required, with the aim of improving security throughout the Mediterranean.[4] Welcoming the new movements, she also placed them in the context of dangers to the region and to the EU.

Here the "Arab Spring" was set in familiar terms, within a framework that had dominated EU policy making vis-à-vis the Middle East for almost 20 years. In 2011 this meant that demands for democratization were welcomed, at least officially: this did not imply, however, that EU leaders accepted the presence in Europe of people from the states affected. Behind the approbation for democratic change was renewed concern about Islamism and unwanted migrations from the South: what challenges would come from people energized by the spirit of Tahrir and eager to explore novel freedoms?

"Biblical" threat

As uprisings spread across the Middle East, affecting Syria, Palestine, Yemen and Bahrain, EU policy advanced on a dual track. In May 2011 Ashton issued a comprehensive policy statement: *A New Response to a Changing Neighbourhood*.[5] The EU wished to consolidate healthy democracies in the region and would help them to pursue sustainable economic growth, she said; at the same time, the Union must carefully manage "cross-border links."[6] In some member states politicians had already set out their concerns more plainly. Italy's interior minister, Roberto Maroni, declared that change in North Africa had prompted a huge increase in migration – "an exodus of biblical proportions" that threatened Italian society and could have "devastating consequences" for the whole continent.[7] According to Bernadino Rubeis, mayor of the Italian island of Lampedusa, migrants from Tunisia were the advance guard of a vast movement that would threaten Europe. He warned: "There is an entire nation trying to escape from Tunisia to reach Italy and then go on to other countries."[8] Italian Foreign Minister Franco Frattini argued that further political change in the Arab states would bring 200,000 to 300,000 migrants to Italy and a future that was "impossible to imagine."[9] The Italian government asked the EU for an urgent joint patrol off the Tunisian coast and for an intervention by Europol, the European law enforcement agency formed "to fight against serious international crime and terrorism."[10] Italian officials demanded action against potential "terrorist-criminal infiltrations" and a contribution from the EU of €100 million to assist in tackling the emergency.[11]

These comments were associated with the highly charged agendas of Europe's extreme Right – organizations such as Maroni's Northern League. Right-wing parties in the EU have pursued increasingly aggressive demands for migration control, reflecting programs of populist racism and Islamophobia that have intensified in proportion to economic crisis, growing unemployment and social tension. The Arab uprisings presented an opportunity to invoke images of invasion from the South; in fact, according to the EU's own border control agency, Frontex, during 2011 only 27,000 people left Tunisia for Europe as irregular migrants, many as part of an annual Spring movement to southern Europe encouraged by employers and governments seeking seasonal supplies of labour.[12] The imagery of the Right, disseminated widely by the European media, had its impact on the mainstream of European politics. German Chancellor Angela Merkel asserted that, "not all people who do not want to be in Tunisia can now come to Europe."[13] French President Nicolas Sarkozy and Italy's Prime Minister Silvio Berlusconi issued a joint statement proposing that uncontrolled migration from North Africa was already subverting Europe's border regime and that the EU's Schengen area of passport-free movement should be suspended. They declared that cross-Mediterranean migration "could swiftly become an out-and-out crisis capable of undermining the trust our fellow citizens place in the free circulation within the Schengen area."[14] EU support for democratic revolutions must be accompanied by renewed efforts to inhibit migration, they said, arguing for "a rapid and efficacious co-operation [of Arab states] with the European Union and its member states in fighting illegal immigration." Meanwhile, Berlusconi warned that Milan, one of his political bases, was "besieged by foreigners" and could turn into "an Islamic city."[15]

Carrera et al. describe the Franco-Italian call to revise EU policies on borders as a "race to the bottom" which subverted European principles of solidarity, cooperation, and fundamental rights.[16] Among the Union's northern states, Denmark meanwhile announced new border controls, Dutch Prime Minister Mark Rutte declared that Tunisians arriving via Italy "must leave the Netherlands," and British Home Secretary Theresa May promised "strong practical action" to inhibit migrants from North Africa.[17] A process of political outbidding was under way, so that more than a year after the first events in Tunisia, anxiety about Arab migrants was being mobilized more and more aggressively within European politics. In France, Sarkozy campaigned throughout the 2012 presidential campaign on issues of migration, linking France to a European campaign of exclusion focused on the Arab states. Illegal immigration threatened European "civilization" and "our way of life", he said: if the EU did not tighten its borders, France would abandon the Schengen area.[18]

Such was the concern with border control that a series of foreign policy initiatives ostensibly focused on political change in North Africa was set in terms of the migration agenda. British Prime Minister David Cameron justified military intervention in Libya by raising the specter of uncontrolled movement across the Mediterranean. Speaking in parliament, he asked:

> Do we want a situation where a failed pariah state [Libya] festers in Europe's southern border, potentially threatening our security, pushing people across the Mediterranean and creating a more dangerous and uncertain world for Britain and for our allies as well as for the people of Libya?[19]

While armed conflict in Libya was still raging, Italy signed a memorandum of understanding with the country's Transitional National Council, the two parties committing to control irregular movements.[20] After the death of Colonel Qaddafi and the final defeat of his armed forces, Italy demanded – and obtained – a further agreement aimed formally to "curtail the flow of migrants."[21]

Bilateral relations

Like most politicians worldwide, Europe's leaders were ill-prepared for the Arab uprisings. For decades they had supported presidents, kings and emirs who partnered Europe in a dual venture – facilitating economic "opening" while maintaining authoritarian regimes which inhibited Islamist opposition and controlled migration. Three cases demonstrate Europe's difficulties as movements for change unfolded: in each, former colonial powers with long-standing interests in North Africa struggled to adjust to new realities. Each had developed specific relations with local regimes: each also pursued strategies which drew on collective approaches adopted by the EU.

France and Tunisia

France was for decades closely linked to the Ben Ali regime. When mass opposition to the dictatorship began to grow in December 2010 Foreign Minister Michèle Alliot-Marie told parliament in Paris that France could "offer the know-how of [its] security forces to help control this type of situation."[22] Her public bid to strengthen the hand of Ben Ali was consistent with a policy by which France attempted to maintain influence in North Africa by exploiting relationships dating back to the colonial era. Alliot-Marie enjoyed close ties with the Ben Ali family and had even taken a Christmas holiday in Tunisia as the uprising gained momentum. Within weeks of Ben Ali's fall, Alliot-Marie had resigned. Mikhail[23] comments that, "The French government's posture towards the Tunisian protests turned into a PR disaster."

Alliot-Marie's embarrassment was shared by President Sarkozy, for whom North Africa was an important arena for foreign policy initiatives. He seemed unable to grasp the scale of the opposition movement and the implications for Ben Ali, justifying his misjudgement by asserting limply that, "one cannot call for the resignation of the leader in question every time there are social movements in a country."[24] Like other political leaders in France, Sarkozy had accepted the Tunisian dictator as a business-friendly ally. Dominique Strauss-Kahn, a leading member of the French Socialist Party and (then) head of the International Monetary Fund (IMF), claimed that Tunisia was a "model for many emerging countries."[25] Ben Ali had embraced neoliberal economic principles favored by the IMF, the World Bank and other international development agencies. In 2010 the French Council of Investors in Africa (CIAN) reported that French companies in Tunisia were thriving: it viewed the business climate as exceptionally favorable, giving Tunisia a "global mark" of 3.2 out of 5, its best for North African states.[26] CIAN praised the country for a "solid economy, coupled with political stability."[27] The regime had also inhibited all forms of opposition and controlled emigration in line with French preferences: in 2008 a bilateral agreement committed Tunisia to control irregular movements. For Paris, Ben Ali was a model North African ruler – hence Sarkozy's fumbled attempts to protect the dictatorship.

Britain and Egypt

Britain had cooperated closely with the Mubarak regime, which was widely seen as the leading economic reformer in the Arab world: in 2007 the World Bank had declared Egypt its annual growth champion. London accommodated several homes for the Mubarak family and provided a safe haven for investment by the president's inner circle. According to the British–Egyptian Chamber of Commerce,[28] by 2008 the United Kingdom had become the largest foreign investor in Egypt; total cumulative investment was $22 billion, with participation by many of the largest corporate players in the United Kingdom, including British Petroleum, British Gas, Shell, GlaxoSmithKline, Cadbury, HSBC, Barclays Bank, Vodafone, and Unilever. In 2011, HSBC – a pillar of the London financial establishment – was said to have been the most active European investment bank in Egypt and to have financed deals valued at almost $1 billion for two of Egypt's biggest and most controversial property developers, each later embroiled in major corruption cases.[29] In the 1990s, HSBC chairman Lord Green had been co-chair of the Egyptian British Business Council, a high-level group that reported to the British and Egyptian governments; Green was later appointed as a minister in the Cameron administration. The British had also shadowed foreign policies developed by their American allies. Under former Prime Minister Tony Blair, Britain had cooperated closely with US military initiatives involving Egypt and was a partner in the highly controversial practice of "extraordinary rendition," by which prisoners seized by US security agencies were transported or "rendered" to torture sites in states such as Egypt and Libya.[30]

Britain viewed Mubarak as a highly congenial ally – a reliable local administrator of neoliberal policies whose authoritarian methods inhibited opposition in general and the Islamist movement in particular. When Egypt's revolution began on January 25, 2011, Prime Minister Cameron balked at the demands of Tahrir Square – that the president must go. As events progressed rapidly, he distanced himself from Mubarak, arguing that the regime should pursue "the path of reform and not repression";[31] Blair meanwhile defended the Egyptian dictator as "immensely courageous and a force for good."[32] When Mubarak eventually fell, Cameron was first among world leaders to travel to Cairo, seeking to identify with popular aspirations for change and what Egyptian writer Ahdaf Soueif has called "the glitter of Tahrir."[33] Cameron's approval was expressed in calculated terms, however: "What is so refreshing about what's been happening," he said, "is that this is not an Islamist revolt, this is not extremists on the streets; this is people who want to have the sort of basic freedoms that we take for granted in the UK."[34]

Italy and Libya

Under Silvio Berlusconi, Italy established close relations with the regime of Muammar Qaddafi. Eager to access Libya's oil resources, Berlusconi resurrected agreements originally negotiated in the late 1990s, when Libyan–Italian relations were restored after decades of suspicion and mutual hostility. Qaddafi began to move Libya into the world economy, using Italy to enter the European market. In 2004 the two countries inaugurated a 520-kilometer gas pipeline to supply Italy's energy needs: a marker for further liaisons. In 2008 relations were normalized when Berlusconi flew to Benghazi to sign a Treaty on Friendship, Partnership and Cooperation (the Benghazi Treaty). Libya received a fulsome apology for the impact of Italian colonisation in the early twentieth century.[35] Italian companies were to undertake major infrastructural projects there over the course of 20 years; meanwhile, sovereign Libyan funds would invest directly in Italian banks and in the construction, telecommunications, and manufacturing sectors.[36] By 2010, Libya had holdings in a series of major Italian companies and provided Italian operators with preferential access to its oil and gas: by 2010, 25 per cent of Italian oil came from Libya.[37] The most controversial aspects of the treaty concerned migration. The "Immigration Chapter" of the agreement provided for joint Libyan–Italian missions in the Mediterranean Sea to intercept irregular migrants, while Libya's land borders were to be controlled by satellite detection systems. A series of further "protocols" followed the 2008 treaty, including agreements that each state would "carry out the repatriation of illegal immigrants from its territory."[38] Italy ignored appeals from human rights organizations which reported widespread abuses of migrants in Libya – in particular of refugees using the Libyan coast in attempts to reach Europe. In 2010, Libya unilaterally suspended operations of the Office of the United Nations High Commissioner for Refugees (UNHCR), leaving migrants in an even more vulnerable position.

The Italian state had pursued a policy of "externalization", extending measures of migration control outside its territory. Migrants were now to be pursued in North Africa with the aim of inhibiting their journeys to Italy. Consistent with the anti-immigration policies of the Berlusconi government, the Italian border had, in effect, been moved to Libya. A programme of "push-back" interceptions was initiated, in which Italian coastguards stopped vessels at sea and returned their occupants directly to Libya. In 2012, the European Court of Human Rights found that these operations violated the European Convention on Human Rights.

When domestic opposition to the Qaddafi regime developed momentum in 2011, the Italian government remained silent. Closely linked to the dictatorship in Tripoli, Berlusconi declined to comment on European intervention:

one academic assessment observed that Italy's silence "is not only unbecoming, it is against Italy's own interests and a renunciation of responsibility."[39]

France, Britain and Italy had developed close relations with North African regimes, and each experienced its own difficulties during the crises of 2011. In each case, there were complex economic links involving European businesses and networks of patronage centered on the dictatorship. Egypt and Tunisia had been pioneers of neoliberal policy in the Middle East, with Britain and France keen to establish a presence which echoed the colonial era. In the case of Libya, a late accommodation with the international economy allowed Italy to advance its commercial interests, albeit on a more modest scale. Each case also revealed the importance to European states of authoritarian regimes that suppressed political opposition in general and Islamist currents in particular, and that policed migration in line with European preferences. It is here that bilateral relations engaged with the EU's wider collective aims and its "neighborhood" strategies.

From "partnership" to "neighborhood"

The European Neighborhood Policy (ENP) was initiated in 2004 as a means of managing relations with countries to the south (North Africa and the Middle East) and to the east (Eastern Europe and the Southern Caucasus). The official purpose was to promote reform in neighborhood states and to press for harmonization of local policies in line with EU practice. The undeclared aim was to pursue the EU's economic and political strategies and to consolidate Europe's cultural influence. The project had limited success. Initiated at a period when other global players were beginning to exert their influence, it also suffered from divisions among the EU states and – most importantly – serious contradictions associated with European governments' own policies for development in the Middle East.

The ENP for the southern neighborhood was a successor to the EU's Barcelona Strategy and its Euro-Mediterranean partnership. These were the outcome of a summit meeting in Barcelona in 1995 at which leaders of EU and Middle Eastern states met for the first time, ostensibly to discuss issues of common regional concern. The formal aim was to develop relations among participating states "based on comprehensive cooperation and solidarity, in keeping with the privileged nature of the links forged by neighbourhood and History."[40] The summit ended with a Barcelona Declaration which pledged movement towards a Mediterranean free trade zone and agreements on security, energy, water, migration, and enhanced cultural relationships between the two regions. The EU was to provide over $6bn in grant aid to Middle East states and a similar sum in loans through the European Development Bank; a further $12bn was to come from individual European states.[41]

The scale of the initiative was startling. So much money was to be redirected towards Middle East governments that European aid strategies for the Global

South as a whole were reshaped. The EU also committed to what it called "decentralized co-operation programs with key players in civil society."[42] These were to link hundreds of institutions across Europe and the Middle East: universities, media organizations, city authorities, and agencies in all manner of policy fields. Neither Eurocrats nor leaders of EU member states provided specific economic rationales, remaining largely silent about measurable outcomes from these investments. Little was revealed to the media: the *Guardian*[43] commented that the Euro-Mediterranean process would soon be wrapped in "the elusive jargon which envelopes EU initiatives." The newspaper proposed that Barcelona and the Euro-Med programs were in fact driven by an overriding political aim: to address religious "fundamentalism"; they were attempts to cope with frustrated ambitions of "the youngsters in Tetouan [Morocco]" and the appeal of religious radicalism across the Middle East.[44] In return for European largesse, Middle East states were to tackle Islamism as a political influence and to work actively to control migration across the Mediterranean.

The initiative for a Euro-Med summit had come from members of the southern tier of EU states, especially France and Spain, in response to political developments in North Africa – the rise of the Islamic Salvation Front (FIS) in Algeria, the French-supported coup in Algiers in 1992, and subsequent refugee movements to Europe. Adamson[45] comments that the conference was designed to address fears that the Algerian conflict would transfer to France and to assuage general anxiety in the EU about the progress of Islamist movements across the Maghreb. In a concerted move, states including the United Kingdom, Germany, Greece and Italy soon introduced legal changes aimed at discouraging applications for refugee status. In Spain, the government set new deadlines for migrants wishing to regularize status. In North Africa, the Spanish enclaves of Melilla and Ceuta were enclosed by new armed border fences. European politicians remained largely silent about the whole initiative; eventually it was a Danish government minister, Ellen Margrethe Loy, who reflected publicly on the strategy:

> The challenges that the [Euro-Mediterranean Partnership] seeks to answer are multiple. From a European perspective one of the most visible challenges is that of Islamic radicalism. The perceived threats of Islamic radicals to Europe as well of the Middle East are sometimes only too real. Acts of terror, internal instability within Muslim countries, a possible increase in migration and export of radical ideas to migrant communities outside the Muslim world [sic].[46]

It was increasingly clear that the EU aimed not only to restrain Islamist movements but also to limit the growth of Muslim communities in Europe. Barcelona had not been inspired by the wish for closer relations with southern "neighbors"; rather, European politicians wished for greater distance from them.

This approach was consistent with a mood of growing anxiety vis-à-vis Islam and Muslims which affected governments, policy institutions and think-tanks in North America and Europe during the early 1990s. The end of the Cold War prompted national and supra-national crises of identity in both. In the case of Europe, the collapse of Communism produced a host of requests for membership in the EU. Ideologues of European unity within the EU struggled to accommodate the change – bereft of the Iron Curtain and the certainties of East and West, the purposes of a pan-European union were unclear. Which states should join? Where are the borders? What defines a common European project? Who is a "European?" EU politicians were heard more and more often invoking the views of Samuel Huntington: that in a post-Cold War world, international affairs would be dominated by a "clash of civilizations" in which the main confrontations would be between "the West" and "Islam."[47] In place of the "Red Menace" of Stalinism and the Communist bloc, they invoked a "Green Menace" of Islam.[48] Delanty[49] commented that although "the East" remained a focus of hostility "it has been pushed further southward." The Iron Curtain was being replaced by a new border – what Huntington called the "fault line" of the Mediterranean.[50]

Gillespie[51] comments on the climate in which the Euro-Mediterranean partnership was developed:

> The Islamist challenge in Algeria and signs of unrest in other Arab countries led some northern Europeans to give expression to phobias about "Islamic fundamentalism" best exemplified by former secretary-general of NATO Willy Claes's controversial statement about the phenomenon being "at least as dangerous" as the former Soviet threat. ... [T]here has been a growing awareness in northern Europe that the conditions that have fuelled the radical Islamist movements are not part of some distant overseas malaise, rather that these conditions affect the European Union as a whole.

For politicians of the Right this approach was consistent with hostility towards Muslims in general. They had long embraced a "xenophobic specter of not only a Muslim-dominated world but an 'Islamization of Europe'."[52] Collective European policy provided opportunities to set these views within the mainstream of EU politics. Some prominent figures were explicit: in Italy Berlusconi called for a stronger European identity based on a common Christian culture.[53] He asserted the "superiority" and "supremacy" of western civilization vis-à-vis Islam, arguing that "Europe must revive on the basis of common Christian roots."[54] In the Netherlands, academic and politician Pim Fortuyn had published *Against Islamization of our Culture*. In 2001 he described himself as the "Samuel Huntington of Dutch politics," adding:

"I am in favour of a cold war with Islam ... If I can legally manage it, I would say: no Muslims [should] come into this country any more."[55] In Denmark, Pia Kjærsgaard, leader of the Danish People's Party, commented that the 9/11 attacks in the US were not the start of a clash of civilizations, as "a clash would indicate that there are two civilizations," when "there is only one civilization, and that's ours."[56] Here a politics of hostility to Others, which for several decades had been largely confined to the extra-parliamentary Right, re-entered the mainstream of public debate. It was further energized by the "war on terror" launched from Washington: this engaged NATO and some European states in alliance with North American allies for new conflicts in the Middle East and Central Asia; it also accelerated policies of securitization which had been part of the Euro-Med program. European governments worked collectively to induce a public mood of imminent threat, "manufacturing consent to increasingly intrusive surveillance and the circumscription of personal freedoms through the evocation of fear."[57]

EU states nonetheless experienced serious problems over policy – especially in relation to the Middle East. European solidarity had been put to the test over the 2003 invasion of Iraq, led by the United States and Britain, and seen by key European leaders as solely an "Atlantic" initiative. In 2002 French President Jacques Chirac warned of "the temptation to legitimize the unilateral and preventive use of force" in relation to military action against Iraq.[58] This was a worrying development, he said:

> It is at odds with France's concept of collective security, one based on cooperation between States and respect for the law and authority of the [United Nations] Security Council. We shall draw attention to these rules whenever necessary and particularly with respect to Iraq.[59]

Germany made vigorous efforts – including in secret talks with Condoleeza Rice, national security advisor to President George W. Bush – to change American plans for invasion and refused to endorse the initiative.[60] The Iraq episode gave testimony to continuing problems faced by the Union in achieving coherence in foreign policy – and credibility for the Union as a major player in international crisis management.

These were the complex circumstances under which a new policy of "neighborhoods" was formalized by the EU. Intent on excluding states of the southern neighborhood from membership of the Union – and their citizens from the territorial space of Europe – EU governments consolidated specific bilateral and multilateral relations with regimes across the Middle East. Aid and programs of collaboration were again focused on the latters' capacities to address Islamism and cross-Mediterranean migration. Here, EU states could find a ready measure of agreement, especially over their dealings with the states of North Africa and in the context of renewed warnings of political instability and the growth of religious activism. In the case of Egypt, said Daniel Korski of the European Council of Foreign Relations, "We have to be honest and accept that we [EU governments] accepted Mubarak's argument that it's better him than the deluge represented by the Brotherhood, the Islamists."[61]

E-borders and the new security regime

From the mid 1990s the pace of economic reform accelerated across the Middle East. With Egypt in the vanguard, states such as Algeria, Syria and Libya – which had long pursued state-centered development strategies – moved sharply towards "liberal" policies, establishing all manner of partnerships with European businesses. Change was to have profound consequences. Commercialization of agriculture, privatization of industry, sharp increases in unemployment, and a huge rise in inequality destabilized authoritarian regimes, setting the scene for radical change in 2011.[62] But as economic reform progressed, European governments were content to accept a yawning democratic deficit: as José Manuel Barroso, president of the European Commission, later admitted, they had "traded democracy for stability."[63] Migration control remained a priority, and at times of heightened political tension a discourse of threat from the South drew on highly charged references: hence Maroni's warning of a "biblical" exodus from North Africa and Berlusconi's image of a European city "besieged" by Muslims. More and more often leaders of Europe's mainstream parties invoked negative images of Islam and Muslims – "phobias profoundly buried in the collective unconscious that trace back to centuries of religious and colonial conflicts."[64] At the same time, EU policy embraced a novel development: implementation of border controls that combined technological innovation with a new corporate security regime.

Europe's external border had been expanded systematically, so that it was policed far into other regions: at ports, airports, embassies, detention centers, and camps; into the seas around southern Europe; and into cyberspace. Since 9/11, Fekete[65] suggests, a distended de-territorialized border has become a key site at which old ideas about nation, ethnicity, and race have been reinvigorated by the language of Huntington and the "culture wars." Migrants have been central to construction of a European identity that requires an alien "non-European" to provide shape and content to an otherwise amorphous concept. Crime, deviance, and alterity provide the vocabulary and images by which migrant threats are identified, enabling construction of a unified figure said to challenge European society. Migrants in general and refugees from the Global South in particular have been placed within a nexus of dangers – transnational networks of organized crime, people smuggling/trafficking mafias, and Islamic terrorism. They are represented variously as sources of cultural dilution, social disintegration, economic disruption, political instability, and direct physical danger.

On Europe's southern borders, Italy and Greece are viewed as a front line to be defended against penetration from the south. In 1999, the EU established an External Border Practitioners Common Unit, composed of members of its Strategic Committee on Immigration, Frontiers and Asylum and heads of national border control services. In 2004, the Union integrated key tasks of the Common Unit by creating the European Agency for the Management of Operational Cooperation at the External Borders of the Member States of the European Union (Frontex). This agency was mandated to manage cross-cutting responsibilities among and between EU member states. These include:

- Joint operations – to coordinate and implement operations using staff and equipment of member states at external borders (sea, land and air);
- Information systems and information sharing – to enhance "situational awareness" for border control across the EU, developing and operating information systems to obtain and exchange key data;
- Joint return operations – to remove foreign nationals deemed to be illegal;
- External relations – to work with border control authorities of non-EU countries, "mainly those countries identified as a source or transit route of irregular migration."[66]

Frontex operates in the opaque world of global security – without regulation, staff accountability or democratic oversight by the European Parliament, the European Court or national parliaments. Amnesty International and the European Council on Refugees and Exiles (ECRE) reported in 2010 that its "joint operations and pilot projects create a gap in accountability and permit member states to engage in border management with impunity." They observed that Frontex implements "technical assistance projects" with third countries by diverting funds intended for humanitarian and development aid to border control.[67] They maintained further that the EU uses Frontex to circumvent international obligations on human rights (preventing forced migrants gaining access to international protection or asylum procedures) by relying on bilateral agreements established in its own name with third countries.[68]

Of seven migratory pathways identified by Frontex as challenging EU borders, six are said to facilitate movements towards the Union from the Mediterranean (along with one from Eastern Europe).[69] The Council of the European Union charges Frontex to "strengthen its operational cooperation with the competent border control authorities of the Southern Mediterranean countries". It also advises that pressure should be exerted to obtain the latters' assent to "accelerated procedures, transit operations, and obligations to readmit third-country nationals and the stateless," in particular through "mobility partnerships" established with Morocco, Tunisia, and Jordan, and "once possible, with other Southern Mediterranean countries" – most urgently, it proposes, with Egypt and Libya.[70] These states are induced to play the role of a European buffer zone in which unwanted would-be migrants to Europe are identified and apprehended.

EU policy is based on a "virtual" border policed by means of complex systems of surveillance and registration. These include the Schengen Information System (known in its upgraded form as SIS II); Eurodac (a database of fingerprints and biometric data of all those seeking asylum in Europe); and the Visa Information System (VIS), each relying on searchable databases. In 2004, the Council of the European Union declared its commitment to "common security standards and interoperable biometric identifiers"[71.] In 2011, a new Frontex regulation specified that the agency would create European Border Guard Teams for deployment in "joint operations and rapid border interventions."[72] They would be empowered to maintain surveillance, to check individual identities, and to intercept incoming vessels suspected of carrying "illegal aliens" – part of an integrated border management system initially targeted at the Mediterranean. In a 2010 statement, Frontex reported that its priorities would include the "dismantling of illegal immigration networks [through] surveillance and intelligence gathering *(particularly on increased migration from Muslim countries)*."[73]

A significant part of the EU security regime is now operated by means of privatized governance of mobility, untroubled by democratic accountability. Lavin and Shapiro[74] describe a process of "remote-control policy-making" through outsourcing to private, transnational, and third-country actors. EU states have continued to harmonize migration policy and simultaneously to outsource asylum and immigration operations to private contractors and multinational corporations involved in the lucrative security/surveillance sector, such as EADS, Finmeccanica, Sagem Sécurité and Geogroup. Deportation in particular has become a lucrative business activity in which private security companies work with state agencies, operating chartered deportation flights for which pre-determined quotas of "illegal" migrants are sought for removal.[75] A mutually beneficial relationship has developed between European government officials and companies operating in this field, inserting the latter into the core of the EU security regime.

European identity

Migration policy is of profound ideological importance to the EU and to European governments – a key means by which "European" identity is asserted. Migrants from the Middle East have become an embodiment of external danger – integral to the European/"alien" dichotomy and to notions of a unified European cultural identity – and of increased importance to the Union during periods of economic crisis and social instability. The world economic crisis that began in 2008 has had a profound impact, raising the prospect of disintegration of the Eurozone and of financial and commercial networks with which it is associated. A series of national governments has collapsed, and others have been replaced after general elections dominated by popular concern about unemployment, welfare and social cohesion. The future of the Union itself has been in question. In 2010, German Prime Minister Angela Merkel warned that pressures on the European currency and the Eurozone threatened the very existence of the EU, asserting: "The Euro is much, much more than a currency. ... The Euro is the guarantee of a united Europe. If the Euro fails, then Europe fails."[76] In 2011, French President

Nicholas Sarkozy argued that: "If the Euro explodes, Europe would explode [sic]," adding: "[The Euro] is the guarantee of peace in a continent where there were terrible wars."[77] According to Polish Foreign Minister Radek Sikorski: "We [in Europe] are standing on the edge of a precipice"; break-up of the EU "would be a crisis of apocalyptic proportions."[78] The choices for Europe, he said, were "deeper integration, or collapse":

> Euro-sceptics are right when they say that Europe will only work if it becomes a polity, a community in which people place a part of their identity and loyalty. *Italy is made, we still have to make Italians*, Massimo D'Azeglio said in the first meeting of the parliament of the newly united Italian kingdom in the nineteenth century. For us in the EU it's easier: we have a united Europe. We have Europeans. What we need to do is to give political expression to the European public opinion. ... We need more "politische bildung" [political education] for citizens and political elite [sic].[79]

In the United States, President Obama's advisors warned of the dangers for global order of developments in Europe.[80] In a strategic assessment for the Brookings Institution, Wright[81] observed:

> The European Union is engaged in a ferocious political, diplomatic, and economic struggle to preserve the future of the single currency, the Euro, and the viability of what has become known simply as "the project," namely the process of integration that has been the bedrock of Western European politics for over half a century. It is distinctly possible that its members' efforts may fail, either in the short or long term, and give way to an era of disintegration.

For Wright, "Failure in Europe would shake the world". Of special concern were the implications for two regions: China and the Middle East. In the latter, he proposed, "populism and revolutionary movements would flourish" and some political systems would collapse, causing major global problems. "Extraordinary steps" were required to find a solution to Europe's crisis.[82]

The EU and its allies fear an historic tendency for instability within member states to find expression in inter-state conflict – an aspect of the Union that former Eurocrat Bernard Connolly[83] has called "the rotten heart" of Europe. Eurocrats and Europhile politicians have long worried about weak popular attachment to the EU and the danger that local nationalisms will respond to crisis by withdrawing from the Union. In the 1970s and 1980s, there were repeated, unsuccessful efforts to stimulate strong popular identification with Europe.[84] In the 1990s, the quest took on greater urgency. The end of the Cold War, unification of Germany and a host of demands from states of the former Eastern Bloc for membership of the Union presented pressing problems, resolved in part by governmental collaboration around a "soft" security agenda – control of immigration. In 1991, the Western European Union (WEU) warned that Europe should address the issue of its "southern neighbours."[85] Collinson[86] notes the importance during this period of "apocalyptic images of a Europe under siege" – media accounts of invasion from the South which set the scene for harmonization of migration policy among national governments. The Barcelona Conference of 1995 subsequently presented a high-profile opportunity to demonstrate commitment to the EU project, cohering an expanded membership and asserting a commitment to protect Europe's citizens and the territorial space of the Union.[87] Migration had become a key area for collaborative ventures: by the late 1990s, notes Fekete,[88] there were some 30 EU projects on border policy.

The "Mediterranean solution" initiated in Barcelona took the form of a foreign policy initiative – it was in fact a key mechanism for stabilisation of the EU, developed continuously over the next 15 years. In 2004, the ENP was accompanied by Euro-Med Migration I, followed in 2008 by Euro-Med Migration II – each aimed at "strengthening cooperation in the management of migration."[89] In 2003, an EU coastal police force was established to patrol the Mediterranean, initially with vessels from Spain, Britain, France, Italy and Portugal: Fekete[90] describes a "Schengen of the Sea." Member states meanwhile undertook bilateral agreements with North African states, notably Italy with Libya, and – in the case of France – with Tunisia. Frontex, operating as a semi-autonomous EU agency, initiated talks on further agreements with Libya, Morocco, Egypt, Tunisia, and Mauritania. Migration control had become a structural feature of the Union, so that accession countries were required to change fundamental laws relating to migration in general and asylum in particular. Policies of exclusion had become key means of aligning states and their citizens with "European" priorities and, in effect, with a putative European identity.

"Barbarian invaders"

The world crisis which began in 2008 reinforced exclusion. According to the International Organization for Migration,[91] immigration to Europe slowed while emigration increased: the EU nonetheless tightened exclusionary policies and increased investment in border control. Over €5.8 billion was allocated to "solidarity and management of migration flows" for the period 2007–13, of which some €3 billion was directed to external border control and deportation: Frontex, established only in 2005, received an additional €500 million.[92] Unprecedented numbers of migrants were expelled by immigration authorities, supra-state agencies and private security corporations – what Fekete[93] terms "the deportation machine." In 2009, parties of the extreme Right made electoral advances in the European Parliament and won seats in Austria, Denmark, Greece, Hungary, Italy, the Netherlands, Slovakia, and Romania. There was a marked intensification of racism in general and Islamophobia in particular: Minority Rights Group International[94] observed that "formerly far-right ideas [moved] into the mainstream." In France, the leader of Front National, Marine Le Pen, proposed that: "The progressive Islamization of our country and the increase in political-religious demands are calling into question the survival of our civilization"; she likened Muslims praying in the streets to the Nazi occupation of France, minus the "tanks and soldiers."[95] As the French general election approached, Le Pen warned of a "tsunami" of illegal immigration; in response President Sarkozy demanded tougher EU migration controls: Europe was a "sieve" through which migrants passed at will, he said.[96] Arno Klarsfeld, of France's Office for Immigration and Integration, demanded construction of a wall on the border between Greece and Turkey to save Europe from "barbarian invaders" entering Europe from the Middle East.[97]

A French government which railed against influences from the South had cultivated relations with rulers of the Arab states. Sarkozy maintained particularly close links with Ben Ali and Mubarak, with whom he shared joint leadership of the Union for the Mediterranean (UfM), initiated through the EU in 2008.[98] In January 2011, Sarkozy backed rulers in both Tunisia and Egypt against the mass movements. Mikhail[99] comments that, "French foreign policy in North Africa sided with autocrats for the sake of short-term interests, with little attention to democracy or human rights." All the core states of the EU had in fact pursued similar policies, so that when the scale and potential of the uprisings became clear, its officials were compelled to make hasty adjustments, formally welcoming democratic aspirations of the movements. Cole[100] observes that change had been precipitated by years of growing inequality across the states of North Africa – the outcome of intensive application of neoliberal policies by authoritarian regimes supported by banks and governments in both North America and Europe:

> Moving public resources into the private sector [in North Africa] created an almost endless range of opportunities for staggering levels of corruption on the part of the ruling families ... International banks, central banks and emerging local private banks aided and abetted their agenda.

Neoliberalism had been pursued with vigor by the most influential states of Western Europe for some 30 years.[101] In the 1990s, it had become an economic orthodoxy in the EU, adopted by all accession states and integrated into the Union's policies vis-à-vis the Global South – in the case of the Middle East this was facilitated by the Euro-Mediterranean partnership and the ENP. The EU was content to work with dictatorships which zealously privatized and marketized while ruthlessly suppressing those who reacted to the consequences – unemployment, landlessness, immiseration and despair.[102] Europe had played an active role in creating conditions which eventually produced the uprisings in Sidi Bouzid and Tahrir. In Tunisia activists expressed fury at the role of foreign banks they believed had provided Ben Ali with vast sums of money borrowed by the state but consumed privately by the ruling family. In Egypt activists formed an influential Popular Campaign to

Drop Egypt's Debt, arguing for independence from all foreign financial institutions.[103] In Cairo, a Judicial Commission was established to investigate the holdings abroad of Mubarak and his associates, while in London leading British banks were implicated in questionable dealings with Mubarak's inner circle.[104]

When the movement spread to Libya, where a series of European states had launched programs of investment, there was further consternation. The possibility of further radical change across North Africa was a nightmare scenario for many of Europe's politicians and brought alarmist reactions. Berlusconi, Sarkozy and others displaced their own responsibilities onto vulnerable and largely powerless people – migrants from North Africa attempting to cross the Mediterranean. They, rather than Europe's former allies in the presidential palaces, were depicted as the real problem of the region. Migrants were targeted with new enthusiasm, record numbers being detained and deported to countries of origin. Others were abandoned at sea, most notoriously in the "left-to-die" boat which in April 2011 – at the height of European panic about migrations from the South – left Libya and drifted for two weeks in the southern Mediterranean. Despite distress alerts and contact with numerous military and commercial vessels, the boat was ignored and 63 people died. A report for the Council of Europe's Parliamentary Assembly noted that neither Italian nor Maltese rescue networks, nor ships in the area under NATO command, responded to the crisis. The author of the report, Assembly member Tineke Strik, concluded that there had been "a catalogue of failures":

> The Mediterranean is one of the busiest seas in the world, and at the same time one of the best monitored. Yet, in 2011, the Mediterranean was also the sea in which the most people disappeared. I am not talking about somewhere in the middle of the Pacific, but about the Canal of Sicily which is full of ships, with many radars [sic] and with satellite imagery available. This boat could and should certainly have been rescued and not left to wash up on the shores of Libya with only a handful of survivors.[105]

The Arab uprisings of 2011 marked an historic development in the Middle East region. They took place as human rights agencies noted a record year for migrant deaths at sea.[106] The two developments were closely associated. For some of Europe's most prominent politicians, the upheaval in North Africa was not only a problem but also an opportunity – to project a powerful discourse of threat, to mobilize a new security regime, and to draw together the disparate elements of a Union in crisis. Apparently careless to the human cost, they invoked public opinion against an imminent encroachment from the South. *Plus ça change, plus c'est la même chose.*

Notes

1 European Commission, High Representative of the Union for Foreign Affairs and Security Policy, *A Partnership for Democracy and Shared Prosperity with the*

Southern Mediterranean. Joint Communication to the European Council, the European Parliament, the European Economic and Social Committee and the Committee of the Regions, March 8, 2011. Brussels: European Commission, p. 2. URL: <http://eeas.europa.eu/euromed/docs/com2011_200_en.pdf> (accessed January 3, 2012).

2 Ibid.

3 Ibid., p. 5.

4 Ibid., p. 6.

5 European Commission, *A New Response to a Changing Neighbourhood: A Review of European Neighbourhood Policy.* Joint Communication by the High Representative of the Union for Foreign Affairs and Security Policy and the European Commission, Brussels, European Union, External Action, May 2011. URL: <http://ec.europa.eu/world/enp/pdf/com_11_303_en.pdf> (accessed January 3, 2012).

6 Ibid., p. 1.

7 "Thousands of Tunisians Arrive in Italy," *Der Spiegel,* February 14, 2011; "Tunisia migrants: Italy puts Europe on alert," BBC News, February 15, 2011. URL: <http://www.bbc.co.uk/news/world-europe-12461866> (accessed January 3, 2013).

8 Ibid.

9 Ibid.

10 See the Europol website. URL: <https://www.europol.europa.eu/content/page/about-europol-17> (accessed January 3, 2012).

11 See the report in *Il Sole 24 Ore,* February 16, 2011.

12 Frontex, *Annual Risk Analysis 2012,* Warsaw: Frontex, 2012, p. 14. URL: <http://frontex.europa.eu/assets/Attachment_Featured/Annual_Risk_Analysis_ 2012.pdf> (accessed July 20, 2012).

13 "Thousands of Tunisians Arrive in Italy," *Der Spiegel,* February 14, 2011. URL: <http://www.spiegel.de/international/europe/biblical-exodus-thousands-of-tunisians-arrive-in-italy-a-745421.html> (accessed January 3, 2013).

14 I. Traynor, "France and Italy in call to close EU borders in wake of Arab protests," *Guardian,* April 27, 2011. URL: <http://www.guardian.co.uk/world/2011/apr/26/eu-borders-arab-protests> (accessed January 3, 2013).

15 "Silvio Berlusconi warns Milan could become 'Gypsytown'," BBC News, May 23, 2011. URL: <http://www.bbc.co.uk/news/world-europe-13507941> (accessed January 3, 2012).

16 S. Carrera et al., *A Race against Solidarity – the Schengen Regime and the Franco-Italian Affair,* CEPS Paper in Liberty and Security in Europe, Brussels: Center for European Policy Studies, 2011, p. 1.

17 N. Morris, "Keep your Arab Spring migrants, May tells France," *Independent,* June 7, 2011. URL: <http://www.independent.co.uk/news/uk/politics/keep-your-arab-spring-migrants-may-tells-france-2293852.html> (accessed January 3, 2013).

18 A. Chrisafis, "Nicolas Sarkozy courts rightwing voters with Schengen zone threat," *Guardian,* March 11, 2012. URL: http://www.guardian.co.uk/world/2012/mar/11/nicolas-sarkozy-french-elections-2012 (accessed January 3, 2013).

19 Ibid.

20 Amnesty International, *S.O.S Europe: Human Rights and Migration Control,* London: Amnesty International, 2012, p. 8. URL: <http://www.amnestyusa.org/research/reports/sos-europe-human-rights-and-migration-control> (accessed January 4, 2012).

21 Ibid.

22 S. Simons, "Dumping Old Friends France Makes Awkward U-Turn on Tunisia Policy," *Der Spiegel,* January 20, 2011. URL: <http://www.spiegel.de/interna tional/world/dumping-old-friends-france-makes-awkward-u-turn-on-tunisia-policy-a-7405 51.html> (accessed Janary 4, 2013).

23 B. Mikail, *France and the Arab Spring: An Opportunistic Quest for Influence,* Working Paper 110, October 2011. Madrid: Fundación para las Relaciones

Internacionales y el Diálogo Exterior (FRIDE0, 2011). URL: <www.fride.org/download/wp110_france_and_arab_spring.pdf> (accessed January 4, 2013).

24 Ibid.

25 Ibid.

26 "CIAN 2008" (report of the French Council of Investors in Africa), quoted by Tunisia News and Press Reviews (2010) "French companies in Tunisia making profits, says last report of French Council of Investors in Africa," *Tunisia News and Press Reviews*, 2010. URL: <http://news.marweb.com/tunisia/economics/business/french-companies-tunisia-profits-council-investors-africa.html> (accessed January 4, 2013).

27 Simons, "Dumping Old Friends."

28 "Investment: Why Egypt?" Egyptian-British Chamber of Commerce. URL: <http://www.theebcc.com/information/investment> (accessed July 20, 2012).

29 N. Mathiason and C. Barr, "HSBC under fire over leading role in land deals for Mubarak regime," *Observer*, April 30, 2011. URL: <http://www.guardian.co.uk/business/2011/may/01/hsbc-egypt-corruption-mubarak-property> (accessed January 4, 2012).

30 Human Rights Watch, "US/UK: Documents Reveal Libya Rendition Details," Human Rights Watch, September 9, 2011. URL: <http://www.hrw.org/news/2011/09/08/usuk-documents-reveal-libya-rendition-details> (accessed July 20, 2012).

31 Morris, "Keep your Arab Spring migrants."

32 C. McGreal, "Tony Blair: Mubarak is 'immensely courageous and a force for good'," *Guardian*, February 2, 2011. URL: <http://www.guardian.co.uk/world/2011/feb/02/tony-blair-mubarak-courageous-force-for-good-egypt> (accessed January 4, 2012).

33 A. Soueif, *Cairo: My City, Our Revolution*, London: Bloomsbury, 2012.

34 Quoted by *Daily Mail*, "Cameron becomes first leader to visit Egypt since uprising brought down Mubarak", February 21, 2011. URL: <http://www.dailymail.co.uk/news/article-1359096/David-Cameron-First-leader-visit-Egypt-Mubarak-protests.html> (accessed January 4, 2013).

35 In an official statement Berlusconi told Qaddafi: "In the name of the Italian people, as head of the government, I feel it my duty to apologize and express my sorrow for what happened many years ago and left a scar on many of your families." Quoted in N. Ronzitti, "The Treaty on Friendship, Partnership and Co-operation Between Italy and Libya: New Pospects for Co-operation in the Mediterranean?" Paper presented at the Mediterranean Strategy Group Conference, "Is Regional Cooperation in the Maghreb Possible? Implications for the Region and External Actors," Genoa, May 11–12, 2009, p. 2, Istituto Affari Internazionali, Istituto Affari Internazionali, Documenti IAI0909. URL: <http://www.iai.it/pdf/DocIAI/iai0909.pdf> (accessed July 20, 2012).

36 According to *Time* magazine, by 2011 the Qaddafi regime owned a substantial share of the Milan stock market, including 7.5 per cent of Unicredit, Italy's largest bank; 2 per cent of the Italian oil company ENI; 2 per cent of the country's second largest industrial group, Finmeccanica; and 7 per cent of the Turin-based Juventus soccer club. S. Faris, "Italy's Bad Romance: How Berlusconi Went Gaga for Gaddafi," *Time*, February 23, 2011. URL: <http://www.time.com/time/world/article/0,8599,2053363,00.html> (accessed January 4, 2013).

37 "For closely tied Italy, Libyan war can't end soon enough," *Globe and Mail*, March 21, 2011. URL: <http://www.theglobeandmail.com/report-on-business/economy/economy-lab/for-closely-tied-italy-libyan-war-cant-end-soon-enough/article612677/> (accessed January 4, 2013).

38 Amnesty International, *S.O.S Europe*.

39 James Walston, professor of international relations at the American University of Rome, quoted in "For closely tied Italy, Libyan war can't end soon enough."

40 "Barcelona declaration adopted at the Euro-Mediterranean Conference – 27–28/11/95." URL: <http://ec.europa.eu/research/iscp/pdf/barcelona_declaration.pdf> (accessed March 15, 2013).

41 P. Marfleet, "A New Orientalism: Europe confronts the Middle East," in T. Ismael, ed., *International Relations of the Middle East in the 21st Century,* London: Ashgate, 2000, p. 261.

42 European Commission, "The Barcelona Conference and the Euro-Mediterranean Association Agreements," memo 95/156, Brussels: European Commission, 1995.

43 *Guardian,* November 25, 1995.

44 Ibid.

45 K. Adamson, *Algeria: A Study in Competing Ideologies,* London: Continuum, 1998, p. 217.

46 Speech to the conference in Copenhagen in 1996 on "Islam in a Changing World: Europe and the Middle East," quoted in A. Jericow and J. Simonsen *Islam in a Changing World: Rethinking Public Religion in the Contemporary World,* London: Routledge, 1997, p. 165.

47 For an assessment of the veracity of interpretations of Huntington's views on cultural "clash," see G. Perry, "Huntington's 'clash of civilizations': rumours and clarification," in T. Ismael, and A. Rippin, eds, *Islam in the Eyes of the West: Images and Realities in an Age of Terror,* London: Routledge, 2010.

48 J. Esposito, *The Islamic Threat: Myth or Reality?* New York: Oxford University Press, 1992, p. 5.

49 G. Delanty, *Inventing Europe,* Basingstoke: Macmillan, 1995, p. 150.

50 P. Marfleet, "Europe's Civilising Mission," in P. Cohen, ed., *New Ethnicities, Old Racisms,* London: Zed, 1999.

51 R. Gillespie, "Northern European Perceptions of the Barcelona Process," *Afers Internacionals,* Madrid: CIDOB 37, 1997, pp. 67–68. URL: <http://www.cidob.org/ca/content/download/5761/55558/ … /37gillespie.pdf> (accessed January 4, 2013).

52 Delanty, *Inventing Europe,* p. 101.

53 J. Hooper and K. Connolly, "Berlusconi breaks ranks over Islam," *Guardian,* September 26, 2001. URL: <http://www.guardian.co.uk/world/2001/sep/27/afghanistan.terrorism7> (accessed 24 April 2013).

54 Ibid.

55 Fortuyn quoted in W. Lunsing, "Islam versus homosexuality? Some reflections on the assassination of Pim Fortuyn," *Anthropology Today* 19, 2003, p. 20.

56 Kjærsgaard, quoted in L. Fekete, "Enlightened Fundamentalism? Immigration, feminism and the Right", *Race and Class,* 2006, Vol. 48, 9.

57 L. Fekete, *A Suitable Enemy: Racism, Migration and Islamophobia in Europe,* London: Pluto, 2009, p. 47.

58 Speech by M. Jacques Chirac, President of the Republic, "10th Ambassadors' Conference," August 29, 2002. URL: <http://www.un.int/france/documents_anglais/020829_mae_chirac_general.htm> (accessed January 5, 2013).

59 Ibid.

60 On the release of secret documents, see K. Wiegrefe, "Classified Papers Prove German Warnings to Bush," *Der Speigel,* November 24, 2010. URL: <http://www.spiegel.de/international/germany/berlin-efforts-to-prevent-iraq-invasion-classified-papers-prove-german-warnings-to-bush-a-730979.html> (accessed January 4, 2013).

61 As quoted in "The struggle to find more than words in Europe's reviewed neighborhood policy: Part 1" *Daily News Egypt,* August 28, 2011. URL: <http://dailynewsegypt.com/2011/08/28/the-struggle-to-find-more-than-words-in-europes-reviewed-neighborhood-policy-part-1/> (accessed January 4, 2013).

62 See R. El-Mahdi and P. Marfleet, eds, *Egypt: The Moment of Change,* London: Zed, 2009.

63 "The struggle to find more than words."

64 E. Balibar, *We, the People of Europe?* Princeton: University of Princeton Press, 2004, p. 231.
65 Fekete, *A Suitable Enemy*.
66 See "Mission and Aims" set out formally at the Frontex website. URL: <http://www.frontex.europa.eu/about/mission-and-tasks> (accessed January 4, 2013).
67 "Amnesty International and ECRE joint briefing on the European Commission proposal amending the Frontex founding Regulation," ECRE (European Council on Refugees and Exiles) website, September 21, 2010. URL: <http://www.ecre.org/topics/areas-of-work/access-to-europe/94-ecre-and-amnesty-international-joint-brief ing-on-the-commission-proposal-to-amend-the-frontex-regulation.html> (accessed January 4, 2013).
68 Ibid.
69 For maps and graphic data, see the "Migratory Routes" page, Frontex website. URL: <http://www.frontex.europa.eu/intelligence/migratory-routes> (accessed January 4, 2013).
70 Council of the European Union 2012.
71 "European Border Guard Teams," Frontex website. URL: <http://www.frontex.europa.eu/operations/european-border-guard-teams> (accessed January 5, 2013).
72 Ibid.
73 Frontex, present authors' emphasis, *Beyond the Frontiers: Frontex: The First Five Years*, Warsaw: Frontex, 2010. URL: <http://www.frontex.europa.eu/assets/Pub lications/General/Beyond_the_Frontiers.pdf> (accessed January 5, 2013).
74 M. Levin and M. Shapiro, *Transatlantic Policymaking in an Age of Austerity*, Washington D.C.; Georgetown University Press, 2004, p. 7.
75 Fekete, *A Suitable Enemy*, p. 140.
76 "Merkel Says EU Must Be Bound Closer Together," *Der Spiegel*, September 7, 2011. URL: <http://www.spiegel.de/international/germany/if-the-euro-fails-europe-fails-merkel-says-eu-must-be-bound-closer-together-a-784953.html> (accessed January 6, 2013).
77 G. Rachman, "The long shadow of the 1930s," *Financial Times*, November 28, 2011. URL: <http://www.ft.com/intl/cms/s/0/79656ee4-19b3-11e1-ba5d-00144feabdc0.html #axzz2H8BH43B1> (accessed January 5, 2013).
78 "Poland and the future of the European Union", Radek Sikorski, Foreign Minister of Poland, Berlin, 28 November 2011. URL: <https://dgap.org/sites/default/files/event_ downloads/radoslaw_sikorski_poland_and_the_future_of_the_eu_0.pdf> (accessed April 25, 2013).
79 (Ibid).
80 See, for example, the comments of Mike Froman, President Obama's deputy national security adviser for international economics. At a White House briefing in June 2012 he warned: "The stakes are so high", proposing that the crisis in Europe was "the dominant risk to the global economy at the moment." A. Gardner, "Obama effort to contain European debt crisis takes on greater urgency," *Washington Post*, June 17, 2012. URL: <http://articles.washingtonpost.com/2012-06-17/politics/ 35459639_1_european-debt-crisis-european-leaders-growth-and-stimulus> (accessed January 5, 2012).
81 T. Wright, "What If Europe Fails?" *Washington Quarterly* 35, 2012, p. 23. URL: <http://www.brookings.edu/~/media/Research/Files/Articles/2012/7/26%20europe %20crisis%20wright/europe%20crisis%20wright.pdf> (accessed January 3, 2013).
82 Ibid., pp. 36–39.
83 B. Connolly, *The Rotten Heart of Europe: The Dirty War for Europe's Money*, London: Faber & Faber, 1995.
84 Delanty describes these campaigns – focused on media events, sports and symbols of the Union such as flags and coinage – as "pathetic exercises in cultural engineering." *Inventing Europe*, p. 128.

85 S. Collinson, *Shore to Shore: The Politics of Migration in Euro-Maghreb Relations*, Washington, DC: Brookings Institution Press, 1996, p. 39.

86 Ibid., p. 40.

87 Austria, Finland and Sweden had joined the EU in 1995, shortly before the Barcelona Conference.

88 Fekete, *A Suitable Enemy,* p. 22.

89 "Euro Med Migration II", at: EU Neighbourhood Info Centre website. URL: <http://www.enpi-info.eu/mainmed.php?id_type=10&id=9> (accessed July 20, 2012).

90 Fekete, *A Suitable Enemy,* p. 153

91 J. Koehler *et al.*, *Migration and the Economic Crisis in the European Union: Implications for Policy*, Brussels: IOM, 2010.

92 Figures collated by the Institute of Race Relations (IRR), *Accelerated Removals: a Study of the Human Cost of EU Deportation Policies, 2009–2010*, European Race Audit, Briefing Paper 4, 2010. URL: <http://www.irr.org.uk/pdf2/ERA_-Briefi ngPaper4.pdf> (accessed January 5, 2013).

93 Fekete, *A Suitable Enemy,* p. 135

94 "Rise of far right in Europe fuels spread of intolerance towards religious minorities, new report," Minority Groups International website, July 1, 2010. URL: <http://www.minorityrights.org/10076/press-releases/rise-of-far-right-in-europe-fuels-spread-of-intolerance-towards-religious-minorities-new-report.html> (accessed July 20, 2012).

95 H. Samuel, "National Front's Marine Le Pen to prove formidable rival to Nicolas Sarkozy," *Daily Telegraph*, December 26, 2010. URL: <http://www.telegraph.co.uk/news/worldnews/europe/france/8225697/National-Fronts-Marine-Le-Pen-to-prove-formidable-rival-to-Nicolas-Sarkozy.html> (accessed May 4, 2013).

96 "Mourning the French victims of terror," *Gulf News*, March 23, 3012. URL: <http://gulfnews.com/opinions/editorials/mourning-the-french-victims-of-terror-1.998515> (accessed January 4, 2013).

97 Ibid.

98 The UfM was an attempt by France to assert its own influence in the Middle East and to accelerate neoliberal policies for development across the region: Sarkozy and Mubarak were the initial joint leaders of the group.

99 Mikail, *France and the Arab Spring*, p. 2.

100 J. Cole, "How neoliberalism created an age of activism," *Aljazeera*, November 15, 2011. URL: <http://www.aljazeera.com/indepth/opinion/2011/11/20111114131340415929.html> (accessed July 20, 2012).

101 P. Marfleet, *Refugees in a Global Era,* Basingstoke: Macmillan, 2006.

102 P. Marfleet, "State and Society," in R. El-Mahdi, R. and P. Marfleet, eds, *Egypt: Tthe Moment of Change*, London: Zed, 2009.

103 "Advocacy group rejects government's IMF-pleasing reform plan," *Al Masry Al Youm*, March 22, 2012.

104 Mathiason and Barr, "HSBC under fire."

105 "Statement from PACE Rapporteur Tineke Strik on Most Recent Deaths in Mediterranean Sea: 'When will this ever end?'" *Migrants by Sea website*, July 12, 2012, p. 24. URL: <http://migrantsatsea.wordpress.com/2012/07/12/statement-from-pace-rapporteur-tineke-strik-on-most-recent-deaths-in-mediterranean-sea-when-will-this-ever-end/> (accessed January 4, 2013).

106 Human Rights Watch, "Hidden Emergency: Migrant Deaths in the Mediterranean," Human Rights Watch website, August 16, 2012. URL: <http://www.hrw.org/news/2012/08/16/hidden-emergency> (accessed August 30, 2012).

9 The United Nations and the Middle East

A guide for the perplexed

Richard Falk

Understanding what the UN can and cannot do in the Middle East

No other region of the world has more clearly disclosed both the need for a proactive United Nations and the presence of formidable political obstacles to a robust UN role that is consistent with the ideals and capabilities of the UN as an organization whose membership consists exclusively of sovereign states. The most obvious explanations for this gap between societal need and institutional performance is associated with the interplay of a dreadful colonial legacy, half of the world's oil reserves, an unresolved Israel–Palestine conflict, severe sectarian tensions that divide Islamic countries, and the frequent intrusion of interventionist geopolitics reflecting the strategic and divergent interests of hegemonic states.

To expect the UN to perform miracles of peacemaking given these regional circumstances is highly unrealistic. At the same time, the UN has made some positive contributions in peace and security situations from time to time, to moderate conflict where the configuration of political forces allows such a constructive role to be played. Beyond this, undoubtedly the most significant contemporary role of the UN in relation to conflict is its underappreciated preeminence is shaping the outcome of symbolic conflicts within the region concerning the legitimacy and illegitimacy of grievances and aspirations. The side that gains the upper hand in the struggle for legitimacy at the UN usually eventually captures the high moral and legal ground in a conflict, and this can often, although not always, offset geopolitical alignments and inferior military capabilities.[1]

The Israel–Palestine conflict illustrates the relevance of the UN as a site of struggle in a legitimacy war, but also underscores the limits that often block translating legitimacy results into appropriate political arrangements. The United States government has demonstrated over and over again that it can shield Israel from the *behavioral* consequences of accountability under international law at the UN. However, despite America's great influence on the global stage, it has been often unable to prevent UN majorities from confirming the inalienable rights of the Palestinian people, including their right of self-determination, and it often cannot prevent the launch of UN-backed inquiries into alleged Israeli wrongdoing despite its vigorous attempts to oppose fact-finding and policy recommendations.[2]

A further point of preliminary clarification is to distinguish between hard and soft power, that is, between reliance on threats and uses of force and reliance on diplomatic and other instruments of coercion and persuasion. In general, the UN is and was intended from the outset of its existence to be primarily a soft power political actor, while hegemonic states were accepted as the preeminent hard power political actors in the world, thereby determining what the UN can and cannot be allowed to do on the level of behavior. It is true also that the UN Charter's modest hopes for a collective security mechanism attached to the Security Council were stillborn, seemingly sidetracked for decades by the Cold War standoff between the US and the Soviet Union. The failure seems deeper and more structural. Since the Soviet collapse in 1992, the absence of any effort to implement these Charter provisions suggests that the main states remain unwilling to transfer military capabilities and sovereign authority to engage in military activities under UN auspices even though any use of force would be subject to the constraints set by the veto power of the five permanent members.[3] That is, despite the language of the Charter, which seems to suggest a blanket prohibition on war making except in strict self-defense situations, world order remains state-centric when it comes to peace and security, and global security continues to be tied to the war system, with geopolitical actors determining when it serves their interests to use force. International law, which claims a universality of application, in practice is deferential to geopolitics in the arena of war/peace issues. This pattern of deference is also expressed by double standards, as in the application of international criminal law, imposing accountability on non-Western leaders while insisting on impunity for hegemonic powers and friends, as well as leaders of states who are "too big to hold accountable."

At the same time, when convenient for legitimating purposes, geopolitical forces have recourse to the UN to receive a mandate to use force from the Security Council. When permanent members, the so-called P5, agree on a response to a conflict situation, the organization accords legitimacy for the use of hard power to control the dynamics of conflict resolution.[4] One dramatic illustration occurred as the Cold War wound down in 1991 when the Security Council authorized an American-led coalition to reverse Iraq's conquest and occupation of Kuwait, a successful process known as the Gulf War. This military operation did seem consistent with the Charter commitment to protect countries from aggression, in this instance Kuwait, although the conduct and goals of the Gulf War were determined in Washington with no attempt to accord the UN supervisory influence as would seem to follow from the mandate.[5] The UN was useful, as it allowed this "coalition of the willing" to gain legitimation, but became superfluous after that – during the conduct of hostilities and in determining the timing and terms of a ceasefire. The UN was reduced to the unsavory role of rubberstamping geopolitical priorities, which in this setting, meant deferring to American foreign policy.

When in Kosovo in 1999 it was anticipated that China and Russia would veto any effort to authorize NATO to embark on a war to dislodge Serbian control over Bosnia and remove a threat of ethnic cleansing, the main backers of the war in Washington and London went ahead with the war under NATO auspices in violation of the letter and intent of the Charter, which prohibits interventions in the internal affairs of sovereign states unless explicitly authorized by the Security Council.[6] When its path was blocked, the NATO consensus created its own ad hoc "coalition of the willing" that was never formally condemned by the UN, suggesting an inability to uphold even verbally its core provisions when these are defied by geopolitics.

The Iraq War of 2003 was another context where a concerted attempt by the US to get the backing of the UN before undertaking an unprovoked attack on Iraq was opposed in dramatic fashion. The rationale given for attacking Iraq was a supposed concern about its possession of weapons of mass destruction, including an alleged program to acquire nuclear weaponry. It was clear that the Bush presidency at the time made a major effort, including doctoring evidence pertaining to alleged purchases of materials relevant to producing nuclear weapons, to convince the Security Council membership of the reasonableness of its proposed invasion of Iraq and overthrow of Saddam Hussein's regime. President Bush lectured the UN that it would lose relevance if it did not give its backing to such an undertaking, despite its manifest unlawfulness.[7] As is known, despite massive civil society protests against recourse to war that took place in an estimated 80 countries and the absence of a UN mandate, the US together with the United Kingdom cobbled together an unimpressive "coalition of the willing" that launched an attack, imposed regime change on Iraq, and undertook a violently contested occupation that lasted almost a decade. The United States finally gave up its combat role at the end of 2011 despite the continuation of significant armed resistance within the country to the post-Saddam Hussein political arrangements established by external fiat.

The UN demonstrated several features of its power(lessness) during the Iraq War and occupation: it withheld support despite heavy geopolitical pressure from the United States, but it did not condemn the attack on Iraq and was a willing partner in the political reconstruction of the country in the early stages of the occupation. In effect, the UN provided a retroactive ratification of unprovoked aggression against a member of the organization. It should not be surprising that UN headquarters were attacked by resistance forces in Iraq, as the UN was accurately perceived after the fall of the Saddam Hussein regime to be a partner of the US in implementing the unlawful occupation of the country, which resulted in a massive and destructive interference with the ethics and politics of self-determination. This is important, as the guiding principle in the long struggle against colonialism in the period after World War II was the illegitimacy of foreign rule, and the primacy of the inalienable right of a people to control their political destiny and defend their territorial integrity by way of self-determination. It is significant in recognition of this primacy that the common Article 1 in the two human rights covenants affirms the right of self-determination as the underpinning for all other rights.

The Arab World was again the scene of a proposed interventionary undertaking in the context of the armed uprising against the Qaddafi regime in Libya in early 2011. Invoking the credible imminence of a massacre of Libyan civilians at the hands of Tripoli and making only a limited claim to provide emergency humanitarian protection via the establishment of a no-fly zone around the threatened city of Benghazi, the pro-intervention members of the Security Council, essentially the US and Europe (minus Germany), which gave approval in constrained language and considerable reluctance exhibited by abstentions cast by five important state members.[8] In arguing in favor of an authorization to use force, great reliance was placed on "the responsibility to protect" norm that had been articulated after NATO's Kosovo War as a way of circumventing opposition to "humanitarian intervention" as a rationale for the use of force.[9] This seemed like a semantic shift to build support for rewriting the Charter so as to allow an expanded use of force under UN authority but on a basis that did not overtly challenge the original social contract that left human rights and civil strife within the domain of "domestic jurisdiction."[10] It is true that unlike Iraq there were good reasons to express a genuine humanitarian concern about the safety of civilians in Libya, especially in Benghazi. This concern was confirmed for many by the genocidal language and brutal tactics of Qaddafi. At the same time, the states advocating emergency protection of endangered civilians misled those members of the Security Council that opposed a regime-changing intervention, and thereby damaged the credibility of both the UN and the proponents of humanitarian protection, as in the subsequent case of Syria. In light of the manipulation of the UN in relation to Iraq and Libya, there was little reason to trust the US and its supporters when they presented evidence that justifiesd a proposed intervention or insisted that intentions were limited to protective goals.

There are two further observations about this pattern that need to be mentioned in order to gain an adequate sense of why intervention under the authority of the United Nations, or otherwise, takes place in some countries in the Middle East but not in others. The first is oil and energy geopolitics. It is notable that the two major interventions in the region have been in Iraq and Libya, both significant oil producers, and that Iran, also an important oil producer, has been threatened with military attacks ever since the Iranian Revolution in 1979, which resulted in hostile relations with the West. The West encouraged Saddam Hussein's Iraq to attack Iran in 1980 with the hope and expectation of toppling the regime in Tehran, and when that goal failed, seemed content to let a devastating war drag on for years so as to weaken both sides in the conflict. It is also notable that the first Gulf War of 1991 was undertaken to restore the sovereignty of Kuwait, an oil producer whose policies were compatible with Western strategic interests. It has also been consistent Western policy not to complain about the human rights abuses associated with the Saudi Arabian government or Bahrain because they were important sources of oil supplies for the world economy and were willing partners in the undertakings of neoliberal globalization, including being large purchasers of arms from Western countries.[11] The oil factor, although rarely acknowledged, seems a major influence in deciding where, when, and to what extent to intervene, preferably with the backing of the UN, but in some instances, without such a mandate. The high costs of the Iraq intervention, in particular, and its lack of satisfying results despite an immense effort, suggest practical limitations on such oil diplomacy, but also reveal the degree to which the UN becomes a partner to these initiatives, before the fact in Libya and after the fact in Iraq. What this pattern shows, additionally, is the extent to which Western geopolitics shapes the behavior of the UN in the Middle East, but not without some outer limits, as was evident in the failure of the US to gain the support of the Security Council for the invasion of Iraq in 2003 or to mobilize a consensus more supportive of the anti-Assad forces in Syria.

The second factor that needs to be acknowledged is the relevance of Israel to what the UN does and doesn't do in the region. Israel's influence is mainly felt by way of the American role in advancing Israel's agenda, which included aggression against Iraq (Saddam Hussein had been an overt supporter of Palestinian resistance and had launched rocket attacks on Israel in the 1991 Gulf War) and, more recently, the successive tightening of sanctions on Iran that has imposed severe hardships on the country and its people. Beyond this, the US shields Israel from censure even when its undertakings are clear violations of international law, as was the case in the Lebanon War of 2006 and the Gaza War of 2008–9. It uses its veto power, sometimes supported by European countries, to avoid condemnation or sanctions that might otherwise be appropriate given Israel's violations of its role as the occupier of Palestinian territories, especially its persistent establishment and expansion of settlements in flagrant violation of Article 49(6) of the 4th Geneva Convention of 1949. Further along these lines, the failure of the UN to protect the 1.6 million Palestinians trapped in Gaza, and subject to an Israeli blockade that has persisted since mid 2007, is to ignore a blatant form of collective punishment, which is unconditionally prohibited by international humanitarian law.[12] In essence, if the US did not wield such a strong influence in the UN, there would be a more balanced approach to the Israel–Palestine conflict and more legitimacy for the organization as guided by considerations of rights and international law, rather than by power and geopolitics.

The UN has the capacity to withhold legitimacy from a proposed attack on a sovereign state, as it did in 2003 in refusing to accede to the American request for a UN mandate for recourse to aggression against Iraq. And it can on certain limited occasions exert delegitimizing pressures, as it did in 1956 when it helped induce France, the United Kingdom, and Israel to withdraw from territory occupied during the Suez War. This is the one and only instance in which the US gave priority to the UN Charter over its allegiance to its NATO allies and Israel. In all subsequent instances involving war/peace issues, the distinguishing feature that determines the level and type of UN influence can be assessed only by reference to geopolitics, that is, by factoring in the priorities and goals of dominant sovereign states – which has meant especially the outlook of the US – in the shaping of a particular UN response. The main conclusion of such an assessment is that the UN retains considerable authority in relation to determinations of the legitimacy of uses of force, but that it can only be effective behaviorally when it has relevant political backing, particularly from the US.

What is helpful, then, by way of background is to understand this dual identity of the UN: as subject to geopolitics and as an institutional setting that is able to manipulate the legitimacy components of a conflict in one direction or another. In this regard, a great early success of the UN was to transform itself from being a bastion of colonialism when it was set up in 1945 to becoming an important site lending support to decolonization struggles only a few years later. Because the Middle East was a geopolitical battleground during the Cold War, its actions in that region were usually gridlocked. Since the collapse of the Soviet Union, the UN seemed more often to serve strategic interests of its West-centric members, especially the US, but not always, and not in every part of the UN System (e.g. the General Assembly and Human Rights Council), and that is what makes this inquiry worthwhile.

The Middle East after the Cold War

The Middle East as a region of concern has certain distinctive features that can push the UN in one direction or the other with respect to addressing either drastic human rights situations or responding to war/peace issues. During the Cold War the Middle East was an arena of superpower bipolar confrontation with countries aligned with either the Soviet Union or the US, and the UN sidelined. In the post-Cold War world a new geopolitical setting emerged that encouraged the United States to claim unilateral prerogatives, especially in the Middle East, that assumed great importance for a series of reasons: upholding Israel's interests; safeguarding Western access to the region's oil reserves; preventing the spread of nuclear weapons beyond Israel; containing the spread of radical Islam; promoting neoliberal globalization; and pushing for liberal Western versions of human rights and democracy.

The geopolitical shift from bipolarity to unipolarity translated itself into a situation in which the US was able to coordinate the priorities of its foreign policy with its predominant influence within the halls of the United Nations, and especially in the Security Council. Such predominant influence was decisive in building support for receiving a mandate to use "all necessary force" to reverse the results of Iraq's invasion, occupation, and annexation of Kuwait in 1990. There was at the time a widely shared regional and global sense that Iraq's act of aggression and acquisition of territory by recourse to force was an unacceptable breach of the most basic norm of the Charter, and in this period after the Cold War, the Soviet Union joined with Western powers to support an American-led intervention.

The military undertaking overwhelmed Iraq's defenses, restored Kuwait's sovereign control, and destroyed much of the civilian infrastructure in Iraq. As the operation proceeded there were regrets expressed at the UN about the degree to which military decisions were shaped in Washington rather than in the UN headquarters in New York. The UN Secretary General at the time, Boutros Boutros Ghali, subsequently wrote that the UN must never in the future relinquish its responsibilities for the conduct of such peacekeeping operations to the extent that occurred during the Gulf War. The US set the terms for the ceasefire and induced the Security Council to impose "a punitive peace" in 1991 that included sanctions that produced great hardships on the civilian population of Iraq over the course of the next decade. The US had claimed that this operation was emblematic of "a new world order" in which the original intention of the UN to protect the victims of aggression had been upheld, and to an extent this was true, but far from encouraging.

But what was also evident was the degree to which the UN role was an extension of American foreign policy rather than an embodiment of the war prevention rationale of the UN Charter. The Charter was premised on an undertaking "to save succeeding generations from the scourge of war." As already argued, geopolitical pressures are responsive to such considerations as strategic alliances and the importance of access to oil and natural gas. This is not to say that the UN is completely subordinated to geopolitics. There are majoritarian capabilities that can be exerted by the General Assembly, although in very limited settings. On November 29, 2012, over the vigorous objections of Israel and the United States, the General Assembly by a vote of 130 to 9 (with 41 abstentions) conferred non-member statehood on Palestine.[13] The prior year the Palestinian Authority had applied for membership in the UN, but was blocked effectively (and undemocratically) by an American threat to use its veto in the Security Council, whose recommendation is required for a state to become a member.[14]

This overall circumstance is highlighted by the approach taken by the UN to the issue of nuclear weapons, which in a manner similar to the relevance of energy geopolitics, is tainted by double standards that can only be understood by reference to the grand strategy of the United States (and its European allies) in the region. Israel has acquired nuclear weapons by stealth, has refused to participate in the non-proliferation regime, and has resisted calls for establishing a nuclear-weapons-free zone in the Middle East. Iran has advocated regional security arrangements that include the desirability of negotiating such a zone and has consistently denied that it intends to produce nuclear weapons. The United States has spearheaded moves in the UN to reinforce Israeli threats of force directed at Iran due to its nuclear program and has indicated its own refusal to remove the military option from the table, backing highly coercive sanctions. The UN, while probably resistant to an attack on Iran, nevertheless is complicit in this one-sided use of its authority to coerce via punitive economic measures and is unable to pursue a set of policies that would bring greater stability and security to the region as a whole through the elimination of nuclear weaponry. In an important respect, the Middle East on the crucial issue of nuclear weapons is a microcosm of a global approach that discriminates in favor of nuclear weapons states in its implementation of the Non-Proliferation Treaty regime.[15]

My argument up to this point can be summarized as follows: in some circumstances the UN does far too little in the Middle East (most notably, regarding Israel–Palestine, and possibly Syria since 2011) and in some other situations it does far too much (most notably, Iraq in 2003, Libya in 2011, and the imposition of sanctions on Iran). The main explanation for these failures of proportion is the intrusion of geopolitical fault-lines. These fault-lines, I am contending, are more significant in the Middle East than elsewhere due to the proportion of oil reserves present in the region, resulting from the American unbalanced support of Israel in the face of the denial of Palestinian fundamental rights, and due to the strategic location of the region at the interface of Europe, Asia, and Africa. In the aftermath of the Cold War, these factors led to a shift in geopolitical preoccupations from Europe, the scene of the great wars of the twentieth century, to the Middle East, which I think has made UN performance more subject to sharp criticisms than in other regions.[16]

There is a natural inclination of critics of the UN performance to write off the organization as nothing but a pawn of Western geopolitics, but this is misguided and simplistic. The UN provides many important services to the peoples and governments of the world as a result of its specialized activities in relation to health, labor standards, wellbeing of children, development, food security, disaster relief, environmental protections and climate change, law-making treaties, auspices for global conferences, international finance including monetary stabilization and credit arrangements, preservation of heritage sites, human rights, and many other areas of concern for human wellbeing, and this is as applicable to the Middle East as elsewhere. But even in relation to the problematic area of war/peace and self-determination, the UN plays constructive roles, although not consistently, especially with regard to mandates to use force to alter conditions within sovereign states. At the same time, the UN is a critical arena in relation to the conduct of legitimacy wars (struggles for the high moral and legal ground in international and internal conflicts), the outcome of which often shape the final results of long conflicts to a greater extent than the military balance of forces.[17]

In this regard, it is notable that the Palestinians have benefited from *symbolic* support at the UN in their effort to shift the balance in the legitimacy war being waged against Israel.[18] The controversial Goldstone Report assessing Israeli and Hamas violations of international law during Operation Cast Lead (the military attack on Gaza at the end of 2008, with a ceasefire agreed upon in January 2009) established in authoritative form Israeli violations of international law, and contributed to the sense that the prolonged occupation of Palestinian territories since 1967 is imprudent, immoral, and unlawful.[19] The Goldstone Report also recommended that the parties establish accountability mechanisms to implement criminal responsibility for violations of international law, including referral to the International Criminal Court if self-enforcement was not forthcoming. These recommendations involved an effort to move from the symbolic battlefield to a program of *behavioral* implementation. It is here that quite predictably the Goldstone Report ran up against a geopolitical brick wall in the form of Israeli and American backroom diplomatic leverage. Where that leverage is stymied by efforts to produce credible fact-finding and critical reports, Israel has resorted to refusals to cooperate with UN activities, including denial of access to those tasked with assessing human rights violations in occupied Palestine or reporting on the Israeli settlement activities in relation to prospects for a peaceful resolution of the underlying conflict. Such denials are inconsistent with the legal obligations of members of the UN, but no adverse consequences have resulted for Israel. In fact, in 2011 Israel severed all relations with the UN Human Rights Council, alleging bias. In my experience, the allegation is unfounded, as almost all HRC initiatives relating to Israel are undertaken in a manner that leans over backwards to give Israel the benefit of the doubt, and this includes the Goldstone Report.[20]

It is not only in the Israel–Palestine context that this distinction between symbolic importance in relation to comparative legitimacy of the claimants and behavioral implementation of UN policies in an evenhanded manner is responsive to law rather than to geopolitics. The UN has been also influential in swaying public opinion and diplomacy in other persisting conflict situations, including even Syria, where the Western liberal democracies have been winning the legitimacy war in relation to the conflict but have so far not been able to mobilize the UN to take action.

The UN and the Arab Spring

The Arab upheavals that started two years ago in Tunisia and Egypt, became known as the "Arab Spring" and represented a regional surge of populist protest against authoritarian and corrupt patterns of governance. These countries shared similar conditions in which their internal situation involved grossly inequitable distributions of income and wealth, with the masses enduring subsistence standards, or worse, and a variety of oppressive abuses, while a tiny minority enjoyed a life of unlimited luxury. While this process of upheaval unfolded, the UN stood aside with no role beyond that of an interested spectator. By and large, although the developments posed serious threats to entrenched strategic and economic interests of the West, there was a strong conviction that such spontaneous democratizing developments in these Arab states should not be opposed, at least not openly. In these respects, the UN's early role in response to the Arab Spring seemed an exercise of appropriate deference to the dynamics of self-determination, as well as dictated by the fundamental Charter notion that the UN should not intervene in the internal dynamics of its members, but limit its peacekeeping activities to conflicts that involved two or more sovereign states.[21]

Over the years, due to the rise of human rights as a constraint on territorial sovereignty, there have been some tensions between respect for self-determination and ideas associated with humanitarian intervention, which has come to be identified as responsibility to protect (R2P).[22] The Libyan, Bahraini, Yemeni, and especially the Syrian cases of upheaval, which did not lead to smooth transfers of power or sufficient reformist responses, pose challenges of this sort to the UN. In a globalized world where atrocities are reported in real time by the media, it is increasingly difficult to stand by while a humanitarian catastrophe is unfolding. At the same time, intervention under UN auspices requires a consensus of the five permanent members of the Security Council. By and large, the US, United Kingdom, and France have opted for more interventionist postures of response, while China and Russia tend to oppose any forcible interference in the internal affairs of sovereign states. This opposition is partly involving ideas about world order, particularly reflecting their own strict sovereignty orientations, and partly tactical or pragmatic, exhibiting differing geopolitical calculations of advantage. Unlike the Cold War, with its bipolarity, the new conflicts are more ideational than ideological, reflecting differing views as to the balance between respect for territorial sovereignty and human rights, as well as the varying historical memories of the colonial West and the post-colonial non-West.

Also there are problems of effectiveness of proposed interventions and of dealing with the aftermath of a successful intervention. As Iraq and Afghanistan have illustrated, even when an intervention is backed by total military supremacy, it is difficult at acceptable costs in a reasonable time interval, to produce the desired outcome. As Kosovo, Iraq, and Libya show, even when the immediate political outcome corresponds with what the intervenors were seeking, it may still over time produce major disappointments in the form of the ascent of illiberal political forces that engage in new cycles of violations of human rights or reject participation in the neoliberal world economy. There are widespread reports that the Serbian minority in Kosovo is not secure in the aftermath of the Kosovo War of 1999, that the sort of West-oriented secular pro-neoliberal forces that Washington hoped to have govern Iraq were dismal failures with the citizenry in national post-invasion elections, and the Libyan victors have been abusive toward the remnants of the Qaddafi epoch and have left the country and its people subject to violence and fragmentation due to the rise of local and tribal militias.

The UN has been called upon to seek a negotiated solution in Syria after attempts at more proactive policies were rejected. The Secretary General (along with the Arab League) has appointed two high profile Special Envoys to discharge what appears to be a "mission impossible," first Kofi Annan, and later Lakhdar Brahimi. Both envoys established a diplomatic connection with Damascus, and sought to propose initiatives that might lead to a sustainable ceasefire and transitional political arrangements, with the overriding goal of alleviating the suffering of the civilian population. This UN role has been frustrated by the unwillingness of either side to be receptive to a genuine compromise or to trust its adversary sufficiently to accept a ceasefire. The marginalization of the UN also reflects the proxy war dimensions of the conflict, with Russia and Iran on the side of the Assad regime, and the West along with Saudi Arabia and Qatar siding with rebel forces. This pattern of rival alignments produced a diplomatic stalemate up to now, as well as facilitating transnational supplies of weaponry that diminish incentives to bring the violence to an end.

Such issues brought to the surface in the Middle East in the failed instances of the Arab Spring raise several questions about the role of the United Nations. The first is whether a more efficient way of enhancing the influence of the UN would be to establish a UN Emergency Peace Force that would be activated by a procedure not subject to a veto, and including an increased role for initiatives proposed on the authority of the Secretary General. Such an innovation could not succeed in freeing UN responses from the grip of geopolitics without being accompanied by the creation of substantial independent funding sources. The neutralization of the UN after the Arab Spring underscores the need for substantial UN reform, especially in the Security Council.

Notes

1 For extensive discussion of the legitimacy dimension of world politics encompassing many perspectives, see R. Falk *et al.*, eds, *Legality and Legitimacy in Global Affairs*, New York: Oxford University Press, 2012.

2 Three recent examples: the US government opposition was unable to block a request to the International Court of Justice for an Advisory Opinion on the Israeli separation wall built on Palestinian occupied territory that led to a 14–1 finding that the wall was in violation of international law; the appointment by the UN Human Rights Council of an inquiry commission on war crimes after the Gaza War of 2008–9 that resulted in the so-called "Goldstone Report"; or the HRC inquiry into Israeli settlements on the West Bank, with a report due in 2013.

3 See Chapter VII provisions of the UN Charter, Articles 39–51, calling for the establishment of standby forces for peacekeeping operations (Article 43) and periodic meetings of senior military officials (Chiefs of Staff of the Permanent Members of the Security Council) to review all aspects of the global peace and security situation (Article 47).

4 For further discussion from this standpoint, see Falk *et al.*, especially pp. 3–71.

5 The Gulf War also raised questions as to whether recourse to force was truly a last resort in upholding the territorial integrity and political independence of Kuwait. There were reports that Iraq was prepared to withdraw and reach a diplomatic solution. Others argued that sanctions combined with diplomacy could have achieved similar results with far less destruction and loss of life. For general analysis, see R. Falk, *The Costs of War: International Law, the UN, and World Order After Iraq*, New York: Routledge, 2008, pp. 37–112.

6 The wording of Article 2(7) is instructive: "Nothing in the present Charter shall authorize the United Nations to intervene in matters which are essentially within the domestic jurisdiction of any state or shall require the Members to submit such matters to settlement under the present Charter; but this principle shall not

prejudice the application of enforcement measures under Chapter VII." The rise of international human rights versus the Westphalian social contract has become a fundamental world order issue.

7 See Falk, *The Costs of War*, pp. 69–82.

8 As authorized by Security Council Resolution 1973 of March 17, 2011.

9 See "The Responsibility to Protect," Report of the International Commission on Intervention and Sovereignty, Ottawa: International Development Research Centre, 2001; for critical assessment of international practice relating to humanitarian intervention, see A. Orford, *Reading Humanitarian Intervention: Human Rights and the Use of Force in International Law,* Cambridge, UK: Cambridge University Press, 2003.

10 As set forth in Article 2(7) of the UN Charter, and listed as one of the seven defining principles of the Organization.

11 Bahrain was also important for the defense of Western regional interests, being the site of a major American naval base.

12 The language setting forth this prohibition in Article 33 of the 4th Geneva Convention is very clear: "No protected person may be punished for an offense he or she has not personally committed. Collective penalties ... are prohibited."

13 As concluded in UNGA Res. A/67/L.28, November 29, 2012.

14 The US has so far been successful in keeping Palestine's membership bid from coming to a vote in the Security Council, which allows the US to avoid casting a veto that would be seen as obstructionist by much of world public opinion.

15 See R. Falk and D. Krieger, *The Path to Zero: Dialogues on Nuclear Dangers,* Boulder, CO: Paradigm, 2012; also the 1996 Advisory Opinion of the International Court of Justice that calls upon parties to the Non-Proliferation Treaty to implement Article VI, which obligates them to seek nuclear disarmament in good faith, a legal duty that has been avoided by successive US administrations over a period of more than 45 years.

16 A recent parallel shift of priorities from Europe to the Asia-Pacific region has been announced by the Obama administration. Such a shift seems to be an example of a traditional geopolitical move to contain China, a rising power that is perceived as a challenger to the existing world power hierarchy.

17 Winners and losers in wars during the period since 1945 have been more often the more legitimate claimant as measured by adherence to prevailing ideas about morality and international law. Contrary to realist thinking, the militarily stronger side in recent conflicts has rarely emerged as a winner; Vietnam is emblematic of this trend, but so are many of the recent struggles against European colonialism and Soviet imperialism, as well as several of the results associated with the Arab Spring.

18 This dimension of the conflict is acknowledged by Israeli sources, and derided as "lawfare," that is, the use of law and legal arguments to weaken Israeli claims of right, and to encourage opposition in civil society and diplomatic circles.

19 For a range of assessments of the Goldstone Report, as well as a large excerpt from the report, see A. Horowitz *et al.*, eds., *The Goldstone Report: The Legacy of the Landmark Investigation of the Gaza Conflict,* New York: Nation Books, 2011.

20 Ibid.; for the argument that the Goldstone Report overlooked several considerations that were favorable to Palestinian claims relating to the Gaza attacks at the end of 2008, see "The Goldstone Report: Ordinary Text, Extraordinary Event," *Global Governance,* 2010, vol. 16, 173–90.

21 Article 2(7) is a basic contractual guaranty that sovereign rights of smaller states would be respected as a constitutive principle of the UN as founded. Various pressures have been claimed to have eroded the authority of this provision, including the growth of efforts to protect peoples vulnerable to gross violations of fundamental human rights or threatened by genocide and the sort of security

claims made by the United States to consider the world as its battlefield in the struggle against global terrorism. It would be a mistake to discard this constraint on UN authority to act without careful consideration of whether it is wise and desirable to so situate smaller societies in relation to the United Nations.

22 For the most comprehensive scholarly analysis to date, see A. Orford, *International Authority and the Responsibility to Protect*, Cambridge, UK: Cambridge University Press, 2011. R2P had been preceded by the advocacy of "responsible sovereignty" as a sequel to "territorial sovereignty," as a way of taking account of the development of international standards of human rights as constraints on the internal authority of governments in relation to people subject to their control. See F. Deng *et al.*, *Sovereignty as Responsibility: Conflict Management in Africa*, Washington, DC: Brookings Institution Press, 1996.

Index

Please note that page numbers relating to Notes will have the letter 'n' following the page number.

268   *Index*

"three no's" formula (Nasser), 117
TIKA (Turkish International
  Cooperation and Development
  Agency), 207, 211
Tobacco Concession, 1890, 67
Transjordan, settlement post-World
  War I, 58–9
Treaty of Turkomanchai, 1828, 66
Triple Entente, 55
Trucial States (UAE), 64
al-Tufayli, Sheikh Subhi, 147
Tunisia: and Arab Spring, 14, 78, 174,
  258; and France, 231–2; migration
  from, 229–30
Turkey, 3, 5; AKP (Justice and
  Development Party), 26, 129, 164,
  202–27; and Arab Spring, 216; and
  Arab states, 129; and Balkans region,
  207, 208, 216–17; and Brazil, 213,
  214; and Caucasus, 208, 216–19; and
  Central Asia, 208, 218; and Cyprus,
  205–6; diplomacy, 206–9; domestic
  factors and ideology, 222–5; economic
  factors, 208–9, 210; and Egypt, 175;
  EU membership issue, 204–5; foreign
  policy, 224; and Greece, 202, 220; and
  Hamas, 211–12; and Iran, 213–14;
  and Israel, 128–9, 210–11, 212;
  modernization, 25; as natural heir of
  Ottoman Empire, 204; relations with
  US and Europe, 220–2; Republic of,
  establishment of borders, 47; role in
  Middle East, 25–6; and Russia,
  217–19; and Saudi Arabia, 129; soft
  power, 207, 208, 217; and Syria, 27,
  130, 210, 216; and US, 220–2, 223;
  "zero problems with neighbors"
  policy, 175, 203, 207, 209–16, 217,
  219, 224
Turkey–Syria High-Level Strategic
  Cooperation Council, 210
Turkish Chamber of Commerce
  (TOBB), 211
Turkish Cypriots, 205–6
Turkish International Cooperation and
  Development Agency (TIKA), 207,
  211
Turkish Petroleum Company (TPC), 61,
  216
Turkish Radio and Television
  Corporation (TRT), 208
Turkmenistan, 218
Turkomanchai, Treaty of (1828), 66
Twelver Shi'ism, 22

UNICEF (UN Children's Fund), 96,
  109n
Union for the Mediterranean (UfM),
  243, 249n
United Arab Emirates (UAE), 64; and
  Iran, 150
United Arab Republic (UAR), 5, 62
United Iraqi Alliance, 153
United Kingdom (UK) *see* Britain;
  British Empire; British imperialism
United Nations Fact Finding Mission
  on the Gaza Conflict (Goldstone
  Report), 2009, 13, 257, 258, 261n
United Nations (UN), 73; and Arab
  Spring, 258–60; Charter *see* Charter,
  UN; Conciliation Commission for
  Palestine, 116; future role, 260;
  General Assembly *see* General
  Assembly (GA), UN; Human Rights
  Council, 260n; and Iran, 151;
  marginalization of, 260; and Middle
  East, 250–62; on nuclear weapons,
  256–7; scope of powers in Middle
  East, 250–5; Security Council *see*
  Security Council, UN; and US, 97–8;
  World Summit, 2005, 98
United States (US), 73–110; Agency for
  International Development, 7; and
  Arab Spring, 78–81; arms sales, 75;
  and Britain, 73; Carter Doctrine, 11,
  104, 105; and Egypt, 176, 179, 187,
  188, 194, 196; "exceptionalism," 98;
  and indigenous movements
  potentially challenging American
  interests, 74; and Iran, 68–9, 74,
  103–7, 145, 168; and Iraq, 5, 74, 94–
  103, 168; and Israel, 8, 9, 10, 74, 81–
  94, 123–4, 187; Jewish population, 8;
  neo-liberal economic models, 76, 100,
  102; oil company profits, 100, 102–3;
  as only remaining superpower, 98;
  radical Islamists, challenge of, 75–8;
  and Saudi Arabia, 11, 12–13, 14–15,
  75, 95, 104–5; and Soviet Union, 73;
  sub-Saharan Africa, aid to, 82, 83;
  and Turkey, 220–2, 223; and UN,
  97–8; "war on terrorism," 14, 65, 188;
  weakening of hegemony, 15, 16, 17;
  and Zionism, 93; *see also* Bush,
  George W.; Carter, Jimmy; Clinton,
  Bill; Clinton, Hillary; Eisenhower,
  Dwight D.; Johnson, Lyndon B.;
  Kennedy, John F.; Nixon, Richard;
  Obama, Barack

prezi